The Big Book of English Grammar for ESL and English Learners

Prepositions, Phrasal Verbs, English Articles a, an and the, Gerunds and Infinitives, Irregular English Verbs, and English Expressions for Real life

by

Thomas Celentano

Copyright

About the Author

Thomas Celentano has written seven books about English grammar for English students worldwide and has taught English as a second language for more than 20 years. He holds university degrees in foreign language studies and anthropology from the University of Hawaii, at Manoa. A novelist, he writes under the pen name, R. Cameron Bryce and is the author of "Killing Tony" and "Under the Giant Mimosa with the Mango Tree Lover" (also published under the title, "When Pigs and Horses Fly")

Dedication

To my students everywhere

Forward

The six English grammar *hotspots* (difficult areas), prepositions, phrasal verbs, English idioms and expressions, English articles, gerunds and infinitives, and irregular verbs are found everywhere in the English language. The correct use of English grammar in English communication can sometimes be difficult because of its unpredictable nature. This text was written as a quick reference guide, and primer, to help students quickly find and correct problem areas. The book was written for low-intermediate through advanced English learners.

Students can find ***audio book*** versions of this content at www.foebooks.com.

Master Table of Contents

Introduction

Focus on English© Mini Series Reference and Textbooks
Making the difficult parts of learning English easy

The Big Book of English Grammar for Every ESL / English Second Language Learner

This book goes beyond just being a guide to the correct use of English grammar. The student can use this text to learn how to correctly use the most difficult and confusing English grammar correctly in situational English communication, in a wide variety of English sentence contexts. In addition to **complete and clear explanations** of the correct way to use difficult areas of English Grammar, there are many **examples** of correct usage and **self reviews** throughout the book.

The student is encouraged to use this book in three ways:

- As *a quick reference resource*. The book layout and design make it easy for the student to quickly search for words or phrases of interest.

- As *a learn-by-example text*. Every step of the way there are many clear examples of usage, making it easy for the student to understand how English speakers use prepositions in everyday communication.

- As *a grammar text*. This book was designed to push the student to the next level in learning English prepositions in their many different usages. The practice and review sections of the book challenge the student to generate communication based on the lesson at hand, helping the student to reinforce his or her new knowledge.

Focus on English© Books for ESL Learners

Making the difficult parts of learning English easy
Use English Grammar Correctly in Every English Sentence

This book is designed for low-intermediate through advanced English Learners who want to clearly understand the use of difficult English grammar in many different kinds of English sentences.

*If English prepositions, phrasal verbs English articles, gerunds and infinitives, irregular English verbs, and English expressions for real life, sound confusing to you, don't worry! This Focus On English Big Book of Grammar will help you to learn and master the six difficult areas (the **hotspots**) of English grammar.*

How to use this grammar book

This book was designed to be both a reference book and an aid for classroom work that can be quickly searched for answers about the correct use in most English sentences of prepositions, articles, irregular verbs, phrasal verbs, gerunds and infinitives, and English expressions. At the beginning of each book there is a full Quick-Find Menu for that book. At the end of some of the books the student will also find a Quick-Find Index where he or she can quickly find something of particular interest in that chapter.

"The Big Book of English Grammar" is broken down into six books: *Prepositions*, *Phrasal Verbs*, *Gerunds and Infinitives*, *Irregular Verbs*, *English Articles*, and *English Expressions*. The student can quickly go to any book from the Master Quick-Find Menu after this section.

The student is encouraged to use the many examples in this book to help understand how we use grammar in particular English sentences, and to practice with the review sections at the end of each chapter.

This book was designed to be used as an aid to classroom study or as a quick-search resource manual.

Book 1 – Prepositions Made Easy
Mastering English Prepositions for Fluency

Book 1 - Quick-Find Menu

Chapter 2 - Using Prepositions when Talking About Place or Location   28

Chapter 3 - Using Prepositions when Talking About Transportation and Traveling

Chapter 4 - Using Prepositions when Giving Directions 40

Chapter 2 - Prepositions Following Verbs Beginning with the letters B and C

Chapter 1 - English prepositions beginning with the letters <u>A</u> and <u>B</u>   **91**

Chapter 2 - English prepositions beginning with the letters <u>C</u> - <u>F</u>   **107**

Chapter 6 - English prepositions beginning with the letters U - Z 146

Forward

English prepositions are everywhere in the English language. The correct use of English prepositions in English communication can sometimes be difficult because of their unpredictable nature. This text was written as a quick reference guide, and primer, to help students quickly find and correct problem areas. The book was written for intermediate and advanced learners.

Notice to all students: a free audio version of this book can be found at https://foebooks.com/index.php/beyond-prepositions-for-esl-learners-audio/

Introduction

Focus on English© Mini Series Books
Making the difficult parts of learning English easy

Beyond Prepositions for ESL Learners - Mastering English Prepositions for Fluency

This book goes beyond just being a guide to the correct use of English prepositions. The student can use this text to learn how to correctly use prepositions, prepositional phrases, prepositions after certain English verbs, and prepositions in situational English communication in a wide variety of English sentence contexts. In addition to **complete and clear explanations** of the correct way to use prepositions, there are many **examples** of correct usage and **self reviews** throughout the book.

The student is encouraged to use this book in three ways:

- As **a quick reference resource.** The book layout and design make it easy for the student to quickly search for words or phrases of interest.

- As **a learn-by-example text.** Every step of the way there are many clear examples of usage, making it easy for the student to understand how English speakers use prepositions in everyday communication.

- As **a grammar text.** This book was designed to push the student to the next level in learning English prepositions in their many different usages. The practice and review sections of the book challenge the student to generate communication based on the lesson at hand, helping the student to reinforce his or her new knowledge.

Focus on English© Books for ESL Learners
Making the difficult parts of learning English easy

*Use **Prepositions** Correctly in Every English Sentence*

This book is designed for English Learners who want to clearly understand the use of prepositions in many different kinds of English sentences.

Why do English speakers say: a person gets <u>on</u> a bus and <u>into</u> a taxi, <u>on</u> a plane and <u>into</u> a car; we arrive <u>in</u> New York <u>at</u> Kennedy Airport <u>on</u> Wednesday <u>at</u> 3 p.m. <u>in</u> November; we sit <u>at</u> a desk but we sit <u>in</u> a chair; our hands are <u>on</u> the desk but our pencil is <u>in</u> our hand; we say we did something <u>for</u> him and then did something <u>to</u> him; I like my friend because he's <u>like</u> my brother; we have been talking <u>about</u> school <u>since</u> 2 p.m. <u>for</u> 3 hours <u>outside</u> the building that is <u>close to</u> the bank; the book is <u>underneath</u> the counter, <u>beneath</u> the bookshelf, <u>under</u> the window, <u>near</u> the door, <u>beside</u> the TV, which is <u>next to</u> the chair that is <u>over</u> the box that is <u>on</u> the floor . . . whew!

Does some of this sound confusing to you? Well, don't worry! This Focus On English lesson is about English prepositions and will help you to understand and use English prepositions correctly in every situation.

How to use this preposition book

This book was designed to be both a reference book and a classroom text book that can be quickly searched for answers about the correct use of prepositions in most English sentences. At the end of this prepositions book there is an Appendix where the student can quickly find the correct prepositions that are used after certain English verbs.

"Prepositions Made Easy" is broken down into three sections.

The **first section** provides the student with the resources to understand the functional use of prepositions in everyday English communication. In this section, the student will find explanations and examples about how to use prepositions when talking about **time, place/location, transportation/travel, giving directions**, and **how things get done** (special uses for the prepositions <u>with</u> and <u>by</u>).

The **second section** is designed to help the student with the difficult area of prepositions following certain common verbs in English. The student may quick-search this second section easily, either by verb or by preposition, using the table of contents at the beginning of this book. This will save the student time and help to get answers quickly.

The **third section** is designed to be a reference resource for all of the most common prepositions used in English. This section contains a comprehensive listing of the prepositions followed by explanations and examples.

This book was designed to be used as a classroom study text or as a quick-search resource manual.

Section 1: Using Prepositions correctly in context

Learn to use English prepositions correctly when talking about time, places, transportation, giving directions, and expressing how things get done.

This first section helps the student to understand the use of English prepositions in real-life situations. In this section, the student will find explanations and examples relating to preposition usage in everyday English usage.

Chapter 1 - Using Prepositions to Talk About Time

Using the prepositions ___ahead___, ___behind___, ___at___, ___on___, ___in___, ___by___, ___within___, ___under___, ___during___, ___over___, ___since___, ___from___, ___for___ and ___after___ when talking about time in English

Directions: Read the brief explanations and then the examples below. *(Note: students are encouraged to use this text in groups, when possible. The student can then practice by listening and speaking, as well as reading, which should make learning easier, faster and more fun.)*

___Ahead___: Use ___ahead___ to talk about being earlier than expected

Examples:

- The train is ___ahead___ of schedule. It was supposed to arrive at 9 a.m. but the time is now 8:55 a.m. and it is here!

- This is my first day of work, so I arrived at the office ___ahead___ of time.

  (Meaning: earlier than I was supposed to be there.)

___Behind___: Use ___behind___ to talk about being later than expected

Examples:

- The train is ___behind___ schedule. It was supposed to arrive at 9 a.m. but the time is now 9:05 a.m. and it's not here yet!.

- My watch says 12:30 p.m., but the time on the bank clock says 12:40 p.m. My watch must be ___behind___.

In this case, meaning: the time on my watch lags the real time. English speakers also say: *my watch is slow*, or *my watch is running slow*.

___On___: Use ___on___ for day names, like Monday or Tuesday

Examples:

- My friends come to visit me ___on___ Wednesday.

- We have an important exam ___on___ Friday.

_On:_ Use **_on_** in expressions like **_on_** time; **_on_** time means at the correct time or agreed upon time.

Example:

- My boss does not want me to come to work late. He wants me to come to work **_on_** time.

_At_ : Use **_at_** to talk about exact clock time.

Examples:

- The exam will start **_at_** 3 p.m..
- The movie starts **_at_** 7:15 p.m..

_At_ : Use **_at_** to talk about midnight, noon, night, daybreak, sunset, sunrise, etc.

Examples:

- We had lunch **_at_** noon.
- We woke up **_at_** dawn (when the sun comes up).
- We went to bed **_at_** dusk (when the sun goes down).

_At_ : Use **_at_** in expressions referring to time: **_at_** the moment, **_at_** the present time, etc.

Examples:

- **_At_** the moment, doctors are not sure what causes cancer.
- **_At_** the present time, we are not hiring any more employees.

_In_ : Use **_in_** to talk about seasons of the year:

Examples:

- We will start school **_in_** the fall.
- Our vacation begins **_in_** the summer

In : Use *in* to talk about centuries, years, and months:

Examples:

- Cars were invented ***in*** the nineteenth century.
- We will finish class ***in*** May.
- We will graduate ***in*** 2012.

In : Use *in* to talk about blocks of time:

Example:

- The woman said that she expects to have children ***in*** the future.

In : Use *in* to talk about named times of the day: morning, afternoon, and evening:

Examples:

- We have tea ***in*** the morning.
- We eat lunch ***in*** the afternoon.
- We have dinner ***in*** the evening.

In : Use *in* to talk about months of the year.

Example:

- I will complete my English course ***in*** February.

In : Use *in* to talk about years.

Example:

- I came to this country ***in*** 2001.

In : Use *in* in expressions like *in* time.

Example:

- He was just *in time* for dinner.

  Meaning: he arrived when dinner was about to be served; at the correct time.

What is the difference between **in time** and **on time**? **In time** means that something has happened approximately at the same time as something else is happening or about to happen. Example: *We are about to have dinner, and you are just **in time** to join us.*

On time means that something has happened exactly at the agreed upon time. Examples: *The student was **on time** for school. School begins at 8 a.m. The student was **on time**.*

Example:

- He was **on time** for dinner. This means that he arrived at **exactly or near the time** when dinner was being served (just before, or exactly when dinner was being served)

Example using *in time*:

- We said dinner was at 6 p.m. and he arrived *in time*. This means that he arrived **sometime approximately around** the agreed upon time of 6 p.m..)

Within : Use **within** to talk about something happening sometime inside of a specific timeframe.

Example:

- The bus should arrive *within* the next 15 minutes.

  Meaning sometime more than 1 minute and less than 15 minutes. So, for example, if it is 8 p.m., the bus should arrive sometime between 8 p.m. and 8:15 p.m. The bus is not expected to arrive at 8:15 p.m. exactly nor at 8 p.m. exactly, but some time in between these two times.

Under : Use **_under_** when talking about something happening in less than a certain amount of time.

Example:

- I'm sure the train will be here in **_under_** an hour. (Meaning in less than an hour)

Over : Use **_over_** when talking about something that takes more than a certain amount of time.

Examples:

- I have been waiting here for you for **_over_** an hour.
- The bus took **_over_** an hour to get to its next stop.

During : Use **_during_** to talk about the time span in which something happened.

Example:

- She cannot sleep well. She woke up several times **_during_** the night. (The time span was the nighttime hours when she was trying to sleep.)

Since : Use **_since_** to talk about situations that began in the past and continue to the present.

Example:

- I haven't felt well **_since_** I left my home country.

  Use since to refer to a specific time in the past like, for example, 1994 or 2 p.m.

For : Use **_for_** to talk about situations that began in the past and continue to the present.

Examples:

- I have been waiting here for the plane **_for_** two hours.

- We have been taking this exam *for* 3 hours and I am tired.

Use for to talk about consecutive time like, for example, for 50 minutes or for 20 years.

From : Use **from** to talk about situations that will begin now or began at a certain time and continue into the future.

Example:

- Last year we lost a very important soccer match to our rival. We were very sad. ***From*** that time on we never lost another game to our rival.

From that time on means *beginning* with that time and *continuing* into the future . . . .

By : When talking about time, use **by** to mean up to a certain time.

Example:

- They will finish building our new house **by** next March.

Practice - *Using Prepositions When Talking About Time*

Directions: Read the story below. Pay particular attention to prepositions **_at_**, **_on_**, **_in_**, **_by_**, **_within_**, **_under_**, **_during_**, **_over_**, **_since_**, **_from_**, **_for_** and **_after_**. Let's begin:

I won the lottery!

Two weeks ago I won the lottery. I'm going to be rich! My life will change forever.

I've got an appointment with the lottery office **_at_** 9 a.m. **_on_** Wednesday. I'm going to the lottery office to pick up my $1,000,000 lottery prize!

During the telephone call, the person at the lottery office told me that I had to be at the lottery office **_on_** January 5th, **_at_** 9 a.m. That's **_on_** a Wednesday. I haven't been able to sleep **_since_** I learned that I won the lottery.

I have been waiting **_for_** two weeks for this appointment. I want to buy many things.

I arrived at the lottery office **_at_** 8:45 a.m. I was really nervous. The lady at the receptionist desk said that the lottery official would give me my prize money **_within_** the next 15 minutes. I really hope he'll be here in **_under_** 10 minutes because I am so excited about receiving this money.

During the time that I was waiting, it has been **_over_** five minutes now, I thought about that money. All that money! I was so excited. **_After_** today, I will be a rich person. I haven't had much money in my life. In fact, I have been poor **_for_** the last five years.

The secretary told me that I was the first person **_in_** the past three years, **_since_** 2005, to win $1,000,000.

I told her about my dream for the future: "**_by_** next Wednesday," I said, "I want to have a new car, and **_in_** three years I want to have a home in Fiji."

I told the secretary: "I won't believe I really won the lottery **_until_** I receive the money in my hands."

Meanwhile, the lottery official opened his door and said, "I'll be out **_in_** five minutes."

I thought to myself: I will buy a brand new car **_by_** Monday, and, **_by_** Wednesday, I will buy a new apartment.

In fact, **_by_** the time you finish reading to this lesson, I will have received my money. I know what I'm going to do! The first thing I'm going to do after I get my money is buy a sailboat and sail around the world!

Quick Review - *Using Prepositions When Talking About Time*
Let's review the use of *on*, *at* and *in* for time sentences

Use **on** for day names, like Monday or Tuesday.

Use **on** in expressions like **on time**.

Use **at** to talk about exact clock time. The exam will start **at** 3 p.m.

Use **at** to talk about midnight, noon, night, day, etc. For example: we had lunch **at** noon. We woke up **at** dawn. We went to bed **at** dusk (when the sun goes down).

Use **at** in expressions referring to time: **at** the moment, **at** the present time, etc. For example: **At** the moment, we are not sure what causes cancer.

Use **in** to talk about what will or may happen in the future: I will arrive **in** Tokyo **in** 4 days.

Use **in** to talk about seasons of the year. For example: we will start school **in** the fall. Our vacation begins **in** the summer

Use **in** to talk about centuries, years, and months. For example: cars were invented **in** the twentieth century. We will finish class **in** May. We will graduate **in** 2012.

Use **in** to talk about blocks of time. For example: I expect to have children **in** the future.

Use **in** to talk about named times of the day. For example: We have tea **in** the morning. We eat lunch in the afternoon. We have dinner in the evening.

Use **in** to talk about months of the year. For example: I will complete my English course **in** February.

Use **in** to talk about years. For example: I came to this country **in** 2001.

Use **in** in expressions like: **in** time. For example: He was just **in time** for dinner.

Snapshot - *Using Prepositions When Talking About Time*

What is the difference between ***in time*** and ***on time?*** ***In time*** means that something has happened approximately at the correct time. ***On time*** means that something has happened exactly at the right time.

He was ***in time*** for dinner. Means that he arrived at some time just before dinner was being served.

We said dinner was at 6 p.m. and he arrived ***on time***. Means that he arrived exactly at 6 p.m.

Chapter 2 - Using Prepositions when Talking About Place or Location

Using the prepositions ***above***, ***across***, ***after***, ***against***, ***along***, ***among***, ***around***, ***at***,

below, ***beside***, ***between***, ***beneath***, ***from***, ***in***, ***off***, ***on***, ***under***, and ***towards*** when talking about place or location.

Above : When talking about place, use ***above*** to mean something that is higher up than something else.

Examples:

- Oh look at that beautiful bird flying ***above*** our heads.
- The president is ***above*** all other managers in the company.
- The ceiling is ***above*** the floor.

Across : When talking about place, use ***across*** to express: from one side to the other.

Examples:

- The chicken walked ***across*** the street to eat some corn.
- The chicken walked ***across*** the busy street safely.
- The cruise ship sailed ***across*** the ocean to Europe.
- The man walked ***across*** the bridge to visit his secret lover.

After : Use ***after*** when talking about the 'next one' when talking about place or location.

Examples:

- The food store is the next building ***after*** the bank.
- The shopping mall is located on the next block ***after*** the high school.

Beside : Use ***beside*** when talking about something that is at the side of or next to something or someone.

Examples:

- The clothing store is ***beside*** the bank.
- The student sat ***beside*** the teacher while the teacher corrected his exam.

Against : When talking about place or location, ***against*** means something contacting or touching something else, pressing on it or pushing on it.

Examples:

- The woman leaned ***against*** the wall waiting for her boyfriend to meet her.
- The traffic was so bad that cars were almost ***against*** one another.

Along : **Along** means over the length of something.

Example:

- The man walked ***along*** the busy road on his way to work.

Among: **among** means something or someone in a group of people or things. There are usually more than two people or things in the group.

Example:

- The woman walked in the park ***among*** the flowers and trees.

Compare: She walked ***between*** two tall trees.

Around : **Around,** first meaning: means in the immediate vicinity. Another way to say this is: something that is close by or near.

Example:

- The new hotel is ***around*** here, but we are not exactly sure where.

Around : **Around,** second meaning: when we talk about a place being on the other side of something (sometimes obscured from your view by something).

Examples:

- The bank is ***around*** the corner from here.
- The police station is ***around*** the other side of the building.

***Around* : *Around*,** third meaning: moving here and there, randomly.

Examples:

- The couple walked ***around*** the neighborhood.
- The boy rode his bicycle ***around*** the town.

At* :** Use ***at to express being in front of, or up to something, but not in it.

Examples:

- He arrived ***at*** the train station ***at*** 3 p.m.. Compare this with: He went ***into*** the train station after he arrived.
- He was ***in*** the train station for 2 hours before his train arrived. The train took him to the airport.
- He was ***at*** the airport by 6 p.m.. He went ***into*** the airport to get his ticket. He was ***in*** the airport for 3 hours before his flight.
- The trash is kept ***at*** the back of the airport building.

In* :** Use ***in to talk about your location within a city, state, country or other named political area.

Examples:

- I will arrive ***in*** Tokyo in 4 days. (Not ***at*** Tokyo)
- He arrived ***in*** New York on Wednesday.

Behind* : *Behind means at the back of or the rear of something or someone.

Examples:

- The trash is kept ***behind*** the building.

- The boy watched the house burn while his little sister hid **_behind_** him.

_On_ : Use **_on_** to talk about something in contact with or over a surface.

Examples:

- The book is **_on_** top of the desk.
- The book is **_on_** the desk.
- The picture is **_on_** the wall.
- The clock is **_on_** the wall.
- The map is **_on_** the wall.
- The light is **_on_** the ceiling.

Under, **_beneath_** and **_below_** : You can use **_under_**, **_beneath_** and **_below_** in similar ways when you want to express something being physically lower than something else.

Examples:

- His feet are **_under_** the desk.
- His feet are **_beneath_** the desk.
- His feet are **_below_** the desk.

Practice - *Using Prepositions when Talking About Place or Location*

Directions: *Read and / or listen (if you are in a group) to this brief story about a college student named Tommy Morgan and his friends to help you further understand how the following prepositions are used:* ***above****,* ***across****,* ***after****,* ***against****,* ***along****,* ***among****,* ***around****,* ***at****,* ***below****,* ***beside****,* ***between****,* ***beneath****,* ***from****,* ***in****,* ***off****,* ***on****,* ***under****, and* ***towards****. After reading and / or listening you will be given some individual example sentences to practice with.*

Tommy Morgan and His Friends

Tommy Morgan sits ***in*** his chair ***at*** his desk. ***On*** his desk there is a book. ***In*** the drawer, ***in*** his desk, there are some school supplies like, for example, pencils and pens. His feet are ***on*** the floor ***below*** the desk and his hands are ***above*** the desk while his elbows rest ***on*** the desk.

His pen is ***between*** the pages of his book. His book is ***on*** his desk. His favorite pen is ***among*** the school supplies ***inside*** the drawer ***in*** his desk. His desk is located ***in*** the middle ***of*** the room.

Tommy Morgan wears very nice shoes ***on*** his feet. ***In*** his right hand there is a pencil. His teacher sometimes tells him he should take his hat off. So he takes his hat off and puts it ***under*** the chair where he sits. His friend Mary sits in front of him ***at*** her desk. His friend Hiro sits ***at*** the desk ***at*** the back of the room. His friend Julio sits ***at*** the desk ***behind*** Tommy.

Today, the teacher is talking to the students about English grammar. ***At*** the top ***of*** the whiteboard, the teacher wrote three irregular verbs. ***At*** the bottom ***of*** the whiteboard the teacher wrote three regular verbs. The teacher asks Tommy to come ***to*** the white board and write a sentence for each verb. She asks him to write the sentences ***in*** the middle of the whiteboard. Tommy leaned ***against*** the whiteboard and thought for a moment. Then he began to write his sentences ***in*** the middle of the whiteboard.

Across from the university, there is a pub. The pub is ***on*** the corner of Warren Avenue and Jackson Place. ***On*** Friday nights, Tommy, Hiro, Julio and Mary meet ***at*** the pub. Mary asked Hiro, "where is the new restaurant that you told me about?' Hiro answered, "I'm not sure, I read about it in the newspaper; it's ***around*** here, not too far away." Mary replied, "oh, so the restaurant is near the pub. Let's go to the restaurant after we go to the pub."

Inside the pub everyone was having a great time. They went ***into*** the pub and had such a good time that they stayed there ***for*** four hours and forgot their idea about going to the restaurant!

Review and Practice - *Using prepositions when talking about location or place*

Directions: Read and / or listen carefully to the sentences below. Fill in the blanks using one of the following prepositions: **above**, **across**, **after**, **against**, **along**, **among**, **around**, **at**, **below**, **beside**, **between**, **beneath**, **from**, **in**, **off**, **on**, **under**, and **towards**. The answers can be found in this chapter (above).

1. Oh look at that beautiful bird flying _____ our heads.

2. The ceiling is _____ our heads.

3. The man walked _____ the street to visit his secret lover.

4. Wal-Mart is the next building _____ the bank.

5. Wal-Mart is _____ the bank.

6. The woman leaned _____ the wall waiting for her boyfriend to meet her.

7. The man walked _____ the busy road on his way to work.

8. The woman walked ____ the park among the flowers and trees.

9. The new hotel is _____ here, but we are not exactly sure where.

10. The couple walked _____ the neighborhood.

11. He arrived ___the train station at 3 p.m.

12. He arrived ___ New York *on* Wednesday.

13. The businesswoman is *in* the car. The man got ____ the train and then ____ a plane to New York.

14. We arrived *at* the train station ____ 2 p.m. Then we went inside the train station. We were *in* the train station when our train arrived ___ 3 p.m.

15. The chicken walked _____ the busy street safely.

16. The trash is kept _____ the building.

17. The trash is kept ___ the back *of* the building.

18. The book is ___ top *of* the desk. The book is **on** the desk

19. His feet are _____ the desk. His feet are **beneath** the desk. His feet are **below** the desk.

Answers: (1) above; (2) above; (3) across; (4) after or beside; (5) beside; (6) against; (7) across; (8) around or in; (9) around; (10) in or around; (11) at; (12) in; (13) on . . . on; (14) at . . . at; (15) across; (16) beside or against; (17) at; (18) on; (19) under

Chapter 3 - Using Prepositions when Talking About Transportation and Traveling

Using the prepositions *in*, *on*, *at*, *into*, *off*, *across*, *from-to*, *along* and ***between*** when talking about transportation and traveling

On: Use ***on*** to talk about trains, buses, and planes. *(Contrast with **in**.)*

Examples:

- I got ***on*** the bus to go to the center of the city.
- When we got ***on*** the plane, we had a difficult time finding our seats.
  - We got ***on*** the train just in time; the train was about to leave.
  - The man got ***on*** the train and then ***on*** a plane to New York.

Using *in* and *inside* note: it *is* true that you are inside the bus, train or plane when you are traveling, but English speakers say "I'm ***on*** a bus to Seattle", for example, if someone calls them on their cell phone. It is more common for English speakers to use ***in*** or ***inside*** when talking about public transportation, for example, when they are talking about things that may have happened while they were traveling, or things that were observed inside the transportation vehicle.

Examples:

- There was a lot of noise ***inside*** the bus while we were going home.
- All of the passengers ***in*** the plane were enjoying the movie.
- The lights ***in*** the train were very bright.

In and ***Into*** : Use ***in*** and ***into*** to talk about taxis, cars and limousines.

Examples:

- The businesswoman left her house at 10 p.m. and then got ***into*** her car and drove to work.

- The two students waved at the taxi to stop.
- When the taxi stopped, they got *in* and told the taxi driver where they wanted to go.

By : Use *by* to talk about how you traveled; what form of transportation.

Examples:

- The family traveled *by* plane to Beijing.
- The boy went to school *by* foot.
- The businesswoman traveled to Frankfurt *by* train.
- We went to the movies *by* bike.

Off : Use *off* in the phrasal verb, *to get off*, to talk about disembarking and arriving at a destination.

Examples:

- The businessman took the train to New Jersey and *got off* in Newark.
- We are taking a plane to Dallas but we are *getting off* in Reno, Nevada.

(Note: Don't use *get off* when referring to a taxi, car, or limousine (for example, don't say "I got off the taxi") Use *get out of* or *arrived in* a taxi, car or limousine. For example: I arrived in New York *in* a taxi. I *got out* of the taxi, paid the taxi driver, and went *inside* the train station to catch the next train to Philadelphia.)

Between : Use *between* to talk about distance from one location to another location.

Example:

- What is the distance *between* New York and Los Angeles? Oh, it's about 2400 miles.

From - to : Use **from - to** to talk about travel plans or distance **from** one location **to** another location.

> **Example:**
>
> - How long does it take to travel **from** New York **to** Chicago?
> - The distance **from** Seattle, Washington **to** Atlanta,
> - Georgia is about 2,900 miles.
> - Could you tell me how to get **to** St. Peters Cathedral **from** here.

Along : Use **along** to talk about traveling over a length of road or train track.

> **Example:**
>
> - We took a train to Miami, Florida. As we traveled **along** the tracks, we could see many farms.

Practice and Review - *Using Prepositions when Talking About Transportation and Traveling*

Directions: *Read this brief story about an English student named Sonya as she travels for the first time in the United States. Read and / or listen carefully to how prepositions are used to talk about transportation and traveling. Fill in the blanks with the correct preposition. Answers are at the end of the chapter.*

Sonya's first trip to Seattle

Sonya came to the U.S. last year to study English (1) _____ New York. She arrived *in* New York (2) ___ May 30th. After studying English *in* New York, she decided to travel *across* the United States using ground transportation like trains, buses, and taxis so that she could see what America looked like.

(3) _____ New York, she decided to take a train *to* Cleveland, Ohio. On the day that she decided to leave, she got (4) _____ a taxi in front of her hotel and told the driver to take her to the railroad station. When she arrived *at* the railroad station she got *out* of the taxi, paid the driver, and went (5) _____ the train station.

After she bought her ticket *at* the ticket counter, she waited *inside* the train station for over an hour, until her train arrived.

When the train arrived and opened its doors, Sonya got (6) ____ the train and found a nice seat *by* the window.

She took many pictures *from* her window seat during the ride to Cleveland. The train was scheduled to stop (7) ___ Pittsburgh, Pennsylvania and Alliance, Ohio before continuing on to Cleveland. When the train stopped *in* Pittsburgh, Sonya got (8) ____ to have a quick look around.

After getting (9) ___ the train again, Sonya had some dinner. As the train traveled (10) _____ the tracks, the sun was going down. Sonya is going to arrive in Cleveland at dusk, just in time to find a hotel room for the evening.

Answers: (1) in ; (2) on ; (3) In ; (4) in ; (5) into ; (6) on ; (7) in ; (8) out ; (9) on ; (10) along

Chapter 4 - Using Prepositions when Giving Directions

Using the prepositions *__in__*, *__on__*, *__at__*, *__near__*, *__down__*, *__towards__*, *__across__*, *__from__*, *__between__*, *__around__* and *__among__* when talking about giving directions

Using prepositions when giving directions

__Towards__ : When giving directions, use *__towards__* to mean in the direction of something.

Example:

- Could you please tell me how to get to the bank?

  Sure. Walk down this street *__towards__* the fountain in the center of the city. Turn left at Warner Street.

__In__ : When giving directions, use *__in__* to mean inside of an area or boundary:

Example:

- Could you please tell me how to get to the bank?

  Sure. Walk down this street *__towards__* the fountain *__in__* the center of the city. Turn left at Warner Street and you will see the bank on your right, *__in__* the financial district.

__On__ : When giving directions, use *__on__* with street, road or highway to indicate location; or use *__on__* in expressions like *on the right*.

Example:

- Could you please tell me how to get to the bank?

  Sure. Walk down this street towards the fountain in the center of the city. Turn left at Warner Street and you will see the bank *__on__* your right, in the financial district. It's *__on__* Warner Street near Sunrise Road.

__Near__ : When giving directions, use *__near__* to mean close to.

Example:

- Could you please tell me how to get to the bank?

  Sure. Walk down this street towards the fountain in the center of the city. Turn left at Warner Street and you will see the bank on your right, in the financial district. It's on Warner Street *__near__* Sunrise Road.

Across : When giving directions, use _across_ to mean from one side to the other side:

Example:

- Could you please tell me how to get to the bank?

  Sure. Walk down this street towards the fountain in the center of the city. Turn left at Warner Street and you will see the bank on your right, in the financial district. It's on Warner Street near Sunrise Road. You may need to walk *__across__* the street. It's *__across__* from the library and between the food store and the computer store.

_At_: When giving directions, use **_at_** to indicate the location of something

Example:

- Could you please tell me how to get to the bank?

  Sure. From here, walk down this street towards the fountain in the center of the city. Turn left *__at__* Warner Street and you will see the bank on your right, in the financial district. It's on Warner Street near Sunrise Road. You may need to walk across the street. It's across from the library and between the food store and the computer store. There are some trees growing at the front of the bank building. The bank is around the corner from the new park.

Around: When giving directions, use **_around_** to talk about something being close, or something located on the other side of something else.

Example:

- Could you please tell me how to get to the bank?

Sure. From here, walk down this street towards the fountain in the center of the city.

Then, turn left at Warner Street and you will see the bank on your right, in the financial district.

It's on Warner Street near Sunrise Road. You may need to walk across the street.

It's across from the library and between the food store and the computer store.

There are some trees growing at the front of the bank building. The bank is ***around*** the corner from the new park, ***around*** where the library is.

Practice and Review - *Using Prepositions when Giving Directions*

Let's read again the discussion about finding the bank. Pay attention to the prepositions and how they are used. See if you can fill in the blanks with the correct answers.

Could you please tell me how to get to the bank?

Sure. **_From_** here, walk **_down_** this street **_towards_** the fountain (1) ___ the center **_of_** the city. Turn left (2) ___ Warner Street and you will see the bank **_on_** your right, **_in_** the financial district. It's **_on_** Warner Street **_near_** Sunrise Road. You may need to walk (3) _____ the street. It's **_across from_** the library and **_between_** the food store and the computer store. There are some trees growing **_at_** the front of the bank building. The bank is (4) _____ the corner **_from_** the new park, **_around_** where the library is.

Answers: (1) in ; (2) on *or* at ; (3) across ; (4) around

Chapter 5 - Using with and by to Express
How Things are Done

 Below we will discuss these important prepositions and provide you with many examples. If you are working in a group, listen carefully to the pronunciation of these expressions in complete sentences.

Some examples of using _**with**_ and _**by**_ to express how things are done:

- The beautiful dress was made _**by**_ hand. Katrina made the beautiful dress _**with**_ her own hands.

- The construction worker dug the hole _**by**_ hand (meaning: manually, with a shovel in his hands; without the help of a machine).

- The construction worker dug the hole _**with**_ his hands (meaning manually, without a shovel or the help of a machine; using his own two hands).

- The family traveled to South Africa _**by**_ air. We sent the letter _**by**_ airmail. We went to school every day _**by**_ foot.

- We walked into the wrong room _**by**_ mistake.

- We paid for the meal _**with**_ a check. We paid for the meal _**by**_ check. We paid for the meal _**in cash**_.

- We were lucky; _**by**_ chance we found the examination room right before the exam was going to begin.

Some rules and examples for using _**with**_ and _**by**_:

_**By**_: _By_ is used to talk about the way you travel or how you travel.

> **Examples:**
- I go to work _**by**_ bus.

- I went to Europe ***by*** plane.

By: ***By*** is used to talk about how you communicate or send mail or packages.

Example:

- We talked ***by*** phone.
- We sent the package to India ***by*** airmail.
- My friend and I communicate ***by*** email.

By: ***By*** is also used in expressions like: ***By mistake*** (meaning: to do something in error) and ***by check*** (meaning: a method of payment)

Example:

- I dialed the wrong number ***by mistake***. I apologized to the person who answered the phone.
- I often pay my bills ***by check***.

Note: if you pay for something with cash, we often say '***in cash***'.

Examples:

- I paid for the new car ***in*** cash.
- I paid the bill ***in*** cash.

It is also possible to say ***with cash***.

Example:

- I paid for the tickets ***with*** cash.

By chance: something that happens that is not planned; luckily or unluckily

Example:

- **_By chance_**, the dress was on sale when we arrived at the shop. We didn't expect to find the dress on sale.

By choice: someone's decision or preference to act in a certain way; a decision originating from one's own free will

Example:

- **_By_** choice, I am single (not married)

  (meaning I choose not to be married).

_By_ : Using **_by_** plus a gerund. Use **_by_** plus a gerund to express a method of doing something

Example:

- I sent an email **_by_** press**_ing_** the send button.
- I repaired the car **_by_** adjust**_ing_** the engine.

With: Use **_with_** when you are talking about using something like a tool or an instrument to do something, or when you are talking about using some part of your body to do something.

Examples:

- I fixed the engine **_with_** a wrench.
- I kicked the door **_with_** my foot.
- I sewed the clothing **_with_** a needle

Let's Practice and Review - *Using the Prepositions <u>by</u> and <u>with</u>*

*Read the following story and fill in the blanks with either <u>**by**</u> or <u>**with**</u>. Answers can be found below.*

1. My friend Jaime and I decided to travel to Hawaii for our vacation. We knew that the flight ____ plane was going to be a long one from Europe, but we really wanted to go to Hawaii.

2. Before we bought tickets, we decided to contact our travel agent in Barcelona (a)____ email to get more information about travel to Hawaii. By chance, out travel agent was working (b)_____ her computer when our email arrived, and she answered our email quickly.

3. She answered our email (a) ____ telling us that she would be happy to give us a brochure about travel to Hawaii. She said that it was probably a good idea to bring a credit card because paying for everything (b) ____ cash was not practical, and it would be dangerous to walk around (c)_____ lots of cash in our pockets. Paying (d) ___ personal check was not a good idea either because many stores in Hawaii do not accept checks that are not from a local bank in Hawaii. She said that going to Hawaii (e)____ Traveler's Checks was a good idea because merchants accepted these in the same way that they accept cash and they were safe to carry in our pockets.

4. When we arrived in Hawaii, we traveled (a)___ bus from the airport to our hotel room. During the ride from the airport we could see Hawaii's beautiful beaches and parks. It smelled like the air was filled (b)_____ flowers, and it was warm and the sky was very blue.

5. The bus let us off in front of a group of hotels (a)_____ all of our luggage. (b)___ mistake, we walked into the wrong hotel. When we asked the clerk at the desk about our reservation, the clerk said that our names were not on the list.

6. ___ chance, there was another person standing at the counter who offered to help. He looked at our itinerary and quickly helped us to find our hotel, which was right next door. He walked with us a little so he could point to the hotel.

7. After getting settled in our hotel room, the rest of the vacation in Hawaii was very exciting. We went ___ bus to see the island.

Answers: (1) by; (2) (a) by; (b) with ; (3) (a) by; (b) with ; (c) with ; (d) by (e) by; (4) (a) by: (b) with ; (5) (a) with (b) by; (6) by; (7) by

Mastering English Prepositions

Section 2: Using Prepositions Correctly After Certain Common English Verbs

Learn to use English prepositions correctly after certain commonly used English verbs.

English has many important expressions that use a combination of verbs plus prepositions or adjectives (beginning with the "be" verb plus prepositions).

How do you know which preposition to use after these verbs? Well, there are no set rules for this. But don't worry! This Focus On English section will help you to understand and then practice and master using these verb-preposition combinations correctly.

Chapter 1 - Prepositions Following Verbs Beginning with the Letter A

In this chapter you will find the English verbs, beginning with the letter 'a,' that are commonly followed by prepositions. An explanation of the verb / preposition combinations is followed by examples of how English speakers typically use these in a wide variety of English sentences.

There are no set rules that might help you to understand which preposition follows a variety of common English verbs. So here you will find the English verbs that are commonly followed by prepositions. Verb / preposition combinations are followed by some examples of how English speakers typically use these in a wide variety of English sentences.

Using prepositions in expressions with certain verbs Verbs beginning with the letter A

Using prepositions in expressions with certain verbs - verbs beginning with the letter A

To be **absent from**:

Examples:

- Students should not **_be absent from_** class.
- Alex **_was_** not **_absent from_** the meeting.

To **_be accustomed to_** (something or someone): similar in meaning to *be used to*

Examples:

- The girl **_is accustomed to_** shopping at the store near her house.
- Kaori **_is accustomed to_** walking home from school.

To be **_acquainted with_** (something or someone):

Examples:

- I *am acquainted with* that man. He is the one who brought the package to our house.
- We *were acquainted with* the school's rules because we went to an orientation.

To *admire for* (something or someone):

Examples:

- I *admire him for* getting a high grade on his exam.
- Gina *admired her mother for* getting a university degree.

To be *afraid of* (something or someone):

Examples:

- I *am afraid of* walking home alone in the dark.
- Lucy *is afraid of* swimming in the ocean.

To *agree with* (something or someone)

Examples:

- I *agree with* my friend. We both have the same opinion about politics.
- Sally *agreed with* her advisor when her advisor told her she should change jobs.

To be *ashamed of* (something or someone)

Examples:

- I *am ashamed of* my friend for stealing the car.
- Clarence *was ashamed of* the bad grade that he got on the exam.

To be **_amazed at_** or **_by_** (something or someone)

Examples:

- I **_am amazed at_** how hard he studied for that exam; almost five hours every night!
- The crowd **_was amazed at_** the circus act.

To be **_angry at_** or **_with_** (something or someone)

Examples:

- I **_am angry with_** / **_at_** my girlfriend for not telling me she was dating someone else.
- The tourists were angry **_with_** / **_at_** the tour guide for speaking too quickly.

To **_apologize for_** (doing something wrong) or **_to_** (something or someone)

Examples:

- I **_apologized_** to the teacher **_for_** being late. I **_apologized for_** being late.
- The policeman **_apologized_** to his boss **_for_** arresting the wrong person.

To **_apply to_** or for

Examples:

- I **_applied to_** the school for admission. I **_applied for_** admission.
- Sam **_applied for_** a new job.

To **_approve of_** (something or someone)

Examples:

- My company **_approves of_** the way I dress when I come to work.
- The passengers on the plane **_approved of_** the way the stewardess did her job.

To **_argue with_** (something or someone)

Examples:

- I **_argued with_** my boss about the project deadline.
- She **_argued with_** her mother about staying out past 10 p.m..

To **_arrive at_** or **_in_** (_at_ a location / building; _in_ a city or country)

Examples:

- I **_arrived at_** school at 8 a.m.. She will **_arrive in_** the United States on Wednesday.
- The hockey team **_arrived at_** the arena at 4:30 p.m..

To **_ask for_** or **_about_** (something or someone)

Examples:

- I **_asked_** him **_for_** a pencil.
- I **_asked_** her **_about_** the exam that she took yesterday.
- The little boy **_asked_** his grandpa **_for_** some candy.

To be **_aware of_** (something or someone)

Examples:

- He **_is aware of_** the penalty for breaking the law.
- We **_were aware of_** the high prices before we entered the store.

To be **_awful at_** (something or someone)

Examples:

- He **_is awful at_** cooking. It's lucky that he has a wife that can cook.
- She **_is awful at_** drawing pictures. She's better at writing.

Let's Practice and Review

Read the following sentences and fill in the blanks with the correct preposition. Answers can be found below.

1. Our boss **_approves_** _____ the way we completed the report.

2. James **_asked_** his teacher _____ the exam yesterday.

3. My friend **_agrees_** _____ me.

4. I **_am ashamed_** _____ our team for losing so badly.

5. I **_admire him_** _____ being brave during the match.

6. Sally **_is afraid_** _____ walking home alone in the dark.

7. Tricia **_is accustomed_** _____ riding the bus home from school.

8. Four students were **_absent_** _____ school.

9. Jim **_was angry_** _____his girlfriend for not telling him that she was dating someone else.

10. The tourists **_were amazed_** _____ how big the building was.

11. The student **_applied_** ___ the school for admission.

12. I **_apologized_** _____ the bus driver **_for_** my extra baggage.

13. Jackie **_argued_** _____ her boss about the new project.

Answers: (1) of; (2) about; (3) with; (4) of ; (5) for; (6) of; (7) to ; (8) from; (9) at; (10) at; (11) to; (12) to; (13) with

Chapter 2 - Prepositions Following Verbs Beginning with the letters B and C

Using prepositions in expressions with certain verbs – beginning with the letters B and C

To be ***bad for*** (something or someone)

Examples:

- Smoking ***is bad for*** your health.
- Factory pollution ***is bad for*** the environment.

To ***believe in*** (something or someone)

Examples:

- I ***believe in*** good luck.
- The people ***believed in*** its government.

To ***belong to*** (something or someone)

Examples:

- The pen ***belongs to*** me.
- The sports car ***belongs to*** the movie star.

To be ***bored with*** or ***by*** (something or someone)

Examples:

- I'm ***bored with*** working every day.
- I'm ***bored by*** that TV show. Can we change the channel?

To ***borrow*** something ***from*** (something or someone)

Examples:

- Tommy Twoshoes ***borrowed*** $10 ***from*** Julio.

(Julio ***lent*** $10 to Tommy Twoshoes.)

- Alicia ***borrowed*** Jim's bicycle ***from*** him.

To be ***careful of*** (something or someone)

Examples:

- ***Be careful of*** the fast-moving cars when you cross the street!
- Calvin told me to ***be careful of*** drinking tap water when traveling.

To ***compare to*** or ***with*** (something or someone)

Examples:

- When I ***compare*** swimming ***with*** (***to***) running, I think that swimming is more difficult.
- ***Compared to*** our team, the opponent's team looks weak.

To ***complain to*** or ***about*** (about something or someone)

Examples:

- I ***complained to*** my teacher ***about*** the cold air conditioning in the room.
- Ginger ***complained about*** the bad food in the restaurant.

To be ***composed of*** (something)

Examples:

- Coke a Cola ***is composed of*** (made of) mostly sugar.
- Bread ***is composed of*** mostly flour.

To ***concentrate on*** (something or someone)

Examples:

- The student has an exam the next day so he ***concentrated on*** studying.
- The athlete ***concentrates on*** winning.

To be ***concerned about*** (something or someone)

Example:

- She ***is concerned about*** her weight. She is gaining weight.
- His parents ***were concerned about*** his poor grades in school.

To ***consist of*** (something) (meaning: made up of certain ingredients)

Examples:

- A good meal ***consists of*** fish, vegetables and rice.
- A good report ***consists of*** lots of research and hard work.

To be ***content with*** (something or someone) (meaning: to be happy with)

Examples:

- The quiet, simple man ***is content with*** his life.
- Amy ***is content with*** her new car.

To be ***crazy about*** (something or someone)

Example:

- She ***is crazy about*** ice cream. She really likes to eat ice cream.
- She'***s crazy about*** her boyfriend.

To be ***curious about*** (something or someone)

Examples:

- The customer ***was curious about*** the price of the car.
- The police detective ***was curious about*** the blood on the floor.

Let's Practice and Review

Read the following sentences and fill in the blanks with the correct preposition. Answers can be found at the bottom of this page.

1. The red Ferrari _belongs_ _____ me.

2. Fiberglass _is composed_ _____ silica fibers.

3. The student _was curious_ _____ the cost of the textbook.

4. Good Italian pasta sauce _consists_ _____ tomatoes, garlic, olive oil, and seasoning.

5. His father _was concerned_ _____ the cost of a new roof for his house.

6. The children _believe_ _____ magic.

7. Drinking too much alcohol _is bad_ _____ your health.

8. Tim Evans _borrowed_ $20 _____ Hiro.

9. _Be careful_ ____ the snake on the ground right next to you!

10. Jenny _complained_ _____ her teacher _____ the noise in the next room.

11. My friend _compared_ his car _____ mine and decided to buy a new car.

The swim team _concentrated_ _____ learning better techniques.

Chapter 3 - Prepositions Following Verbs Beginning with the letters <u>D</u> and <u>E</u>

Using prepositions in expressions with certain verbs – beginning with the letters D and E

Using prepositions in expressions with certain verbs - verbs beginning with the letters D and E

To ***depend on*** (something or someone)

Examples:

- Car motors ***depend on*** gasoline or diesel fuel to run.
- She ***depends on*** her friends for help with her homework.

To be ***devoted to*** (something or someone; to be loyal to)

Examples:

- She ***is devoted to*** her husband.
- The professor ***is devoted to*** his research.

To be ***different from*** (something or someone)

Examples:

- Coffee ***is different from*** tea.
- Apples ***are different from*** oranges.

To ***disagree with*** (something or someone)

Examples:

- I ***disagreed with*** him about smoking in the classroom.
- The lawyers ***disagreed with*** each other in court.

To be ***disappointed in*** (something or someone)

Examples:

- I ***was disappointed in*** our team. They lost the game.
- Jenny ***was disappointed in*** the quality of the fruit at the market.

To ***discuss*** (something) ***with*** (someone)

Examples:

- I ***discussed*** the problem ***with*** my boss.
- The students ***discussed*** the assignment ***with*** the teacher.

To ***divide into*** (divide something into)

Examples:

- I ***divided*** the cake ***into*** two pieces so my friend could have some.
- The manager ***divided*** the workers ***into*** three groups.

To be ***divorced from*** (something or someone)

Examples:

- The woman ***was divorced from*** her husband.
- They ***have been divorced from*** each other for two years.

To ***dream of*** (something or someone)

Examples:

- She ***dreamed of*** going to the South Pacific for a vacation.
- The couple ***dreamed of*** having their own house in the future.

To be ***engaged to*** (someone)

Examples:

- The man and woman ***were engaged to*** each other. They planned to get married in one month.

- Alex and Cynthia ***were engaged to*** each other in March, but broke off the engagement in April.

To be ***equal to*** (something or someone)

Examples:

- His English skills ***are equal to*** her English skills.

- The two soccer teams ***are equal to*** each other in match records.

To ***escape from*** (something or someone)

Examples:

- The prisoner ***escaped from*** prison and the police cannot find him.

- The young dog ***escaped from*** the cage and ran away.

To be ***excited about*** (something or someone)

Examples:

- I ***am excited about*** my summer vacation. I am going to Asia.

- We ***are excited about*** going to Hawaii.

To ***excuse*** (someone) ***for***:

Examples:

- My boss ***excused*** me ***for*** being late for work.

- Frank ***excused*** his friend ***for*** not wanting to go on the hike.

To be ***exhausted from*** (something)

Examples:

- I ***was exhausted from*** working in the garden all day.

- Our team ***was exhausted from*** playing so hard in the competition.

Let's Practice and Review

Read the following sentences and fill in the blanks with the correct preposition. Answers can be found at the bottom of page.

1. I ***divided*** the cake _____ five pieces so all of my friends could have some.

2. Our team lost. I ***was*** really ***disappointed*** _____ our team.

3. We ***discussed*** the plan _____ our superior.

4. The players ***disagreed*** _____ the referee.

5. Monty ***is devoted*** _____ playing the violin.

6. Airline pilots ***depend*** _____ ground control to help them land safely.

7. Surfing ***is different*** _____ snow boarding.

8. My brother ***dreamed*** ____ becoming an engineer.

9. Toby's grades ***are equal*** _____ the best grades in the school.

10. We are in love. My girlfriend and I ***are engaged*** _____ each other.

11. The gorilla ***escaped*** _____ its cage and is now somewhere in the city.

12. The child ***was excited*** _____ going to the zoo.

13. The workers ***were exhausted*** _____ working in the sun all day.

Answers: (1) into; (2) in; (3) with; (4) with; (5) to; (6) on; (7) from ; (8) of or about (9) to; (10) to; (11) from; (12) about ; (13) from

Chapter 4 - Prepositions following verbs beginning with the letters <u>F</u>, <u>G</u>, <u>H</u>, and <u>I</u>

Using prepositions in expressions with certain verbs – beginning with the letters F, G, H, and I

Using prepositions in expressions with certain verbs - verbs beginning with the letters F, G, H and I

To be *familiar with* (something)

Examples:

- I *am familiar with* the laws in my country

  (meaning: I know what the laws are in my country).

To *forgive* (someone) *for* (something)

Examples:

- I *forgive* you *for* coming late.
- Rodney *forgave* the barber *for* the bad haircut.

To be *fond of* (something)

Examples:

- I *am fond of* Italian food. I eat it almost every night.
- Sarah *is* very *fond of* her boyfriend.

To be *friendly with / to* (someone)

Examples:

- The people of New Zealand *are* very *friendly to* foreigners.
- The woman who works at the pub *is* very *friendly with* the customers.

To be *frightened of* or *by* (something)

Examples:

- I *am frightened of* the dark.
- She *is frightened by* his behavior.

To be *full of* (something)

Examples:

- The car *is full of* gas.
- The arena *is full of* people.

To *get rid of* (something)

Examples:

- I am going to *get rid of* my old pants because they have too many holes in them.
- The company president wants to *get rid of* employees who are not working hard.

To be *glad about* (somewhere)

Examples:

- Your team just won the game! Wow, I'*m glad about* that.
- Kathy *was glad about* finishing school.

To be *good at* (something)

Examples:

- He'*s good at* speaking English.
- Mr. Frankel *is good at* teaching English.

To be *good for* (something)

Examples:

- That hammer *is good for* pounding nails into wood
- Yoga *is good for* your health.

To be *gone from* (somewhere)

Examples:

- I'll *be gone from* the office for two hours.
- Hiromi *was gone from* school for a week because of illness.

To *graduate from* (somewhere)

Examples:

- She *graduated from* university last year with a degree in mathematics.
- John and I *graduated from* high school last year.

To *happen to* (do something)

Examples:

- When you were in school, did you *happen to* see your friend, Kazu? (*Happen to* means 'by chance').
- When Joy was at the mall she *happened to* see her friend Alice.

To be *happy about* (something)

Examples:

- The student *was* very *happy about* getting an A on the exam.
- The shopkeeper *was happy about* all the customers that came to his store.

To *hear about* (something)

Examples:

- Did you *hear about* the bank robbery yesterday?
- We *heard about* the cancellation of the concert and we were not happy.

To *hear from* (someone)

Examples:

- She ***heard from*** her good friend in Japan. She got an email from her yesterday.

- I haven't ***heard from*** my brother in six months. I hope he's okay.

To ***help*** (someone) ***with*** (something)

Examples:

- I will ***help*** you ***with*** your homework.

- The clerk ***helped*** me ***with*** filling out the form.

To ***hide*** (something) ***from*** (someone)

Examples:

- He ***hid*** her birthday gift ***from*** her until the day of her birthday.

- The boy ***hid from*** his friend in order to surprise him when he arrived.

To ***hope for*** (something)

Examples:

- We ***are hoping for*** nice weather tomorrow because we want to have a picnic.

- The students who didn't study were ***hoping for*** an easy exam.

To ***insist on*** (something)

Examples:

- Because it was dark, the kind taxi driver ***insisted on*** walking us to our door.
- The young man ***insisted on*** driving the car before buying it.

To be ***interested in*** (something or someone)

Examples:

- The business student ***is interested in*** learning to speak English well.

- My sister and I ***are interested in*** investing in real estate.

To *introduce* (someone) *to* (someone)

Examples:

- I would like to *introduce* you *to* my friend, Stephan.
- Stefan *introduced* his friend *to* me.

To *invite* (someone) *to* (something)

Examples:

- I would like to *invite* you *to* my party.
- Shawn was *invited to* William's party.

To be *involved in* (something) *with* (someone)

Examples:

- We are working together to finish this school project; we *are involved in* this school project.
- The beautiful lady *is involved with* the prince of England. (Meaning: she is having a relationship with the prince.)

Let's practice and review:

Read the following sentences and fill in the blanks with the correct preposition. Answers can be found at the bottom of the page.

1. She's *good* _____ English grammar.

2. My friend Bill is going to *get rid* ____ his old pants because they have too many holes in them.

3. Gene *is frightened* ____ lizards.

4. You just won the lottery! Wow, I am sure you *are glad* _____ that.

5. Brad *graduated* _____ English school last year and can now speak English very well.

6. The boss *will be gone* _____ the office for a day.

7. When you were shopping, did you *happen* _____ see your friend, Aiko?

8. Janet *was* very *happy* _____ getting a passing grade on the exam.

9. Did you *hear* _____ the terrible news yesterday?

10. The doorman *insisted* ____ carrying our luggage.

11. Jeff *hid* his girlfriend's birthday gift _____ her until the day of her graduation.

12. Claudia *is interested* ____ learning to speak English well.

13. The boss wants to *invite* you _____ the company party.

14. Four of us *are involved* ____ the community project.

15. I would like to ***introduce*** you _____ my friend, Frank.

16. He ***was familiar*** _____ the design of the engine.

Answers: (1) at; (2) of; (3) of; (4) about; (5) from; (6) from; (7) to; (8) about; (9) about (10) on; (11) from; (12) in; (13) to; (14) in; (15) to; (16) with

Chapter 5 - Prepositions following verbs beginning with the letters <u>K</u>, <u>L</u>, and <u>M</u>

Using prepositions in expressions with certain verbs – beginning with the letters K, L, and M

To be ***kind to*** (someone)

Examples:

- The young boy ***was*** very ***kind to*** the old lady and helped her to walk across the busy street.
- The clerk in the candy store ***was*** always ***kind to*** children. He gave them a free piece of candy when they came into the store.

To ***know about*** (something)

Examples:

- The students didn't ***know about*** the test that the teacher planned for next Tuesday.

- We were new students and didn't ***know about*** the rules in the school.

To ***laugh at*** (something or someone)

Examples:

- The people on the sidewalk ***laughed at*** the funny car driving down the street.

- All the students ***laughed at*** him because he said something funny.

To ***listen to / for*** (someone or something)

Example:

- We ***listened to*** the rap music.

- We walked along the street late at night in the dark and we ***listened for*** any unusual noise.

Meaning: we *listened for* something means that we were trying to hear something

To *look at / for* (something or someone)

Examples:

- We *looked at* the ocean for a hour.
- We were *looking for* the little girl. She was lost in the big department store.

To *look forward to* (something)

Examples:

- We are *looking forward to* going to Hawaii next month.
- Janice and Hiro were *looking forward to* the hiking trip.

To be *mad at* (someone)

Examples:

- My boss *was mad at* me because I didn't finish my work on time.
- The customer *was mad at* the bartender for giving him the wrong drink.

To be *made of* (something)

Examples:

- The house *was made of* wood.
- The jar *was made of* glass.

To be *made for* (someone)

Examples:

- The dress *was made for* that lady.
- These shoes *were made* especially *for* me.

To be *married to* (someone)

Examples:

- Ted *is married to* Alice.

- Darlene *is married to* Don.

To *matter to* (someone)

Examples:

- The project seemed small, but it *mattered to* the company.

  means: the project was important to the company even though it was a small project.

- Money doesn't *matter to* some people.

  means: money is not important to some people.

To be *the matter with* (someone or something)

Examples:

- I don't know what *is the matter with* this car, it won't start up!

  Means: The car has a problem and the motor won't start

- My brother was sick, but the doctors didn't know what *was the matter with* him.

To *multiply* (this) *by* (that)

Examples:

- If you *multiply* 10 *by* 10 the answer will be 100.

- *Multiply* 2 *by* 27 and the answer is 54.

To *add* (this) *to* / *and* (that)

Examples:

- If you *add* 10 *to* 10 the solution will be 20.

- *Add* 5 *and* 45 and the answer is 50.

To *subtract* (this) *from* (that)

Example:

- *Subtract* 10 *from* 15 and the answer is 5.
- If you *subtract* 100 *from* 1000 you get 900.

To *divide* (this) *by* (that)

Example:

- *Divide* 10 *by* 2 and the answer is 5.
- When 20 is *divided by* 2 the answer is 10.

Let's practice and review

Read and / or listen to the following sentences and fill in the blanks with the correct preposition. Answers can be found at the bottom of this page.

1. **_Subtract_** 15 _____ 30 and the answer is 15.

2. If you **_add_** 20 _____ 30 the solution will be 50.

3. What **_is the matter_** _____ this pen? It doesn't write!

4. Kaori **_is married_** _____ Kazu.

5. His wife **_was mad_** _____ him because he didn't take the garbage outside.

6. The building **_was made_** _____ stone.

7. The wedding dress **_was made_** ____ Yukiko.

8. If you **_multiply_** 5 ___ 5 the answer will be 25.

9. **_Divide_** 100 ___ 50 and the answer is 2.

10. The children are **_looking forward_** ____ going to the park tomorrow.

11. The people at the circus **_laughed_** ___ the funny clown.

12. We sat in the audience and **_listened_**_____ the orchestra.

Answers: (1) from; (2) and; (3) with; (4) to; (5) at (6) of; (7) for; (8) by *or* times; (9) by (10) to; (11) at; (12) to

Chapter 6 - Prepositions following verbs beginning with the letters <u>N</u>, <u>O</u>, <u>P</u>, and <u>Q</u>

Using prepositions in expressions
with certain verbs – beginning with the letters N, O, P, and Q

To be ***nervous about*** (something)

Examples:

- The actress ***was nervous about*** going on stage.
- The students ***were nervous about*** the exam.

To be ***nice to*** (someone)

Examples:

- The owner of the store ***was nice to*** the children and gave them some candy bars.
- Chris *is* always ***nice to*** his cousins.

To be ***opposed to*** (something)

Examples:

- The people of that country ***were opposed to*** high taxes.
- The local people of the island ***were opposed to*** having visitors.

To ***pay for*** (something)

Examples:

- The clerk in the food store waited for the man to ***pay for*** the food.
- Please ***pay for*** your groceries at the checkout counter.

To be ***patient with*** (something or someone)

Examples:

- The teacher ***was patient with*** the new student.
- My sister didn't do well in school, but the teachers were patient with her.

To be ***pleased with*** / ***about*** (something or someone)

Examples:
- Tomoko ***was pleased with*** the new bracelet that she just bought.
- She ***was*** also ***pleased about*** getting such a good price.

To ***point at*** (something or someone)

Examples:
- The little girl ***pointed at*** the bird in the sky.
- It is not polite to ***point at*** someone.

To be ***polite to*** (someone)

Examples:
- Jim was very ***polite to*** the older woman.
- It is not ***polite to*** point at someone.

To be ***prepared for*** (something)

Examples:
- Students, please ***be prepared for*** the final exam next week.
- The people of the town ***were prepared for*** the big storm.

To ***protect*** (something / someone) ***from*** (something / someone)

Examples:
- The mother ***protected*** the child ***from*** the cold rain with an umbrella.
- The police ***protect*** us ***from*** crime.

To be ***proud of*** (someone or something)

Examples:

- Keoki was very ***proud of*** his daughter because she received good grades on her exams.

- We are ***proud of*** our soccer team.

To be *qualified for* (something)

Examples:

- Eric ***was qualified for*** his new computer job. He had 4 years of training in the computer field.

- Joel was not ***qualified for*** the job he was doing.

Let's practice and review:

Read the following sentences and fill in the blanks with the correct preposition. Answers can be found below.

1. Jerry was very **_polite_** _____ the monks.

2. The teacher **_was patient_** _____ the beginning English students.

3. We **_paid_** _____ the food and left the restaurant.

4. Allison **_was pleased_** _____ the clothes she bought at the mall.

5. The guide **_pointed_** _____ the mountains in the east.

6. We **_weren't prepared_** _____ the big storm that came quickly.

7. The applicant **_wasn't qualified_** _____ the job he wanted.

8. My friend was very **_proud_** _____ his sister because she received good grades on her exams.

9. The business **_was nervous_** _____ making the investment.

10. The shop owner **_was nice_** _____ everyone who shopped there.

11. The president of the company _is opposed_ _____ hiring more employees.

Answers: (1) to; (2) with; (3) for; (4) with; (5) at; (6) for; (7) for; (8) of; (9) about (10) to; (11) to

Chapter 7 - Prepositions following verbs beginning with the letters R and S

Using prepositions in expressions with certain verbs – beginning with the letters R and S

To be *ready for* (someone or something)

Examples:

- The doctor *was ready for* the next patient. We *are ready for* the long hike up the mountain. We have out boots and hiking equipment.

- When you are camping in the wild, you should be prepared for anything.

To be *related to* (someone or something)

Examples:

- Bob Moore *is* not *related to* Kathy Moore. They come from different families.

- This bad weather *is* not *related to* the storm that we heard about.

To *rely on* (someone or something)

Examples:

- The employee was never on time and could not do his job right. His boss could not *rely on* him (could not trust him) to do a good job.

- We *relied on* our tour guide to take us back to the hotel.

To be *responsible for* (someone / something)

Examples:

- Jim was the manager of his division in his company. He *was responsible for* his employees and their work.

- Peter *is responsible for* bringing the potato chips to the party.

To be ***sad about*** (something)

Examples:

- The little girl ***was sad about*** loosing her dog.

- Jennifer ***was sad about*** missing the bus.

To be ***safe from*** (something)

Examples:

- The family went into the storm shelter to ***be safe from*** the hurricane.

- Janet uses an anti-virus program on her computer to ***be safe from*** viruses.

To be ***satisfied with*** (someone /something)

Examples:

- Tomoko just bought a new car. She ***was*** very ***satisfied with*** the car. The car was just the right color and was easy to operate.

- Julie ***was satisfied with*** her grade on the exam.

To be ***scared of / by*** (someone / something)

Example:

- The people in the city ***were scared of*** the monster.

- The young children ***were scared by*** the loud noise on the street.

To ***search for*** (someone / something)

Examples:

- Jane could not find her car keys. She ***searched for*** them in her bedroom, living room and bathroom, but she could not find them.

- The police ***searched for*** the missing child.

To ***separate*** (someone / something) ***from*** (someone / something)

Examples:

- The woman bought some beautiful red flowers and green flowers. The florist put all of the flowers together in one bag. When the woman took the flowers home she **_separated_** the green flowers **_from_** the red flowers.

- The contest judges **_separate_** the good performances **_from_** the bad performances.

To be **_sick of_** (someone / something)

Examples:

- The student **_was sick of_** doing homework.

- Jack **_was sick of_** eating the same thing for lunch every day.

To be **_similar to_** (someone / something)

Examples:

- Janet went to the clothing shop to buy a dress. The clerk showed her a dress that **_was_** very **_similar to_** a dress that she already owned.

- This sports car **_is_** very **_similar to_** that one.

To be **_slow at_** (something)

Examples:

- The student **_was slow at_** learning math.

- In the beginning, the visitors **_were_** a little **_slow at_** understanding our culture.

To be **_surprised at / by_** (someone / something)

Examples:

- Hiroko **_was surprised at_** the store's high prices for food.

- Everyone **_was surprised at_** how expensive the dress was.

To **_be_** / **_feel sorry for_** (someone / something) **_about_** (something)

Examples:

- The family lost all of their possessions in the terrible storm. We _**feel**_ very _**sorry for**_ them.

- The boy broke the window with his soccer ball. He _**was**_ very _**sorry for**_ doing this.

- The thief _**was very sorry about**_ stealing the little girl's money.

To _**speak to**_ (someone) _**about**_ (something)

Examples:

- Nicole _**spoke to**_ Tom about the problem she was having at work.

- Maya _**spoke to**_ her travel agent about her trip to Europe.

To _**stare at**_ (someone / something)

Examples:

- Never _**stare at**_ the sun.

- The two lovers _**stared at**_ each other for a long time.

To be _**sure of**_ (someone / something)

Examples:

- The student _**was sure of**_ his answer. He wrote the answer on the test paper.

- Sandra was a confident person; she _**was sure of**_ herself.

Let's practice and review

Read the following sentences and fill in the blanks with the correct preposition. Answers can be found on the bottom of the page.

1. Christine Smith _is related_ ____ Allen Brock. They are brother and sister. Smith is Christine's married name.

2. You should not _rely_ ____ other people to help you.

3. Stephan _was responsible_ _____ maintenance of the company's cars.

4. Julie _was sad_ _____ having to leave Hawaii after her vacation.

5. I went to my doctor and got a flu vaccine to _be safe_ _____ the flu virus.

6. Allan's job at the factory is to _separate_ the large parts _____ the small parts.

7. Annja _searched_ _____ her car keys but could not find them.

8. The children at the zoo _were scared_ _____ the lion.

9. Peter _was satisfied_ _____ the car he just bought.

10. The operator _was sick_ ____ hearing complaints from callers.

11. Jean _was surprised_ _____ the number of people who came to her party.

12. We _feel_ very _sorry_ _____ people who lose family members.

13. The students _were slow_ ____ learning the new lesson.

14. A girl came to the party wearing a dress that _was_ very _similar_ ___ the dress that Kyoko was wearing.

15. The team _was sure_ ____ it's ability to win the soccer match.

16. Never _stare_ _____ a stranger. It's impolite.

Answers: (1) to; (2) on; (3) for; (4) at; (5) from; (6) from; (7) for; (8) of; (9) with (10) of; (11) at; (12) for (13) at; (14) to; (15) of; (16) at

Chapter 8 - Prepositions following verbs beginning with the letters <u>T</u> through <u>Z</u>

Using prepositions in expressions
with certain verbs – beginning with the letters T through Z

To *take care of* (someone / something)

Examples:
- The mother *took care of* the child.
- The businessman *took care of* the details needed to complete the business transaction.

To *talk to / with* (someone) *about* (something)

Examples:
- The boy's father *talked to* him about his poor grades in school.
- The new employee *talked with* some of her colleagues about her new job.

To *tell* (someone) *about* (someone / something)

Examples:
- The police *told* everyone *about* the prisoner that escaped.
- Mary told Christine about the new family who moved into the neighborhood.

To be *terrible at* (something)

Examples:
- Jack *was terrible at* math. He never got good grades on his math exams.
- When I was in high school, I *was terrible at* history.

To be *terrified by* / *of* (someone / something)

Examples:

- The little girl *was terrified of* the dark. She would never go outside of the house after dark.

- Jan's mother *was terrified by* snakes.

To *thank* (someone) *for* (something)

Example:

- The old lady *thanked* the boy *for* helping her to cross the street.

To be *tired of* (someone or something) (*similar to* *sick of*):

Example:

- The little boy *was tired of* eating vegetables at dinner time.

To be *tired from* (something)

Examples:

- The man *was tired from* working so hard.

- Andrew *was tired from* the workout.

To *travel to* (somewhere)

Examples:

- The girl and her boyfriend *traveled to* Las Vegas together.

- We plan on *traveling to* Indonesia this summer.

To be *used to* (something)

Examples:

- Jim walks to school every day. Walking to school was not a problem for Jim because he *was used to* doing it. (Same meaning as accustomed to)

- Megumi *is used to* spending many hours studying English.

To *wait for* (someone or something)

Examples:

- The people in the theater ***waited for*** the show to begin.

- We ***waited for*** the train for one hour.

To ***wait on*** (someone)

Examples:

- The waiter in the restaurant ***waited on*** the customers.

- The stewardess ***waited on*** the airline passengers.

To be ***worried about*** (someone or something) (similar to ***worry about***):

Examples:

- The mother ***was worried about*** her sick child.

- Toby ***was worried about*** his friend who was in the hospital.

Let's practice and review

Read the following sentences and fill in the blanks with the correct preposition. Answers can be found at the bottom of this chapter .

1. The nurse _**waited**_ _____ her seriously ill patients.

2. The principal of the school _**was used**_ _____ hearing the excuses of the late students.

3. We _**traveled**_ _____ Honolulu last year.

4. The hikers _**were tired**_ _____ walking so much.

5. The big, strong man _**was terrified**_ _____ spiders.

6. The manager _**thanked**_ his workers _____ their hard work.

7. The policeman _**talked**_ _____ Jenny _____ her expired drivers license.

8. Fred _**was terrible**_ _____ English grammar.

9. The lady next door _**told**_ everyone _____ Mika's new boyfriend.

10. The baby sitter _**took care**_ _____ the two children.

11. Everyone at the bus stop _**waited**_ _____ the 12:05 bus.

12. The students **were worried** _____ the exam.

Answers: (1) on; (2) to; (3) to; (4) of; (5) of; (6) for; (7) to . . . about; (8) at; (9) about (10) of; (11) for; (12) about

Mastering English Prepositions

Section 3: Understanding the meanings and correct usage of all common English prepositions

Learn to use English prepositions correctly in all kinds of English sentences and conversation.

In this section, the student will find a comprehensive listing of the most commonly used prepositions in the English language, along with clear explanations about how to use them in different types of English sentences and plenty of examples to reinforce understanding.

Chapter 1 - English prepositions beginning with the letters <u>A</u> and <u>B</u>

This is a comprehensive listing of the most common English prepositions. The prepositions are followed by a usage explanation. After each explanation there are examples to help reinforce the correct use of the preposition in common English sentences.

Common English prepositions beginning with the letters A and B

Below we will explain these commonly used prepositions, give you many examples and give you some practice at the end of the chapters.

About

About: usually we use the word ***about*** before a topic or person

Examples:
- They are talking ***about*** the plan for next week.
- The newspaper story is ***about*** the bank robbery that took place last night.
- She is not talking ***about*** you she is talking about Betty.

About can also mean preparing to or getting ready to do something:

Example:
- She was ***about*** to leave when suddenly it began to rain.

Sometimes we use the word ***about*** to help describe a noun:

Example:
- There is something scary ***about*** that dark house.

Some **non**-prepositional uses for the word ***about:***

Examples:

- He did an ***about***-face (meaning: he changed his direction by 180 degrees).

- It's ***about*** time! You're late! We have been waiting for more than three hours.

Note: ***about*** can also be used as an adverb. The adverb ***about*** means almost:

Example:

- They are ***about*** done with the exam.

Above:
(the opposite of **above** is **below**)

Above: usually, ***above*** means higher than or over:

Examples

- Oh look at that bird flying ***above*** our heads.

- Look, this is very easy to understand. The ceiling is ***above*** us and the floor is beneath us. Got it?

- There are no subways in this city; all the trains travel ***above*** ground. (Our city has a good subway system; the trains travel ***below*** ground.)

Above: Sometimes ***above*** is used in a sentence to talk about a good person that has good values and judgment and would not do something wrong:

Example:

- The Buddhist monk is ***above*** stealing.
- A virtuous person is ***above*** hurting others.

Above: Sometimes ***above*** is used like in the above sentence but to mean that a person wrongly believes that they are better than, for example, the law.

Example:

- The politician thought that he was **_above_** the law. (meaning: the politician wrongly believed that he could commit crimes because he thought that he was higher than the law).

Above: Sometimes when you are reading something and it says to see something **_above_**. This means to look for something that was written before the section you are now reading.

Example:

- If you are having trouble using your new mp3 player, please see the **_above_** instructions.

Across

Across is usually used to talk about movement from one side to the other side of a space, area, or location:

Examples:

- The man walked **_across_** the street to visit his secret lover.
- The tiny boat sailed **_across_** the great Pacific Ocean.
- The satellite flew **_across_** the sky at great speed.

Across is often used to mean directly facing something or someone:

Example:

- The bank was directly **_across_** from the food store. (*Meaning: the bank's location and the food store's location were across from or facing each other*)

Across: Other uses for the preposition **_across_**:

Example:

- I came **_across_** a big sale while I was at the shopping mall.

  (Meaning: I discovered something I didn't expect to find while I was shopping.   Please see Phrasal Verbs for more information.)

After
(the opposite of **after** is **before**)

After is usually used to mean following or later than:

Examples:

- There was a big dinner **after** the wedding ceremony, and the bride and groom were toasted many times.
- Dessert came **after** the main course, and it was delicious.
- I will be ready to go **after** 9 a.m.; please don't rush me.
- **After** breakfast, we went to the zoo and saw the new baby elephant.

After is used to mean something that happens continuously:

Example:

- The student studied night **after** night for the final exam.

After is often used to mean to chase or to be in pursuit of:

Example:

- The soccer player ran **after** the ball.

After can be used as a conjunction to connect two parts of a sentence:

Example:

- The teacher congratulated me **after** I received a high mark.

Please see Gerunds and Infinitives for more information about gerunds that follow prepositions.

Against

Against can mean something forcibly hitting into or touching something else:

Example:

- He hit the tennis ball *__against__* the wall, but he didn't hit it very hard.

__Against__ is usually used to mean to lean on or touch something or someone for support:

Example:
- You are such a lazy husband. The ladder is *__against__* the wall in the garage. Use this ladder to help to paint the house.

__Against__ can mean in opposition to something:

Example:
- The people of the town were *__against__* higher taxes.

__Against__ can also mean something that may not be an advantage; a disadvantage:

Example:
- They tried to repair the railroad tracks as quickly as possible, but time was *__against__* them; the next train would soon arrive.

__Against__: Other uses for the preposition **__against__** as in this English expression meaning 'impossible or unlikely':

Example:
- *__Against__* all odds, Hiro won the tournament.

Ahead of

__Ahead of__ usually means to be located in front of:

Example:
- Kazu was ahead of Katrina in the lunch line. (Meaning, Katrina was closer to where lunch was being served than Kazu was.)

__Ahead of__ can sometimes mean that someone or something is more advance than someone or something else:

Example:

- The student registered for classes one week late and so the other students were ***ahead of*** him.

Meaning: the other students had already been studying for one week. The new student was new to the class work.)

Along

Along usually means following the boundary of something:

Example:

- There were beautiful flowers (all) ***along*** the road.

Along can mean together:

Example:

- My friend Don decided to drive to Dallas, Texas. I decided to go ***along*** for the ride.

Please refer to "Beyond Phrasal Verbs" book, for more information about the word ***along***.

Among

Among usually means surrounded by, included in a group, or many things or people in a group:

Examples:

- See, over there. You can see the house ***among*** the trees. There are ghosts in that house.
- The party was a lot of fun. I was ***among*** my friends so I felt very comfortable. We had a blast.

Around

Around can mean: follow a route (sometimes almost circular) to a desired location; located on the farther side of:

> **Example:**
> - The shopping center is **_around_** the corner from the bank, and two stores down from Wal-Mart. It's close to the park.

Around can mean following a boundary in a circular direction:

> **Examples:**
> - For exercise we walk **_around_** the park, and then we do yoga and tai chi.
> - The man traveled **_around_** the world by foot.

Around can mean walking or moving in many different directions randomly:

> **Example:**
> - We walked **_around_** the car show for about an hour and then we went home. We saw many interesting concept cars there.
>
> *Please refer to the Focus on English book about "Beyond Phrasal Verbs" for more information about the word **_around_**.*

As

_As_ *can mean: in the role of:*

> **Example:**
> - Marco works **_as_** a mail clerk for the postal service.
>
> *Please refer to the Focus on English book "Beyond Phrasal Verbs" for more information about the word **_as_**.*

At

_At_ is often used in expressing time:

Example:

- I have to be at the dentist office *at* 10 o'clock. Oh, I don't want to go!

At is often used in talking about location:

Examples:

- He sat *at* his desk and sent emails to his girl friends.
- Example: There was someone *at* the door with a big package. I was so surprised.
- Example: We have to be *at* the show at 9 p.m., otherwise they will not allow us to enter the theater.

At is used to express a level or rate:

Examples:

- The food store is selling tomatoes *at* $1.00 per pound. Boy, that's cheap!
- She is a good student. She is *at* the top of her class.

At is sometimes used to express rate of speed:

Example:

- The policeman stopped Martin and told him that he was driving too fast. Martin was traveling *at* 75 miles per hour when the policeman saw him.

There are many uses for the word at after certain English verbs, in English phrasal verbs, and in English expressions (or idioms). Please refer to our "Beyond Phrasal Verbs" book.

Before
(the opposite of **before** is **after**)

Before is sometimes used in expressions of time, as in: earlier than a certain time:

Examples:

- The new student arrived in class *__before__* 9 a.m..
  - The bus usually arrives *__before__* 4 p.m..
  - Oh no, we have to be at school *__before__* 8 a.m. tomorrow morning because we have to prepare a presentation for the class. Oh, I can't get up that early!

__*Before*__ is sometimes used to express order:

Examples:
- The B train comes *__before__* the J train. If you miss the B train you will have to wait for 1 hour for the next B train.
- The letter A comes *__before__* the letter B in the English alphabet.

__*Before*__ is sometimes used to express the position of someone or something in relationship to something else:

Examples:
- The student was asked to stand *__before__* the class and give her presentation.
- The politician stood *__before__* the crowd and gave a speech.

Behind
(the opposite of **behind** is **ahead**)

__*Behind*__ is sometimes used to express on the other side of something or someone; or to the rear of something:

Examples:
- The mouse is *__behind__* the wall, and it sounds like he's playing a clarinet.
- She hid her face *__behind__* her scarf because she was laughing at the boy who seemed so interested in her.

__*Behind*__ is sometimes used in expressions of time, meaning late or not on schedule:

Example:

- We were supposed to finish the project yesterday, but we are ***behind***.

Below
(the opposite of below is above)

Below is used to talk about rank, position or location in comparison to something or someone else:

Examples:

- We live in a valley ***below*** a big mountain. (location)
- The dish soap is in the cabinet ***below*** the sink. (location)
- The assistant director is ***below*** (lower in rank) the director. (rank)

Beneath
(similar in meaning to the preposition **underneath**)

Beneath means under something and sometimes hidden or concealed by something:

Examples:

- Your feet are ***beneath*** the desk. Do I need to tell you that?
- The rug is ***beneath*** your feet. Please take off your shoes because the rug is new.

Beneath can be used to mean that something or someone is less worthy than someone or something else:

Examples:

- I am well educated and have plenty of experience. That job is for people with no education or experience. That job is ***beneath*** me. I am better than that.
- How dare you accuse me of stealing! I come from a very good family with high virtues. Stealing is ***beneath*** me.

(🖊 Meaning: I am too virtuous to commit a crime).

Beside
(similar in meaning to **_next to_**)

Beside means very close by, next to:

Examples:

- My friend stood **_beside_** me while I applied for citizenship.
- Your bicycle is **_beside_** the house.
- The pencil is there, **_beside_** your book.

Beside can also be used to mean very upset, agitated or emotional:

Examples:

- The mother was **_beside_** herself when she heard that her daughter was in the hospital.
- The man who won the lottery was **_beside_** himself with joy.

Besides

Besides can mean *in addition to or apart from*; :

Examples:

- **_Besides_** being the best student in the school, she was also a good athlete.

  (🖊 meaning: **_in addition to_** being the best student . . .)

- You are not old enough to drink alcohol, and **_besides_** that, alcohol is not good for you.

  (🖊 meaning: another reason why you shouldn't drink alcohol (**apart from** the fact that you are not old enough . . .)

Between

Between is used to talk about location of something, usually in the middle of two other things or people:

> **Examples:**
>
> - The grocery store is located ***between*** the bank and the library.
> - I found my homework. It was ***between*** the first and second page of my grammar book.

Between is sometimes used in expressions of time: from (beginning with) one time to (ending with) another time :

> **Examples:**
>
> - We eat lunch ***between*** 12 p.m. and 1 p.m. every day.
> - School is closed ***between*** June 1st, and August 1st.

Between is sometimes used to express sharing:

> **Examples:**
>
> - We went on our vacation with about $500 ***between*** us.
>
>   (Meaning: together we had $500).
> - The ice cream cone costs $1.75, but we only had $1.50 ***between*** us.
>
>   (Meaning: together we only had $1.50, 75 cents each, not enough for the ice cream cone)

*There are other uses for the word **between** in English phrasal verbs and in English expressions (or idioms). Please refer to our book, "Beyond Phrasal Verbs".*

Beyond

Beyond is used to express that something's or someone's location is further ahead or on the other side of something / someone else :

> **Examples:**
>
> - Hello, I'm looking for the bank. Is it much further ahead?

No, only a kilometer ***beyond*** the gas station.

- Excuse me, where is the restroom?

  The restroom is located just ***beyond*** the water fountain in that direction.

Beyond is sometimes used to express lack of understanding about something:

Examples:

- That math example was so hard. It was ***beyond*** me.

  (🐒 Meaning: the math example was beyond my understanding, or my ability to understand it).

- I heard that Keiko got a passing grade on the exam.

  How she ever passed that exam without studying is ***beyond*** me!

Beyond can also be used to express being ahead of something or someone:

Example:

- She is a very good English student; she is ***beyond*** me in grammar and writing.

  (🐒 Meaning: she is better than me at English grammar and writing)

By

By can be used in expression of time with the meaning not later than:

Examples:

- Why are you so worried?
  The teachers said that we have to have the homework done ***by*** Wednesday at 8am!

- Hurry, we have to be there ***by*** 5 p.m. or we will miss the show.

By can be used to talk about a way or method of doing something:

Examples:

- You can calculate the solution to that problem **by** adding 5 and 8 together.
- I have to go to school **by** bus tomorrow because my car broke down.
- I went to Fiji **by** boat. Boy, that was a long trip!

By can be used to can be used to mean near or next to:

Examples:

- My dog was sitting **by** my side.
- He parked his car **by** my car.

  (Meaning: he parked his car next to my car.)

By can be used to express who or what caused something (usually used in passive sentences):

Examples:

- This house was built **by** a carpenter.
- The building was destroyed **by** the typhoon.
- The fingerprint marks on the wall were made **by** the child.

By can be used when talking about math, multiplication, division and expressing the measurements of rooms and geometric shapes:

Examples:

- The teacher told us that when we multiply 5 **by** 6 the answer is 30.
- All four pieces of candy cost $1.00. To calculate how much each piece of candy costs, divide $1.00 **by** 4. Each piece of candy costs 25 cents!
- The room measures 10 feet **by** 50 feet. That's a big room!

*There are other uses for the word **by** in English phrasal verbs and in English expressions (or idioms). Please refer to our book, "Beyond Phrasal Verbs".*

Chapter 1 *review*

Prepositions beginning with the letters **A** and **B**

Instructions: read the sentences below. Decide whether the use of the preposition is correct or incorrect. If incorrect, which of these prepositions **best** fits the sentence: ***about, above, across, after, against, ahead of, along, among, around, as, at, before, behind, below, beneath, beside, besides, between, beyond, by***. The answers can be found at the bottom of this page.

1. Alfred is talking **about** the exam he took last night. ☐correct ☐incorrect

2. The military planes are flying **beneath** our heads. ☐correct ☐incorrect

3. The grocery store was directly **by** the street from the library. ☐correct ☐incorrect

4. The policeman ran **among** the criminal. ☐correct ☐incorrect

5. The new bicycle is **against** the wall in the garage. ☐correct ☐incorrect

6. Lila was **ahead** of Alicia and Tommy in the registration line. ☐correct ☐incorrect

7. There were many people **among** the road during the marathon. ☐correct ☐incorrect

8. Many people walk **around** the mall for exercise. ☐correct ☐incorrect

9. William works as a pizza maker for the pizza shop **on** the corner. ☐correct ☐incorrect

10. Mika sat **between** the table and read a book. ☐correct ☐incorrect

11. You are not late for work if you arrive **before** 9 a.m.. ☐correct ☐incorrect

12. The vice president is **about** the president in rank. ☐correct ☐incorrect

13. The new floor tile is **beneath** my feet. ☐correct ☐incorrect

14. Your bicycle is **<u>above</u>** the house. ☐correct ☐incorrect

15. You can find the bank **<u>between</u>** the pet store and the fire station. ☐correct ☐incorrect

16. The grocery store is located just **<u>along</u>** the water fountain. ☐correct ☐incorrect

Answers: (1) correct; (2) incorrect; should be <u>above</u>; (3) incorrect; should be <u>across</u>; (4) incorrect; should be <u>after</u>; (5) correct; (6) correct; (7) incorrect; should be <u>along</u>; (8) correct; (9) correct (10) incorrect; should be <u>at</u>; (11) correct; (12) incorrect; should be <u>above</u> (13) correct; (14) incorrect; should be <u>by</u> *or* <u>beside</u>; (15) correct; (16) incorrect; should be <u>beside</u>

Chapter 2 - English prepositions beginning with the letters <u>C</u> - <u>F</u>

This is a comprehensive listing of the most common English prepositions beginning with the letters **C** through **F**. The prepositions are followed by a usage explanation. After each explanation there are examples to help reinforce the correct use of the preposition in common English sentences.

Common English prepositions beginning with the letters C - F

Below we will discuss the commonly used prepositions beginning with the letters **C** through **F**.

Close to

Close to is used to express nearness or nearly (almost):

Examples:

- Where is the shopping mall?
  The shopping mall is ***close to*** the park.

- I am very ***close to*** my family.

- I received ***close to*** 100 emails this morning (meaning, almost 100 emails)! I'm tired of spam!

Despite

Despite (In Spite Of) is used with a similar meaning to even though or notwithstanding:

Examples:

- ***Despite*** the rain, we will still have a picnic.

- He did well on the exam ***despite*** the difficult questions.

- He can kick a soccer ball hard ***despite*** the fact that he has weak legs.

Down

Down is used with a similar meaning to along when talking about travel:

> **Examples:**
> - We walked **_down_** the road for about 2 miles and then stopped at the lake.
> - My friend drove **_down_** the highway at about 100 miles per hour. I was really scared!

Down is used to talk about going from a higher place to a lower place:

> **Examples:**
> - The divers went **_down_** to the bottom of the lake.
> - He was playing cards with his friends and he was loosing money. He threw the cards **_down_** on the table in anger.

*There are other uses for the word **_down_** in English phrasal verbs and in English expressions (or idioms). Please refer to our book, "Beyond Phrasal Verbs".*

During

During is used in expressions of time; meaning within a period of time or meaning at the same time as something else is happening:

> **Examples:**
> - I wrote my friend an email **_during_** the morning break. (within a period of time)
> - I got up **_during_** the show and bought my girlfriend some popcorn. (at the same time as the show was occurring)

Far From

Far From is used to talk about distance with the meaning that something is located a long way apart from something else:

> **Examples:**
> - The airport was **far from** the city center.
> - Everyone moved **far** away **from** the entrance so that other people could enter the room easily.

For

For: Use **for** in conversation to indicate a special purpose for something or someone:

> **Examples:**
> - He uses a motorcycle **for** transportation.
> - She wears that outfit **for** the beach.
> - Do you give a gift to your girlfriend when she gets a good grade on her exams? No, I usually don't give gifts **for** that reason.
> - My friend gave me a gift **for** Christmas.
> - We wore costumes **for** Halloween.

For: Use **for** in conversation to talk about time (usually length of time or to indicate future time):

> **Examples:**
> - I have been in New York **for** 3 months. (length of time)
> - I have been studying English **for** 2 years. (length of time)
> - I am studying now **for** the test next week. (future time)

For: Use **for** to express who or what is the recipient:

> **Examples:**
> - They played the song **for** him.
> - My wife has a gift **for** me.

- The engineer has some information *for* his boss.
- I bought gas *for* the car.

For: Use *for* to explain the reason or benefit of doing something:

Examples:

- The student apologized *for* getting a bad grade. (reason)
- The woman was paid *for* cleaning the house. (reason)
- The boy was scolded *for* stealing the apple. (reason)
- We go surfing *for* fun. (benefit)
- We speak English to everyone *for* practice. (benefit)

For: Use *for* to talk about financial transactions:

Examples:

- Apples are $5 *for* 3 pounds.
- After he repaired the woman's car, he handed her a bill *for* $1,000!
- How much does he get paid?
  He works *for* $10 an hour.

For: Use *for* to express an unusual talent or sense:

Examples:

- Marco can sing any song just by listening to it! He has an ear *for* music.
- That woman has an eye for good art. She buys and sells art *for* an art gallery.

For: Use *for* to express an unusual fact:

Examples:

- That woman has big feet *for* such a small person.
- Boy, it's really cold *for* July!

*There are other uses for the word **for** in English phrasal verbs and in English expressions (or idioms). Please refer to our book, "Beyond Phrasal Verbs".*

From
(the opposite of *from* is *to*)

From can be used in expressions of time:

Examples:

- The advanced English course runs *from* April 1st through April 30th. (*From*, in this example, has the meaning of 'beginning on.')

- The celebration runs *from* 5 p.m. on. (Meaning: *From* 5 p.m. until an unknown time in the future)

- We will see the exhibit one month *from* today. (Meaning: one month's time, beginning today)

From can be used to indicate where something came from, source:

Examples:

- I got a letter *from* my friend in China.
- Peaches come *from* Georgia.
- The brother and sister get money *from* their parents.
- He doesn't come *from* Europe. He comes *from* South Africa.

From can be used to indicate source + separation:

Examples:

- She borrowed money *from* her friend. (The friend was the source and money was separated *from* her and was lent to her friend).
- The scientists tried to protect the whales *from* harm. (Separating the whales from harm)

From can be used to indicate distance (and separation) away:

Examples:

- My aunt lives 25 miles *from* here.
- New York City is 2,905 miles *from* San Francisco.
- The racing cars raced passed us and then disappeared *from* view very quickly.

From is used in discussing math, especially subtraction:

Examples:
- Two *from* four equals two.
- 100 *from* 1000 = 900

From can answer the question why; **from** can mean because of:

Examples:
- Why are they tired? They are tired *from* running all day.
- Why are they so overweight? They are overweight *from* eating too much.

From can be used to talk about what something is made of:

Examples:
- The sweater was made *from* wool.
- The shoes were made *from* leather.
- The apple tree was grown *from* a seed.

From can be used to talk about position in relation to something or someone else (usually referring to viewing or listening):

Examples:
- We can see the fireworks *from* our window.
- I could hear the speech *from* the back of the room.

*There are other uses for the word **from** in English phrasal verbs and in English expressions (or idioms). Please refer to our book, "Beyond Phrasal Verbs".*

Chapter 2 *review*

*Prepositions beginning with the letters **C** through **F***
*Instructions: read and / or listen carefully to the sentences below. Decide whether the use of the preposition is correct or incorrect. If incorrect, which of these prepositions **best** fits the sentence: **close to**, **despite**, **down**, **during**, **far from**, **for**, **from**. The answers can be found at the bottom of this page.*

1. Go **down** the road for about 3 miles, and then turn left at the red light.
   ☐correct ☐incorrect

2. A student raised his hand **close to** the class and asked a question.
   ☐correct   ☐incorrect

3. The library is **far from** the school building. ☐correct   ☐incorrect

4. The workers use the machine **except** digging the earth. ☐correct
   ☐incorrect

5. Jean received an email **close to** her friend in Spain. ☐correct   ☐incorrect

6. The members of the soccer team are tired **from** the workout. ☐correct
   ☐incorrect

7. **Despite** the bad weather, our team won the match. ☐correct   ☐incorrect

8. I went for a swim **during** the afternoon. ☐correct   ☐incorrect

9. Alex borrowed money **down** Tricia. ☐correct   ☐incorrect

10. The company sells products **for** a profit. ☐correct   ☐incorrect

Answers: (1) correct; (2) incorrect; should be during; (3) correct; (4) incorrect; should be for; (5) incorrect; should be from; (6) correct; (7) correct; (8) correct; (9) incorrect; should be from; (10) correct

Chapter 3 - English prepositions beginning with the letters I - N

This is a comprehensive listing of the most common English prepositions beginning with the letters *I* - *N*. The prepositions are followed by a usage explanation. After each explanation there are examples to help reinforce the correct use of the preposition in common English sentences.

Common English prepositions beginning with the letters I - N

Below we will discuss these commonly used prepositions and provide you with many examples.

In

In is used to talk about a person's or thing's location inside of something:

Examples:

- She was sitting *in* the room.
- He was watching television *in* his house.
- The pen was *in* the drawer.

In is used to talk about a location direction:

Examples:

- The sun sets *in* the west.
- Beautiful woven rugs are made *in* the east.

In is used to talk about being inside of a location boundary, city, country, state, etc:

Examples:

- Right now, we are *in* New York City.

- My friend lives *in* San Francisco.
- Tokyo is *in* Japan.
- We are *in* the park.

  (What is the difference between *at* the park and *in* the park? We say that we are *in* the park when we are within the boundaries of the park. We often say we are *at* the park when we have arrived near to the park boundary. Sometimes, English speakers use *in* and *at* interchangeably when referring to locations like airport, library, school, park, etc. Example: Where are you now? I'm *at* the park; or, I'm *in* the park. Generally, *at* refers to being located close to or on the border of a location, whereas *in* refers to being inside the boundaries of the location.)

In is used to talk about time:

Examples:

- He was born in Okinawa, *in* 1983.
- I'm late! I have to be at school *in* 10 minutes!
- My wife should be home *in* 2 hours.
- We usually start school *in* September.
- My mother will be arriving *in* two weeks.
- They take their shower *in* the morning.
- We watch the sun set *in* the evening.
- I think we were happier *in* the 1970s. (or: *in* the 70s)

In: Use *in* when talking about weather:

Examples:

- We like to walk *in* the rain.
- It's hot *in* the sun.

In: Use *in* when talking about what someone is wearing:

Examples:

- She went to dinner *in* a beautiful black dress.
- They went to the Halloween party *in* a funny costume.

In: Use *in* when talking about a location on the body:

Examples:
- He was hit *in* the chest.
- She put her contact lens *in* her eye.
- The soccer player has a pain *in* his foot.

In: Use *in* when talking about how people relate to each other:

Examples:
- They were *in* an argument last night.
- All of the members of the group worked *in* cooperation with each other to solve the problem.
- The mother asked the little boy why his shirt was torn. The little boy told his mother that he was *in* a fight.

In: Use *in* when talking about the current status of something or someone:

Examples:
- The old book is still very popular. It is still *in* print.
- That recipe is very famous and is *in* demand. (Meaning: many people would like to have it)

In: Use *in* when you want to be clear about measurement:

Examples:
- He is very heavy. I don't know what he weighs *in* kilos, but *in* pounds he weighs more than 300.
- The car is very tall *in* height.

There are many other uses for the word __in__ in English phrasal verbs and in English expressions (or idioms). To learn more, please refer to our book, "Beyond Phrasal Verbs".

In Back of

In __Back__ of means to the rear of or behind:

Examples:

- They keep the garbage cans **in __back__ of** the building.
- The garage is **in __back__ of** the house.

In Front of

In __Front__ of refers to something or someone that is located before or facing something or someone:

Examples:

- The woman stood **in __front__ of** the mirror combing her hair.
- The car was parked **in __front__ of** the school building.

Inside

Inside refers to something or someone that is located within something else:

Examples:

- The pencils are **inside** that red box.
- The two girls are **inside** that house.

Instead of

Instead __of__ means to substitute something for something else:

Examples:

- We went swimming ***instead of*** surfing.
- Kazu studied English ***instead of*** Italian.

Into

Into is used to mean enter:

Examples:

- The businessman stepped ***into*** the cab.
- The English student went ***into*** the classroom.
- The flower shop girl put the flowers ***into*** a bag.

Into is sometimes used to mean something of interest or an occupation or preoccupation:

Examples:

- The students are really ***into*** learning English. (The students really enjoy learning English.)
- He loves soccer; he is really ***into*** soccer!

Into is sometimes used to talk about math division:

Examples:

- 12 ***into*** 48 equals 4.
- Ten ***into*** one hundred equals ten.

Into is used to talk about a condition change:

Examples:

- The student got ***into*** trouble for cheating on the exam.
- Kyoko got ***into*** debt after buying the expensive home.

Into is used to talk about sudden, hard contact, or forced contact with something or someone:

Examples:

- The motorcycle crashed ***into*** the building but the driver was not seriously hurt.
- The girl ran ***into*** the tree and had to be taken to the hospital.

*There are many other uses for the word **into** in English phrasal verbs and in English expressions (or idioms). Please see our book, "Beyond Phrasal Verbs".*

Like

Like is used to talk about similarities:

Examples:

- There is no other person ***like*** him.
- Places ***like*** New York and Los Angeles can be interesting vacation stops.
- He is ***like*** his brother. They both enjoy playing sports.

Like is used to talk about examples:

Examples:

- There are many forms of transportation, ***like*** cars, trains and planes.
- There are many things you can do to improve your English, ***like*** talking to native speakers, studying grammar, and attending classes regularly.

Near

Near is used to talk about distance from or location; something that is close by:

Examples:

- Oh, look at the tall buildings, we must be ***near*** Dallas.
- The whiteboard is ***near*** the door.

Next to

Next to is used to talk about something or someone that is near, close to, or in very close proximity to

Examples:

- She parked her car **_next to_** mine in the mall parking lot.
- Could you tell me where the grocery store is?
  Yes, it is **_next to_** the bank on Smith Street.

Chapter 3 *review*

*Prepositions beginning with the letters **I** - **N***

*Instructions: read the sentences below. Decide whether the use of the underlined preposition is correct or incorrect. If incorrect, which of these prepositions **best** fits the sentence: **in**, **in back of**, **in front of**, **inside**, **instead of**, **into**, **like**, **near**, **next**. The answers can be found at the end of the practice.*

1. I waited <u>in near of</u> the taxi stand for two hours, but no taxi came.
    ☐correct   ☐incorrect

2. The car is <u>inside</u> the garage. ☐correct   ☐incorrect

3. The businessman went <u>into</u> the building. ☐correct   ☐incorrect

4. Places <u>like</u> Honolulu and Cancun can be nice for vacations. ☐correct ☐incorrect

5. Long Island is a place <u>instead of</u> New York City. ☐correct   ☐incorrect

6. The bus stopped <u>next to</u> the shopping center. ☐correct   ☐incorrect

7. One hundred <u>near</u> one thousand equals ten. ☐correct   ☐incorrect

8. We went swimming <u>instead of</u> surfing. ☐correct   ☐incorrect

9. Jim and Nancy got <u>into</u> debt when they bought the expensive sports car.
    ☐correct   ☐incorrect

10. The garbage bins are <u>in back of</u> the store . ☐correct   ☐incorrect

Answers: (1) incorrect; should be <u>in front of</u>; (2) correct; (3) correct; (4) correct; (5) incorrect; should be <u>near</u>; (6) correct; (7) incorrect; should be <u>into</u>; (8) correct; (9) correct; (10) correct

Chapter 4 - English prepositions beginning with the letter O

This is a comprehensive listing of the most common English prepositions beginning with the letter *O*. The prepositions are followed by a usage explanation. After each explanation there are examples to help reinforce the correct use of the preposition in common English sentences.

Common English prepositions beginning with the letter O

Below we will discuss these commonly used prepositions and provide you with many examples.

Of

Of is used to talk about belonging to or being connected to a group, something, someone or time:

Examples:

- Who is that tall man there?
  He is the dean *of* this college.
- That monk is *of* the Buddhist religion.
- That man is a citizen *of* the USA.
- Who is she?
  She is a doctor *of* medicine.
- The author is writing a book on the trees and plants *of* Australia.
- We watched fireworks on the fourth *of* July.
- April Fools day is on the first day *of* April.
- I finished my English studies in March *of* last year.

Of is used to help talk about categories or types of things or people:

Examples:

- He was very embarrassed; the color *of* his face was red.
- The cost *of* the home was very high.
- Before you can order shoes, you have to know the size *of* your foot.
- I don't like the smell *of* that fish. I think it is bad.
- My mother bought two bags *of* rice yesterday.

Of is used to help talk about quantity:

Examples:

- Are we going to be late?
  No, we have plenty *of* time.
- Many *of* the people who listen to EnglishMP3 audio books learn English well.
- We have hundreds *of* products in our store.
- Don't worry about breaking the dish; we have plenty *of* dishes.

*There are many other uses for the word **of** in English phrasal verbs and in English expressions (or idioms). Please refer to our book, "Beyond Phrasal Verbs".*

Off

Off is used to talk about a condition or state of being; that something is not on or has stopped functioning:

Examples:

- The stove is cool. It must be *off*.
- Would you please turn *off* all the lights? Electricity is expensive.
- Well, that show was terrible. I think I will turn *off* the TV now.
- Did we turn the stove *off* before we left home?
  Yes, remember? I turned it *off* 10 minutes before we left the house.

Off is used to talk about movement that represents change in location:

Examples:

- The papers blew **_off_** the table.
- The motorcycle ran **_off_** the road but the driver was not hurt.

Off can be used to mean to remove or separate:

Examples:
- Mary, did you take your books **_off_** the counter? Yes mom, my books are **_off_** the counter.
- My father shaved **_off_** his beard. Boy, his appearance really changed!

Off can be used to mean to stop doing something:

Examples:
- Do you want to go to the club with me?
  I can't because I'm **_off_** alcohol.

  (Meaning: I don't want to drink alcohol any more.)
- What time do you get **_off_** work?

  (Meaning: What time do you stop work.)
  I get **_off_** at 4 p.m..

Off is used to mean not far from:

Examples:
- The bank is just **_off_** Elm Street.

  (Meaning: A little bit further past or in the vicinity of Elm Street.)
- Oh, that was a terrible golf shot. You're a little **_off_** today.

  (Meaning: You are not playing like you usually do; your golf game is not as good as usual.)

Off is sometimes used in commands and warning signs to mean do not have contact with:

Examples:
- Please keep **_off_** the grass!
- Wet concrete, keep **_off_**!

*There are many other uses for the word **off** in English phrasal verbs and in English expressions (or idioms). Please see our book "Beyond Phrasal Verbs".*

On

On can mean contact with a surface or surface location:

Examples:

- The books are **on** the desk.
- The picture is **on** the wall.
- The fly is **on** the window.
- The writing is **on** the wall.
- The woman is driving her car **on** the street.
- The boy is riding his skateboard **on** the sidewalk.

On can mean in contact but above something else:

Examples:

- Please print your name **on** the line.

On can mean a location, usually outdoors:

Examples:

- The parking garage is **on** the side of the building.
- Where are you?
  We're **on** the corner of Elm and Second Avenue.
- We went **on** the roof to get the cat.
- We all live **on** the planet called Earth.

On is used to talk about time:

Examples:

- I have to go to the doctor's office **on** Wednesday.
- My family is coming to visit **on** Christmas day.

- We will arrive **on** Monday.

On is used when talking about transportation and traveling:

Examples:

- They got **on** the bus.
- She was **on** the train for two hours.
- The family spent four hours **on** the plane.

(Note: use **in** when talking about a taxi or car. Example: The businessman was **in** the taxi for an hour because of heavy traffic.)

On is used to talk about membership or being part of *something:*

Examples:

- My name is **on** the good student list.
- He is **on** the soccer team.

On is used to talk about means or resource:

Examples:

- The space shuttle rocket runs **on** special fuel.
- My wife and I live **on** my paycheck.
- The three mountain climbers survived **on** little water.

On can sometimes indicate the cause of a mishap or problem:

Examples:

- The boy hurt himself **on** his skateboard.
- She got sick **on** the bad food she ate at the restaurant.

On can sometimes indicate a reason for doing something:

Examples:

- They went to Fiji **on** vacation.
- Michael went to New York **on** business.

On is sometimes used to indicate subject or topic; meaning about:

Examples:

- I read an article ***on*** how to learn English quickly.
- Their class presentation was ***on*** the environment.

On can be used to indicate possession:

Examples:

- Can I borrow $5?
  Sorry, I don't have any money ***on*** me.
- Excuse me. Do you have a pen ***on*** you? I need to write down a phone number.

On is used to indicate a special occasion:

Examples:

- Congratulations ***on*** getting married.
- They celebrated by going out dancing ***on*** their anniversary.

On can indicate status, condition, or state:

Examples:

- Your new shoes are ***on*** order and should arrive next week.
- The woman is ***on*** a diet. She is trying to lose 30 pounds.

On can be used to indicate a continuation of what was being done:

Examples:

- After stopping at the motel, we drove ***on*** to our next destination.
- We stopped to look at the accident, but the police told us to move ***on***.

On is used to talk about how something was communicated:

Examples:

- I learned about the new job opportunity ***on*** the Internet.

- I saw the advertisement **_on_** TV.

- Stefan and his brother heard the news **_on_** the radio.

On is used to talk about behavior towards something or someone:

Examples:

- The long days without food or water were hard **_on_** the survivors. It was the biggest challenge of their lives.

- The test was too easy **_on_** the students. Everyone got a very high mark!

On can help to express adding to something or acquiring something:

Examples:

- Jim wants to add **_on_** a bedroom to his house.

- The school added **_on_** five new teachers.

On can be used to express two things happening at the same time (in this usage, on and upon can be used interchangeably):

Examples:

- **_On_** second thought, he decided not to buy the car.

- He called the fire department **_on_** seeing the fire in the house.

On can be used to help express feelings or attitude towards something or someone:

Examples:

- The girl in the second row has a crush **_on_** the boy in the front of the class. (Meaning: she has a romantic interest in him.)

- The man took pity **_on_** the homeless man and gave him some money.

*There are many other uses for the word **_on_** in English phrasal verbs and in English expressions (or idioms). Please see our book "Beyond Phrasal Verbs".*

Onto

Onto *is used to talk about moving from one place to another place:*

Examples:

- The spider jumped ***onto*** the table.
- It was raining so they moved all of the picnic food ***onto*** a table that was under an umbrella.

Opposite

Opposite is used to mean across from:

Examples:

- Excuse me. Could you tell me where the bank is located?
  Yes. The bank is up that street ***opposite*** the grocery store.
- She sat ***opposite*** her boyfriend at the fancy restaurant.

Out

Out is used when talking about passing something around or distributing something:

Examples:

- Sally, would you please pass ***out*** these forms to the class.
- We mailed ***out*** about 1,000 brochures to advertise our new business.

Out is used when talking about removing something or someone:

Examples:

- I brought the gift ***out*** to the car. I'm bringing it to my sister's birthday party.
- She opened the box and took ***out*** the new dress.

*****Out*** *is often used with the preposition **of** in expressing different ideas in English. Below are some usage explanations and examples for **out of**.*

Out of can be used to express absence:

Examples:

- Three ***out*** of five people today do not exercise regularly.
- Two ***out*** of every three of these apples are bad. We should take this bag of apples back to the market.

Out of can be used to express a percentage or fraction of something:

Examples:

- Hello Marta. I haven't seen your sister in a week. Where is she? Oh, she is ***out of*** the country. She will be back next week.
- Mr. Yoshida is ***out of*** the office at the moment, may I take a message for him?
- Hello? No, Gerhard is not here right now. He is ***out of*** town.

Out of can be used to express not being normal or not what is usually expected:

Examples:

- Oh my gosh, that coat is so ***out of*** style!
- What happened?

  That car went ***out of*** control and hit the telephone pole!

Out of can be used to express what something was made of or what ingredients went into making something:

Examples:

- That company makes surfboards ***out of*** bamboo.
- Cotton candy is made ***out of*** pure sugar.

Out of can be used to express a lack of or no longer available or in supply:

Examples:

- I drove to the gas station to get some fuel for my car, but the gas station was ***out of*** fuel.
- I would like to have a vanilla ice cream cone, please.

  Sorry. We are all ***out of*** vanilla.

  (Note: the word ***all*** used with ***out of*** means ***completely***.)

Out of can mean away from, similar to distance from:

Examples:

- Excuse me. Could you tell me where the nearest gas station is? Yes. It's on this road about four miles ***out of*** town.
- If you want to buy alcohol, you will have to go ***out of*** state because it is illegal in this state to sell alcohol.

Out of can be used to express a reason for doing something:

Examples:

- I went to Bali ***out of*** curiosity. I've always wanted to see what that island was like.
- I adopted the stray cat ***out of*** pity.

*There are many other uses for the word **out** in English phrasal verbs and in English expressions (or idioms). Please see our book, "Beyoind Phrasal Verbs".*

Outside

Outside is often used with the preposition *of*. Outside means not within the confines of something:

Examples:

- We could hear strange noises ***outside*** the house.
- The man put his wet boots ***outside*** the door.

Over

Over means above something or someone; it usually indicates being higher than:

Examples:

- We flew ***over*** New York on our way to Boston.

- The branch of the tree hung ***over*** the house.

- The price of that car is expensive. It's way ***over*** my head because I don't earn that much money.

- I don't understand Einstein. His theories are way ***over*** my head.

  (Meaning: I can't understand his theories because they are too complicated for me.)

Over is used to mean to cover something or someone:

Examples:

- The workers put a steel plate ***over*** the hole in the road.

- It was cold in the room so she put a sweater on ***over*** her blouse.

Over is used to express above and then to the other side of something or someone:

Examples:

- The runner jumped ***over*** the branch that was in the road.

- The football player kicked the ball ***over*** the wall.

- We had to climb ***over*** the fence to get into the park.

- Is it possible to jump ***over*** a rainbow?

- You should drive your car slowly ***over*** a speed bump.

Over is used to express control over something or someone:

Examples:

- The emperor rules ***over*** the people in his country.

- The general manager of the company is ***over*** all employees.

Over is used to express location away from and on the other side of something or someone else:

Examples:

- The market is ***over*** there.
- I work in a building that is just ***over*** the bridge.

  (Note: the word ***just*** is used to mean ***a small distance from***.)

Over can be used to indicate topic or subject:

Examples:

- We fought ***over*** who should pay the check at the restaurant.
- The leader of the country worried ***over*** the shortage of food.

Over (adverb) can mean finished:

Examples:

- The show is ***over***.
- School is ***over***.

*There are many other uses for the word **over** in English phrasal verbs and in English expressions (or idioms). Please see our book, "Beyond Phrasal Verbs".*

Chapter 4 *review*
*Prepositions beginning with the letter **O***

*Instructions: read the sentences below. Decide whether the use of the preposition is correct or incorrect. If incorrect, which of these prepositions **best** fits the sentence: **of**, **off**, **on**, **onto**, **on top of**, **opposite**, **out**, **outside**, **over**. The answers can be found at the bottom of this page.*

1. The priest is <u>of</u> the Catholic faith. ☐correct ☐incorrect

2. The final semester ends in June <u>on top of</u> this year. ☐correct ☐incorrect

3. My friend shaved the hair <u>off</u> his head. ☐correct ☐incorrect

4. The butter is <u>on</u> the table. ☐correct ☐incorrect

5. She was <u>out</u> the train for two hours. ☐correct ☐incorrect

6. The dancer jumped <u>onto</u> the stage. ☐correct ☐incorrect

7. The two buildings are <u>opposite</u> each other. ☐correct ☐incorrect

8. The student turned <u>of</u> the lights in the classroom. ☐correct ☐incorrect

9. Jonathan is <u>out of</u> the country. ☐correct ☐incorrect

10. The two girls fought <u>over</u> the good-looking boy. ☐correct ☐incorrect

Answers: (1) correct; (2) incorrect; should be <u>of</u>; (3) correct; (4) correct; (5) incorrect; should be <u>on</u>; (6) correct; (7) correct; (8) incorrect; should be <u>off</u>; (9) correct; (10) correct

Chapter 5 - English prepositions beginning with the letters P - T

This is a comprehensive listing of the most common English prepositions beginning with the letters **P** - **T**. The prepositions are followed by a usage explanation. After each explanation there are examples to help reinforce the correct use of the preposition in common English sentences.

Common English prepositions beginning with the letters P - T

Below we will discuss these commonly used prepositions and provide you with many examples.

Past

Past is used to mean beyond:

Examples:

- Excuse me. How do I get to the theater.
  Just go up this street **past** the stop light and the theater is on your left.

- The director's office is just **past** classroom number 3 on the right side of the hall.

Past can mean to go by something or someone:

Examples:

- The girl walks **past** the pastry shop on her way to school every day.
- We drove **past** Lincoln Center in New York City.

Since

Since means continuously or intermittently from a time in the past until the present:

Examples:

- I haven't been in Tokyo ***since*** last September.
- The school has been open ***since*** 1995.
- He hasn't said hello ***since*** we had that argument.

Through

Through can be used to express passage, or movement, across or under a potential barrier or obstacle:

Examples:

- The five limousines passed ***through*** the open gate.
- I got a ticket for going ***through*** a red light.
- As we walked ***through*** the door, our whole family was there to greet us.
- We drove ***through*** the tunnel without our lights on. Boy, it was dark in there.

Through can be used to mean contiguous or sequential

(*Meaning: one thing occurring in exact order after the other*) *with a beginning and an ending:*

Examples:

- The students were asked to read pages 24 ***through*** 31 for their homework.
- My dad works Monday ***through*** Friday at the factory.
- The sale will continue on ***through*** Tuesday of next week.

Through can be used to express passage or movement within a confining space or borders:

Examples:

- We passed ***through*** the long, dark hallway as we walked to the waiting room.
- We walked ***through*** the park on our way home.

Through can relate to vision; being able to see something beyond the initial surface:

Examples:

- We looked ***through*** the window and saw the city below.
- My car needs new paint. I can see the metal showing ***through*** the paint in some spots.

Through is used to express completing something that may require hard work to finish:

Examples:

- I want to travel a lot, but first I have to get ***through*** school.
- That was a bad storm. I didn't think we were going to get ***through*** it.
- She went ***through*** a bad experience, but now she feels better.

Through is used with the word all to have the same meaning as throughout (Meaning: in all parts, or during an entire event):

Examples:

- My girlfriend and I walked all ***through*** the park looking at the gardens and enjoying the sunshine.
- That cat was crying all ***through*** the night. I hardly got any sleep!

Through is used to express the reason for something:

Examples:

- The student achieved high grades ***through*** hard work and study.
- The woman was overcharged for her purchase ***through*** a computer error.

Through is used to express the means by which something happens:

Examples:

- We got the information ***through*** his website.
- I got the job ***through*** an employment agency.

Throughout

Throughout is used to express that something is occurring everywhere, in all parts of:

Examples:

- There are yoga centers ***throughout*** New York City.
- There are fire alarm boxes ***throughout*** the building.

Throughout is used to talk about something occurring during an entire period of time:

Examples:

- He has been a very successful person ***throughout*** his life.
- We ask that students remain silent ***throughout*** the exam.
- We partied ***throughout*** the whole Christmas holiday.

To

To is used to indicate a response or reaction to something or someone:

Examples:

- I hope you will agree ***to*** my offer.
- The teacher hoped that the students paid attention ***to*** the lesson.
- Her reaction ***to*** that comment was negative.
- The old man was grateful ***to*** receive the help.

To is used to indicate a destination:

Examples:

- The plane ***to*** L.A. will arrive at 5 a.m..

- She wants sail **_to_** the South Pacific.
- The letter was **_to_** her.
- The sisters go **_to_** school every day, five days a week.

_To_ is used to talk about time:

Examples:
- We work from 9 a.m. **_to_** 5 p.m. every day.
- They worked on the project from morning **_to_** night.

*Here is another way **to** is used to talk about time:*
- The time is now 15 minutes **_to_** 6. (a quarter to six)
- It's 20 minutes **_to_** noon.

_To_ is used to help express who or what receives something; meaning, beneficiary of something:

Examples:
- His company awarded the prize **_to_** him for his hard work.
- The city dedicated the monument **_to_** the memory of its famous writer.
- The school gave a scholarship **_to_** the student because of her good work.

_To_ is used to help express transferring and exchanging something from a person or a place:

Examples:
- The secretary brings the mail **_to_** the office every day.
- The student read his presentation **_to_** the class.
- The hair dresser recommended the hair conditioner **_to_** the woman.
- "Would you please give that **_to_** me," said Oliver Hardy to Stan Laurel. "Thank you."

_To_ is used to help express what effect someone or something has on someone or something else:

Examples:

- Please stop having loud parties every night! You are a nuisance *to* the neighborhood. (And, besides, you never invite me.)
- The new park has been a pleasing experience *to* everyone.
- To my embarrassment, I sent the email *to* the wrong person.

To can be used to refer to one's self in a sentence:

Examples:

- *To* her disappointment, she didn't get a good grade on the final exam.
- The work was completed *to* their satisfaction.

To is used to help express repetition:

Examples:

- Our boat trip across the bay was really uncomfortable. The boat rolled side *to* side.
- The homeless man went from house *to* house asking for food.

To is used to help express attaching something to something, or attachment:

Examples:

- She stapled the picture *to* the form.
- The carpenter nailed the wood *to* the floor.

To is used to help express comparison:

Examples:

- The sun is very bright here, compared *to* where I live.
- Your essay is very similar *to* mine.

To is used to indicate action caused by sound:

Examples:

- The next morning they woke up *to* the sound of the ocean.
- She tapped her fingers *to* the sound of the music.

To is used to help express relationship of one thing to another:

Examples:

- I'd like to introduce you to the new assistant *to* the director.
- These are the keys *to* my car. Please don't crash it.
- The school building is close *to* the mall.
- This street runs parallel *to* that one.
- There are 3.8 liters *to* one gallon.

To is used to help express extremes:

Examples:

- She was so mad that she tore the contract *to* bits.
- I'm trying to study and the noise from the party next door is driving me *to* madness.

To is used to help indicate problems or solutions:

Examples:

- Our water reservoirs are almost dry. This is a threat *to* our survival.
- What is your solution *to* this problem?

To is used to help express ownership or connectedness:

Examples:

- That house belongs *to* me.
- This issue is important *to* me.
- He is married *to* that woman.

To is used to help express restrictedness:

Examples:

- The teenager was confined ***to*** her room for disobeying her mother.

- The prisoners were restricted ***to*** two meals a day.

*Please refer to Focus On English, "Mastering English Gerunds and Infinitives", for more uses of the word **to**. There are also many other uses for the word **to** in English phrasal verbs and in English expressions (or idioms). Please refer to our book "Beyond Phrasal Verbs".*

Toward(s)

Toward(s) is used to help express the direction to a location or place:

Examples:
- The tourists headed ***toward*** the beach.
- We sailed our boat ***toward*** the island.
- How do I find the iPod store?
  To find the iPod store, walk ***towards*** the bank for about 5 minutes, and then look to your left. It's the third store past the bank.
- The plane took off and headed ***toward*** Paris, France.
- See, over there. Look ***towards*** the intersection. You can see a man playing music on the street corner and dancing in his bare feet.

Toward(s) is used to help express contribution or making a partial payment:

Examples:
- The couple made a contribution of $1,000 ***towards*** the sick man's medical bills.
- The boy pays $50 every month ***towards*** his car payment.

Toward(s) is used to help express nearness to a certain time:

Examples:

- We always get excited about going skiing ***towards*** the middle of the winter.
- The math student was getting nervous ***towards*** the end of the exam because time was running out.

Toward(s) is used to help express attitude:

Examples:

- The parents are very loving ***towards*** their children.
- The students were very respectful ***towards*** their teacher.

Toward(s) is used to help express movement in the direction of some kind of action:

Examples:

- They are working ***towards*** an agreement.
- Peter is heading ***towards*** a decision to leave the company.

Chapter 5 <u>review</u>
*Prepositions beginning with the letters **P** – **T***

*Instructions: read the sentences below. Decide whether the use of the preposition is correct or incorrect. If incorrect, which of these prepositions **best** fits the sentence: <u>past</u>, <u>since</u>, <u>through</u>, <u>throughout</u>, <u>to</u>, <u>towards</u>. The answers can be found at the bottom of the page.*

1. I haven't been in Tokyo ***<u>since</u>*** 1999. ☐correct   ☐incorrect

2. The students passed ***<u>through</u>*** the museum and looked at the works of art.
    ☐correct   ☐incorrect

3. There were many questions ***<u>throughout</u>*** the company meeting. ☐correct
    ☐incorrect

4. The student was grateful ***<u>to</u>*** receive tutoring from the teacher. ☐correct
    ☐incorrect

5. As soon as we got to Hawaii we headed ***<u>since</u>*** the beach. ☐correct
    ☐incorrect

6. Barbara is married ***<u>past</u>*** Alex Smith. ☐correct   ☐incorrect

7. Our group sang songs ***<u>throughout</u>*** the train journey. ☐correct
    ☐incorrect

8. Every time I walk ***<u>past</u>*** the pastry shop I get hungry. ☐correct
    ☐incorrect

9. We attend school Monday ***<u>through</u>*** Friday every week. ☐correct
    ☐incorrect

10. The leader of the country has been kind ***to*** everyone.   ☐correct
    ☐incorrect

Answers: (1) correct; (2) correct; (3) correct; (4) correct; (5) incorrect; should be <u>to</u>; (6) incorrect; should be <u>to</u>; (7) correct; (8) correct; (9) correct; (10) correct

Chapter 6 - English prepositions beginning with the letters U - Z

This is a comprehensive listing of the most common English prepositions beginning with the letters *U* - *Z*. The prepositions are followed by a usage explanation. After each explanation there are examples to help reinforce the correct use of the preposition in common English sentences.

Common English prepositions beginning with the letters U - Z

Below we will discuss these commonly used prepositions and provide you with many examples.

Under

Under is used to mean being in a lower position than, or beneath something or someone else:

Examples:
- The pen is ***under*** the table.
- The man is walking ***under*** the bridge.
- The submarine can travel ***under*** water.

Under is used to help express being under the supervision of or control of something or someone:

Examples:
- She has been very sick. Currently, she is ***under*** the supervision of a doctor.
- We are working ***under*** a manager that does not give us very much freedom.
- That country continues to suffer ***under*** bad leadership.

Under is used to express less than:

Examples:

- You can buy that car for ***under*** $20,000.
- Sorry, we can't sell you beer because you are ***under*** age 21.

Under can mean the same as **underneath** meaning hidden or covered by something else:

Examples:

- The cats hid ***under*** the house. We couldn't find them for days.
- She hid her purse ***under*** the bed.
- Sand crabs are found ***underneath*** the sand at the beach.
- He found his driver's license ***underneath*** a pile of papers on his desk.

Under can be used to express a situation, condition or state:

Examples:

- The website is ***under*** construction and should be done next month.
- The man was sent to jail for causing trouble while ***under*** the influence of alcohol.

Under can be used to identify categories:

Examples:

- You can find her name in the directory ***under*** the letter P.
- Porpoises can be found in the encyclopedia ***under*** mammals.

Underneath

Underneath is used to help express when something is being hidden or covered by something else:

Examples:

- ***Underneath*** her jacket she wore a sweater.
- I was very warm and cozy ***underneath*** the blankets of my bed.

Until

Until helps to express the beginning or end of an action, activity, situation or time:

Examples:

- I'm sorry sir, but the bank is closed. You will not be able to withdraw money ***until*** tomorrow.

- (Students taking an exam): Please do not leave your seats ***until*** the teacher gives you permission.

Up

Up can mean movement to a higher place:

Examples:

- The price of gasoline has really gone ***up***.

- The champagne cork flew ***up*** into the air when it was removed.

Up can be used to express movement against a current of water:

Examples:

- Salmon always swim ***up*** stream.

  Meaning: against the current of a river or stream

- We rowed the canoe ***up*** the river.

Up can be used to express forward movement towards a location further away:

Examples:

- The new park is ***up*** the road about ten miles and on your right.

- The bikers rode ***up*** the bike trail another five miles before they stopped and rested.

Up can be used to express forward movement along a route or path:

Examples:

- The truck traveled **_up_** the road.
- The two friends jogged **_up_** the path.

_Up_ can be used to express division or cutting of something into pieces:

Examples:

- My mother chopped **_up_** the onion and then chopped **_up_** some garlic and put all the pieces in the sauce.
- The bank robbers divided **_up_** the money and then ran away.

*There are also many other uses for the word **_up_** in English phrasal verbs and in English expressions (or idioms). Please refer to our book, "Beyond Phrasal Verbs".*

Upon

Upon can be used in many of the same situations where <u>on</u> can be used:

Examples:

- **_Upon_** entering the room, everyone yelled, "surprise!"
- The stone was resting **_upon_** two supports

With

With can be used to express things being added on:

Examples:

- I like my tea **_with_** milk.
- How much is a hamburger **_with_** French fries.

With is used to express being together or in the company of:

Examples:

- I went *with* my brother to see the show.

- The students went *with* their teacher to the student auditorium.

- Did you see a man *with* a small boy within the last hour?

- Sally came to the party *with* her friend.

- Did you go *with* her?

With is used to express a type of behavior:

Examples:
- They accepted the new jobs *with* gratitude.

- Children have to be handled *with* care.

- The teacher congratulated the class *with* pride.

- The girl was being honest *with* her friend.

With is used to help **ex**press feelings:

Examples:
- The office worker was bored *with* her job.

- The newly wed couple were filled *with* joy to be moving into a new home.

With is used to help express affiliation or relationship:

Examples:
- He has been working *with* the International Red Cross for two years.

- Melissa works *with* blind children.

With is used to help express conflict or struggle:

Examples:
- The children are always arguing *with* each other.

- Our football team is going to compete *with* the champion team next week.

- He had trouble *with* the car. The motor wouldn't start.

With is used to help express filling or covering something or an area:

Examples:
- The waitress filled the glass **_with_** water.
- The whole side of the mountain was covered **_with_** wild flowers.

With helps to express which tool or implement is used to accomplish an action:

Examples:
- The artist painted a picture of the flower **_with_** his paintbrush.
- The worker dug a hole in the ground **_with_** a shovel.

With helps to express simultaneous (occurring together at the same time) time and direction:

Examples:
- The teacher always starts the class **_with_** a quiz.
- The monks always start their day **_with_** prayer.
- The boat sailed **_with_** the current.

With helps to express parting or separation:

Examples:
- Toshiko is finished **_with_** her company and is now looking for a new job.
- She broke up **_with_** her boyfriend because they didn't spend enough time together.

With helps to express cooperation:

Examples:
- All of the neighbors helped **_with_** cleaning the park.
- We decided to work **_with_** them on this important project.
- The car company has decided to form a partnership **_with_** their main parts manufacturer.
- We no longer do business **_with_** them.

With helps to express comparisons:

Examples:

- Stefan's shirt didn't go ***with*** his pants. (Meaning: the colors of his shirt didn't look good ***with*** the color of his pants.)
- The value of the U.S. dollar is comparable ***with*** the value of the Canadian dollar.
(Meaning: they are approximately equal in value.)
- Two different stores have the computer we want. We should compare one price ***with*** the other before we buy the computer.

With helps to express reason or cause:

Examples:
- The graduates were smiling ***with*** joy.
- The man was trembling ***with*** fear.

There are other uses for the word ***with*** *in English phrasal verbs and in English expressions (or idioms). Please refer to our book "Beyond Phrasal Verbs".*

Within

Within usually means inside of some area:

Examples:

- ***Within*** the room there were many fine paintings.
- ***Within*** the United States there are many fine universities.

Within can be used to express less than a specified period of time:

Examples:

- We should be finished ***within*** the hour.
- The bus usually comes ***within*** 15 minutes of the last bus.
(Meaning: in less than 15 minutes after the last bus left.)

Within can be used to express less than a specified distance:

Examples:

- The library is ***within*** two miles of the university.
- We are ***within*** two miles of our destination.

Without

Without can mean not having:

Examples:

- She gets to school ***without*** a car. She walks.
- ***Without*** your help, I couldn't have finished the project.
- ***Without*** water, we would not be able to live long.

Without can be used to express the absence of someone or something:

Examples:

- The worker finished the project ***without*** his colleagues.
- The baby tiger won't survive long ***without*** its mother.

Without can be used to express the absence of action:

Examples:

- He received a lot of money ***without*** working.
- She is famous ***without*** doing anything extraordinary.

Chapter 6 *review*
*Prepositions beginning with the letters **P** – **T***

*Instructions: read the sentences below. Decide whether the use of the preposition is correct or incorrect. If incorrect, which of these prepositions **best** fits the sentence: **under**, **underneath**, **until**, **up**, **with**, **within**, **without**. The answers can be found on the bottom of the practice.*

1. Prices of food have really gone <u>up</u> □correct   □incorrect

2. The boats were sailing <u>upon</u> the water. □correct   □incorrect

3. The teacher worked <u>with</u> students to help them understand the new chapter. □correct   □incorrect

4. My friend arrived home <u>with</u> her groceries. I helped my friend <u>until</u> her groceries. □correct   □incorrect

5. <u>Without</u> the help of my family, I could never have finished school. □correct   □incorrect

6. We won't complete the project <u>with</u> next Wednesday. □correct   □incorrect

7. Our bus traveled <u>up</u> the highway at high speed. □correct   □incorrect

8. The water passes <u>under</u> the bridge. □correct   □incorrect

9. Alice bought the car for <u>under</u> $30,000. □correct   □incorrect

10. She repaired her car <u>without</u> the help of her brothers. □correct   □incorrect

Answers: (1) correct; (2) correct; (3) correct; (4) correct; (5) incorrect; should be <u>to</u>; (6) incorrect; should be <u>to</u>; (7) correct; (8) correct; (9) correct; (10) correct

Book 2 - Phrasal Verbs for Real-Life English

English Phrasal Verbs Made Easy for English Learners

Book 2 - Quick-Find Menu

Chapter 5 *Phrasal verbs beginning with*
the letter H **253**

Phrasal verbs beginning with the letter H 253

Chapter 6 *Phrasal verbs beginning with the letter K* **265**

Phrasal verbs beginning with the letter K...........265

Chapter 7 Phrasal verbs beginning with the letter L 273

Chapter 8 Phrasal verbs beginning with
the letters M, N, and O 287

**Chapter 13 Phrasal verbs beginning with
the letter U, W, and Z.................................. 360**

Notice to Students

A free audio version of this book can be found at:
https://foebooks.com/index.php/beyond-phrasal-verbs-audio/

Introduction

Focus on English© Mini Series Books
Making the difficult parts of learning English easy

Beyond Phrasal Verbs:
Mastering Phrasal Verbs in Context for ESL Learners

Efficient and ubiquitous, English phrasal verbs provide the ESL learner with a window onto the world of fluent English communication. Found in English idioms of all descriptions, the ESL learner who masters phrasal verbs will have access to vast areas of every day English communication. Much of informal English expression, slang, and jargon are structured around phrasal verbs.

This Focus on English© book not only contains a comprehensive listing of common English phrasal verbs, but also goes to lengths to explain meanings and variations of usage, including slang and informal expressions. The student will find clear, simple, explanations for each of the phrasal verbs, followed by examples of their correct usage in a sentence.

*A digital audio book version of this book (for smart phones and other digital devices), available separately, **free**, at www.FOEBooks.com (click on AUDIO in main menu). If the student has this Focus on English© digital audio book, then he or she will be able to listen to how these phrasal verbs are actually spoken by a native English speaker. This method helps the student remember the lesson more easily and also helps the student with pronunciation.*

Chapter 1 *Phrasal verbs beginning with the letters A and B*

In this and following sections you will learn how to use many different phrasal verbs correctly in a sentence.

There are two kinds of phrasal verbs, separable and inseparable. Separable phrasal verbs can take an object between the verb and the preposition. For example: *My father **picked** me **up** after school and drove me home.* Inseparable phrasal verbs cannot take an object between the verb and the preposition. For example: I asked my friends to **come along** with me to the Christmas party. **Come along** cannot be separated by an object.

The numbers in front of the examples that are in parenthesis (), correspond the to number of the explanation found directly above. So, for example: 1. *explanation . . .* refers to (1) *example . . . .* If there is only one explanation or meaning given for the phrasal verb, then there will be two examples given for the one explanation. Both examples will be marked with (1).

If you have the Focus on English digital audio book version of this book (available separately from www.FOEBooks.com) listen to each of the phrasal verbs, followed by their meanings and then some examples of how they are used in real English sentences. Each example will be spoken twice. There will be a review at the end of this chapter.

Phrasal verbs beginning with the letters A and B

Aim at
(separable):

1. To point something at something or someone; usually a gun or other weapon, as in this example: *The soldier **aimed** his rifle **at** the target.* 2. Intending to finish at a certain destination or goal, as in this example: *We're hoping to finish this evening. We're **aiming at** 8pm.*

More examples:

❑ (1) The man **aimed** the gun **at** the bank teller.

❑ (2) The president of the company *__aimed at__* increasing his bank customers by 15%.

Ask for
(separable):

1. To request something from someone, as in this example: *I __asked__ the waitress __for__ the bill.*

2. To be due something, sometimes used to express consequence for something you did or did not do, as in this example: *Allan never insured his car. When he had an accident, he had to pay for the damage. He really __asked for__ it.*

   More examples:
   ❑ (1) The customer *__asked__* the store clerk *__for__* a box for her new dress.
   ❑ (2) Bill lost all of his money gambling. He really *__asked for__* it when he bet all

   of his money in one night. (Meaning: he was really tempting bad luck when he decided to bet all of his money the way he did)

Ask out
(separable):

1. To invite someone to go somewhere (usually used in romantic situations), as in this example: *I __asked__ the new girl in school __out__ for dinner.*

   More examples:
   ❑ (1) My boyfriend *__asked__* me *__out__*. We are going to the movies tonight.
   ❑ (1) My sister told me that that new boy in the school *__asked__* her *__out__*.

Ask over
(separable):

1. Usually used to invite someone to one's home, as in this example: *I __asked__ my colleagues __over__ for dinner on Friday.*

   More examples:
   ❑ (1) Let's *__ask__* your teacher *__over__* for dinner Saturday night.
   ❑ (1) My girlfriend *__asked__* me *__over__* to her house to meet her parents.

Back down
(inseparable):

1. Means to give up; to shy away from, usually, some kind of challenge, as in this example: *The students wanted the teacher to change the exam date because the exam date was the same date as the concert. The teacher didn't **back down**.*

More examples:

- ❑ (1) We are not going to ***back down***, we want a pay raise from the company or we will strike.
- ❑ (1) My mother told me I couldn't go out this weekend. I argued with her but she didn't ***back down***.

Back off
(inseparable):

1. *(informal)* To stop being persistent, as in this example: *My sister asked my father many times if she could go to the concert. Finally, my father told her to **back off** and stop asking so much.* 2. To move away from in a reverse direction, as in this example: *The car **backed off** of the ferry.*

More examples:

- ❑ (1) The police asked the girl many questions and she began to cry. When she began crying, the police ***backed off*** and stopped asking her questions.
- ❑ (2) Realizing she was walking on very thin ice, the girl carefully ***backed off*** the ice and onto land.

Back up
(separable):

1. To move or go in reverse, as in this example: *The car **backed up** into the parking spot.*

More examples:

- ❑ (1) I had to ***back*** the car ***up*** to get out of my parking space.
- ❑ (1) Some of the students didn't understand Fedor's story, so he had to ***back up*** and tell some of it again.

Beat up
(separable):

1. To subject someone or something to rough treatment, as in this example: *The thief tried to take the woman's purse, but the woman surprised him, **beat** him **up**, took his wallet, and then ran away—a most unfortunate day for the thief.*

More examples:

- ❑ (1) My friend really ***beat up*** the book that I lent him.
- ❑ (1) The gang of boys ***beat up*** the old man and then robbed him.

Beef up
(separable):

1. To make stronger, more resilient, as in this example: *The soldiers had to **beef up** their fort against enemy attack.*

More examples:

- ❑ (1) We decided to make some changes to the motor in my car. We decided to ***beef up*** the motor so it would make the car go faster.
- ❑ (1) The leader of the country gave the order to ***beef up*** the military because he was afraid there might be an attack from a neighboring country.

Believe in
(inseparable):

1. To have confidence in something or someone, as in this example: *If you **believe in** yourself and your abilities, you will be successful.*

More examples:

- ❑ (1) I did well on the exam because I ***believed in*** the idea that if I studied, I would do well on the exam.
- ❑ (1) Many Hindus ***believe in*** Krishna, a deity worshiped across many traditions of Hinduism.

Bite off
(inseparable):

1. To accept responsibility or work, or agree to do something; usually used when someone is agreeing to do more than normal, as in this example: *I **bit off** quite a bit when I agreed to do the project without help.*

More examples:

- ❑ (1) According to an old saying: Don't ***bite off*** more than you can chew. Meaning, don't accept or agree to more responsibility than you can actually accomplish.
- ❑ (1) The student ***bit off*** quite a lot when he agreed to do the whole presentation by himself.

Blow away
(separable):

1. To win by overwhelming odds, to impress in a very big way, as in this example: *The swimmer **blew away** the competition with a new world record.*

2. *(informal)* To kill, as in this example: *The drug dealers tried to **blow away** their rivals.* 3. To move something from one location to another via the wind or moving air, as in this example: *The hurricane **blew** the houses **away**.*

More examples:

□ (1) We ***blew away*** the competition in that last soccer match! (☝Meaning they won by a large score.)

□ (2) The gangsters ***blew away*** rival leader. (☝Meaning that they killed their rival).

□ (3) The wind came up and ***blew*** the papers ***away***. We had to run and catch them before they went into the street.

Blow off
(separable):

1. *(informal)* To ignore a result, as in this example: *When Sally got home from shopping she discovered that the clerk did not give her the right change. She didn't worry about it; she **blew** it **off** because it was only five cents.*

2. To vent or release built up pressure, as in this example: *Sometimes Hiro goes to the gym to **blow off** the frustrations of the day.*

3. To remove with explosive force, as in this example: *The tornado **blew** the top **off** that building.*

More examples:

□ (1) His boss yelled at him for loosing the sale, but he ***blew*** it ***off*** because his boss was having a bad day. (☝Meaning he ignored his boss' anger because his boss was not having a good day, which caused him to yell at his employees.)

□ (2) He knew that his boss was just ***blowing off*** steam. (☝Meaning, he knew that his boss was suffering from stress and was yelling at people because of this stress.

□ (3) The force of the explosion ***blew off*** the roof of the building.

Blow out
(inseparable):

1. To extinguish or be extinguished by wind or the force of moving air, as in this example: _The woman **blew out** the candle._

2. To suddenly or abruptly stop working or fail, as in this example: _The switch **blew out** and now the washing machine doesn't work._

More examples:

- ❑ (1) The wind came through the window and **_blew out_** the candles.

- ❑ (2) We **_blew out_** a fuse when we plugged in the oven.

Blow up
(inseparable or separable depending on usage):

1. _(separable)_   To explode with a bomb, to destroy something usually with explosives, as in this example: _The soldiers **blew up** the enemy trucks._

2. _(inseparable)_   To lose your temper; to have a discussion turn violent, as in this example: _Kaori **blew up** after learning that her boyfriend was dating another girl._

3. _(separable)_   To amplify, make something bigger, to enlarge, as in this example: _We **blew** the photograph **up** so we could see more details._

More examples:

- ❑ (1) They **_blew_** the building **_up_** so they could build a new building on that location.

- ❑ (2) The men couldn't come to an agreement and one of them finally **_blew up_** (Meaning, one of the men finally got very angry.)

- ❑ (3) He really **_blew_** that story **_up_**. That is not how it happened. (Meaning: he added things to the story that weren't true; he made they story sound more important than it really was.)

Boil down (to)
(inseparable or separable depending on usage):

1. _(separable)_ To reduce by boiling, as in this example: _My mother made great chicken soup. She would **boil** a chicken **down** and then add vegetables._

2. *(inseparable)* To summarize (**_boil down to_**), as in this example: *What it **boils down to** is that we can't go on our vacation this year because of the airline strike.*

More examples:

❑ (1) The cook **_boiled_** the vegetables **_down_** until they were soft and then made a nice soup.

❑ (2) We have not been able to pay our bills and the demand for our products is getting smaller. What it **_boils down to_** is that our business is in trouble.

Break down
(inseparable or separable depending on usage):

1. *(separable)* To divide into parts or pieces for analysis or in order to make repairs or upgrades, as in this example: *The scientists **broke** the problem **down** to try to understand it better.*

2. *(inseparable)* To suddenly collapse emotionally or physically; to become or cause to become upset or distressed, as in this example: *When the police told the suspected criminal that they knew he was guilty, he **broke down** and told them the truth.*

3. *(inseparable)* When something no longer functions; to become incapable of functioning, as in this example: *The car **broke down** at 2 o'clock in the morning and we had to wait until sunlight before we could get help.*

4. *(separable)* To eliminate, destroy, or abruptly remove a barrier, as in this example: *The police **broke down** the door to get inside the house.*

5. Used to mean weaken, reduce resistance to something, or cause to be ineffective, as in this example: *I didn't have enough money for a new car, but the salesman said it wouldn't be a problem. Eventually, I **broke down** and bought the new car with credit.*

More examples:

❑ (1) The mechanic is **_breaking down_** the engine to make a major repair.

❑ (2) When she heard of the accident involving her parents, she **_broke down_** and cried.

❑ (3) The car was **_broken down_** on the side of the road.

❑ (4) Don't be afraid to **_break down_** the barriers that prevent you from being successful.

❑ (5) I asked my mother many times if I could go to the rock concert. She finally **_broke down_** and let me go.

Break in(to)
(separable):

1. To acclimatize something or someone to a task or action, as in this example: *The manager **break in** the new employee, explaining to her the rules and procedures of their office.*

2. To enter an area or building by force, as in this example: *We forgot our keys and had to **break into** own house in order to get in.*

   More examples:

❑ (1) It is important to **_break_** a new horse **_in_** before racing it. (Meaning: to help the horse become accustomed to its new job and surroundings.)

❑ (2) The robber **_broke into_** the house and stole the painting.

Break off
(separable):

1. To stop something that was ongoing; to quit doing something, as in this example: *Our company **broke off** relations with the company from New York.*

2. To separate something from another thing by twisting or tearing, as in this example: Alex **_broke off_** *a piece of bread and then ate it.*

   More examples:

❑ The couple decided to **_break off_** their wedding engagement because they decided they would not be happy together.

❑ The farmer **_broke off_** a branch of a tree and used it to make a mark on the ground.

Break out
(inseparable or separable depending on usage):

1. *(informal) (separable)* To take something out for use; to cause something to appear suddenly, as in this example: *After hiking for two hours, we sat down under a tree, **broke out** a bottle of water and drank.*

2. To become infected with a disease, illness, or condition that is visible on the skin, such as red blotches or rashes, or pimples, as in this example: *The little girl's skin **broke out** in measles.*

3. *(inseparable)* To escape from, as in this example: *The hostages **broke out** of the room where they were being held and escaped.*

More examples:

❑ (1) Okay, let's ***break out*** the beer and begin this party! (Meaning, let's take the beer out of the cooler, refrigerator, or other location and let the party begin.)

❑ (2) Every student in the class ***broke out*** with a red rash. The doctor said it was not a serious disease.

❑ (3) The prisoner ***broke out*** of prison.

Break through
(inseparable):

1. *(informal) (separable)* To advance or move through, usually suddenly and with force, some kind of barrier or obstacle, as in this example: *The rescuers broke through the wall to save the children in the burning building.*

More examples:

❑ (1) The miners finally ***broke through*** the hard rock and began digging their mine.

❑ (2) Aiko was having difficulty understanding the math problem. Finally, after hours of work, she ***broke through*** her misunderstanding and solved the problem.

Break up
(separable):

1. *(separable)* To divide or separate into pieces or parts, as in this example: *We **broke up** the candy bar and gave a piece to the children.*

More examples:

❑ (1) The workers ***broke up*** the concrete sidewalk with their machine.

❑ My father used to ***break up*** a cracker and put the pieces in his soup.

Bring back

(separable):

1. To return something, as in this example: *I lent my friend my book and he **brought** it **back** this morning.*

2. To recall, as in memory, as in this example: *Seeing those students sitting in a classroom **brings back** the days when I was a teacher in high school.*

More examples:

❑ (1) The girl ***brought*** the music CD ***back*** after borrowing it from her friend for two weeks.

❑ (1) The old man would like to ***bring back*** the days when life was simple.

Bring over
(separable):

1. To carry or move something to a specific location, usually a location that is close to the speaker, as in this example: *Would you **bring** the pencil **over** here please.*

More examples:

❑ (1) Please ask Kaori to ***bring*** her CD ***over*** so we can listen to it. (Meaning, ask Kaori to bring her CD to this location.)

❑ (1) Son, would you ***bring*** that tool ***over*** here, please. (Meaning, bring that tool to my location.)

Bring up
(separable):

1. To raise, as with a child or pet, as in this example: *I was born in New York, but I was **brought up** in California.*

2. To introduce into a discussion, as in this example: *During our discussion about grades, the teacher **brought up** the subject of homework.*

More examples:

❑ (1)The couple ***brought up*** two children, a girl and a boy.

❑ (2) *During a meeting:* I would like to ***bring up*** a question. When are we going to get a paycheck?

Brush up
(inseparable):

1. To review something for the purpose of becoming familiar with it again, as in this example: *In order to get my driver's license, I had to **brush up** on my driving skills again.*

More examples:

❑ (1) I need to **brush up** on my Mandarin Chinese before we travel to China.

❑ (1) Students should **brush up** on the rules for taking exams before taking an important exam.

Brush off
(separable):

1. To wipe something off of the surface of something else, as in this example: *The man lifted himself off of the ground, **brushed off** his jacket and walked away.*

2. To not be affected by something, as in this example: *Julian lost his job, but he didn't worry about it. He just **brushed** it **off** and looked for a new job.*

More examples:

❑ (1) The lady tried to **brush** the lint **off** of her dress before going to the party.

❑ (2) When I was learning to ski I would fall down frequently. I just **brushed** it **off** and continued to practice until I got good.

Build in
(separable):

1. To construct something integral to or inside of something else; to have one thing be a part of and in close working relationship to another, as in this example: *The fan was **built into** the computer to keep the computer cool during operation.*

More examples:

❑ (1) That stove had an exhaust fan **built in**.

❑ (1) The electrician **built** the electrical outlet **into** the wall.

Bump into
(inseparable):

1. To meet by surprise, as in this example: *I **bumped into** my teacher while I was in town.*

2. To run into lightly, as in this example: *I **bumped into** one of the other passengers while on the bus.*

More examples:

- ❏ (1) I ***bumped into*** my friend at the mall. (Meaning, I met my friend at the mall by surprise.)

- ❏ (2) There was a lot of traffic and the white car ***bumped into*** the red one in front of it at the traffic light. (Meaning, the white car lightly hit the red one in front of it.)

Burn down
(separable):

1. To raze; to destroy by fire, as in this example: *The store **burned down**, but fortunately all of the customers and employees escaped without injury.*

More examples:

- ❏ (1) The house next door ***burned down***. The family lost everything.
- ❏ (1) The firefighters had a difficult time putting out the fire in the building and the building finally ***burned down***.

Burn up
(separable):

1. To be destroyed by fire, as in this example: *My car **burned up** when the motor caught fire.*
2. To use up or deplete, as in energy, as in this example: *The runner **burned up** all of his energy running up the hill.*
3. To make angry, as in this example: *The driver of that car turned in front of me. Boy, that really **burns me** up!*

More examples:

- ❏ (1) I'm going to take the trash out in the back yard and ***burn*** it ***up***.

- ❏ (2) That big SUV really ***burns up*** the gas. (Meaning, the car really uses a lot of gasoline to operate.)

- ❏ (3) I was really ***burned up*** that I got such a low grade on the exam.

Burst out

(inseparable):

1. To erupt suddenly (emotional), as in this example: *While watching the horror movie, my friend **burst out** with a scream during the scary part.*

2. To suddenly escape or exit from somewhere, as in this example: *When the little girl entered her bedroom, her brother **burst out** of the closet to try to scare her.*

More examples:

❑ (1) When she heard that she got a failing grade on the exam she **burst out** crying.

❑ (2) The policeman **burst out** the door in pursuit of the thief.

Butt in
(inseparable):

1. To interrupt; an unwanted or unsolicited interruption, as in this example: *Can't you see that I am talking to this gentleman over here. Please don't **butt into** our conversation.*

More examples:

❑ (1) I was talking to my wife when you **butted in**. (Meaning: The person interrupted a conversation when he or she was not being spoken to.)

❑ (2) Please don't **butt in**; this is between Bill and me. (Meaning: Bill and I were having a discussion that didn't have anything to do with the other person.)

Chapter 1 review

*Phrasal verbs beginning with the letters **A** and **B***

Instructions: read and /or listen carefully to the sentences below. Fill in the blank spaces with the correct **preposition, particle,** or **adverb**. The answers can be found below.

1. The president of the company aimed ___ increasing his bank customers by 15%.

2. The customer asked the store clerk _____ a box for her new dress.

3. Please don't butt _____; this is between Bill and me.

4. When Martha heard that she got a failing grade on the exam she burst ____ tears.

5. That big American car really burns ___ gas.

6. The house next door burned _____. The family lost everything.

7. I bumped _____ my friend at the mall.

8. The girl brought the music CD _____ after borrowing it from her friend for two weeks.

9. Every student in the class broke _____ with a red rash. The doctor said it was not a serious disease.

10. The couple decided to break _____ their wedding engagement because they decided they would not be happy together.

11. It is important to break a new horse _____ before racing it.

12. The car was broken _____ on the side of the road.

13. We have not been able to pay our bills and the demand for our products is getting smaller. What it boils _____ ___ is that our business is in trouble.

14. He really blew that story _____. That is not how it happened.

15. The wind came through the window and blew _____ the candles.

16. The force of the explosion blew ____ the roof of the building.

17. The wind came ____ and blew the papers away. We had to run and catch them before they went into the street.

18. I did well on the exam because I believed ____ the idea that if I studied, I would do well on the exam.

19. My friend really beat ___ the book that I lent him.

20. I had to back the car _____ to get out of my parking space.

Answers: (1) at; (2) for; (3) in; (4) into (5) up; (6) down; (7) into; (8) back; (9) out; (10) off; (11) in; (12) down; (13) down to; (14)up; (15) out; (16) off (17) up; (18) in; (19) up; (20) up

Chapter 2 *Phrasal verbs beginning with the letter C*

In this section you will learn how to use many different phrasal verbs that begin with the letter C correctly in a sentence.

There are two kinds of phrasal verbs, separable and inseparable. Separable phrasal verbs can take an object between the verb and the preposition. For example: *My father **picked** me **up** after school and drove me home.* Inseparable phrasal verbs cannot take an object between the verb and the preposition. For example: I asked my friends to **come along** with me to the Christmas party. **Come along** cannot be separated by an object.

The numbers in front of the examples that are in parenthesis (), correspond the to number of the explanation found directly above. So, for example: 1. *explanation . . .* refers to (1) *example . . . .* If there is only one explanation or meaning given for the phrasal verb, then there will be two examples given for the one explanation. Both examples will be marked with (1).

If you have the Focus on English digital audio book version of this book (available separately from www.FOEBooks.com) listen to each of the phrasal verbs, followed by their meanings and then some examples of how they are used in real English sentences.

There will be a review at the end of this chapter.

Phrasal verbs beginning with the letter C

Call back
(separable):

1. To return a phone call, as in this example: *Kyoko **called** me **back** to confirm the date of the picnic.*

2. Request to return, as in this example: *The military commander **called** his men **back** from the battle.*

More examples:

- ❑ (1) I called the dentist but he didn't answer his phone. He ***called*** me ***back*** in about ten minutes.

- ❑ (2) The construction company ***called*** their men ***back*** after finding out that they could not do the job. (Meaning: The construction company asked its workers to return to the office because the company was unable to do the job that they had been requested to do.)

Call in
(separable):

1. Request to assemble, as in this example: *The manager **called in** the workers for a meeting.*

2. To make a telephone call usually in a business or formal setting, as in this example: *Jon didn't feel well so he **called in** sick.*

More examples:

- ❑ (1) The military officer ***called in*** his best soldiers to fight the attackers.

- ❑ (2) The repairman ***called in*** his parts order to the warehouse.

Call off
(separable):

1. To cancel or postpone, as in this example: *They **called off** the concert because of the bad weather.*

2. Request that someone or something stops doing something and returns, as in this example: *The military commander **called off** its troops because there was no longer a threat by the enemy.*

More examples:

- ❑ (1) The policeman ***called off*** his police dog after the thief surrendered. (Meaning, the policeman gave the dog the command to attack the thief. When the thief surrendered, then the policeman ordered the dog to stop attacking.)

❏ (2) ***Call off*** the picnic, it's going to rain. We'll postpone the picnic until next weekend.

Call up
(separable):

1. To initiate a telephone call, as in this example: *I **called up** my sister in Kansas to discuss her wedding.*

2. To request to assemble, to summon, as in this example: *The government **called up** all of its soldiers to fight the war.*

More examples:

❏ (1) I ***called*** Janice ***up*** yesterday and asked her to lend me her history book.

❏ (2) The military is ***calling up*** all eligible young men to serve in the Army.

   (Meaning, The military is requesting that all young men who are physically able and are of a certain age to report to military headquarters for service.)

Calm down
(separable):

1. To cause to become tranquil or calm, as in this example: *The storm had **calmed down** and the sun came out so we decided to go outside.*

More examples:

❏ (1) The man ***calmed down*** after the police recovered his wallet.

❏ (1) The children were nervous after hearing the explosion, so the teacher had to ***calm*** them ***down***.

Care for
(inseparable):

1. To provide needed assistance or watchful supervision, as in this example: *The nurse **cared for** the patient.*

2. To indicate preference, as in this example: *My sister usually doesn't **care for** tomatoes.*

More examples:

❏ (1) The nanny ***cared for*** the children.

❑   (2) I don't ___care for___ that kind of food. I like Japanese food better.

Carry on
(separable):

1. To continue without stopping, as in this example: *The teacher told the student to* ___carry on___ *doing the exercise for ten more minutes.*

2. To act or behave in an improper, excited or silly way, as in this example: *She* ___carried on___ *for a half an hour about how she was almost robbed in the city.*

More examples:

❑   (1) The lottery winner said that he would ___carry on___ working for his company.

❑   (2) When Kaori found out that she got the best grade in the class on the exam, she ___carried on___ for ten minutes.

Carry out
(separable):

1. Complete or finish something, as in this example: *The sales group carried* ___out___ *their mission to increase sales. Sales were up 25%.*

2. To follow or obey a command, order, or request, as in this example: *The commander of the military asked his soldiers to* ___carry out___ *his command.*

More examples:

❑   (1) The president of the company asked the manager if he could complete the project on time. The manager said that he could ___carry out___ the request without a problem.

❑   (2) The police dog was expected to ___carry out___ the command of his trainer.

Catch on
(inseparable):

1. To understand, to learn, as in this example: *The German Shepherd dog is very smart. It* ___catches on___ *quickly and is easy to train.*

More examples:

❑   (1) The new worker ___caught on___ quickly.

❑   (1) He was a smart student who could ___catch on___ quickly.

Catch up
(inseparable):

1. To come up from behind; overtake, as in this example: *The runner in second place **caught up** with the leader.*

2. When wrongdoings or mistakes are detected by someone else and then made known, as in this example: *The businessman didn't pay taxes for years, but the Tax Department finally **caught up** with him.*

3. To become involved with something, often unwillingly, as in this example: *As the sunset I got **caught up** in the beauty of the sky.*

4. To become up to date or current with something, as in this example: *I talked to my girlfriend yesterday to **catch up** with the latest gossip.*

More examples:

- ❑ (1) After thirty minutes, the racing car in 3rd place **caught up** with the leader.

- ❑ (2) I never studied in English class. When I took the exam I go a low grade. All of those weeks of not studying finally **caught up** with me. My parents were really mad.

- ❑ (3) The crowd was cheering every time our team played well. I got **caught up** in all of this excitement and began cheering with the crowd.

- ❑ (4) I was sick for two weeks and didn't go to school. My teacher gave me some homework assignments so that I could **catch up** with the rest of the class.

Cheat on
(inseparable):

1. To act dishonestly; to deceive by trickery; swindle, as in this example: *The business owner **cheated on** his tax form.* (Meaning: *the business owner put the wrong income on his tax form so that he wouldn't have to pay everything he owed to the tax department.*)

More examples:

- ❑ The student was caught **cheating on** the exam.

❑ Susan accused her boyfriend of ***cheating on*** her. (🐛 Meaning: Susan accused her boyfriend of dating another girl).

Check in
(separable):

1. To register, as at a hotel, as in this example: *When I **checked in** at 8:30am the clerk reminded me that checkout time was 12pm tomorrow.*

2. *(informal)* To contact someone for the purpose of confirming your presence, or exchanging information, as in this example: *I **checked in** with my parents to let them know where I was.*

More examples:

❑ 1. We ***checked in*** at the hotel around 10pm.

❑ 2. I ***checked in*** with my colleagues to see if I could help with our project.

(🐛 Meaning: I visited with my colleagues to find out if there was something I could do to help with the project.)

Check out
(inseparable or separable depending on usage):

1. *(inseparable)* To settle one's bill and then leave, as at a hotel, as in this example: *We asked the hotel clerk if we could **check out** an hour later than normal.*

2. *(separable) (informal)* To scrutinize or look over carefully, as in this example: *We went to the mall to **check out** the sales.*

More examples:

❑ (1) We ***checked out*** of the hotel at noon.

❑ (2) We decided to go to the auto showroom and ***check out*** the new BMWs.

Chop up
(separable):

1. To cut into small pieces, as in this example: *We **chopped up** the tomatoes and made a nice salad.*

More examples:

- ❑ (1) The cook ***chopped up*** the garlic and the onions and put them into a saucepan.
- ❑ (1) Then, the cook ***chopped up*** the beef and put that into the saucepan.

Clean out
(separable):

1. To remove clutter or everything from a room or area; sometimes implies that the area is in critical need of cleaning, or that the area has to be made ready for another occupant by removing everything, as in this example: *I **cleaned** **out** my car because it was a mess.*

More examples:

- ❑ (1) I have to ***clean out*** my house to get ready for spring cleaning.
- ❑ (1) They had to ***clean out*** the warehouse so that the new business could move in.

Clear up
(separable):

1. To make free from doubt or confusion, as in this example: *I was confused about the test date, but the teacher **cleared** that **up**.*

2. When a disease condition heals and goes away, especially a skin condition, as in this example: *When I went back to the doctor I showed him that the rash had **cleared up**.*

More examples:

- ❑ (1) We have to ***clear up*** the misunderstanding between us. (Meaning: we have to have a discussion so that we can understand each other's point of view better.)
- ❑ (2) The rash ***cleared up*** after I took the medicine.

Clog up
(separable):

1. To obstruct movement on or in something; when obstructions (something that blocks an opening) prevent something from working properly, as in this

example: *The bathtub drain is **clogged up** and water won't drain out of the tub.*

More examples:

❑ (1) The sink drain is ***clogged up***. Water will not pass out of the drain.

❑ (1) The roads were all ***clogged up*** with traffic.

Close off
(separable):

1. To block or obstruct an area, usually deliberately, so that something or someone cannot pass, as in this example: *Main Street was **closed off** to car traffic because of the street celebration.*

More examples:

❑ (1) The police ***closed off*** the main street because of the big parade.

❑ (1) The workers ***closed off*** one of the entrances to the building because of construction inside the building.

Come across
(inseparable):

1. To encounter or discover; to find unexpectedly, as in this example: *While traveling in China, I **came across** a man who was kind enough to show me the ancient temple.*

More examples:

❑ (1) The man ***came across*** some old photographs while searching through his closet.

❑ (1) The workers ***came across*** some old coins while digging a hole in the ground.

Come along
(inseparable):

1. To accompany; to go with someone, as in this example: *The mother told the child to **come along** with her into the car.*

2. To make progress, as in this example: *The company's new project was **coming along** nicely.*

More examples:

❑   (1) The tour guide told the tourists to ***come along*** with him so that he could show them some interesting things about the city.

❑   (2) The new building is really ***coming along***. (Meaning: the construction on the new building is progressing very well.)

Come apart
(inseparable):

1. To separate, to fall to pieces or fall apart because of poor condition or construction, as in this example: *Her old dress looked nice but it **came apart** when she tried to put it on.*

2. To lose control emotionally, as in this example: *When the man discovered that his wife was seeing another man, he **came apart**.*

More examples:

❑   (1) The old book ***came apart*** when I tried to open it.

❑   (1) When she found out that the school would not accept her she really ***came apart***. (Meaning: she became emotionally upset when she found out the school would not accept her.)

Come back
(inseparable):

1. To return, as in this example: After going to the theater, Nancy ***came back*** home about 11:30pm.

2. To have a consequence, as in this example: *Not doing your homework will **come back** to you in a bad way. Maybe you will do poorly on an exam.* (Note: we use come back to mean return in many ways. In this case it means: Your laziness will return to you when you take an exam and discover you don't know the answers.)

More examples:

❑ (1) Our daughter was away at school for two years. She ***came back*** yesterday.

❑ (2) The salesman's laziness ***came back*** on him when he was fired for a poor sales record.

Come down
(inseparable):

1. Movement from a higher level to a lower level, as in this example: *He **came down** off of the ladder and stepped on the ground.*

2. Socially moving from a good position to a lesser position, as in this example: *Boy, I remember when she was a great actress. Now no one knows who she is. She has really **come down**.*

3. Business: when pricing is reduced, as in this example: *Clothing prices have really **come down** at the mall. Let's go shopping!*

More examples:

❑ (1) My friend from New York is ***coming down*** to visit me here in Florida.

❑ (2) Poor Ted, he's lost his job and now he has to move out of his apartment. Boy, he's really ***come down***.

❑ (3) During the sale, the prices ***came down***.

Come down with
(inseparable):

1. To get sick, as in this example: *Many of the students in the same class **came down with** a cold.*

More examples:

❑ (1) My head is hot and my throat hurts, I think I am ***coming down with*** the flu.

❑ (1) While visiting Thailand, my friend ***came down with*** malaria.

Come from
(inseparable):

1. Origin; location where something or someone originated, as in this example: *He **came from** the south of the country.*

2. Can also be used to refer to a person's reference point when they are giving their opinion to another, as in this example: *Your boss seems mean and nasty, but you must understand where he is **coming from**.* The president of the company will fire your boss if your boss doesn't enforce the rules.

More examples:

❑ I just ***came from*** the grocery store. I bought some food for dinner tonight.

❑ In Mark's opinion, international aid should be sent to that nation. I think that he is ***coming from*** a place of compassion. (Meaning: the reason why he is saying this is because he feels compassion for the people of the poor nation.)

Come in
(inseparable):

1. To enter or to request or give permission to enter, as in this example: *Julia **came in** the front door soaking wet because of the heavy rain outside.*

2. Used to talk about including or inserting an idea, activity, event, etc., into an existing situation, as in this example: *We are planning an outdoor celebration. We are going to have food and competitions. The bike race will **come in** between the swimming race and the running race.*

More examples:

❑ (1) There is someone knocking at our door. It must be our dinner guests, please ask them to ***come in***.

❑ (2) Getting good grades on exams takes hard work. This is where doing homework ***comes in***.

Come off
(inseparable):

1. To result in; to end up, as in this example: *If we don't sell our products more cheaply, we will **come off** the losers in this market.*

2. To happen or occur, as in this example: *The picnic **came off** perfectly because of the beautiful weather.*

3. To separate away from, as in this example: *The cover **came off** of that book.*

More examples:

❑ (1) If we don't score some points in this soccer match we are going to ***come off*** looking like a bad team.

❑ (2) The party ***came off*** poorly because there wasn't enough food.

❑ (3) The handle ***came off*** of the cheap cooking pot.

Come on
(inseparable):

1. Request to accompany, motivational imperative, or used in the imperative to mean hurry up, as in this example: ***Come on***, *we're going to be late for the movies!*

2. (slang) to show romantic or sexual interest in someone, as in this example: *The guy at the bar **came on** to me, but I wasn't interested.*

More examples:

❑ (1) ***Come on*** with me and I'll show you the office.

❑ (2) The guy looked like a movie star. All the girls at the party ***came on*** to him.

Come out
(inseparable):

1. The results of; as in this example: *The total for all of the groceries **came out** to $52.*

2. First appearance, as in this example: *This fashion line of dresses **came out** last month.*

3. Make an appearance, as in this example: *The sky was clear and you could see the stars **come out**.* 4. Remove or come away from, as in this example: *Lots of sand **came out** of my pocket when I returned from the beach.*

More examples:

❑ (1) You blood test ***came out*** negative. You are not sick.

❑ (2) The book ***came out*** last week. It was really exciting.

❑ (3) It was a beautiful night. The moon ***came out***.

❑ (4) The dirt ***came out*** easily when she washed the soiled dress.

Come through
(inseparable):

1. To pass (usually successfully) from the beginning to the end of an experience, as in this example: *The student **came through** the exam okay.*

2. To move from one place to another; pass by and then continue on to a destination; to pass under or between a structure on your way to somewhere, as in this example: *I knew a lot of people that **came through** that door.*

3. To be successful at completing something, or getting something done for someone else, as in this example: *I can always rely on my best friend to **come through** for me.*

More examples:

❑ (1) He **came through** a really bad experience. He was hospitalized after a bad car accident. But today he is finally well.

❑ (2) During our party, people that I didn't know **came through** the door

❑ (3) Our team won the championships. They **came through** for us.

Come up
(inseparable):

1. Moving from a lower position to a higher position, physically or socially, as in this example: *He **came up** the stairs in a hurry. He was late for the meeting.*

2. New or unexpected appearance of an idea or event, as in this example: *A sudden storm **came up** and ruined our picnic.*

3. Anticipation of an event, holiday, or other situation, as in this example: *The Cherry Blossom celebration is **coming up** this week.*

More examples:

❑ (1) They **came up** to Canada from Texas to visit us.

❑ (2) Thank you for the invitation to your party. I'm sorry I can't go, something important has **come up**. (Meaning that an unexpected situation has arisen for the speaker.)

❑ (3) Christmas is **coming up** next week.

Come up with
(inseparable):

1. To originate, to think of, to invent, as in this example: *Yolanda **came up with** a good idea. She would go to America with her friends to study English.*

More examples:

- ❑ (1) We need to ***come up*** with some good ideas for the party next week.

- ❑ (1) Rudolf Diesel ***came up*** with the idea for the diesel engine.

Con into
(separable):

1. Use a deceitful method to get someone to do something (Note: sometimes this expression is used playfully), as in this example: *My friends **conned** me **into** helping them clean up the house.*

More examples:

- ❑ (1) The woman was ***conned into*** sending money to an organization that did not exist.

- ❑ (1) My boss ***conned*** me ***into*** doing the large project. (The speaker does not mean that his boss used negative trickery; only that his boss persuaded him to do a project that he hadn't planned to do.)

Con out of
(separable):

1. Use a deceitful method to get something from someone. (Note: sometimes this expression is used playfully) , as in this example: *My girlfriend **conned** me **out of** my last $20.*

More examples:

- ❑ (1) The phony advertisement on the Internet ***conned*** us ***out of*** our money.

- ❑ (1) My wife ***conned*** me ***out of*** $50 for a new dress. (Note: The speaker does not mean that his wife used negative trickery; only that his wife persuaded him to give her money for the new dress.)

Cool off
(separable):

1. To become more relaxed (usually after being upset), as in this example: _It took me two hours to_ **_cool off_** _after the policeman gave me a ticket._

2. To reduce temperature, as in this example: _It took me two hours to_ **_cool off_** _after jogging in the sun._

More examples:

❑ (1) After the argument, he left the room and tried to **_cool off_**. (Tried to become more calm)

❑ (2) After boiling the eggs, the cook left them out to **_cool off_**.

Count in
(separable):

1. To include, as in this example: _My father asked us if we wanted to go to a nice restaurant tonight. I told him to_ **_count_** _me_ **_in_**_!_

More examples:

❑ (1) The project seemed interesting. I asked the group to **_count_** me **_in_**. (Meaning: I wanted to be included in the project.)

❑ (1) Who wants to have ice cream now? **_Count_** me **_in_**, I love ice cream!

Count on
(inseparable):

1. To rely on, as in this example: _I could always_ **_count on_** _my brother to help me when I was in trouble._

More examples:

❑ (1) I knew that I could **_count on_** my friend to pick me up from work.

❑ (1) An employer likes to hire someone they can **_count on_**.

Count up
(separable):

1. To tally; to add up, as in this example: *After the swap meet we **counted up** the money and discovered that we made over $500.*

Examples:

- ❏ (1) At the end of the day, the business **counts up** the amount of money it made.

- ❏ (1) We **counted up** the number of holidays we have every year.

Cover up
(separable):

1. To hide something, to be blocked from view, as in this example: *I couldn't find my car keys because they were on the table **covered up** by my purse.*

More examples:

- ❏ The politician tried to **cover up** his connection to the criminal. (Meaning: the politician didn't want people to know he had a connection to a criminal)

- ❏ She put some makeup on to **cover up** the red marks on her face.

Crack down
(inseparable):

1. To more strictly enforce law, order, or rules, sometimes suddenly, as in this example: *The school **cracked down** on smoking in the building.*

More examples:

- ❏ (1) The government **cracked down** on protesting in the city.

- ❏ (1) The company **cracked down** on lateness by employees. (Meaning: the company more strictly enforced the rules about being late to work.)

Cross off
(separable):

1. To draw a line through; eliminate, as in this example: *I decided to **cross** my name **off** of the list of students who wanted to take the TOEIC exam.*

More examples:

- ❏ (1) She made a list of places that she wanted to visit. After she visited Rome, she **crossed** that city **off** of her list.

❑ (1) My boss asked us to put our names on a list if we wanted a new position in the company. I hope they don't ***cross*** my name ***off*** of this list.

Cut back
(separable):

1. To reduce; to make shorter or smaller, as in this example: *Because of the high price of petroleum, we had to **cut back** the amount of time that we were driving.*

More examples:

❑ (1) We were spending too much money so we had to ***cut back*** on spending.

❑ (1) The company had to ***cut back*** on bus services because they weren't making enough money.

Cut down
(separable):

1. To reduce; not use so much, as in this example: *It is important for farmers to **cut down** on the amount of pesticides that they use on our food.*

2. To remove by sawing or by using a knife or ax or other sharp tool, as in this example: *The bushes in my yard were too tall, so we **cut** them **down**.*

3. *(informal)* To ridicule, as in this example: *Tanya's friend really **cut** her **down** for being so mean to her boyfriend.*

More examples:

❑ (1) We were spending too much money on our vacation so we had to ***cut down*** our spending.

❑ (2) They ***cut down*** the tree to make room for the new house.

❑ (3) Some of the students ***cut down*** the girl for wearing an old dress to school.

Cut off
(separable):

1. To stop; discontinue, as in this example: *The government **cut off** aid to the poor.*

2. To move in front of someone or something else so as to interfere with their progress, as in this example: *The tall building directly in front of our window **cut off** our view of the ocean.*

3. To cut and completely remove with scissors or knife or other sharp instrument, as in this example: *The cook **cut off** the bad parts of the vegetables and threw them out.*

More examples:

❑ (1) His parents **cut off** his allowance because of his bad grades.

❑ (2) The car moved into the left lane and **cut off** the bus, which caused an accident.

❑ (3) The barber **cut off** Jim's hair. Jim had a bald head after visiting the barber.

Cut out
(separable):

1. *(informal)* Leave unexpectedly, as in this example: *The students **cut out** a 2pm to go to a concert.*

2. To remove part of something like, for example, a section from a piece of paper with a scissors, as in this example: *The dressmaker **cut out** a sleeve from the cloth.*

3. To stop unexpectedly, as in this example: *The electric generator **cut out** and the city was without electricity for two hours.*

4. To stop using something, as in this example: *The doctor told me to **cut out** smoking because it wasn't good for my health.*

More examples:

❑ (1) The meeting was longer than expected so Stefan **cut out** early. (Means he left early)

❑ (2) The children **cut out** star shapes from the colored paper.

❑ (3) I was racing along the freeway when suddenly the car engine **cut out** and I had to turn the car off the road.

❑ (4) The woman was dieting so she **cut out** all sweets.

Cut up
(separable):

1. Separate into pieces, usually with a knife or other sharp instrument, as in this example: *We **cut** the cake **up** into four equal pieces.*

2. *(informal)* To make jokes, as in this example: *My friends and I sat around the table and **cut up** all night.*

More examples:

❑ (1) The cook ***cut up*** the celery.

❑ (1) When my friends get together we always ***cut up***. (Meaning: we always make a lot of jokes.)

Chapter 2 review
Phrasal verbs beginning with the letter C

*Instructions: read and /or listen carefully to the sentences below. Fill in the blank spaces with the correct **preposition, particle,** or **adverb.** The answers can be found below.*

1. I called the dentist but he didn't answer his phone. He called me _____ in about ten minutes.

2. The repairman called ___ his parts order to the warehouse.

3. The children were nervous after hearing the explosion, so the teacher had to calm them _____.

4. The nanny cared _____ the children.

5. When Kaori found out that she got the best grade in the class on the exam, she carried _____ for ten minutes.

6. I don't care _____ that kind of food. I like Japanese food better.

7. The student was caught cheating _____ the exam.

8. We checked _____ at the hotel around 10pm.

9. We decided to go to the auto showroom and check _____ the new BMWs.

10. Then, the cook chopped ___ the beef and put that into the saucepan.

11. The project seemed interesting. I asked the group to count me ___.

12. The phony advertisement on the Internet conned us _____ of our money.

13. The government cracked _____ on protesting in the city.

14. She made a list of places that she wanted to visit. After she visited Rome, she crossed that city _____ of her list.

15. The company had to cut _____ on bus services because they weren't making enough money.

16. They cut _____ the tree to make room for the new house.

17. The car moved into the left lane and cut _____ the bus, which caused an accident.

18. The cook cut _____ the celery.

19. Some of the students cut _____ the girl for wearing an old dress to school.

20. The company cracked _____ on employees who were spending too much time at the water cooler.

Answers: (1) back (2) in; (3) down (4) for; (5) on; (6) for; (7) on; (8) in; (9) out; (10) up; (11) in; (12) out; (13) down; (14) off; (15) back; (16) down; (17) off; (18) up; (19) down; (20) down

Chapter 3 *Phrasal verbs beginning with the letters D, E, and F*

In this section you will learn how to use many different phrasal verbs that begin with the letters D, E, and F correctly in a sentence.

There are two kinds of phrasal verbs, separable and inseparable. Separable phrasal verbs can take an object between the verb and the preposition. For example: *My father **picked** me **up** after school and drove me home.* Inseparable phrasal verbs cannot take an object between the verb and the preposition. For example: I asked my friends to ***come along*** with me to the Christmas party. ***Come along*** cannot be separated by an object.

The numbers in front of the examples that are in parenthesis (), correspond the to number of the explanation found directly above. So, for example: 1. *explanation . . .* refers to (1) *example . . . .* If there is only one explanation or meaning given for the phrasal verb, then there will be two examples given for the one explanation. Both examples will be marked with (1).

If you have the Focus on English digital audio book version of this book (available separately from www.FOEBooks.com) listen to each of the phrasal verbs, followed by their meanings and then some examples of how they are used in real English sentences.

There will be a review at the end of this chapter.

Phrasal verbs beginning with the letters D, E, and F

Deal with
(inseparable):

1. To do business with, as in this example: *When we want to buy clothing we only **deal with** the best stores.*

2. To interact with someone or something, as in this example: *The teacher always **dealt with** his students in a fair way.*

3. *(separable)* To do what is necessary to solve a problem, as in this example: *The police always **deal** harshly **with** drug dealers.*

4. About or concerning, as in this example: *There is an excellent book on the environment. It **deals with** the topic of global warming.*

More examples:

❑ (1) When we need laundry services we **deal** with Ajax Cleaners.

❑ (2) When there was a problem between them, Marco always **dealt with** his wife in a compassionate way.

❑ (3) My home had a leaky roof so I **dealt with** this problem by calling a roofing company.

❑ (4) The newspaper article **deals with** the problem of drugs in big cities.

Do away with
(inseparable):

1. To end, as in this example: *The school **did away with** the old system of grading students.*

2. To kill, as in this example: *The gangsters **did away with** the rival leader.*

More examples:

❑ (1) The teacher **did away with** homework in his classes. (Meaning: the teacher no longer gave homework in his classes)

❑ (2) The military commander **did away with** the traitor. (Meaning: had him killed for being a traitor)

Do over
(separable):

1. Do again, to repeat something, as in this example: *If the teacher did not approve the project, the student was allowed to **do** it **over**.*

More examples:

❑ (1) The owner didn't like the paint job on his house and asked the painter to **do** it **over**.

❑ (1) As the golfer swung the club someone in the crowd made a loud noise. The golfer was allowed to ***do*** that shot ***over***.

Do without
(inseparable):

1. To be deprived of; to continue living minus some of the things you have been used to in your life in the past, as in this example: *When I was young, we had to **do without** nice clothes and fine food because we had very little money.*

More examples:

❑ (1) The water heater stopped working so we will have to ***do without*** hot water tonight.

❑ (1) The survivors of the shipwreck had to ***do without*** clean water for many days.

Dress up
(separable):

1. To put nice clothes on, as in this example: *My wife and I **dressed up** and went to a nice restaurant for dinner.*

2. To fix something up to look better, as in this example: *The company **dressed up** its headquarters to make a better impression on visitors.* (Meaning: The company improved the looks of the building where their main headquarters was located so that visitors would be impressed.)

More examples:

❑ (1) Tonight is the night that we are going to the big dance. We are going to have to ***dress up*** tonight.

❑ (2) The chef will often ***dress up*** his dishes (meals) to look more delicious. (Meaning: the chef will arrange the food on the plate to look more appealing.)

Drink down
(separable):

1. Drink all of something, usually in one pass, as in this example: *The marathon runners stopped at the water table, **drank down** the water, and continued running.*

   More examples:

   ❑ (1) During a beer-drinking contest, the competitors will ***drink down*** their mug of beer.

   ❑ (1) The medicine doesn't taste good so you will have to ***drink*** it ***down*** quickly.

Drink up
(separable):

1. Finish drinking something, as in this example: *We were so thirsty that we **drank up** all of the ice tea in the refrigerator.*

2. To take in, to absorb, as in this example: *We took the dog out to play with a ball. When he came back to the house, he **drank up** all of his water in his water bowl.*

   More examples:

   ❑ (1) I told my children to ***drink up*** their milk so we could leave for the beach.

   ❑ (2) The ground was so dry that it ***drank up*** the moisture from the new rain.

Drop in
(inseparable):

1. To visit unexpectedly or with little warning, as in this example: *After work, I **dropped in** at the library and got a book.*

   More examples:

   ❑ (1) On the way home, we decided to ***drop in*** on our friends.

   ❑ (1) It is usually not polite to ***drop in*** on someone unless they are a relative or a very close friend.

Drop off
(separable):

1. To leave something somewhere without spending much time at the location; to stop somewhere unexpectedly and leave something, as in this example: *On the way home from school I **dropped** my laundry **off** at the cleaners.*

   More examples:

   ❑ (1) On the way to work I ***dropped*** my daughter ***off*** at school.

   ❑ (1) The postman ***dropped off*** a package at our house.

Drop out
(inseparable):

1. To stop participating in something; to quit, as in this example: *The student **dropped out** of the advanced class because it was too difficult for him.*

2. To stop doing what everyone else is doing; to ignore the rules of normal society and live a life based on your own ideas, as in this example: *The hippies **dropped out** in the 1960s and 1970s because they didn't trust the ways of normal society.*

   More examples:

   ❑ (1) The runner ***dropped out*** of the race in exhaustion.

   ❑ (2) Marco decided to ***drop out*** and sail around the world on his own sailboat.

Dry off
(separable):

1. To remove water or moisture from someone or something, as in this example: *I **dried off** the table with a towel.*

   More examples:

   ❑ (1) After we got out of the swimming pool we ***dried*** ourselves ***off***.

   ❑ (1) My cell phone fell in the water so dried it off and took the battery out.

Dry out
(separable):

1. All moisture evaporating out of something over time; all the moistness leaves something, as in this example: *I stepped in some water during the rainstorm. When I returned home I **dried out** my shoes with the help of a hair dryer.*

More examples:

- ❑ (1) Rain came in the window and got the rug wet. It took two weeks to ***dry*** the rug ***out***.

- ❑ (1) Sometimes the skin can ***dry out*** during the winter season. Some women put skin moisturizer on themselves to prevent their skin from ***drying out***.

Dry up
(separable):

1. When moisture leaves something because of evaporation, as in this example: *The sun came out and the ground **dried up**.*

2. When the amount of something gets smaller and disappears, as in this example: *Our supply of corn chips has **dried up**. Would someone go to the food store and get some more.*

More examples:

- ❑ (1) The towel that was wet yesterday has ***dried up*** over night.
- ❑ (2) Our coffee supply has ***dried up***, someone better go to the store and get some more coffee.

Eat up
(separable):

1. To eat all of something, as in this example: *I **ate up** all of the cake in the refrigerator. My roommates were really mad.*

2. To use resources usually at a high rate of speed, as in this example: *Shopping at that expensive store really **eats up** my bank account.*

3. *(slang)* To really enjoy or embrace something, as in this example: *The political candidate told the people they wouldn't have to pay taxes if they elect him. The people were **eating** it **up**.*

More examples:

- ❑ (1) The sushi was great. We ***ate*** it all ***up***. (English speakers use "all" to mean "completely.")
- ❑ (2) That car really ***eats up*** gas.

❑ (3) When we were doing our song on stage the audience was really *eating* it *up*. (Meaning: the audience really liked our song)

Eat out
(inseparable):

1. To eat at a location away from home, at a restaurant or elsewhere, as in this example: *We **ate out** at the club last night.*

More examples:

❑ (1) We **ate out** last night. I really liked that restaurant.

❑ (1) I'm tired of cooking, let's **eat out**.

Empty out
(separable):

1. Completely removing the contents of something, as in this example: *I **emptied out** my closet trying to find my ice skates.*

More examples:

❑ (1) We **emptied out** the refrigerator so that we could clean it.

❑ (1) The woman **emptied out** her purse looking for her driver's license.

End up
(inseparable):

1. To finish with a result; resulting in; resulting outcome regardless of the choices that were available, as in this example: *Sabine **ended up** going to university in Cologne.*

More examples:

❑ (1) We **ended up** going to California for our vacation because we didn't have enough money to go to Paris.

❑ (1) The school **ended up** closing because it didn't have enough money to pay the teachers.

Fall apart
(inseparable):

1. To break down, collapse, as in this example: *The old building was **falling apart** because of lack of care.* 2. To become emotionally unstable or weak, usually due to some situation or circumstance, as in this example: *The woman **fell apart** and started to cry when she talked about her mother.*

More examples:

❑ (1) The old chair ***fell apart*** when Jason tried to sit in it.

❑ (2) My colleague ***fell apart*** when he was told that he would be laid off in two months.

Fall behind
(inseparable):

1. To fail to keep up a pace, to lag behind, as in this example: *The student **fell behind** the rest of the class because he was always absent.*

More examples:

❑ (1) The tired runner ***fell behind*** the rest of the runners.

❑ (1) We ***fell behind*** in our car payments and the bank was angry. (Meaning: we could not continue to make payments when the bank required.)

Fall down
(inseparable):

1. To drop or come down from a higher position, usually to the ground, as in this example: *The runner **fell down** during the marathon competition.*

2. Fail to meet expectations, as in this example: *The company **fell down** on its obligation to complete the production of its product.*

More examples:

❑ (1) Gina ***fell down*** and hurt her knee while trying to learn how to ice skate.

❑ (2) Jim's boss was really mad with him because he ***fell down*** on the job that he was given. (Meaning: Jim did not do his job right and because of this his boss was mad at him.)

Fall for
(inseparable):

1. To believe something that was not true and sometimes act on that belief; to be deceived or swindled, as in this example: *I can't believe I **fell for** that advertisement.* The advertisement said that I would get a free car if I bought one of their products.

2. To feel love for, as in this example: *I really **fell for** the girl with the red hair.*

More examples:
- (1) My friend **fell for** that work-at-home advertisement on the Internet and lost $100.

- (2) The first time I saw my wife I **fell for** her immediately.

Fall off
(inseparable):

1. To become less, decrease, as in this example: *Our store sales **fell off** by 50% last week. We have to advertise more.*

2. To drop from a higher level to a lower place, usually the thing or person was perched on something above the ground, like a chair or the branch of a tree, etc., as in this example: *The book **fell off** the table and onto the floor.*

More examples:
- (1) The boy **fell off** the chair.

- (2) Stock prices **fell off** sharply. (Meaning: stock prices went down rapidly.)

Fall out
(inseparable):

1. To leave a military formation, as in this example: *After the military exercise was finished, the commander asked the men to **fall out** and go have dinner.*

2. To quarrel, as in this example: *The shopkeeper and the customer **fell out** over the price of bread.*

3. To fall or drop from something you were in, like a chair, car or plane, and fall to the ground or a lower elevation, as in this example: *I **fell out** of my chair when I heard that my daughter was getting married.* (Note: sometimes this

phrasal verb is used in a light, playful way, meaning that a person was surprised about something).

More examples:

- ❑ (1) The captain ordered his men to _**fall out**_ and go back to their barracks.
- ❑ (2) The two women _**fell out**_ over the same man.
- ❑ (3) The man was laughing so hard he _**fell out**_ of his chair.

Fall over
(inseparable):

1. To tumble or drop from a higher place to a lower one with the help of gravity and sometimes because of an obstacle (the feeling of "fall over" is that there is usually motion, movement or some causative element first and then, unexpectedly, someone or something tumbles to the ground or down with the help of gravity, sometimes because of an obstacle in their path), as in this example: _The flower pot **fell over** and broke._

2. To _**fall over**_ oneself means to make a lot of effort to help someone out (the feeling of this phrase is that someone really wants to please someone else by showing them how much they want to help or accomplish something for them), as in this example: _The student **fell over** himself trying to make a good impression on the rest of the class._

More examples:

- ❑ (1) The children ran into the table and the lamp _**fell over**_ and broke.
- ❑ (2) The new employee _**fell over**_ herself trying to please her boss.

Fall through
(inseparable):

1. To drop down into an opening and continue to the ground or lower location, as in this example: _The workman **fell through** a hole in the roof._
2. When something fails or is not completed, as in this example: _The business deal between the two companies **fell through**._

More examples:

- ❑ (1) The sailor _**fell through**_ the open hatch and had to be taken to the hospital.

❑　(2) We were going to go to Japan for our vacation but those plans ***fell through*** and we decided to go somewhere else.

Feel up to
(inseparable):

1. To be in the mood, to have the energy, to be healthy/well enough to do something (🖾 a variation of this phrase with the same meaning is ***to be up to)***, as in this example: *I didn't **feel up to** going to work today so I stayed home.*

More examples:
❑　(1) I told my friends that I wasn't ***feeling up to*** playing soccer this afternoon. They would have to find someone else for their team.

❑　(1) We were excited about going snowboarding. We were ***feeling up to*** trying some new techniques.

Fight back
(inseparable):

1. To defend oneself in a conflict. (🖾 You get the feeling from this phrase that someone really wants to fight back because they were attacked), as in this example: *Our soccer team was losing 1-0. We decided to **fight back** because we wanted to win.*

More examples:
❑　(1) Our football team was losing 3 to 1 and we really wanted to ***fight back*** and win.

❑　(1) The woman ***fought back*** against her attacker and then ran away.

Figure on
(inseparable):

1. To plan on, as in this example: *We **figure on** completing our English studies by next June.*

More examples:
❑　(1) We had to cut our vacation short because we didn't ***figure on*** the high cost of hotel accommodations.

❑ (1) You should ***figure on*** spending at least two hours at the airport for checking in and security checks.

Figure out
(separable):

1. To uncover the answer, to think something through and come up with the answer, as in this example: *I **figured out** why we cannot get a visa to enter that country. They just changed governments.*

More examples:

❑ (1) We couldn't ***figure out*** the math problem.

❑ (1) I couldn't ***figure out*** why my mother was so mad at me.

Fill in
(separable):

1. To give information, usually the information is new, as in this example: *I was absent from work for two weeks. My colleague **filled** me **in** on what happened in the office while I was gone.*

2. To substitute, as in this example: *Nancy Yee filled in for her colleague, Wendy, while Wendy was in Europe.*

3. To put something like dirt or water into a void or hole to build up to an even level, as in this example: *After putting the fuel tank in the ground, the company **filled in** the hole.*

More examples:

❑ (1) My classmate ***filled*** me ***in*** on what homework was due today. (Meaning: One classmate told the other classmate about the homework assignment due today.)

❑ (2) Janice stayed home sick so Yuki ***filled in*** for her. (Yuki substituted for Janice because Janice was sick.)

❑ (3) The workers shoveled dirt into the hole to ***fill*** it ***in***. (Meaning: the workers put dirt back into the hole.)

Fill out

(separable):

1. To complete, as in this example: *The school secretary asked me to **fill out** the form.*

2. To gain weight, as in this example: *I stopped exercising three months ago and now I'm starting to **fill out**.*

   More examples:

   ❑ (1) The custom's official asked me to **fill out** the form.

   ❑ (2) My friend Paco really **filled out**. (Meaning: Paco gained weight.)

Fill up
(separable):

1. To put liquid or other substance into a container to replenish supply, as in this example: *I **filled up** the ice tea pitcher and put it in the refrigerator.*

2. **Fill up** can refer to eating enough food, as in this example: *I **filled up** on salad and didn't feel like eating anything else.*

3. **Fill up** can refer to a room or building being crowded with people, as in this example: *The room **filled up** to capacity.* (*Meaning: The room was full of people. The number of people legally allowed in the room, or the comfort of the people already in the room, would determine if it was filled up.)*

   More examples:

   ❑ (1) Erika went to the gas station to **fill** her car **up** with gas. (Note: Americans say, "fill the car up with gas" when they mean fill the gas tank of the car up with gas.")

   ❑ (2) The father told his daughter not to **fill up** on chocolate because they were going to have dinner in one hour.

   ❑ (3) It was a great celebration. There were so many people at the party that the room was **filled up**.

Find out
(separable):

1. To discover, to learn of, as in this example: *We just **found out** that our flight was cancelled.*

   More examples:

   ❑ (1) His classmates **found out** that his birthday was next week and they decided to have a party for him.

   ❑ (1) The police **found out** that the thief was hiding in the building.

Fix up
(separable):

1. To renovate, to put in good condition, as in this example: *They **fixed up** the meeting room. They painted it and bought new furniture.*

   More examples:

   ❑ (1) When they finished **fixing up** the old car it looked like new.

   ❑ (1) The old house looked terrible before they **fixed** it **up**.

Flip out
(inseparable):

1. To get angry or very anxious, as in this example: *He really **flipped out** when he saw his electric bill.*

2. To become emotional, as in this example: *Rita **flipped out** when they told her she won the lottery.*

   More examples:

   ❑ (1) My mother **flipped out** when she found out I spent the money on a new dress. I was supposed to buy groceries with that money.

   ❑ (2) The student **flipped out** when she got her exam back with a perfect score.

Float around
(separable):

1. When something or someone moves through space as if they were supported by liquid or air, moving from one location to another with no real focus, as in this example: *The leaves were **floating around** in the swimming pool.*

   More examples:

❑ (1) The hostess of the party was ***floating around*** talking to this couple and then that couple.

❑ (1) The toy sailboat was ***floating around*** in the bathtub.

Follow through
(inseparable):

1. To complete an action or responsibility, as in this example: *The four of us were able to **follow through** with our promise to travel around the world in eight months.*

2. In sports to continue a movement after contact, for example, ***follow through*** with a golf swing, as in this example: *When you kick a soccer ball you have to **follow through** the ball with your foot.*

   More examples:

❑ (1) Our project failed because we didn't ***follow through*** and complete the work that was necessary.

❑ (2) After Martina hits the tennis ball she ***follows through***.

Follow up
(separable):

1. When someone makes an additional effort to check on or complete something that he or she was interested in, or interested in doing (this phrase is usually used to talk about someone continuing to do something or research something for the purpose of solving a problem, getting a job done, or learning more about something), as in this example: *Jack did some research about the company on the Internet and then **followed** that **up** with a phone call to the company.*

   More examples:

❑ (1) Hiro called the cell phone company to find out if they had the model and color cell phone that he wanted. A salesman at the company ***followed up*** on Hiro's request and called him back to tell him they did have the model and color he wanted.

❑ (2) The police ***followed up*** on a tip that the Main Street bank was going to be robbed at 5pm. When the robbers came, the police were waiting for them.

Fool around
(inseparable):

1. Usually someone not taking something seriously, as in this example: _We will never get our work done because we are **fooling around** too much._

2. Can mean that a girlfriend or boyfriend, husband or wife, is cheating on the other, as in this example: _Hilde's boyfriend caught her **fooling around** with another man and told her he didn't want to see her again._

   More examples:
   - ❑ (1) The students **fooled around** the whole day and didn't learn anything.
   - ❑ (2) The wife found out that her husband had been **fooling around** with another woman.

Freak out
(inseparable):

1. _(informal)_ Becoming emotionally unstable because of something that happened (Note: Americans can use this phrasal verb in a playful way, not meaning it in a serious way), as in this example: _I **freaked out** when my friend told me that the cute boy in our class was interested in me._

   More examples:
   - ❑ (1) My mother **freaked out** when I brought the lizard home.
   - ❑ (1) Billy wore the Halloween mask to school to **freak out** his classmates.
   - ❑

Chapter 3 review

*Phrasal verbs beginning with the letters **D, E, and F***

*Instructions: read and /or listen carefully to the sentences below. Fill in the blank spaces with the correct **preposition, particle,** or **adverb**. The answers can be found below.*

1. The newspaper article deals _____ the problem of drugs in big cities.

2. The wife found out that her husband had been fooling _____ with another woman.

3. After Martina hits the tennis ball she follows _____.

4. The toy sailboat was floating _____ in the bathtub.

5. The police found _____ that the thief was hiding in the building.

6. The old house looked terrible before they fixed it _____.

7. The student flipped _____ when she got her exam back with a perfect score.

8. The custom's official asked me to fill _____ the form.

9. We had to cut our vacation short because we didn't figure ___ the high cost of hotel accommodations.

10. The woman fought _____ against her attacker and then ran away.

11. The new employee fell _____ herself trying to please her boss.

12. The sailor fell _____ the open hatch and had to be taken to the hospital.

13. The boy fell _____ the chair.

14. Gina fell _____ and hurt her knee while trying to learn how to ice skate.

15. The school ended ____ closing because it didn't have enough money to pay the teachers.

16. We emptied _____ the refrigerator so that we could clean it.

17. That American car really eats _____ gas.

18. The towel that was wet yesterday has dried ___ over night.

19. The runner dropped _____ of the race in exhaustion.

20. On the way to work I dropped my daughter _____ at school.

Answers: (1) with; (2) around; (3) through; (4)around; (5) out; (6) up; (7) out; (8) out; (9) on; (10) back; (11) over; (12) through; (13) off; (14) over; (15) up; (16) out; (17) up; (18) out; (19) out; (20) off

Chapter 4 *Phrasal verbs beginning with the letter G*

Read and / or listen to each of these phrasal verbs beginning with the letter G, followed by their meanings and then some examples of how they are used in real English sentences.

There are two kinds of phrasal verbs, separable and inseparable. Separable phrasal verbs can take an object between the verb and the preposition. For example: *My father **picked me up** after school and drove me home.* Inseparable phrasal verbs cannot take an object between the verb and the preposition. For example: I asked my friends to **come along** with me to the Christmas party. **Come along** cannot be separated by an object.

The numbers in front of the examples that are in parenthesis (), correspond the to number of the explanation found directly above. So, for example: 1. *explanation . . .* refers to (1) *example . . . .* . If there is only one explanation or meaning given for the phrasal verb, then there will be two examples given for the one explanation. Both examples will be marked with (1).

If you have the Focus on English digital audio book version of this book (available separately from www.FOEBooks.com) listen to each of the phrasal verbs, followed by their meanings and then some examples of how they are used in real English sentences.

There will be a review at the end of this chapter.

Phrasal verbs beginning with the letter G

Get ahead
(inseparable):

   1. To improve your position or situation; to make progress, as in this example: *The man worked at two jobs to try to **get ahead** and improve his monthly income.*

More examples:

- ❏ (1) It is difficult to ***get ahead*** if you don't work hard.

- ❏ (1) After I got a raise at work, I was able to ***get ahead*** and pay all of my bills.

Get along
(inseparable):

1. Usually refers to humans or animals and means to coexist harmoniously, as in this example: *The coworkers liked each other and **got along** very well.*

2. Can also mean to get older, as in this example: *My grandfather is **getting along** in years and has to be helped when he enters or leaves a car.*

3. Sometimes refers to economics with the following meaning: a person or group is able to exist without undue hardship, as in this example: *I don't make much money at work, but I **get along** okay.*

More examples:

- ❏ (1) We have a dog and a cat and they ***get along*** just fine.

- ❏ (2) We all ***get along*** in years as time goes by.

- ❏ (3) The couple living in the old house is able to ***get along*** on their pension checks.

Get around to
(inseparable):

1. To do something whenever the person is in the mood, or has time to do it. The feeling of this usage is that the person or group is lazy or very busy and will not do something until the time is right or until they feel like it, as in this example: *The road out in front of our house needs urgent repair, but the Roads Department said that they are not in a hurry and will fix the road when they **get around to** it.*

More examples:

- ❏ (1) My daughter thinks that she should do her chores when she ***gets around to*** it.

- ❏ (1) I'll do my homework when I ***get around to*** it.

Get away

(inseparable and separable depending on the content of the sentence):

1. To leave to go on vacation (the feeling of this expression is that you need a rest or a real change and you are leaving everything behind for a little while and going on vacation), as in this example: *I've had enough of work; I need to **get away** for a short vacation;*

2. To **get away with** something is when no one detects or catches or cares about something that was done that was sneaky or not the usually accepted way of doing something, as in this example: *Tom **got away** with not doing his homework because the teacher did not check homework today.*

3. *(separable)* To separate something or someone from something or someone, as in this example: *I hate snakes, **get** that snake **away** from me!*

More examples:
- ❑ (1) It is nice to leave the city for a while and **get away** to the country.
- ❑ (2) The clerk **got away** with not giving the customer the correct change.
- ❑ (3) **Get** that cat **away** from me; I am allergic to cat hair!

Get back
(inseparable and separable depending on the content of the sentence):

1. Usually a command that means to keep a distance from something or someone usually because there is danger, as in this example: ***Get back**! It is dangerous to enter this area;*

2. To return to where one was before, as in this example: *The party lasted almost all night and I didn't **get back** home until 5am;*

3. To have something returned that one once owned or possessed before, as in this example: *I **got** my exam paper **back** from the teacher yesterday. I got an A on the exam.*

More examples:
- ❑ (1) **Get back**, the building may collapse any time!
- ❑ (2) When I **got back** to my home country, my family was waiting for me.
- ❑ (3) The thief took my purse, but I **got** my wallet **back** when the police found it in the trash.

Get back at
(inseparable):

> 1. To retaliate against., as in this example: *The soccer team from Newbury beat us last week, but this week we **got back at** them with a 4-2 win.*

More examples:
- ❑   (1) The little girl was mad at her mom, so she ***got back at*** her by not cleaning her room.
- ❑   (1) If you complain to the government, the government may ***get back at*** you by increasing your taxes.

Get back to
(inseparable):

> 1. To return to some place or something that was being said or done, as in this example: *I like talking about this subject, but I would like to **get back to** the subject that we were talking about in the beginning.*

More examples:
- ❑   (1) To ***get back to*** our hotel we had to take a taxi.
- ❑   (1) We should not have gone on a long hike because now we won't ***get back to*** the camp for at least four hours.

Get behind
(inseparable):

> 1. To support; to give support to something or someone, as in this example: *We really **got behind** our team during the game.*
> 2. To position oneself or something to the rear of something or someone; frequently used as a command to emphasize urgency or danger, as in this example: *If you **get behind** me you will be safe from harm.*

More examples:
- ❑   (1) Cancer research is important so my family ***got behind*** the Cancer Society when they asked for volunteers.
- ❑   (2) The soldiers ***got behind*** the wall to protect themselves from the enemy bullets.

Get by
(inseparable):

1. When someone or a group is able to survive (but not much more) by their efforts, or create barely acceptable action results, as in this example: *While we were lost in the woods we **get by** on berries and whatever we could find to eat.*

2. To move around or by someone or something on the way to a destination beyond, as in this example: *May I **get by** you? I want to sit in the front row.*

More examples:

❏ (1) The survivors **got by** on very little food and water.

❏ (2) The soccer play ran down the field, **got by** one player and kicked the ball towards the goal.

Get down
(inseparable and separable depending on the content of the sentence):

1. To climb or move downward or from a higher place to a lower place, as in this example: *The workers **get down** off of the roof and went home.*

2. *(separable)* To make feel melancholy or depressed, as in this example: *I got a poor grade on the exam, but I didn't let that **get** me **down**.*

More examples:

❏ (1) The cat **got down** off the table and ate dinner.

❏ (2) The boxer hated to lose. Losing really **gets** him **down**.

Get in (into)
(inseparable and separable depending on the content of the sentence):

1. To climb into or enter usually an enclosed area of some kind like a building or a car, as in this example: *I **got in** (or into) the taxi and asked the driver to take me to River Street.*

2. To fit something or someone in or into something, as in this example: *We couldn't **get** all of the milk **in** (or into) the jar.*

3. To arrive, as in this example: *After the long drive, we **got in** at 2am;*

4. To find time for something, an event or activity, as in this example: *We were able to **get in** some tennis during our business trip to Spain.*

More examples:

❑   (1) We all ***got in*** the bus and began singing.

❑   (2) I really gained weight; I couldn't ***get into*** that size 9 dress.

❑   (3) The train ***got in*** at 4:56pm, almost 1 hour late!

❑   (4) We were supposed to be working, but we ***got*** some shopping ***in*** during the day.

Get off
(inseparable and separable depending on the content of the sentence):

1. To disembark, as in this example: *When we reached Frankfurt, everyone **got off** the train.*

2. Used in expressing the time when you stop doing something, like working, as in this example: *We **got off** work at 5pm.*

3. When someone stops talking on the phone and hangs up, as in this example: *My daughter was on the phone for about an hour. She finally **got off** at 8:30pm.*

4. Used to express difficulty in removing something, as in this example: *I can't **get** this stain **off** of my blouse.*

More examples:

❑   (1) Driver, I would like to ***get off*** at 23rd Street.

❑   (2) We're going to the movies tonight, what time do you ***get off*** school? Maybe you can go with us.

❑   (3) As soon as my wife ***gets off*** the phone I will call the doctor and make an appointment to see him.

❑   (4) I took the pants to the cleaner to see if they could ***get*** the black mark ***off*** of my pants.

Get off on
(slang) (inseparable):

1. Used to express one's pleasure at doing something, as in this example: *I really **get off on** walking in nature.*

More examples:

❑ (1) I really ***get off on*** doing math.

❑ (1) This is the third time we've seen that movie; ___we___ really ***get off on*** it.

Get on
(inseparable):

1. To board transportation, as in this example: *We **got on** the bus and went to the city center.*

2. To move towards and then sit, stand or recline on something, as in this example: *When the actress **got on** the stage she sang a love song.*

3. To take action to do something or continue doing something (common British usage), as in this example: *It is important to **get on** with taking the exam because you only have five minutes left.*

More examples:

❑ (1) We ***got on*** the plane at 2pm and flew to Tokyo.

❑ (2) She ***got on*** the table and started dancing.

❑ (3) Let's ***get on*** with finishing this project so that we can go home.

Get out
(inseparable or separable depending on usage):

1. Used to express leaving or disembarking, as in this example: We got out of the taxi and went into the restaurant.

2. Used to express the feeling of rescue or helping to leave or escape someplace, as in this example: *There was a practice fire drill in our building and we had to **get out** of the building as quickly as possible.*

3. Used to have the same meaning as get away, to take a rest, vacation or break and go somewhere that is different than where you usually are as in this example: *We have been working too hard. We need to **get out** and enjoy ourselves more.*

4. To make known, to make information widely available, information that was usually private, kept secret, or not generally known, as in this example: *When the news **got out** about Paul and Debbie's wedding, everyone was very surprised.*

More examples:

- ❑ (1) We told the Taxi drive to stop on Broadway. Then we **_got out_** of the taxi and went to a theater.

- ❑ (2) When the earthquake came we **_got out_** of the building quickly.

- ❑ (3) We **_got out_** of the city for a while to enjoy ourselves in the country.

- ❑ (4) When the news about John getting fired **_got out_**, we were all shocked.

Get out of
(inseparable or separable depending on usage):

1. (inseparable) To remove oneself from something or some obligation, as in this example: _The student **get out of** having to take the exam because he already had a high mark in that class._

2. (inseparable) Used to express the idea of reward for doing something, as in this example: _This is what we **get out of** working for that company: a high salary and good benefits._

3. (separable) Used to express the idea of forcibly getting something from someone or something, as in this example: _She **got** the information she needed **out of** the old woman by threatening her._

More examples:

- ❑ (1) I **_got out of_** having to go to the meeting because I had a dental appointment at that time.

- ❑ (2) He didn't sell his house because he couldn't **_get_** enough money **_out of_** it.

- ❑ (3) The police **_got_** the information about the robbery **_out of_** the witness.

Get over
(inseparable):

1. To recover, as in this example: _I just **get over** the flu._

2. Used in commands or to express urgency when you want someone to come to where you are located, as in this example: **_Get over_** _here, I want to show you something interesting in the water!_

More examples:

- ❑ (1) Miho was hospitalized for an infection; I hope she **_gets over_** it soon.

❑ (2) You'd better ***get over*** to the office, the director wants to talk to you.

Get over with
(separable):

1. Used when you want to express wanting to complete something or finish something, as in this example: *Boy, I'm worried about this exam. I can't wait to **get** it **over with***.

   More examples:

❑ (1) I have to go to the dentist tomorrow. I hate going to the dentist. I want to ***get*** it ***over with*** as soon as possible.

❑ (1) That medicine tastes terrible, so I'd better drink it fast and ***get*** it ***over with***.

Get through
(inseparable):

1. Used to express struggling to finish something, as in this example: *This has been a bad day, I will be glad when I **get through** it.*

2. Used to express the need to communicate something to someone, or communication with someone, as in this example: *The teacher **got through** to us that we needed to study for the difficult exam.*

   More examples:

❑ (1) Try to ***get through*** the first part of the exam as quickly as possible, because you only have one hour to finish.

❑ (2) The parents tried to ***get through*** to their daughter that it was dangerous to walk home alone in the dark.

Get to
(inseparable):

1. To arrive at or reach a place, idea or situation, as in this example: *Excuse me, how do we **get to** the center of town?*

2. Used to express time when one is talking about starting to do something, as in this example: *I am really busy now, I will cut the grass when I **get to** it.*

   More examples:

❑ (1) The men looked at the map to decide how to ***get to*** the top of the mountain.

❏   (2) I have about ten things to do right now, I will ***get to*** that project in about an hour.

Get together
(separable):

1. To meet and spend time with, as in this example: *The family **got together** for Christmas.*

2. To become organized for the purpose of accomplishing a task or action, as in this example: *We **got** the papers **together** so that we could meet with the company representative.*

3. To focus or bring your emotions together so that you are calm and rational, as in this example: *Before taking a big exam, I am always very nervous. My solution to this is to spend a couple of minutes relaxing and **getting** it **together** so that I am calm and can think clearly.*

   More examples:
❏   (1) The students ***got together*** and had a party.

❏   (2) We have to ***get*** our plan ***together*** so that we can defeat the other team.

❏   (3) After about two hours of crying, my sister finally ***got*** it ***together***, had a cup of tea, and calmed down.

Get up
(inseparable):

1. To awaken, as in this example: *I **got up** at 6:30am and went for a walk.*

2. To raise, for example, money or resources, as in this example: *Our organization had to **get up** enough money to help the poor in our town.*

3. To rise up from a lower position, as in this example: *I **got up** and turned off the TV.*

   More examples:
❏   (1) We all had to ***get up*** at 8 o'clock to go to breakfast.

❏   (2) Our group had to ***get up*** enough money to pay for the tickets.

❏   (3) She ***got up*** and left the room.

Give away
(separable):

1. To make a gift of, as in this example: *The company **gave away** free samples of their product.*

2. To present a bride to the groom at a wedding ceremony (The father is the presenter in American custom), as in this example: *The father **gave** the bride **away** at the alter of the church.*

3. To reveal or make known, often accidentally, as in this example: *She drank too much at the party and **gave away** our secret.*

4. To betray, as in this example: *The captured soldier **gave away** our hiding place to the enemy (Meaning: the captured soldier, under pressure, told the enemy where we were hiding).*

   More examples:
   - (1) We **gave away** Christmas presents to the poor children.
   - (2) Her father **gave** her **away** on her wedding day.
   - (3) While speaking to her boss, I accidentally **gave away** the real reason why my friend was absent from work yesterday.
   - (4) Our loud talking **gave away** our location in the building.

Give back
(separable):

1. To return, as in this example: *I **gave** the tools **back** to my friend.*

   More examples:
   - (1) I borrowed a bicycle from my friend and, two days later, I **gave** it **back**.
   - (2) After the purchase, the shopkeeper **gave** me $1.10 **back** as change.

Give in
(inseparable):

1. To relent, to cease opposition to, to yield, as in this example: *After arguing for two hours, I finally **gave in**.*   2. To submit or hand in, as in this example: *The students **gave in** their homework.*

   More examples:

❑ (1) My friend asked me to lend her money and after three hours I finally ***gave in*** and lent her $10.

❑ (2) Everyone had to ***give in*** his or her exam after one hour.

Give out
(separable):

1. To run out of energy or to fail while proceeding with some action, as in this example: *The car finally **gave out** after four hours of trying to climb the mountain.*

2. To distribute something, as in this example: *The teacher **gave out** the exams.*

3. To emit as a noise, as in this example: *The alarm clock **gave out** a loud ringing noise.*

   More examples:

   ❑ (1) I ***gave out*** after two hours of running.

   ❑ (2) My boss ***gave out*** our paychecks.

   ❑ (3) The gun ***gave out*** a loud bang!

Give up
(separable):

1. To surrender; to admit defeat, as in this example: *The enemy soldiers **gave up** after a long fight.* 2. To stop doing or performing an action, as in this example: *The wolf **gave up** chasing the rabbit.*

3. To part with something or someone, as in this example: *The family had to **give up** everything to leave their country and move to Europe.*

4. To express losing hope or opportunity, as in this example: *I **give up**, I will never understand math!*

5. To abandon doing something, or abandon the idea of doing something, as in this example: *We **gave up** the idea of hiking to the top of the mountain.*

   More examples:

   ❑ (1) The police chased the thief until he ***gave up***.

   ❑ (2) After two hours, I ***gave up*** riding my bike in the rain.

   ❑ (3) I went on a diet; I had to ***give up*** eating candy.

- ❑ (4) After two days without food or water, the survivors almost ***gave up*** hope.

- ❑ (5) We ***gave up*** the idea of going to Asia.

Go about
(inseparable):

1. To do or to undertake a responsibility, action or project; this phrase also has the feeling of 'continuing' an action as usual, as in this example: *After the meeting, we went back to our offices and **went about** our usual business.*

   More examples:
   - ❑ (1) We ignored all of the noise outside and ***went about*** our business.
   - ❑ (2) We didn't get upset by the small earthquake and ***went about*** our business after the shaking stopped.

Go after
(inseparable):

1. To pursue or chase, as in this example: *The police **went after** the escaped prisoner.*

2. Try to get or obtain something, for example, like a sales goal, university degree, or English proficiency, as in this example: *After high school, I **went after** my degree in economics at the University of Hawaii.*

   More examples:
   - ❑ (1) During the game, two of our players ***went after*** their star player to try to stop the goal.
   - ❑ (2) After attending university, I ***went after*** a career in teaching.

Go ahead
(inseparable):

1. Proceed forward or move forward or take action, as in this example: *We decided to **go ahead** with the project.*

2. Permission to do something, as in this example: *My daughter asked me if she could play with her friends and I told her to **go ahead** but come home in about two hours.*

More examples:

❑ (1) We ***went ahead*** with the competition even though it was raining.

❑ (2) Mom, can I go to the movies?
   Go ahead, but be home by 10pm.

Go along with
(inseparable):

1. To agree with, as in this example: *My boss **went along** with my idea.*

2. To accompany, as in this example: *We **went along** with the tour group to see the ancient ruins.*

   More examples:

   ❑ (1) We ***went along*** with the committee's decision.

   ❑ (1) Stefan ***went along*** with his friend to the pizza parlor for lunch.

Go around
(inseparable):

1. To go here and there, move from place to place, as in this example: *We **went around** the mall looking at different things.*

2. To avoid something by moving in a curve pattern, as in this example: *We **went around** the obstacle in the road.*

3. To spin, as in this example: *We almost got sick on the amusement park ride because it **went around** very fast.*

4. To be in plain sight of other people while in a certain condition or situation, as in this example: *I **went around** with the ketchup stain on my shirt all day. I was so embarrassed.*

5. Something being distributed or communicated, as in this example: *The bad news about the economy **went around** very quickly.*

   More examples:

   ❑ (1) We spent the day ***going around*** the city, first to the different historic buildings, and then to the different stores.

   ❑ (2) On our way to lunch, my colleagues and I found a way to quickly ***get around*** the construction blockades in the middle of the walkway.

❑ (3) The wheels of the machinery ***went around*** very quickly.

❑ (4) Marco ***went around*** all day with two different colored socks on.

❑ (5) When Shino quit the company, the news ***got around*** quickly.

Go away
(inseparable):

1. To leave, to take leave of, as in this example: *We **went away** for the holiday.*

2. Also used to express ceasing or stopping an annoyance as in this example: *I wish this noise would **go away**.*

   More examples:

   ❑ (1) When I asked where Kazu was, his colleagues told me that he ***went away*** to New York.

   ❑ (2) The smell coming from the other room was terrible, we hoped it would ***go away***.

Go back
(inseparable):

1. To return to (this can refer to physically returning to a place, as in this example: *We liked Los Vegas so much we **went back** again.*

2. Can refer to returning in one's mind to a time, as in this example: *In our minds, we **went back** to the time when we were in high school.*

3. (***go back on***) to renege, especially relating to promises or agreements, as in this example: *The politician **went back on** his word that he would help everyone get health insurance.*

   More examples:

   ❑ (1) We ***went back*** to our office after lunch.

   ❑ (2) The history book talked about things that happened in the past: it ***went back*** to the Roman times.

   ❑ (3) She left her boyfriend because he ***went back on*** his word that he would marry her.

Go beyond

(inseparable):

1. To do more than the required amount; to exceed the intended goal or to do more than was expected, as in this example: *The way to succeed in business is to **go beyond** your customers' expectations.*

2. To go further than a physical location, as in this example: ***Go beyond** the water fountain and the English classroom is on your right.*

   More examples:
   - (1) She ***went beyond*** her boss' expectations when she folded all of the letters and put them into envelopes.
   - (2) ***Go*** three stores ***beyond*** the restaurant and you will find the bookstore.

Go by
(inseparable):

1. To pass usually close to you or a group; or elapse (as with time), as in this example: *Sometimes it seems that time **goes by** very quickly; In Rome, we **went by** a group of tourists who were looking at the coliseum.*

2. Similar to drop by, meaning to stop for a short visit, as in this example: *Let's **go by** my sister's house for a little visit.*

   More examples:
   - (1) In the town center, we ***went by*** a group of political demonstrators.
   - (1) When you are taking an exam, time seems to ***go by*** too quickly.
   - (2) On the way to town, we ***went by*** an Italian restaurant to look at the menu.

Go down
(inseparable):

1. Referring to something dropping below the horizon, as in this example: *The sun **went down** and it was a beautiful evening.*

2. To go to a lower position or location, as in this example: *The wine maker **went down** into the cellar to get some wine.*

3. When a computer, computer network or machinery stops working, as in this example: *I'm sorry but I cannot get your information right now because my computer **went down***.

4. Referring to swallowing something, as in this example: *The cough medicine **went down** easy.*

   More examples:
   - ❑ (1) The moon ***went down*** over the horizon and the sun started to come up.
   - ❑ (2) The secretary ***went down*** to the second floor to get the papers.
   - ❑ (3) The electrical generator ***went down*** and the town didn't have electricity.
   - ❑ (4) If you take this medicine with a little honey, it will ***go down*** easily.

Go for
(inseparable):

1. To attack, as in this example: *The dog **went for** the child and bit her on the leg.*

2. To have a special liking for something or someone, as in this example: *When I first met my wife I really **went for** her.*

3. To make an attempt to achieve or get something, as in this example: *The student studied hard for the exam because he wanted to **go for** the highest possible mark.*

4. Used to express equality, for example: *What **goes for** me **goes for** you (meaning, rules apply equally to me and to you).*

   More examples:
   - ❑ (1) The opponents ***went for*** each other.
   - ❑ (2) She ***really goes*** for chocolate.
   - ❑ (3) The runner ***went for*** first place in the competition.
   - ❑ (4) What ***goes for*** one employee should ***go for*** all employees.

Go in
(inseparable):

1. To enter into something, usually an enclosed area, as in this example: *We **went in**(to) the dark room.*

2. Used to mean that something belongs in a certain place, as in this example: *The book **goes in** the drawer.*

3. Used to mean ***to advance into an area*** for the purpose of defeating an enemy or stopping a riot, as in this example: *The police **went into** the riot area to stop the destruction.*

4. Go in *for* is used to show preference for something, for example: *I don't **go in** for tennis.*

    More examples:

    ❑ (1) The tour group ***went in***(to) the cathedral.

    ❑ (2) The pencils ***go in*** the drawer.

    ❑ (3) The soldiers ***went in***(to) the war zone.

    ❑ (4) The students didn't ***go in*** for the long homework assignment.

Go off
(inseparable):

1. Used to express a sudden loud reaction as in, for example: *The bomb **went off** early in the morning.*

2. When a plan or an event occurs as planned as in, for example: *The school dance was fun, it **went off** well.*

3. To stop operating as in this example: *The light **went off** after the big storm hit.*

    More examples:

    ❑ (1) My alarm ***went off*** at 3:30am by accident.

    ❑ (2) The fund raising event ***went off*** well. We collected over $2,000!

    ❑ (3) The refrigerator ***went off*** and all of the food spoiled.

Go on
(inseparable):

1. Continue, as in the example: *I can't **go on** working at this job.*

2. To initiate operation of something, as in this example: *After the storm, the lights **went on** again.*

3 Used to inquire about what happened, as in this example: *What **went on** in class yesterday, I couldn't be there.*

4. To initiate some action, like, for example: Silvia went on a diet yesterday.

5. Can be used as encouragement, as in this example: ___**Go on**___, give it a try, I think you'll like this kind of food.

   More examples:
   - ❑ (1) We couldn't ___**go on**___ paying the employee because he wasn't doing his job.
   - ❑ (2) The refrigerator ___**went on**___ when we turned on the main electrical breaker.
   - ❑ (3) What ___**went on**___ at the business meeting this morning?
   - ❑ (4) We ___**went on**___ a two-day hike in the mountains.
   - ❑ (5) ___**Go on**___, you can win that game.

Go out
(inseparable):

1. To leave or exit someplace, as in this example: *During the exam, no one was allowed to **go out** of the room.*

2. To stop burning or illuminating, as in this example: *all of the lights **went out** when the storm hit.*

3. Used to express what people do for leisure or romantic situations, as in this example: *My boyfriend and I **went out** last night and saw a movie.*

   More examples:
   - ❑ (1) I ___**went out**___ and smoked a cigarette during the movie.
   - ❑ (2) The fire ___**went out**___ when it started raining.
   - ❑ (3) My wife and I ___**went out**___ and had dinner.

Go over
(inseparable):

1. Moving from one place to another place, as in this example: *My sister wants to go to Mary's house. Do you mind if I **go over** there with her?*

2. Used when expressing movement from one place to another place which usually is a home or familiar-feeling location, as in this example: *Last night we **went over** to the Yamaguchi's house for dinner;*

3. To review, as in this example: *Let's **go over** the exam and see where you made your mistakes.*

4. Used to express approval, as in this example: *Our financial report **went over** very well and the boss took us all out to dinner.*

More examples:
- ❏ (1) I **went over** to the other side of the room so I could hear the teacher better.
- ❏ (2) My wife and I **went over** to our daughter's house last night.
- ❏ (3) The colleagues **went over** the report before having the meeting.
- ❏ (4) His resume (CV) **went over** very well with the company.

Go through
(inseparable):

1. To commit to an action, usually in a difficult situation, as in this example: *We **went through** with the adoption of the child even though we knew the child was sick.*

More examples:
- ❏ (1) I just **went through** a divorce that was very difficult.
- ❏ (1) We just **went through** two weeks of rainy weather and now we are ready for sunshine!

Go up
(inseparable):

1. Moving to a higher place or to a place that is located north of your location, as in this example: *We **went up** to New York for our vacation (from Virginia). I **went up** the stairs to the second floor.*

2. Used to express increase in value or quality, as in this example: *Wow, the gas prices really **went up**!*

3. To approach something or someone, as in this example: *She **went up** to her teacher and asked when the exam was going to be given.*

More examples:
- ❏ (1) Claudia **went up** to Canada for a vacation (from New York).

- ❏ (2) The price of food ***went up*** because the price of fuel went up.
- ❏ (3) I ***went up*** to the tour guide and asked a question about the old building.

Go with
(inseparable):

1. To compliment, one thing with another, as in this example: *Kaori bought a blouse to **go with** her skirt.*

2. To accompany, as in this example: *The chaperones **went with** the students to the dance.*

3. To accept something or someone, or support someone or someone's idea or action, as in this example: *We had a choice between the red car and the green one, and we **went with** the red one. I'll go with Jane for class president.*

More examples:
- ❏ (1) Denise was shopping for a purse that would ***go with*** her black shoes.
- ❏ (2) In an American breakfast, eggs usually ***go with*** bacon.
- ❏ (3) We ended up ***going with*** the blue car because the red car was too big for us.

Goof around
(inseparable):

1. To not take something seriously, or, having aimless fun; can also mean wasting time doing foolish things, as in this example: *He hasn't finished his work yet because he has been **goofing around** all day.*

More examples:
- ❏ (1) The students who ***goof around*** usually don't learn English very quickly.
- ❏ (1) ***Goofing around*** is the fastest way to get fired from a job.

Gross out
(separable):

1. Used to express causing to be disgusted or sickened by something or someone, as in this example: *He **grossed out** everyone at the table when he spit his food back onto his plate.*

More examples:
- ❏ (1) We saw a dead cat in the road and it really ***grossed*** us ***out***.

❑   (1) The toilet facilities were very dirty; they really ***grossed*** me ***out***.

Grow out
(separable):

1. To become too mature or old for a certain thing, behavior, or way of acting, as in this example: *Kazu couldn't fit into his high school clothes any more; he's **grown out** of them.*

2. When a person becomes too physically big to wear certain clothing, as in this example: *Our children are growing quickly, they have already **grown out** of all of their clothing and now we have to buy all new clothing.*

More examples:

❑   (1) My children are ***growing out*** of playing with dolls. Now they want more expensive toys.

❑   (2) This dress is too tight for me; it looks like I ***have grown out*** of this dress and I will have to buy a new one.

Grow up
(inseparable):

1. A request by someone that someone acts more mature, as in this example: *Please **grow up** and act your age!*

2. To become older in age, as in this example: *Silvia **grew up** in California and now lives in Hawaii.*

More examples:

❑   (1) I wish you would ***grow up*** and accept the responsibilities that you have.

❑   (2) I ***grew up*** in New York and now live in Philadelphia.

Chapter 4 review
Phrasal verbs beginning with the letter G

*Instructions: read and /or listen carefully to the sentences below. Fill in the blank spaces with the correct **preposition, particle,** or **adverb**. The answers can be found below.*

1. The couple living in the old house is able to get _____ on their pension checks.

2. It is difficult to get _____ if you don't work hard.

3. I'll do my homework when I get _____ to it.

4. To get _____ to our hotel we had to take a taxi.

5. Cancer research is important so my family got _____ the Cancer Society when they asked for volunteers.

6. Driver, I would like to get _____ at 23rd Street.

7. We told the Taxi drive to stop on Broadway. Then we got _____ of the taxi and went to a theater.

8. She got _____ the table and started dancing.

9. I really get _____ on doing math.

10. I borrowed a bicycle from my friend and, two days later, I gave it _____.

11. Everyone had to give ___ his or her exam after one hour.

12. We gave ___ the idea of going to Asia.

13. We went _____ with the competition even though it was raining.

14. Marco went _____ all day with two different colored socks on.

15. Go three stores _____ the restaurant and you will find the bookstore.

16. The electrical generator went _____ and the town didn't have electricity.

17. When you are taking an exam, time seems to go ___ too quickly.

18. The fire went _____ when it started raining.

19. When I asked where Kazu was, his colleagues told me that he went _____ to New York.

20. I grew ____ in New York and now live in Philadelphia.

Answers: (1) along (2) ahead; (3) around (4) back (5) behind; (6) off; (7) out; (8) on; (9) off (10) back; (11) in; (12) into(13) through; (14) around; (15) down; (16) out (17) by (18) out; (19) over (20) up

Chapter 5 *Phrasal verbs beginning with the letter H*

In this section you will learn how to use many different phrasal verbs that begin with the letter H correctly in a sentence.

There are two kinds of phrasal verbs, separable and inseparable. Separable phrasal verbs can take an object between the verb and the preposition. For example: *My father **picked** me **up** after school and drove me home.* Inseparable phrasal verbs cannot take an object between the verb and the preposition. For example: I asked my friends to **come along** with me to the Christmas party. **Come along** cannot be separated by an object.

The numbers in front of the examples that are in parenthesis (), correspond the to number of the explanation found directly above. So, for example: 1. *explanation . . .* refers to (1) *example . . . .* If there is only one explanation or meaning given for the phrasal verb, then there will be two examples given for the one explanation. Both examples will be marked with (1).

If you have the accompanying Focus on English mp3 audio book (available separately from the school store or from www.FOEBooks.com) listen to each of the phrasal verbs, followed by their meanings and then some examples of how they are used in real English sentences. Each example will be spoken twice. There will be a review at the end of this chapter.

Phrasal verbs beginning with the letter H

Hand back
(separable):
   1. To return something, as in this example: *The teacher **handed back** the exams.*

   More examples:
   - ❏ (1) The customs official ***handed back*** my passport.
   - ❏ (1) The sales clerk ***handed*** me ***back*** my change.

Hand in
(separable):

1. To give something to someone or a group that was expected, as, for example, in this sentence: *The students **handed in** their homework assignments. The applicants **handed in** their forms when they completed them.*

2. When you are quitting a job, sometimes you say you are **handing in** your resignation or your letter of resignation, as in this example: *I didn't like my job, so I **handed in** my resignation to my boss.*

   More examples:
   - (1) When we finished the exam, we **handed** it **in** to the teacher.
   - (2) The manager **handed in** his letter of resignation on Friday.

Hand out
(separable):

1. To distribute, as in this example: *The student **handed out** the forms for the other students to complete.*

   More examples:
   - (1) The teacher **handed out** the corrected exams.
   - (1) The man on the sidewalk **handed out** advertising to people who walked by.

Hand over
(separable):

1. To release, give or relinquish to another, as in this example: *The police told the criminal that he had to **hand over** his gun.*

   More examples:
   - (1) The customs official asked the tourist to **hand over** her passport.
   - (1) The principal of the school told the student to **hand over** her cigarettes.

Hang around
(inseparable):

1. To spend time idly or to loiter, as in this example: *We **hung around** the coffee shop talking about school.*

2. To keep company (with), to consort, as in this example: *The four friends have* ***hung around*** *together for ten years.*

More examples:

❑ (1) The students ***hung around*** the pizza parlor after school.

❑ (2) The two sisters ***hang around*** together like best friends.

Hang on
(inseparable):

1. To wait, as in this example: I asked the customer to ***hang on*** while I looked for her size; often used in telephone conversations, as in this example: *Hello. Mr. Liu? Yes, he is here, please* ***hang on*** *while I connect you.*

2. To grab onto or cling tightly to something or someone, as in this example: *The wind was very strong, I had to* ***hang onto*** *my umbrella.*

More examples:

❑ (1) ***Hang on***; you've taken the wrong luggage out of the baggage claim area!

❑ (2) The amusement park ride was fun. We had to ***hang on*** really tightly!

Hang out
(separable):

1. Similar meaning to *hang around* (above): to spend time idly or to loiter, as in this example: *We* ***hung out*** *at the coffee shop talking about school.*

2. Can also mean to keep company (with) or to consort (with), as in this example: *The four friends have* ***hung out*** *with each other for years.*

3. To suspend something or someone from something usually for the purpose of drying, as in this example: *The housewife* ***hung*** *the clothes* ***out*** *to dry.*

More examples:

❑ (1) Students often ***hang out*** at the local Internet cafe.

❑ (2) The friends ***hung out*** with each other after school.

❑ (3) We ***hung*** the wet towel ***out*** to dry on the clothesline.

Hang up
(separable):

1. To finish a phone conversation, as in this example: *She **hung up** the phone after talking to her friend for an hour.* 2. To cause to delay, as in this example: *The bad traffic in the city **hung** us **up** for at least two hours.*

   More examples:
   - ❑ (1) The secretary **hung up** the phone after giving the customer travel directions to the office.
   - ❑ (2) On Friday we were **hung up** in Houston because of a flight delay.

Have on
(separable):

1. To wear something, as in this example: *The woman **had on** a beautiful black dress.*

   More examples:
   - ❑ (1) The secretary **had** a blue dress **on**.
   - ❑ (1) The cat **had** a little cat sweater **on**.

Head back
(inseparable):

1. To return, as in this example: *We **headed back** to the city after spending 5 hours in the country.*

   More examples:
   - ❑ (1) After spending a day at the beach, we **headed back** home.
   - ❑ (1) We **headed back** to our home country after studying English in America.

Head for
(inseparable):

1. To go towards, as in this example: *We got in our car and **headed for** the night club.*

2. You can also use this phrase to mean going towards a situation or consequence, as in this example: *Playing with that poisonous snake is a bad idea; he is **headed for** trouble.*

   More examples:

- ❏ (1) On our vacations we usually like to ***head for*** the mountains.
- ❏ (2) If he keeps doing well on his exams, he is ***headed for*** top honors at his school.

Head off
(separable):

1. To block the progress of something or someone, intercept or to block the completion of, as in this example: *When the water pipe broke we turned off the main water valve to **head off** more damage to the house.*

   More examples:
   - ❏ (1) The soldiers ***headed off*** the enemy before they got to the city.
   - ❏ (1) The police ***headed off*** the thief before he could jump over the fence.

Head towards
(inseparable):

1. Similar to *head for* with the meaning going in the direction of, as in this example: *I asked the taxi driver to **head towards** the center of town.*

   More examples:
   - ❏ (1) After work, we ***headed towards*** our favorite pub for some beer and conversation.
   - ❏ (1) This country is ***headed towards*** disaster if that politician wins the election.

Hear about
(inseparable):

1. To learn of, or to get information concerning something or someone, usually verbally transmitted, as in this example: *Did you **hear about** the big sale down at the mall? Yes, I **heard about** it on the news.*

   More examples:
   - ❏ (1) Everyone ***heard about*** the big traffic accident.
   - ❏ (1) I ***heard about*** the new tax that we will have to pay next year.

Hear of

(inseparable):

1. Similar in meaning to *hear about* but is commonly used between speakers attempting to identify something specifically, as in this example: *Did you ever **hear of** a pillow tax? No, what **kind of** tax is this?*

   More examples:
   - ❑ (1) Did you ever **hear of** the number 56 train?
   - ❑ (1) Have you ever **heard of** Sally Little? No, I have never **heard of** her. Where is she from?

Heat up
(separable):

1. To make hotter or warmer, as in this example: *The car was really cold, so we turned on the heater to **heat** the car **up**.*

2. Also used to mean make more intense, agitated, or more competitive, as in this example: *The contest has begun to **heat up** with the three top competitors all in the same round.*

   More examples:
   - ❑ (1) If you put some wood on the fire it will **heat up** the room.
   - ❑ (2) The conversation between the two men **heated up** and then someone called the police when the men started fighting.

Help out
(separable):

1. To provide assistance to, as in this example: *We offered to **help** the old woman **out** with her shopping.*

   More examples:
   - ❑ (1) The daughter **helped** her mom **out** in the kitchen.
   - ❑ (2) Many people from the community came to **help out** the poor family.

Hit on
(inseparable):

1. To arrive at an idea, conclusion, or solution, as in this example: *After days of thinking about the problem we finally **hit on** a solution.*

More examples:

- ❏ (1) The problem was complicated but we ***hit on*** a solution after talking about it for two days.

- ❏ (1) The chef ***hit on*** just the right combination of ingredients to make a delicious pasta dinner.

Hold against
(inseparable):

1. To restrain or contain something or someone by forcing or pressing them against an object, as in this example: *The police **held** the robber **against** the wall while they searched his pockets for a gun.*

2. To blame, to be upset with someone or something for some wrongdoing, as in this example: *My business partner ruined our business, something I've always **held against** him.*

   More examples:

   - ❏ (1) The woman ***held*** her purse tightly ***against*** her side as she walked through the bad area of town.

   - ❏ (2) I was absent from the important meeting and my boss ***held*** that ***against*** me for a long time.

Hold off
(separable):

1. To prevent or delay something from happening, as in this example: *We decided to **hold off** making our travel plans until after the summer.*

2. To keep at a distance, to resist, as in this example: *We **held** the reporters **off** by telling them that we had no comment.*

   More examples:

   - ❏ (1) The teacher ***held off*** giving the exam because some students needed more time to prepare.

   - ❏ (2) The actress's bodyguard ***held off*** the paparazzi while the actress got into the car.

Hold on

(inseparable):

1. To cling or maintain one's grip, as in this example: *The amusement park ride was scary; we had to **hold on** with both hands!*

2. To persist or continue, as in this example: *The plane ride was long, but we **held on** and tried to relax until the plane finally landed.*

   More examples:
   - ❑ (1) The passenger **held on** to the handrail as the train came to a stop.
   - ❑ (2) Our soccer team **held on** until the final minute but lost by one point.

Hold out
(inseparable):

1. To continue to resist, as in this example: *The Indians attacked the fort but the soldiers in the fort were able to **hold out** for four more days.*

2. To refuse to reach an agreement, as in this example: *The employees wanted more money, but the management **held out** against their demand.*

3. To present or show, usually as proof of something, as in this example: *The politician said that health care was improving and to prove this he **held out** the new hospital as an example.*

   More examples:
   - ❑ (1) The soldiers were outnumbered by the enemy, but they **held out** until help arrived.
   - ❑ (2) The workers would not go back to work. They were **holding out** for more benefits.
   - ❑ (3) The company **held out** the possibility that workers would get an extra holiday with pay if they went back to work.

Hold over
(inseparable):

1. To remain the same from an earlier time, as in this example: The music was a **hold over** from the baroque period.

2. To suspend, as in this example: They **held** the marshmallows **over** the fire to warm them up.

3. To continue or prolong, as in this example: The movie was ***held over*** for an additional two weeks.

   More examples:
   - ❑ (1) This custom is a ***hold over*** from ancient times.
   - ❑ (2) She ***held*** the pot ***over*** the fire to heat up the potatoes.
   - ❑ (3) The sale was ***held over*** for another week.

Hold up
(separable):

1. To obstruct or delay, as in this example: *The work was **held up** because we did not have the correct materials.*

2. To rob someone, usually with a weapon, as in this example: *The thief **held up** the tourists and took all of their money.*

3. To continue to function under duress or pressure, as in this example: *The survivors **held up** well during their week without food.*

   More examples:
   - ❑ (1) The exam was ***held up*** because one of the exam sheets was missing.
   - ❑ (2) The bank was ***held up*** yesterday. The thieves got more than $10,000.
   - ❑ (3) The woman did not ***hold up*** well after surviving the storm with no food or water, and had to be hospitalized.

Hook up
(separable):

1. To connect to, as in this example: *The fireman **hooked up** the water hose to the fire hydrant.*

2. *(informal)* To meet, make a new contact, or join, as in this example: *I needed to learn English faster, so I **hooked up** with a good English tutor.*

3. To assemble a mechanism with wiring, as in this example: *The electrician **hooked up** our wall socket in the kitchen.*

   More examples:
   - ❑ (1) The worker ***hooked up*** the new washing machine to the water system.
   - ❑ (2) We ***hooked up*** with some new friends when we studied English abroad.

❑   (3) The electrician ***hooked up*** the dishwasher to the electrical mains.

Hurry up
(separable):

1. Often used as a command to demand that someone go faster, as in this example: ***Hurry up****! The movie is going to start in three minutes!*

2. To hasten something, or make something or someone go faster, as in this example: *The teacher wanted the students to work faster on the practice exam, so he **hurried** them **up** by telling them they only had two minutes left to finish.*

   More examples:

   ❑   (1) ***Hurry up***! Class starts in five minutes.

   ❑   (2) We ***hurried*** our project ***up*** by eliminating some of the less important items.

Chapter 5 review
Phrasal verbs beginning with the letter H

*Instructions: read and /or listen carefully to the sentences below. Fill in the blank spaces with the correct **preposition, particle,** or **adverb**. The answers can be found in this chapter (above).*

1. The customs official handed _____ my passport.

2. The manager handed ____ his letter of resignation on Friday.

3. The customs official asked the tourist to hand _____ her passport.

4. The two sisters hang _____ together like best friends.

5. We hurried ____ our project by eliminating some of the less important items.

6. The electrician hooked ____ the dishwasher to the electrical mains.

7. The bank was held ____ yesterday. The thieves got more than $10,000.

8. The sale was held _____ for another week.

9. The actress's bodyguard held _____ the paparazzi while the actress got into the car.

10. Our soccer team held ____ until the final minute but lost by one point.

11. The workers would not go back to work. They were holding ____ for more benefits.

12. Many people from the community came to help _____ the poor family.

13. Did you ever hear ____ the number 56 train?

14. The soldiers headed ____ the enemy before they got to the city.

15. After spending a day at the beach, we headed _____ home.

16. The secretary had a blue dress _____.

17. On Friday we were hung ____ in Houston because of a flight delay.

18. If he keeps doing well on his exams, he is headed ____ top honors at his school.

19. This country is headed _____ disaster if that politician wins the election.

20. The woman held her purse tightly _____ her side as she walked through the bad area of town.

Answers: (1) back (2) in; (3) over (4) out (5) up; (6) up; (7) up; (8) over; (9) off (10) on; (11) out; (12) out(13) of; (14) off; (15) towards; (16) on (17) up (18) for; (19) for (20) against

Chapter 6 *Phrasal verbs beginning with the letter K*

In this section you will learn how to use many different phrasal verbs beginning with the letter K correctly in a sentence.

There are two kinds of phrasal verbs, separable and inseparable. Separable phrasal verbs can take an object between the verb and the preposition. For example: *My father **picked me up** after school and drove me home.* Inseparable phrasal verbs cannot take an object between the verb and the preposition. For example: I asked my friends to **come along** with me to the Christmas party. **Come along** cannot be separated by an object.

The numbers in front of the examples that are in parenthesis (), correspond the to number of the explanation found directly above. So, for example: 1. *explanation . . .* refers to (1) *example . . . .* If there is only one explanation or meaning given for the phrasal verb, then there will be two examples given for the one explanation. Both examples will be marked with (1).

If you have the Focus on English digital audio book version of this book (available separately from www.FOEBooks.com) listen to each of the phrasal verbs, followed by their meanings and then some examples of how they are used in real English sentences.

There will be a review at the end of this chapter.

Phrasal verbs beginning with the letter K

Read and /or listen carefully to the examples, as they will give you a good idea as to how to use the phrasal verb in real English sentences.

Keep at
(inseparable):

1. To continue or persist at something, as in this example: *Building the home was difficult, but we **kept at** it until we were done.*

More examples:

- ❑ (1) Just *__keep at__* it! You'll get it done soon.
- ❑ (1) The children made a castle in the sand; they *__kept at__* it all day.

Keep away
(separable):

1. To deliberately maintain a distance from someone or something, as in this example: *The tour group was told to __keep away__ from the edge of the cliff.*

   More examples:

   - ❑ (1) *__Keep away__* from that man because he is very dangerous.
   - ❑ (1) Children are told to *__keep away__* from alcohol.

Keep down
(separable):

1. To diminish, suppress, or restrict from rising, as in these examples: *I can't eat chocolate any more because I am trying to __keep__ my weight __down__. They are trying to __keep__ the price of rice __down__ but it has been difficult.*

   More examples:

   - ❑ (1) Please *__keep down__* the noise; we are trying to study!
   - ❑ (1) The child was sick and couldn't *__keep__* his food *__down__*. (Meaning that the child had to throw up a lot.)

Keep from
(separable):

1. To prevent, sometimes under pressure, as in this example: *My love of chocolate __keeps__ me __from__ losing weight.*

   More examples:

   - ❑ (1) The heat in this room *__keeps__* me *__from__* thinking clearly.
   - ❑ (1) That team's poor attitude *__keeps__* them *__from__* being number one.

Keep off
(seperable)

1. To stay clear of, to not stand, sit or lay on something, as in this example: *The sign said to __keep off__ the grass because the ground was wet.*

More examples:

❑ (1) The mother told her child to ***keep*** her elbows ***off*** of the table.

❑ (1) We had to ***keep off*** the playing field because it was wet.

Keep on
(inseparable):

1. To continue an action, as in this example: *We wanted to stop our car and look at the sunset but we had to **keep on** going because of the traffic.*

   More examples:

   ❑ (1) Son, if you ***keep on*** tapping the table with your finger I'm going to get upset.

   ❑ (1) I was so tired, but I had to ***keep on*** running because the race was not over.

Keep to
(separable):

1. To restrict to certain guidelines, as in this example: *During our vacation, we **kept** our spending **to** a minimum because we didn't have a lot of money.*

2. To guard as a secret, to restrict knowledge of something, as in this example: *I saw a strange object in the sky but I **kept** it **to** myself because I didn't want people to think I was crazy.*

   More examples:

   ❑ (1) We played the radio but ***kept*** the noise ***to*** a minimum because students were studying in the next room.

   ❑ (2) I saw my friend's girlfriend with another boy but I ***kept*** it ***to*** myself because I didn't want my friend to be hurt.

Keep up
(separable):

1. To maintain the condition of something, as in this example: *He **kept** his car **up** by washing and waxing it regularly.*

2. To carry on or persevere in something, as in this example: *Her foot was hurting her but she **kept up** with the other runners.*

3. To match the success of someone or something, as in this example: *Jennifer spent a lot of money to **keep up** with her friends. She has a nice car, nice clothes and a nice apartment.*

   More examples:
   - ❑ (1) He ***kept up*** the house by painting it.
   - ❑ (2) The runner ***kept up*** his strong performance during the race.
   - ❑ (3) We have a saying in English: Everyone is trying to ***keep up*** with the Jones. 🔦 The meaning of this saying is that everyone is trying to have all of the possessions and nice things that more successful families have.

Kick back
(separable and inseparable depending on usage):

1. *(separable) (slang)* To give something, usually not ethical or legal, to someone for a favor, as in this example: *If you can get me a job with that company, I'll **kick** you **back** some cash.*

2. *(inseparable)* To recoil violently and usually unexpectedly, as in this example: *I fired the big rifle at the target, and it **kicked back** and hurt my shoulder.*

   More examples:
   - ❑ (1) The criminal ***kicked back*** some money to the police for not arresting him.
   - ❑ (2) The soldiers fired the big cannon, which ***kicked back*** immediately.

Kick out
(separable):

1. To reject, fire, get rid of, or remove someone or something from an organization or operation, as in this example: *We voted to **kick** that member **out** of the club because he was using drugs.*

2. *(slang in the sport of surfing)* Deliberately removing oneself from a wave, as in this example: *When she was done surfing on the wave so she **kicked out**.*

   More examples:
   - ❑ (1) They ***kicked*** him ***out*** of the bar because he was drunk.
   - ❑ (2) The surfer ***kicked out*** of the wave just before it came crashing down.

Knock off
(separable or inseparable depending on usage):

1. *(separable)* To forcibly remove someone or something from a position of being on top of something, as in this example: *The boy* kicked *the ball in the house and accidentally* ***knocked*** *the cook pot* ***off*** *of the stove.*

2. *(informal) (inseparable)* To take a break or rest, as in this example: It's lunch time, lets ***knock off***;

3. *(informal) (inseparable)* To finish working, as in this example: *What time do you* ***knock off*** *work?*

4. *(Informal) (separable)* To rob or steal from, as in this example: *The bank robbers* ***knocked off*** *the local bank and got away with $10,000 cash.*

More examples:
- ❑ (1) The student accidentally ***knocked*** the book ***off*** of the desk.
- ❑ (2) The workers decided to ***knock off*** at ten for a cup of coffee.
- ❑ (3) I usually ***knock off*** work around 4:30pm.
- ❑ (4) The young thief ***knocked off*** the convenience store.

Knock out
(separable):

1. To remove material from within material or an object, as in this example: *The construction workers* ***knocked out*** *a section of the wall to make room for a new window.*

2. To cause someone to lose consciousness, as in this example: *The boxer* ***knocked out*** *his opponent.*

3. *(Informal)* To finish a job quickly, as in this example: *It was an easy job; we* ***knocked*** *it* ***out*** *in an hour.*

4. To render useless, as in this example: *The lightening strike* ***knocked out*** *our electrical power.*

5. To exhaust oneself doing something, as in this example: *Stefan* ***knocked*** *himself* ***out*** *trying to finish the project before 10am.*

More examples:

❏ (1) The electrician ***knocked out*** a small hole in the wall to install a receptacle.

❏ (2) One fighter ***knocked out*** the other fighter in the championship match.

❏ (3) The homework wasn't difficult and I was able to ***knock*** it ***out*** in about 20 minutes.

❏ (4) The storm ***knocked out*** the power in the community.

❏ (5) Mei Ling really ***knocked*** herself ***out*** working on that project because she wanted to finish it before her vacation.

Knock over
(separable):

1. To cause to tumble over or fall to the ground, as in this example: *The young boy **knocked over** the lamp while playing with his sister.*

More examples:

❏ (1) Keiko accidentally ***knocked over*** the orchid at the flower show.

❏ (1) The big football player easily ***knocked over*** his opponent.

Know about
(inseparable):

1. To be familiar with, to have knowledge of, as in this example: *The students **knew about** the final exam date next week.*

More examples:

❏ (1) The students ***knew about*** the problem the school was having with the bathrooms.

❏ (1) The visitor ***knew about*** the visa restrictions and had made plans to visit the country according to these restrictions.

Chapter 6 review
*Phrasal verbs beginning with the letter **K***

*Instructions: read and /or listen carefully to the sentences below. Fill in the blank spaces with the correct **preposition, particle,** or **adverb**. The answers can be found below.*

1. I was so tired, but I had to keep ___ running because the race was not over.

2. I saw my friend's girlfriend with another boy but I kept it ___ myself because I didn't want my friend to be hurt.

3. We had to keep ___ the playing field because it was wet.

4. That team's poor attitude keeps them _____ being number one.

5. The runner kept ___ his strong performance during the race.

6. I usually knock ___ work around 4:30pm.

7. They kicked him ____ of the bar because he was drunk.

8. The criminal kicked _____ some money to the police for not arresting him.

9. One fighter knocked ____ the other fighter in the championship match.

10. Please keep the noise _____; we are trying to study!

11. Children are told to keep _____ from alcohol.

12. Just keep ___ it! You'll get it done soon.

13. The big football player easily knocked _____ his opponent.

14. The students knew _____ the problem the school was having with the bathrooms.

15. The children made a castle in the sand; they kept ___ it all day.

Answers: (1) on (2) to; (3) off (4) from (5) up; (6) off; (7) out; (8) back; (9) out (10) down; (11) away; (12) at (13) over; (14) about; (15) at

Chapter 7 *Phrasal verbs beginning with the letter L*

In this section you will learn how to use many different phrasal verbs beginning with the letter L correctly in a sentence.

There are two kinds of phrasal verbs, separable and inseparable. Separable phrasal verbs can take an object between the verb and the preposition. For example: *My father **picked** me **up** after school and drove me home.* Inseparable phrasal verbs cannot take an object between the verb and the preposition. For example: I asked my friends to **come along** with me to the Christmas party. **Come along** cannot be separated by an object.

The numbers in front of the examples that are in parenthesis (), correspond the to number of the explanation found directly above. So, for example: 1. *explanation . . .* refers to (1) *example . . . .* . If there is only one explanation or meaning given for the phrasal verb, then there will be two examples given for the one explanation. Both examples will be marked with (1).

If you have the Focus on English digital audio book version of this book (available separately from www.FOEBooks.com) listen to each of the phrasal verbs, followed by their meanings and then some examples of how they are used in real English sentences.

There will be a review at the end of this chapter.

Phrasal verbs beginning with the letter L

Read and / or listen carefully to the examples, as they will give you a good idea as to how to use the phrasal verb in real English sentences.

Lay down
(separable):

1. To put or place in a horizontal position, or in a position lower than the current position, as in this example: *The workers **laid** the window frame **down** so they could make some adjustments to the size.*

2. To specify rules, guidelines or parameters, as in this example: *The camp counselor **laid down** the rules to the young campers (meaning: the camp counselor explained the rules of the camp to the young campers).*

3. Used in expressing surrender of an opposition force, as in this example: *The enemy was told to **lay down** their arms and surrender.*

   More examples:
   - (1) The student **laid** the papers **down** on the desk.
   - (2) The immigration officer **laid down** the rules to the new visitors.
   - (3) The crook was told to **lay down** his weapon and put his hands up.

Lay off
(separable or inseparable depending on usage):

1. *(separable)* To terminate the employment of a worker, as in this example: *The company **laid** the workers **off** because of lack of work.*

2. *(inseparable) (slang)* Stop doing something, usually a forceful request to stop doing something, as in this example: ***Lay off**! Stop yelling at her. Can't you see that she is upset?*

   More examples:
   - (1) Five workers were **laid off** because the company was not making enough money.
   - (2) **Lay off** alcohol because it makes you sick.

Lead up to
(inseparable):

1. To proceed towards something, to lay the foundation for, as in this example: *The civil unrest and the burning of the flag all **led up to** the overthrow of the government.*

2. In books and movies, earlier parts of a story or article can lay a foundation for later parts, as in this example: *The first and second chapters of the book **led up to** the exciting events in the third chapter.*

More examples:

❏ (1) The health food store clerk told the girl that candy had a lot of sugar and bad chemicals in it. The clerk was ***leading up to*** the idea that candy is not good for you.

❏ (2) The first part of the movie ***led up to*** the climax in the middle of the movie.

Leave behind
(separable):

1. To not take something or someone with you when moving to another location, as in this example: *When we moved to our new country, we had to **leave** all of our possessions **behind**.*

2. To advance ahead of others, as in this example: One student in the class was so smart that he advanced quickly and he ***left*** the others ***behind***.

   More examples:

   ❏ (1) When I left the theater, I ***left*** my purse ***behind***.

   ❏ (2) I learned the material quickly, ***left*** the other students ***behind***, and quickly rose to the top of my class.

Leave off
(separable):

1. To stop temporarily, as in this example: *Okay class, we will **leave off** here in our reading and continue again tomorrow.*

   More examples:

   ❏ (1) We stopped working on the project and went to lunch. When we get back, we'll pick up where we ***left off*** (meaning: we will continue working from the place where we ***left off*** when we went to lunch).

   ❏ (1) The teacher told the class that they would ***leave off*** at chapter ten and continue again tomorrow beginning with chapter 10.

Leave out
(separable):

1. To omit, as in this example: *This chocolate cake doesn't taste right. I think we **left** out an ingredient.*

   More examples:
   - ❑ (1) We invited all of our friends to the party. We didn't **leave out** anyone.
   - ❑ (1) Please study chapters three through seven but **leave out** chapter four.

Let down
(separable):

1. To disappoint, as in this example: *Our soccer team really **let** us **down** by not winning that game!*

2. To lower something to a lower position gradually, as in this example: *The workers gently **let** the bundle of wood **down** until it reached the floor.*

   More examples:
   - ❑ (1) My daughter **let** me **down** when she got a bad grade on her exam.
   - ❑ (2) At the end of the day they **let down** the flag.

Let in
(separable):

1. To admit, to allow something or someone enter, as in this example: *I hear someone knocking at the door; I'll **let** them **in**.*

   More examples:
   - ❑ (1) Please don't open the window because you'll **let** the mosquitoes **in**.
   - ❑ (1) It is never a good idea to **let** strangers **in**(to) your home.

Let in on
(inseparable):

1. To include, usually other people, in sharing knowledge or ownership, as in this example: *Does Jim know the secret? No. Let's **let him in on** this.*

   More examples:
   - ❑ (1) I **let** my friend **in on** the secret about my new girlfriend.
   - ❑ (1) I think that it's a good time to **let** your colleagues **in on** this news.

Let off

(separable):

1. To release from, as in this example: *The police officer stopped the man for speeding, but **let** him **off** (didn't give him a ticket) with a warning.*

2. Similar to *drop off;* to leave someone somewhere after riding on transportation, as in this example: *The taxi driver **let** me **off** at the library.*

3. To vent or release, as in this example: *The city **let off** fireworks for the Fourth of July celebrations.*

   More examples:
   - ❑ (1) The student didn't do his homework, but the teacher **let** him **off** because the student was sick.
   - ❑ (2) The bus **let** him **off** in front of the bank.
   - ❑ (3) The little boy **let off** his firecracker in the back yard.

Let out
(separable):

1. To release, to release with permission, as in this example: *The principal **let** the students **out** of school during lunch break.*

2. To make bigger or larger as with clothing, as in this example: *As her children got a little older, their mother **let** the seams **out** of their clothing so that she would not have to buy new clothing so often.*

3. To release a noise, especially to express an emotion, as in this example: *When her boyfriend came up behind her and covered her eyes, she **let out** a scream.*

   More examples:
   - ❑ (1) The girl **let** her cat **out** of the house.
   - ❑ (2) The seamstress **let out** the dress so it would fit the girl.
   - ❑ (3) The cat **let out** a cry when I stepped on its tail.

Let up
(separable):

1. To pause, as in this example: *The workers continued building the engine without **letting up**, because the deadline was very near.*

2. To release someone or something from a lower position, as in this example: *Okay, you win the wrestling match. Now **let** me **up**.*

   More examples:
   - ❏ (1) The rain didn't ***let up*** for even a minute.
   - ❏ (2) The little girl in the swimming pool held her ball under water for a minute and then ***let*** it ***up***.

Lie around
(inseparable):

1. To lounge or rest without concern for anything in particular, as in this example: *What did you do last weekend? I just **lay around** and didn't do much of anything.*

2. A way to express disorganization especially when talking about possessions or items that usually belong in an area, as in this example: *He desk was a mess. There were folders and papers and office equipment **lying around** all over his desk.*

   More examples:
   - ❏ (1) During our vacation we just ***lay around*** and did nothing.
   - ❏ (2) Papers were ***lying around*** everywhere and his room was really messy.

Lie down
(inseparable):

1. To recline, as in this example: *The dog went over to his corner and **lay down**.*

   More examples:
   - ❏ (1) I went to my bedroom and ***lay down*** on the bed.
   - ❏ (1) The dog was ***lying down*** next to the door.

Lift up
(separable):

1. To raise something from a lower position to a higher position, as in this example: *We **lifted up** the hood of the car and looked at the motor.*

   More examples:
   - ❏ (1) The mother ***lifted up*** the little boy into her arms.

❑ (1) When I ***lifted*** the piece of wood ***up***, there was a spider underneath.

Light up
(separable):

1. To illuminate, as in this example: *We turned on the lights to **light up** the area.*

2. To become or cause to become cheerful or animated, as in this example: *She really **lit up** when her boyfriend asked her to marry him.*

3. To start smoking a cigarette or cigar, as in this example: *Let's go outside and **light up** (a cigarette).*

   More examples:

   ❑ (1) The moon was so bright that it ***lit up*** the sky.

   ❑ (2) When I asked my friend to go to the concert with me, she really ***lit up***.

   ❑ (3) Workers are not permitted to ***light up*** in the building.

Line up
(separable):

1. To arrange things or people in a line, or to form a line, as in these examples: *I **lined up** the coins on the table and counted them. We **lined up** to buy tickets for the show.*

2. To arrange for or to arrange, as in this example: *We planned to have a festival in six months, so we **lined up** the location, food vendors, and equipment that we would need to have a successful festival.*

3. To align one thing with another thing, as in this example: *We have two boxes with a hole in each corner of each box. You have to place one box on top of the other box and **line up** the holes in the top box with the holes in the bottom box.*

   More examples:

   ❑ (1) The people ***lined up*** to buy tickets..

   ❑ (2) We have to ***line up*** our flight and accommodations for our vacation in six weeks.

   ❑ (3) The men building the new section of road ***lined up*** the new section with the old section.

Live with
(inseparable):

1. To cohabitate, or to reside at the same location as someone or something, as in this example: *I **live with** my parents.*

2. To endure something that usually not pleasant or agreeable, as in this example: *My brother has been **living with** his disease for ten years.*

   More examples:
   - ❏ (1) My grandmother **lives with** my parents.
   - ❏ (2) We have to **live with** the noise coming from that construction site every day.

Lock in
(separable):

1. This term is often used in finances and investing and means to commit to an investment or financial transaction at a certain price, usually by giving money, as in this example: *I just bought stocks in a manufacturing company and I **locked in** at $56 per share.*

2. To close in and secure by lock, as in this example: *I was not allowed to bring my dog into the store, so I opened the car windows a little and **locked** my dog **in** the car.*

   More examples:
   - ❏ (1) When we bought our new house we **locked in** a mortgage at an interest rate of 2.5%.
   - ❏ (2) My father **locked** his tools **in** the shed.

Lock out
(separable):

1. To keep someone out of an area by means of securing by lock the entrance, as in this example: *I left the keys in my car and accidentally **locked** myself **out**.*

2. To withhold work from employees during a labor dispute, as in this example: *The company **locked out** its employees because of a disagreement about wage and benefits.*

   More examples:

   ❑ (1) In my class, the teacher will **lock** you **out** of the classroom if you are late.

   ❑ (2) The clothing company **locked out** its sewing machine operators because of a disagreement with their union about pay.

Lock up
(separable):

1. To secure by lock in a, for example, box, room, building, or institution, something or someone to prevent escape or to protect valuables, as in these examples: *We **locked up** the diamonds in the bank vault. The police locked the criminal up in jail.*

   More examples:

   ❑ (1) The clerk **locked up** his store and went home at the end of the day.

   ❑ (1) The woman **locked up** her car and went shopping in the mall.

Look around
(inseparable):

1. To use your vision and to turn your head in different directions to see things on different sides of you, as in this example: *I **looked around** to see where that loud noise came from.*

2. Often used when shopping for something or when searching for something. To first go here and then go there to try to find something or someone, as in this example: *I **looked around** for the best price for a new car.*

   More examples:

   ❑ (1) When we arrived at the parking lot, we **looked around** for a parking spot.

   ❑ (2) Before purchasing a new house, we decided to **look around** and see what was available.

Look at
(inseparable):

1. To focus with your eyesight on something or someone, as in this example: *We **looked at** the sunrise as we stood on the beach together.*

2. Used in expressing opinion or point of view, as in this example: *The way I **look at** it, we should not have spent all of our money on gambling.*

3. Sometimes used informally to talk about how much of something in an estimate, as in this example: *How much do you think the house will cost? I think you're **looking at** approximately $200,000.*

   More examples:
   - ❑ (1) When I asked the clerk for a discount, he **looked at** me as if I was crazy.
   - ❑ (2) The two groups agreed on the idea; they both **looked at** it the same way.
   - ❑ (3) The policeman told me that I was **looking at** a $500 fine for speeding.

Look down on
(inseparable):

1. To regard with contempt or condescension, as in this example: *The rich people in the neighborhood **looked down on** their poorer neighbors.*

   More examples:
   - ❑ (1) The company manager **looked down on** the idea of giving someone a raise for no reason.
   - ❑ (1) The two girls **looked down on** other girls who didn't wear current fashions.

Look for
(inseparable):

1. To search for, to seek, as in this example: *I **looked for** my car keys, but I could not find them.*

   More examples:
   - ❑ (1) The children **looked for** hidden gifts during the treasure hunt.
   - ❑ (1) We drove along the coastline **looking for** a hotel.

Look forward to
(inseparable):

1. To anticipate something in the future, usually in a positive way, as in this example: *I am **looking forward to** my vacation.*

   More examples:
   - ❑ (1) The children **looked forward to** opening their presents.
   - ❑ (1) We **looked forward to** resting after the long drive.

Look into
(inseparable):

1. To research, to investigate, as in this example: *My wife and I were **looking into** buying a house in another country.*

   More examples:
   - ❑ (1) The students are **looking into** attending school in Hawaii.
   - ❑ (1) We **looked into** renting an apartment downtown, but it's too expensive.

Look out
(inseparable):

1. To use caution, to be vigilant, as in this example: *This is a wonderful hike through the jungle, but you have to **look out** for snakes.*

   More examples:
   - ❑ (1) **Look out**! Stop the car! The road ends just ahead.
   - ❑ (1) Our bird watching group was **looking out** for brightly-colored birds.

Look over
(separable):

1. To review something or someone carefully, as in this example: *The businessman **looked over** the contract before signing it.*

   More examples:
   - ❑ (1) We **looked over** the apartment before renting it.
   - ❑ (1) My girlfriend and I **looked over** the display of jewelry before making a selection.

Look up
(separable):

1. To search for and find, as in a reference book, as in this example: *I took out my dictionary and **looked up** the meaning of the English word.*

   More examples:
   - (1) We **looked up** the telephone number in the directory.
   - (1) When I went to New York, I **looked up** an old friend.

Look up to
(inseparable):

1. To admire, to respect, as in this example: *The people of the town **looked up to** Kimo because he was a successful, generous and kind man.*

   More examples:
   - (1) The young worker **looked up to** his boss.
   - (1) The violinist **looked up to** her teacher.

Luck out
(inseparable):

1. To have good fortune, as in this example: *Boy, he really **lucked out**; he won the lottery!*

   More examples:
   - (1) He **lucked out** and got a good job.
   - (1) The thief **lucked out** and escaped the police.

Chapter 7 review
*Phrasal verbs beginning with the letter **L***

*Instructions: read and /or listen carefully to the sentences below. Fill in the blank spaces with the correct **preposition, particle,** or **adverb**. The answers can be found in this chapter (above).*

1. Please don't open the window because you'll let the mosquitoes ____.

2. The bus let him ____ in front of the bank.

3. I let my friend ____ on the secret about my new girlfriend.

4. My daughter let me ____ when she got a bad grade on her exam.

5. We invited all of our friends to the party. We didn't leave ____ anyone.

6. When I left the theater, I left my purse _____.

7. The first part of the movie led ____ to the climax in the middle of the movie.

8. In my class, the teacher will lock you ____ of the classroom if you are late.

9. My father locked his tools ____ the shed.

10. The woman locked ____ her car and went shopping in the mall.

11. When we arrived at the parking lot, we looked _____ for a parking spot.

12. We looked _____ renting an apartment downtown, but it's too expensive.

13. The policeman told me that I was looking ____ a $500 fine for speeding.

14. The two girls looked ____ on other girls who didn't wear current fashions.

15. The children looked ____ hidden gifts during the treasure hunt.

16. The children looked _____ ____ opening their presents.

17. We looked _____ the apartment before renting it.

18. The students are looking _____ attending school in Hawaii.

19. Look _____! Stop the car! The road ends just ahead.

20. We looked _____ the telephone number in the directory.

Answers: (1) in (2) off; (3) in (4) down (5) out; (6) behind; (7) up; (8) out; (9) in (10) up; (11) around; (12) at (13) at; (14) down; (15) for; (16) forward to; (17) over (or at); (18) into (19) out; (20) up

Chapter 8 *Phrasal verbs beginning with the letters M, N, and O*

In this section you will learn how to use many different phrasal verbs beginning with the letters M, N, and O correctly in a sentence.

There are two kinds of phrasal verbs, separable and inseparable. Separable phrasal verbs can take an object between the verb and the preposition. For example: *My father **picked** me **up** after school and drove me home.* Inseparable phrasal verbs cannot take an object between the verb and the preposition. For example: I asked my friends to **come along** with me to the Christmas party. **Come along** cannot be separated by an object.

The numbers in front of the examples that are in parenthesis (), correspond the to number of the explanation found directly above. So, for example: 1. *explanation . . .* refers to (1) *example . . . .* . If there is only one explanation or meaning given for the phrasal verb, then there will be two examples given for the one explanation. Both examples will be marked with (1).

If you have the Focus on English digital audio book version of this book (available separately from www.FOEBooks.com) listen to each of the phrasal verbs, followed by their meanings and then some examples of how they are used in real English sentences.

There will be a review at the end of this chapter.

Phrasal verbs beginning with the letters M, N, and O

Read and / or listen carefully to the examples, as they will give you a good idea as to how to use the phrasal verb in real English sentences.

Make for
(inseparable):

1. To create conditions or environment for a situation, action or event, as in this example: *This cool weather **makes for** very nice hiking.*

More examples:

- ❑ (1) The comfortable chair ***made for*** a nice place to sit and watch TV.

- ❑ (1) The beautiful weather ***made for*** a nice day to go to the beach.

Make of
(inseparable):

1. Interpret something, an event, action, or situation, as in this example: *Person A: What do you **make of** all of that smoke on the horizon? Person B: I think that there is a big fire in the bush.*

2. How something is built, or what something consists of, as in this example: *The house is **made of** wood.*

    More examples:

    - ❑ (1) When we first arrived in Rome we didn't know what to ***make of*** all the winding streets.

    - ❑ (1) The students didn't know what to ***make of*** the first part of the exam because it didn't have anything to do with the material they studied.

    - ❑ (2) The vase is ***made of*** glass.

Make out
(inseparable or separable depending on usage):

1. *(inseparable)* To be successful at something, as in this example: *I made $20,000 on that investment; I really **made out** well!*

2. *(separable)* To be able to see and identify something, as in this example: *As we were approaching the city, I could just **make out** the Empire State Building.*

3. *(separable)* To fill in, as with a form, application, check, etc., as in this example: *I paid my landlord for rent. I **made** the check **out** to his company.* (Meaning: *The name that I wrote on the check was the name of my landlord's company.*)

4. *(separable)* To represent something or someone as being a certain way, as in this example: *The cake in that restaurant wasn't as bad as you **made** it **out** to be.*

    More examples:

- ❏ (1) We got the tickets at half price; we really ***made out*** well.

- ❏ (2) Standing on the seashore, we could ***make out*** the outline of a ship far at sea.

- ❏ (3) My wife ***made*** a check ***out*** for $1500 to pay the rent.

- ❏ (4) The concert wasn't very good but my friend ***made*** it ***out*** to be fantastic.

Make up
(inseparable or separable depending on usage):

1. To invent or create a story, explanation, or reason for something, sometimes used for deceitful purposes, as in this example: *My son **made up** an excuse for why he didn't go to school today. Unfortunately, no one believed him.*

2. To do or complete something that should have been completed earlier, as in this example: *Sally didn't do her homework, so she had to **make** it **up** and give it to the teacher the next day.*

3. Comprised of or to be part of a larger something, group, or action, as in this example: *This drink is **made up** of soda and alcohol.*

4. To make a decision, as in this example: *I **made up** my mind to never go back to that restaurant.*

5. To put on cosmetics, as in this example: *The woman went into the rest room and **made** herself **up**.*

   More examples:
   - ❏ (1) I don't think that was the real reason why he quit the company. I think he ***made*** that ***up***.
   - ❏ (2) The teacher said that everyone who didn't take the exam yesterday has to ***make*** it ***up*** tomorrow.
   - ❏ (3) The business group is ***made up*** of executives from different companies.
   - ❏ (4) My boss ***made up*** her mind never to hire poorly qualified applicants.
   - ❏ (5) The clown ***made*** himself ***up*** before the show.

Mess up
(separable):

1. To make a mistake or error, as in this example: *I really **messed up** on my exam and my grade was low.*

2. To make dirty or disorganized, as in this example: *Stephan made a great meal but he really **messed up** the kitchen.*

   More examples:
   - (1) I really **messed up** the exam and ended up getting a low grade.
   - (2) The child spent the day in his room and really **messed** it **up**.

Mix up
(separable):

1. To confuse, as in this example: *I got really **mixed up** during the exam and got a poor grade.*

2. To blend two or more things together, as in this example: *We **mixed up** the ingredients for the cake, put them in a pan, and then baked them in an oven.*

   More examples:
   - (1) I always **mix up** the names of the twin sisters.
   - (2) **Mix** rice **up** with vegetables for a delicious meal.

Move in
(inseparable or separable depending on usage):

1. *(separable* To begin to occupy a place of residence or business; usually you bring your furniture and personal belongings into the new location and then begin to occupy the new location, as in this example: *We **moved in**(to) our new home on the 4th of December.*

2. *(inseparable* To advance towards something, as in this example: *The enemy was **moving in** on the military camp.*

   More examples:
   - (1) We are **moving into** our new business headquarters tomorrow.
   - (2) The police **moved in** on the criminal hideout.

Move out
(separable):

1. To leave a location, usually with belongings, equipment, or other things that may be important to you or a group, as in this example: *Our company **moved out** of the building and moved into a new, much larger building.*

   More examples:
   - ❑ (1) We are ***moving out*** of our rental tomorrow.
   - ❑ (1) The company is ***moving out*** of the city.

Narrow down
(separable):

1. To reduce in size or in scope, as in this example: *We are going on vacation in two months but we had to **narrow down** the list of things we wanted to do because we don't have enough time.*

   More examples:
   - ❑ (1) The company ***narrowed down*** the list of applicants to just two.
   - ❑ (1) We ***narrowed down*** our choices to two: go to the beach or relax at home.

Open up
(separable):

1. To remove a cover or top or to open a door to reveal something inside of an enclosed area, as in this example: *We **opened up** our gifts at the beginning of the holiday.*

2. To speak very honestly to someone because you trust them with certain information, as in this example: *I **opened up** to my teacher and told him why I am having trouble in class.*

3. To make available or accessible, as in this example: *The prime minister **opened up** his country for trade with the rest of the world.*

4. To spread out or unfold, as in this example: *The student **opened up** the book and read the paragraph.*

5. To begin operation, as in this example: *The store **opened up** last week and is having a big sale.*

   More examples:
   - ❑ (1) The young boy ***opened up*** the box and found a soccer ball inside.

❑ (2) I ***opened up*** to my friend about my recent bad luck.

❑ (3) The new corporation in our city ***opened up*** many opportunities for employment.

❑ (4) We ***opened up*** the map and found our location.

❑ (5) The school ***opened up*** two years ago and is already very popular with students.

Chapter 8 review
*Phrasal verbs beginning with the letters **M, N, and O***

*Instructions: read and /or listen carefully to the sentences below. Fill in the blank spaces with the correct **preposition, particle,** or **adverb**. The answers can be found in this chapter (above).*

1. The company is moving _____ of the city.

2. We are moving _____ our new business headquarters tomorrow.

3. Mix rice _____ vegetables for a delicious meal.

4. I really messed _____ the exam and ended up getting a low grade.

5. We opened _____ the map and found our location.

6. The company narrowed _____ the list of applicants to just two.

7. The clown made himself _____ before the show.

8. We got the tickets at half price; we really made _____ well.

9. When we first arrived in Rome we didn't know what to make ___ all the winding streets.

10. The beautiful weather made _____ a nice day to go to the beach.

Answers: (1) out (2) into; (3) with (4) up (5) up; (6) down; (7) up; (8) out; (9) of (10) for

Chapter 9 *Phrasal verbs beginning with the letter P*

Reminder: There are two kinds of phrasal verbs, separable and inseparable. Separable phrasal verbs can take an object between the verb and the preposition. For example: *My father **picked** me **up** after school and drove me home.* Inseparable phrasal verbs cannot take an object between the verb and the preposition. For example: I asked my friends to **come along** with me to the Christmas party. **Come along** cannot be separated by an object.

The numbers in front of the examples that are in parenthesis (), correspond the to number of the explanation found directly above. So, for example: 1. *explanation . . .* refers to (1) *example . . . .* If there is only one explanation or meaning given for the phrasal verb, then there will be two examples given for the one explanation. Both examples will be marked with (1).

If you have the Focus on English digital audio book version of this book (available separately from www.FOEBooks.com) listen to each of the phrasal verbs, followed by their meanings and then some examples of how they are used in real English sentences.

There will be a review at the end of this chapter.

Phrasal verbs beginning with the letter P

Pass on
(separable):

1. To relay from one to another, as in this example: *When my mother died she **passed** her jewelry **on** to her daughters.*

2. To die; a polite way of saying that a person has died, as in this example: *Last night her grandfather **passed on**.*

   More examples:
   - ❑ (1) When my brother grew older, he **passed** his clothes **on** to his little brother.

❑ (2) My father ***passed on*** some years ago, but he left me with a wonderful education.

Pass out
(separable or inseparable depending on usage):

1. *(separable)* To distribute something, as in this example: *The immigration officer **passed out** booklets explaining immigration law.*

2. *(inseparable)* To lose consciousness, as in this example: *It was so hot in the room that some people **passed out**.*

   More examples:
   ❑ (1) The teacher ***passed out*** the exams.
   ❑ (2) The mountain climber ***passed out*** for lack of oxygen.

Pass over
(separable):

1. To be left out, omitted, or disregarded as in this example: *Some of the employees at the company were **passed over** for a raise because they were too new.*

   More examples:
   ❑ (1) During our vacation, we ***passed over*** going to Las Vegas because it was too expensive.
   ❑ (1) There was so much food at the buffet that we ***passed over*** on trying many things.

Pass up
(separable):

1. To forego, to not accept, to let go, as in this example: *I **passed up** the chocolate cake for dessert because I was full.*

   More examples:
   ❑ (1) I ***passed up*** an opportunity to go to France because I had to finish a project at work.
   ❑ (1) I ***passed up*** the pudding at dinner last night; I heard it was good.

Pay back
(separable):

1. To return something, usually a debt of some kind, as in this example: _Keone **paid** the bank **back** the money he borrowed from them._

2. Retribution, sometimes used to express returning or giving something back for something negative received earlier, as in this example: _We **paid** the thief **back** by calling the police._

   More examples:
   - ❑ (1) Christina **_paid back_** her credit card debt.
   - ❑ (2) I paid her **_back for_** starting that rumor.

Pay for
(inseparable):

1. Remuneration, to exchange money or something of value for something else of value, as in this example: _Jeff **paid for** the groceries and left the store._

2. Used to express retribution, to refer to the penalty you have to pay when you do something wrong, too much of something, too little of something etc., as in this example: _I ate way too much chocolate cake and now I am **paying for** it with a stomachache!_

   More examples:
   - ❑ (1) We traded the farmer some clothes to **_pay for_** the oranges he gave us.
   - ❑ (2) People who break the law have to **_pay for_** it by going to jail.

Pay off
(separable):

1. To finish paying for something, as in this example: _I finally **paid off** my car!_

2. Sometimes used to express bribery, or paying someone to do something that may not be legal or ethical, as in this example: _The music company **paid** the radio station **off** for playing their music on the radio._

   More examples:
   - ❑ (1) We traded the farmer some clothes to **_pay for_** the oranges he gave us.
   - ❑ (2) The lady driver tried to **_pay_** the police officer **_off_** for not giving her a ticket.

Pay up
(inseparable):

1. To settle a debt or pay an amount of money that is demanded, as in this example: *Hey, you owe me $20; __pay up__!*

   More examples:
   - (1) My roommate told me that we needed to __pay up__ our light bill or the electric company would turn off the electricity next week.
   - (1) The bartender asked the group to pay for their tab: "__Pay up__, or I'll call the police."

Pick on
(inseparable):

1. To tease or bully, as in this example: *My older brother always used to __pick on__ me.*

   More examples:
   - (1) I don't know why the teacher always __picks on__ me.
   - (1) Mother: "Please don't __pick on__ your little sister!"

Pick out
(separable):

1. To choose or select, as in this example: *Mary went shopping and __picked out__ a beautiful black dress.*

2. To discern or to distinguish from the surroundings, as in this example: *I __picked__ the criminal __out__ from a picture of twenty suspects.*

   More examples:
   - (1) I needed a new tie so I went to the clothing shop and __picked__ one __out__.
   - (2) While we watched the sun set over the ocean, I was able to __pick out__ a sailboat far out at sea.

Pick up
(separable):

1. To take something up by hand or by mechanical device as in this example: *The student **picked up** the book and put in on the desk.*

2. To clean up, as in this example: Mom picked up the room after we left.

3. To take on passengers or freight, as in this example: *The train **picked up** the passengers at 3pm.*

4. *(informal)* To acquire in a casual way, as in this example: *I **picked up** a CD at the record shop on my way home.*

5. To learn or to acquire knowledge (the feeling of this is meant to be casual and not formal), as in this example: *I **pick up** languages easily.*

6. Can be used to mean: claim something that you left behind, as in this example: K*imo **picked up** his pants at the dry cleaners.*

7. To catch a disease or sickness, usually passed on from someone else, as in this example: *I **picked up** malaria while in the south of the country.*

8. To take into custody, or to capture (usually used with police or military), as in this example: *The police **picked up** the robber and took him to the police station.*

9. Casual relationship; used to express meeting someone in a casual environment like a bar, as in this example: *I **picked up** a girl at the pub last night.*

10. To encounter or come upon and observe, as in this example: *The ship **picked up** the enemy aircraft on their radar.*

11. To continue something after a break, as in this example: *Let's **pick** this discussion **up** after a lunch break.*

12. To improve a situation or condition, as in this example: *Her attitude really **picked up** after getting that good grade on the exam!*

13. *(slang)* To leave unexpectedly, as in this example: *He was so mad he just **picked up** and ran out of the room.*

More examples:
- (1) The crane **picked** up the old car and put it on a pile of old cars.
- (2) After the party we all helped to **pick up** the room.
- (3) The taxi **picked** us **up** at the train station.
- (4) I **picked up** some popcorn on the way to the party.

❑ (5) I'm good at math; I ***pick*** it ***up*** easily.

❑ (6) Kathryn gave the shoemaker her claim check so that she could ***pick up*** her shoes that were repaired.

❑ (7) My brother said that he ***picked up*** the flu on the flight from Houston to Cleveland.

❑ (8) The military police ***picked up*** the drunken sailors.

❑ (9) My friend told me he ***picked up*** two women last night.

❑ (10) The police ***picked up*** the speeder on their radar.

❑ (11) We ***picked up*** where we left off in our meeting after we had lunch.

❑ (12) Business really ***picked up*** after the holiday.

❑ (13) My girlfriend said that she ***picked up*** and left her boyfriend because of his abuses.

Pile up
(separable):

1. To accumulate or amass things, as in this example: *My wife **piled up** all the books and took them back to the library.*

   More examples:
   ❑ (1) Claudia ***piled up*** traffic tickets, mostly because she drove too fast.
   ❑ (1) Kelly loved ice cream. She ***piled up*** ice cream on her plate for dessert.

Piss off
(separable) (slang):

1. To make angry, as in this example: *People who throw garbage out of their car window **piss** me **off**.*

   More examples:
   ❑ (1) Kaori was ***pissed off*** that she got a poor grade on her exam.
   ❑ (1) The police officer was really ***pissed off*** and gave the guy a ticket for driving recklessly.

Plan ahead
(inseparable):

1. To think about and organize for things that you would like to happen in the future, as in this example: *We would like to have a successful party next month so we are **planning ahead**.*

   More examples:
   - (1) The festival organizers ***planned ahead*** for the big celebration.
   - (1) We wanted to avoid unpleasant surprises during our vacation so we ***planned ahead*** very carefully.

Plan for
(inseparable):

1. To prepare for something, as in this example: *We **planned for** the long, cold winter season by cutting lots of wood for the fireplace.*

   More examples:
   - (1) We knew the company was going to lay us off; we ***planned for*** it.
   - (2) We ***planned for*** the food shortage by storing lots of food on our shelves last year.

Plan on
(inseparable):

1. To be prepared for or to anticipate something that will occur in the future, as in this example: *We **planned on** staying in school an extra hour.*

   More examples:
   - (1) When we went to the theater, we ***planned on*** waiting on a long line for tickets.
   - (1) We ***plan on*** going to China next summer.

Play around
(inseparable):

1. *(informal)* To be disloyal to a significant other, boyfriend, girlfriend, wife or husband in particular, as in this example: *My wife was **playing around** with another man; I'm going to ask for a divorce.*

2. *(informal)* To tinker with something without really understanding how it works, or what the nature of a problem is, as in this example: *The lawnmower stopped working so I **played around** with it for a while to see if I could fix it.*

3. *(informal)* To not be serious, joking, jesting, teasing, etc., as in this example: *I was only **playing around** with you when I said I didn't like your clothes.*

More examples:

❑ (1) I caught my boyfriend ***playing around*** with my best friend.

❑ (2) The car wouldn't start this morning so I ***played around*** with the battery until I got it started.

❑ (3) I hope my friend understands that I am only ***playing around*** when I brag about how good I am at that game.

Plug in
(separable):

1. To connect an electrical to a wall receptacle, as in this example: *We **plugged in** the toaster so we could have breakfast.*

2. *(slang)* Used to talk about one's connection to, or one's awareness of information from a social or professional network, as in this example: *If you really want to be up to date in your field, you should be **plugged into** your professional association.*

More examples:

❑ (1) The workman ***plugged in*** the electric drill.

❑ (2) I'm ***plugged into*** the local gossip network so I know everything that's going on in this town.

Plug up
(separable):

1. To stop and restrict the flow of something, as in this example: *The plumber temporarily **plugged up** the leak in the hose.*

More examples:

❑ (1) Hair and other things ***plugged up*** the shower drain.

❑ (2) The major roads into town were ***plugged up*** with traffic.

Point out
(separable):

1. To direct one's attention to something, as in this example: *The tour guide __pointed out__ the 2000-year-old statue to the tourists.*

2. To stress or emphasize certain information to someone, as in this example: *The teacher __pointed out__ to the students that the homework would be due next Tuesday.*

   More examples:
   - ❑ (1) The store clerk __*pointed out*__ the casual blue dress to her customer.
   - ❑ (2) I would like to __*point out*__ to you that this is not the first time your son was caught cheating on an exam.

Point to
(inseparable):

1. To cause to focus one's attention on an area of concern, as in this example: *The unusual weather, the heavy rains, the melting ice all __point to__ global warming as a possible cause.*

2. When you use your hand or finger to direct one's attention to something or someone, as in this example: *When the clerk in the candy store asked the boy what he wanted, the boy __pointed to__ the red candy.*

   More examples:
   - ❑ (1) The student always looked out of the window and did not pay attention while in class, __*point to*__ the fact that the student was not interested in the subject.
   - ❑ (2) The boy's mother __*pointed to*__ his bedroom and said, "Clean it up, now!"

Print out
(separable):

1. To print by mechanical means something produced in a computer, as in this example: *The manager __printed out__ his report after completing it on the computer.*

   More examples:

❑ (1) The student couldn't get his report to ***print out*** because there wasn't enough memory in the printer.

❑ (1) The office worker ***printed out*** the work schedule for the following month.

Pull off
(separable):

1. *(informal)* To succeed at something despite difficult conditions, or low probability of success, as in this example: *I **pulled off** an A on the exam.*

   More examples:
   ❑ (1) The workers moved a house from one state to another without damaging anything; everyone was surprised that they ***pulled*** it ***off***.
   ❑ (1) I can't believe that I ***pulled off*** that double back flip.

Pull out
(separable):

1. To remove, sometimes with force, as in this example: I ***pulled*** the young boy ***out*** of the water.

2. To leave, or to vacate an area, as in this example: *The military **pulled out** of the area because it was finished with its operations.*

   More examples:
   ❑ (1) The firemen ***pulled*** the woman ***out*** of the burning house.
   ❑ (2) The Navy ***pulled*** its ships ***out*** of the area because they were needed elsewhere.

Pull over
(separable):

1. To drive a vehicle over to the side of the road, as in this example: *I **pulled** the car **over** to let the ambulance go by.*

   More examples:
   ❑ (1) The policeman told me to ***pull*** my car ***over*** to the side of the road.
   ❑ (1) The truck driver ***pulled over*** so he could check his tires.

Pull through
(inseparable):

1. To recover from for survive something, as in this example: *My friend was sick for a month, but he finally **pulled through** and he's okay now.*

    More examples:
    - ❑ (1) The shipwrecked survivors ***pulled through*** the long ordeal, and they are recovering now in a hospital in New York.
    - ❑ (1) My sister ***pulled through*** a long bout with the flu.

Punch in
(inseparable):

1. To register your time of entry to a job or other organization, usually with a time clock or other mechanical time-keeping device, as in this example: *We **punch in** at 8 o'clock every day at our company.*

    More examples:
    - ❑ (1) I ***punched in*** five minutes late yesterday; the boss wasn't happy about this.
    - ❑ (1) We usually ***punch in*** ten minutes early every day.

Punch out
(inseparable):

1. To register your time of exit from a job or other organization, usually with a time clock or other mechanical time-keeping device, as in this example: *We **punched out** at 5 o'clock and then left the building.*

    More examples:
    - ❑ (1) We ***punched out*** early yesterday so we could go to the concert.
    - ❑ (1) Jason ***punches out*** a 6pm every night; he's a hard worker.

Put away
(separable):

1. To return something to a usual location, as in this example: *We **put** the books **away** back on the shelf. (Note: when we use "back," in this context we mean "where something usually is located.")*

2. *(informal)* Used to express eating large quantities of food or drink, as in this example: *Wow, you can really **put** it **away**! You've eaten two plates of food!*

3. To put someone in jail or to place someone in an mental institution, as in this example: *The murderer was **put away** for life.*

More examples:
- (1) After I looked at the new CD player the sales clerk **put** it **away** in the showcase.
- (2) Jack **put** two pizzas **away**; now he's sick.
- (3) She was acting crazy so they **put** her **away** for a while. (Meaning: they put her in a mental institution.)

Put back
(separable):

1. Similar to put away, to return something to a usual location, as in this example:

*We **put** the books **back** on the shelf. (Note: when we use "back," in this context we mean "where something usually is located.")*

More examples:
- (1) After looking at the pictures in the book, I **put** it **back** on the shelf.
- (1) The mother said to the little boy: "Please **put** the cookie **back**; you're going to eat dinner in ten minutes!"

Put down
(separable):

1. To take something you are holding and place it in a lower , sometimes horizontal, position, as in this example: *Katrina **put** the book **down** and walked to the white board.*

2. To criticize, as in this example: *I don't mean to **put** you **down** but your pants don't match your shirt.*

3. To make a partial payment on something, or a payment to hold something for future purchase, as in this example: *I bought the house. The bank asked me to **put down** $10,000 and they would lend me the rest of the money needed to purchase the house.*

4. To add something in writing to something else, like a list, as in this example: *I **put down** my name on the signup list.*

5. To attribute an action or occurrence to something else, as in this example: *The student failed the exam. He **put** it **down** to not studying enough.*

6. To land an aircraft, as in this example: *The passengers were surprised when the pilot announced he would **put** the plane **down** in a different city.*

More examples:
- (1) After playing with the baby, the father ***put*** it ***down*** in its bed.
- (2) All the children used to ***put*** her ***down*** for being so small.
- (3) I ***put down*** $50 so the store would hold the bicycle for me until I purchased it in June.
- (4) I ***put*** my full name ***down*** on the top of the exam.
- (5) I don't understand why people drink alcohol and then drive a car. I just ***put*** it ***down*** to stupidity.
- (6) The pilot ***put*** the plane ***down*** in New York.

Put in
(separable):

1. To cause to make a formal offer, or to offer, as in this example: *Soo Woo **put in** an offer of $100,000 for the house.*

2. To contribute to, to add to, as in this example: *Each student **put in** $2 towards the purchase of the pizza.*

3. To arrive at a port, especially a commercial or military ship, as in this example: *The cruise ship **put in** at Pago Pago, American Samoa.*

4. To install something, as in this example: *The workers **put in** a new computer system for the company.*

5. To spend time, as in this example: *The employee **put in** thirty years at his company.*

More examples:
- (1) I ***put in*** a bid (offer) of $5000 for the blue car at the car auction.
- (2) We all ***put in*** $10 to help pay for the food at the party.

❑ (3) The military ship ***put in*** at Guam.

❑ (4) The government ***put in*** a new bridge over the river.

❑ (5) The criminal ***put in*** twenty years in jail for the robbery.

Put off
(separable):

1. To delay or postpone something, as in this example: *Pablo **put off** going on vacation until all of his work was done.*

2. To repel or repulse, as in this example: *Joan's awkward behavior at the party **put** the other guests **off**.*

   More examples:

   ❑ (1) The teacher ***put off*** giving the exam today because there were too many students absent.

   ❑ (2) The dirty restaurant really ***put*** us ***off***.

Put on
(separable):

1. To dress or put on clothes, or to apply something, as in this example: *Jeremy **put on** his jacket and left the house.*

2. *(informal)* To fool, tease or mislead in a playful way, as in this example: *My friends were **putting** me **on** when they told me they saw a ghost.*

3. To attach something to something, as in this example: *The Yorimoto family **put** a new addition **on**(to) their house.*

4. Can be used to talk about weight gain, as in this example: *I saw Sally the other day and it looked like she had **put on** some weight.*

   More examples:

   ❑ (1) Reiko ***put on*** her best perfume for the party.

   ❑ (2) My brother told me there were ten thousand people at the concert last night; he was ***putting*** me ***on***.

   ❑ (3) The librarian ***put*** the sticker ***on*** the book for identification.

   ❑ (4) My mother is a good cook and I think I ***put on*** some weight.

Put out

(separable):

1. To take something from inside of a close area and put it outside of the enclosed area, as in this example: *The garbage man is coming tomorrow morning, so we **put** the garbage **out** for him to pick up.*

2. To extinguish a fire or switch off a light, as in this example: *The firemen **put out** the house fire.*

3. To be inconvenienced or annoyed, as in this example: *I hope that we didn't put you out by our unexpected visit to your house.*

4. To distribute something like a magazine, newspaper, or printed advertising, as in this example: *The publishing company **put** the magazine **out** last May.*

   More examples:

   ❑ (1) The bartender ***put*** the two boys ***out*** of the pub for being under age.

   ❑ (2) The mother asked her son to ***put out*** the lights in the living room before going to bed.

   ❑ (3) We were really ***put out*** by all of the road construction in front of our house.

   ❑ (4) We plan to ***put*** the advertising ***out*** in about a month.

Put past

(separable):

1. Used to express doubt and sometimes mistrust about the actions of someone, or to talk about someone's capacity to do something that is not quite right, as in this example: *I wouldn't **put** it **past** him to find a way to get his certificate without taking an exam, while the rest of us have to take the exam.*

   More examples:

   ❑ (1) That guy has been in jail for theft before and I wouldn't ***put*** it ***past*** him to do steal again.

   ❑ (2) I wouldn't ***put*** it ***past*** mom to check on where we go at night.

Put to

(separable):

1. Usually refers to placing some part of your body or something in your hand against something else in order to accomplish some action, as in this example: *I **put** my ear **to** the wall to listen to my neighbor's conversation.*

2. Used to express causing an inconvenience to someone else, as in this example: *Sorry to **put** you **to** the trouble, but may I use your phone?*

3. To confront with a question or information, as in this example: *We didn't know when we were going to get our grades, so I **put** that question **to** the teacher.*

   More examples:
   - ❑ (1) I **put** my pencil **to** paper and made a list of the things I needed for the trip.
   - ❑ (2) They really **put** my brother **to** a lot of trouble when they asked him to help out with the fund raising.
   - ❑ (3) When my friend **put** his idea **to** me that way, I could understand it better.

Put together
(separable):

1. To assemble, or to build, as in this example: *My younger brother **put** the pieces **together** and completed the puzzle.*

2. To organize something, usually an event or activity, as in this example: *The students **put together** a nice party for all of the students in the school.*

3. To place in close proximity, or close together, as in this example: *The teacher **put** students from different countries **together** to practice their English.*

   More examples:
   - ❑ (1) We **put** the model airplane **together** in about four hours.
   - ❑ (2) The town leaders **put together** a really nice Fourth of July celebration.
   - ❑ (3) The teacher **put** the older students together and the younger students **together** to work on separate projects.

Put up
(separable):

1. To provide accommodations or a place to stay, as in this example: *When my cousin arrived from Ohio, we **put** him **up** for a week.*

2. To build or construct something, as in this example: *The workers **put up** the house in a short time.*

3. To provide funds or funding in advance, as in this example: *The rich man **put up** the money to build the new art museum.*

4. To attach something to something else, like a notice on a bulletin board, as in this example: *The housewife **put up** the curtains on the window.*

5. To upload, especially website files, as in this example: *We **put up** our new website last Tuesday.*

6. To display, carry on, or engage in something, as in this example: *She really **put up** a good argument as to why she should be paid more money.*

   More examples:
   - (1) When my brother visited from Minnesota, I **put** him **up** for a week.
   - (2) The construction company **put up** apartment buildings.
   - (3) We had a good idea for a business, but we needed someone to **put up** the money to help us start it.
   - (4) We **put up** signs all over town to advertise the loss of our dog.
   - (5) We **put up** some files that added two more pages to our website.
   - (6) The boxer **put up** a good fight, but lost the match in the third round.

Put up with
(inseparable):

1. To tolerate something or someone, or be patient with an uncomfortable situation, as in this example: *The price for the hotel room was cheap so we **put up with** the bad service, noise, and uncomfortable bed.*

   More examples:
   - (1) We **put up with** the noise from the construction for a week.
   - (1) The flight to Rome from Frankfurt was really cheap, so we **put up with** the uncomfortable seating on the aircraft.

Chapter 9 review
*Phrasal verbs beginning with the letter **P***

*Instructions: read and /or listen carefully to the sentences below. Fill in the blank spaces with the correct **preposition, particle,** or **adverb**. The answers can be found in this chapter (above).*

1. My roommate told me that we needed to pay _____ our light bill or the electric company would turn _____ the electricity next week.

2. We traded the farmer some clothes to pay _____ the oranges he gave us.

3. Christina paid _____ her credit card debt.

4. We traded the farmer some clothes to pay _____ the oranges he gave us.

5. Mother: "Please don't pick ___ your little sister!"

6. I needed a new tie so I went to the clothing shop and picked one _____.

7. Kathryn gave the shoemaker her claim check so that she could pick ___ her shoes that were repaired.

8. Claudia piled ___ traffic tickets, mostly because she drove too fast.

9. Jack put two pizzas _____; now he's sick.

10. The government put ___ a new bridge over the river.

11. We were really put _____ by how dirty the restaurant was.

12. The bartender put the two boys _____ of the pub for being under age.

13. We put ___ some files that added two more pages to our website.

14. We put _____ _____ the noise from the construction for a week.

15. Hair and other things plugged ___ the shower drain.

16. I caught my boyfriend playing _____ with my best friend.

17. We plan ____ going to China next summer.

18. We knew the company was going to lay us ____; we planned ___ it.

19. The festival organizers planned _____ for the big celebration.

20. Claudia piled the cheese ____ the pizza. It was good.

Answers: (1) up (2) for; (3) off (4) for (use *off* when you finish paying a debt) (5) on; (6) out; (7) up; (8) up; (9) down (10) up; (11) off; (12) out (13) up; (14) up with; (15) up; (16) around; (17) on; (18) off (19) ahead; (20) on

Chapter 10 *Phrasal verbs beginning with the letter R*

In this section you will learn how to use many different phrasal verbs beginning with the letter R correctly in a sentence.

There are two kinds of phrasal verbs, separable and inseparable. Separable phrasal verbs can take an object between the verb and the preposition. For example: *My father **picked me up** after school and drove me home.* Inseparable phrasal verbs cannot take an object between the verb and the preposition. For example: I asked my friends to **come along** with me to the Christmas party. **Come along** cannot be separated by an object.

The numbers in front of the examples that are in parenthesis (), correspond the to number of the explanation found directly above. So, for example: 1. *explanation . . .* refers to (1) *example . . . .* If there is only one explanation or meaning given for the phrasal verb, then there will be two examples given for the one explanation. Both examples will be marked with (1).

If you have the Focus on English digital audio book version of this book (available separately from www.FOEBooks.com) listen to each of the phrasal verbs, followed by their meanings and then some examples of how they are used in real English sentences.

There will be a review at the end of this chapter.

Phrasal verbs beginning with the letter R

Read and / or listen carefully to the examples, as they will give you a good idea as to how to use the phrasal verb in real English sentences.

Rip off
(separable):

1. To tear or pull away, sometimes violently, as in this example: *Chama **ripped** the top **off** of the flour box and poured the flour into a bowl.*

2. *(informal)* To steal or take something without authorization from its owner (recently: means to download music files from the Internet, sometimes without complete authorization from the owners of the music), as in this example: *My bicycle was **ripped off** yesterday and I had to walk home from school.*

More examples:
- ❑ (1) The check-in clerk at the airport ***ripped*** the old tags ***off*** of my luggage and put new ones on.
- ❑ (2) Somebody ***ripped off*** my jacket from the back of my chair.

Rip up
(separable):

1. To tear paper or cardboard, as in this example: *Alex **ripped up** the traffic ticket and said he wasn't going to pay the fine.*

More examples:
- ❑ (1) The clerk ***ripped up*** the cardboard box into small pieces and then threw it away.
- ❑ (1) The worker ***ripped up*** the old clothing and used it for rags.

Rule out
(separable):

1. To exclude from consideration, to exclude as a possibility, as in this example: *We **ruled out** going to Majorca this year because it was too expensive.*

More examples:
- ❑ (1) The teacher ***ruled out*** giving extra homework because it was a holiday.
- ❑ (1) Tim ***ruled out*** going to his friend's house because it was too late at night.

Run across
(inseparable):

1. To encounter or meet, usually unexpectedly, as in this example: *I **ran across** my classmate from school while I was shopping at the mall.*

More examples:
- ❑ (1) Patrick ***ran across*** a problem while doing his homework.

❏ (1) Megumi **_ran across_** a diamond earring lying in the sand while walking at the beach.

Run around
(inseparable):

1. To hurriedly go here and there, as in this example: *Just before the party, I **ran around** looking for a new jacket at some of the clothing stores in town.*

   More examples:
   ❏ (1) Right before the exam I **_ran around_** asking people to lend me a pencil.
   ❏ (1) Mattias **_ran around_** the beach asking people if they knew what time it was.

Run down
(separable):

1. Can mean to find or locate something that you were looking for, as in this example: *I finally **ran down** that diamond necklace I was looking for.*

2. To hit with a vehicle, as in this example: *The woman was hurt badly when the car **ran** her **down**.*

3. To chase and catch someone or something, as in this example: *The police **ran** the criminal **down** and put him back in jail.*

   More examples:
   ❏ (1) I finally **_ran down_** that computer software I was looking for.
   ❏ (2) In the early morning, the milk truck accidentally **_ran down_** the dog that was lying in the street.
   ❏ (3) The crowd **_ran down_** the purse snatcher and held him until the police arrived.

Run into
(separable):

1. Can mean to meet or encounter unexpectedly; similar, but not identical in meaning to **_run across_**, as in this example: *I **ran into** my best friend while I was shopping in town.*

2. To hit or collide with something, as in this example: *The car **ran into** the telephone pole because the driver was drunk.*

3. To amount to or to be approximately valued at, as in this example: *The owner's net worth **runs into** the millions of dollars.* (Note: *we often use a noun phrase after using the expression run into with this meaning.*)

   More examples:
   - ❏ (1) Toshiko **ran into** an old friend while walking downtown.
   - ❏ (2) The drunken man **ran into** the door while leaving the pub.
   - ❏ (3) The cost of rebuilding the city after the storm will **run into** the millions of dollars.

Run out
(separable):

1. To exhaust, to deplete, to have no more of something, to be out of something, as in this example: *My car **ran out** of gas on the way to work.*

2. To leave unexpectedly; sometimes used in a negative context to mean permanently, as in this example: *My wife **ran out** on me, and now I am all alone.*

3. To put out by force, to force someone to leave, as in this example: *The townspeople **ran** the thief **out** of town.*

   More examples:
   - ❏ (1) I couldn't complete the race because I **ran out** of energy.
   - ❏ (2) Jim's partner **ran out** on him and took all of his money.
   - ❏ (3) The bartender **ran** the troublemaker **out** of the pub.

Run over
(separable):

1. To collide with, knock down, and often pass over, as in this example: *The car **ran over** the chicken that was crossing the road.*

2. To review something, usually quickly, as in this example: *The politician **ran over** his speech before going on stage.*

3. To exceed a limit, usually used with time, as in this example: *We had to pay extra because we **ran over** our time limit.*

More examples:

❑ (1) The car ***ran over*** a nail in the road and got a flat tire.

❑ (2) The student ***ran over*** his presentation before giving it to the class.

❑ (3) The policeman gave us a parking ticket because we ***ran over*** our time.

Run up
(separable):

1. To accumulate a tab or bill, as in this example: *We **ran up** a big bill at the bar and the bartender asked us to pay before we have any more drinks.*

2. To run to a higher level, as in this example: *Jack and Jill **ran up** the hill.*

3. To approach someone or something quickly, as in this example: *The concert fan **ran up** to the rock star and asked for an autograph.*

More examples:

❑ (1) We really ***ran up*** a big bill when we went shopping today.

❑ (2) The marathon runners ***ran up*** the steep hill.

❑ (3) My son ***ran up*** to me and asked me if he could have a new bicycle like his friend has.

Chapter 10 review
*Phrasal verbs beginning with the letter **R***

*Instructions: read and /or listen carefully to the sentences below. Fill in the blank spaces with the correct **preposition, particle,** or **adverb**. The answers can be found in this chapter (above).*

1. Mattias ran _____ the beach asking people if they knew what time it was.

2. We really ran _____ a big bill when we went shopping today.

3. The car ran _____ a nail in the road and got a flat tire.

4. Toshiko ran _____ an old friend while walking downtown.

5. I couldn't complete the race because I ran _____ of energy.

6. I finally ran _____ that computer software I was looking for.

7. Patrick ran _____ a problem while doing his homework.

8. Tim ruled _____ going to his friend's house because it was too late at night.

9. The worker ripped _____ the old clothing and used it for rags.

10. Somebody ripped _____ my jacket from the back of my chair.

Answers: (1) down (2) up; (3) over (4) into (5) out; (6) into; (7) into; (8) out; (9) up (10) off

Chapter 11 *Phrasal verbs beginning with the letter S*

In this section you will learn how to use many different phrasal verbs beginning with the letter S correctly in a sentence.

There are two kinds of phrasal verbs, separable and inseparable. Separable phrasal verbs can take an object between the verb and the preposition. For example: *My father **picked** me **up** after school and drove me home.* Inseparable phrasal verbs cannot take an object between the verb and the preposition. For example: I asked my friends to **_come along_** with me to the Christmas party. **_Come along_** cannot be separated by an object.

The numbers in front of the examples that are in parenthesis (), correspond the to number of the explanation found directly above. So, for example: 1. *explanation* . . . refers to (1) *example* . . . . If there is only one explanation or meaning given for the phrasal verb, then there will be two examples given for the one explanation. Both examples will be marked with (1).

If you have the Focus on English digital audio book version of this book (available separately from www.FOEBooks.com) listen to each of the phrasal verbs, followed by their meanings and then some examples of how they are used in real English sentences.

There will be a review at the end of this chapter.

Phrasal verbs beginning with the letter S

Read and / or listen carefully to the examples, as they will give you a good idea as to how to use the phrasal verb in real English sentences.

Screw on(to)
(separable):

1. To fasten something to something else using screws, as in this example: *We screwed the bulletin board on(to) the wall.*

2. To tighten a top on a jar or other container with a screw top, as in this example: *After removing the beans from the jar, Sophie **screwed** the top back **on**.*

 (*Note: We use the word "back" in English a lot, usually with the meaning "return."*)

 More examples:
 - (1) We ***screwed*** the part ***on***(to) the car motor and then started up the motor.
 - (2) Mark unscrewed the top from the sugar jar, got one tablespoon of sugar, and then ***screwed*** the top back ***on***.

Screw out of
(separable):

1. *(informal)* To cheat or defraud someone out of something, as in this example: *The ticket seller sold us invalid tickets; we got **screwed out of** $20 each.*

 More examples:
 - (1) The investors were ***screwed out of*** millions of dollars because the stocks they bought had no value.
 - (1) My brother counted the change that the vendor returned to us and discovered that the vendor tried to ***screw*** us ***out of*** $5.

Screw up
(separable):

1. *(informal)* To make a mistake or miscalculation, as in this example: *The vendor **screwed up** and gave us the wrong change.*

2. *(informal)* Is also used to mean contort or change a facial expression, as in this example: *When I told the vendor that he had made a mistake and had given me the wrong change, the vendor **screwed up** his face and then gave me the correct change.*

3. *(informal)* Another meaning is to injure, as in this example: *My friend **screwed up** his ankle while skiing.*

 More examples:

❑ (1) I ***screwed up*** and got a bad grade on the exam.

❑ (2) The teacher ***screwed up*** his face and then gave the student the bad news about his exam results.

❑ (3) I ***screwed up*** my thumb trying to stop a soccer goal from getting into the goal.

___See about___
(inseparable):

1. English speakers will use the word see to mean *talk to in person*, as in this example: *The teachers said that he wanted to **see** me **about** my exam grade.*

2. Can also be used to refer to the future, when someone is interested in experiencing the results of something that is or has been said, or that is happening or has happened in the near past, as in this example: *My brother said he was going to be a better person in the future. I told him that we would have to wait and **see about** that.*

   More examples:

   ❑ (1) I went to ___see___ my doctor ___about___ my sore arm.

   ❑ (2) My classmate said that I would probably not get a good grade on the exam. I told her that we would ___see about___ that.

___Sell out___
(separable):

1. To sell all of something that you had to sell, as in this example: *The price of apples was cheap and people came and bought all his apples. He was **sold out** in about two hours.*

2. To betray someone, especially when the betrayer was someone you trusted; to betray an idea or principle, as in this example: *During the war we were safely hidden in the mountains until someone we knew and trusted **sold** us **out** to the enemy. The enemy then found our hiding place, captured us, and then put us in jail.*

   More examples:

   ❑ (1) Excuse me, do you have any mp3 players left?

   I am sorry, but we are all ___sold out___ of that item.

❑ (2) My classmates *__sold__* me *__out__* and told the teacher I didn't hand in the homework assignment.

Set out
(inseparable):

1. To embark on or undertake; to begin a journey, venture, or project; to have the intention to do something, as in this example: *The explorer __set out__ to find the lost continent of Atlantis.*

2. To carefully and systematically lay out plans, rules or ideas, as in this example: *My girlfriend and I entered a cooking contest. Before the contest began, the judge __set out__ the rules of the competition so that everyone was clear about them.*

More examples:
❑ (1) In 1492 Columbus *__set out__* to find a shorter route to India.

❑ (2) The coach of our soccer team *__set out__* plans for playing our competition today.

Set up
(separable):

1. To assemble, build or erect something, as in this example: *The mechanics __set up__ the new machine.*

2. To establish someone with authority or power, as in this example: *After the war, the military __set up__ the dictator.*

3. *(informal)* To be tricked or deceived into doing something that could be dangerous, as in this example: *The gangsters __set__ him __up__ to do something illegal. The police will probably catch him and he will go to jail.*

More examples:
❑ (1) The students *__set up__* a table at the science fair.

❑ (2) Powerful and wealthy businessmen *__set__* their representative *__up__* to lead the country.

❑ (3) His friends *__set__* him *__up__* to meet the girl. They convinced him that the girl liked him and wanted to meet him. Really, they knew that the girl had no interest in him and they knew that the girl would get mad at him if he spoke to her.

Settle down
(separable):

1. To begin living a more stable life, a more settled life, as in this example: *Jim thought that it was time for him to **settle down** and make a nice life for himself, so he asked his girlfriend to marry him.*

2. To calm down, to become less nervous or restless, as in this example: *Silvia was really upset about the traffic accident that she witnessed. Her mother finally talked to her and helped her to **settle down** a little.*

    More examples:
    - (1) The salesman traveled from city to city for his job, but dreamed about the day when he could **settle down** in one location.
    - (2) Gina's purse was stolen. She was so upset she couldn't describe the thief to the police. Finally, the police asked her to **settle down**, relax and have a cup of water.

Settle for
(inseparable):

1. To accept what is offered, even though it is not what you really want; To accept less than what was expected, as in this example: *Rita advertised her car for $5000, but she **settled for** $4500 when a buyer made the offer.*

    More examples:
    - (1) The house was up for sale for $100,000, but the owner told the salesman to **settle for** a little less money to make a fast sale.
    - (1) Mika was hoping to get a perfect score on the exam, but she had to **settle for** 98% because of a small error she made.

Shake off
(separable):

1. To get rid of something; to free yourself of something, as in this example: *The dog came in from the rain and **shook** himself **off**. He made everything we around him!*

2. To deliberately ignore bad feelings or pain and, usually, continue doing what you were doing, as in this example: *The runner fell at the beginning of the competition but he __shook__ it __off__, got up and continued racing.*

   More examples:
   - (1) After two hours of hiking we arrived back at our cabin, __shook__ the mud __off__ of our shoes and then took them off.
   - (2) Marta felt a little sick when she began the exam, but she __shook__ it __off__ and worked hard to get a good grade.

__Shake up__
(separable):

1. To vigorously mix, as in this example: *I combined some oil and vinegar with some other ingredients, __shook__ them __up__ and made a nice salad dressing.*

2. The result of being badly frightened or emotionally upset by something or someone, as in this example: *The race car driver was __shaken up__ by the accident.*

3. To drastically reorganize or rearrange something, as in this example: *Company sales were down and the president __shook up__ the management. Some managers lost their jobs and other managers had to take a different position.*

   More examples:
   - (1) After putting the ingredients into the jar, Sarah put the lid on and __shook__ them __up__.
   - (2) The businessman was __shaken up__ by the sudden downturn in the economy.
   - (3) The voters in the country __shook up__ the government with a new leadership and many new faces. (Note: We use the word "faces" in English to mean people; "new faces" to mean who have never been in a certain position before.)

__Show off__
(separable):

1. To act or behave in a way that deliberately tries to bring the attention of others to yourself, as in this example: *The boy was riding his bicycle on only one wheel and __showing off__ to all the people that were watching.*

   More examples:
   - ❏ (1) Jean wanted to __*show off*__ her new clothes at the school party.
   - ❏ (2) Yolanda likes to __*show off*__ by riding her skateboard around town.

__*Show up*__
(separable):

1. To arrive somewhere, sometimes unexpectedly, or at an unexpected time, as in this example: *We had a birthday party for my aunt but she __showed up__ late.*

2. To do better than someone or something else, to surpass, as in this example: *We __showed up__ the competition by beating them 5 to 1.   3.* When something can be easily or clearly seen, as in this example: *When you've had too much alcohol to drink, alcohol __shows up__ in the blood during a test.   If too much alcohol shows up in your blood, the police will not allow you to drive your car.*

   More examples:
   - ❏ (1) The police __*showed up*__ just in time. The mugger tried to run away but the police caught him.
   - ❏ (2) The new student __*showed up*__ the class by getting the highest mark on the exam.
   - ❏ (3) When some professional athletes are tested, illegal drugs __*show up*__ in their blood and they are punished for violations.

__*Shut off*__
(separable):

1. To stop the flow of or passage of something, as in this example: *The cook filled the pot with water and then __shut off__ the faucet.*

2. To close off, or to block access or block passage, as in this example: *Access to the street was __shut off__ due to construction.*

   More examples:
   - ❏ (1) The damage from the storm __*shut off*__ the electricity.

❑ (2) The entrance to the building was ***shut off*** to the public because of a police investigation.

Shut up
(separable and inseparable depending on usage):

1. *(inseparable)* To stop talking, as in this example: *I told my sister to **shut up** when she said bad things about my boyfriend.*

2. *(separable)* To cause to stop talking, as in this example: *We didn't believe that she was a good student, but her high exam grade really **shut us up**.*

More examples:

❑ (1) The boy tried to explain why he as late but his father told him to ***shut up***.

❑ (2) My boss tried to ***shut*** me ***up*** when I told him that his information was incorrect.

Sign in
(separable):

1. To record your entrance by writing your name down on a piece of paper or by typing in a user ID or password (or both), as in this example: *Everyone was required to **sign in** before entering the exam room.*

More examples:

❑ (1) All guests were required to ***sign in*** at the check-in desk.

❑ (1) I asked my friend to ***sign*** me ***in***(to) the forum with his password and username.

Sign out
(separable):

1. To record you exit or departure from a formal meeting, a workplace or location by writing your name on a piece of paper, as in this example: *After the meeting, everyone was required to **sign out** before leaving.*

2. To register the removal of something like a book or merchandise, from a location, as in this example: *I **signed out** two really interesting books from the library.* 3. Sometimes used in radio communications when the speaker

informs the listener that he or she will no longer be talking, as in this example: *This is Ai Tanaka **signing out** until our broadcast next week at this time.*

More examples:

- ❑ (1) After using the employment services computer, you are required to ***sign out*** before leaving.

- ❑ (2) My sister ***signed out*** two library books about gardening.

- ❑ (3) The radio announcer ***signed out*** long after I went to sleep.

Sign up
(separable):

1. To agree to participate, or receive something by signing your name, as in this example: *I **signed up** for a two-week free trial of the gym membership.*

    More examples:

    - ❑ (1) My brother ***signed up*** to join the Army.

    - ❑ (1) Sarah ***signed up*** for the two week vacation in Trinidad.

Sit down
(separable or inseparable depending on usage):

1. *(inseparable)* To take a seat or to change your position to one of sitting, as in this example: *The students **sat down** when the teacher entered the room.*

2. *(separable)* To cause to be in a sitting position, usually when one person needs information from or needs to give advice or admonishment to another, as in this example: *The teacher **sat** the student **down** and gave him the bad news about his low grade on the exam.*

    More examples:

    - ❑ (1) I got on the bus and ***sat down***.

    - ❑ (2) The detective ***sat*** the criminal ***down*** and began to ask him some questions.

Slip up
(inseparable):

1. To make a mistake or error; the feeling of this expression is "accidental," as in this example: *I **slipped up** and got four wrong on the exam.*

More examples:

❑ (1) When you are mountain climbing, you cannot afford to ***slip up***.

❑ (1) I ***slipped up*** and told my brother about the ending to the movie before he had a chance to see it.

Slow down
(separable):

1. To move more slowly, to cause to move more slowly," as in this example: *We **slowed** the car **down** when we arrived in the city.*

   More examples:

   ❑ (1) The policeman ***slowed*** the traffic ***down*** around the accident.

   ❑ (1) I have been running around all day and now I just want to ***slow down*** and take a rest.

Sneak in(to)
(inseparable or separable depending on usage):

1. *(inseparable)* To enter a building, event, or restricted area without being seen or heard, as in this example: *Every Saturday night the kids would **sneak into** the dance party held at the beach club.*

2. *(separable)* To cause something or someone to enter someplace without the knowledge of those in authority, as in this example: *Two of the boys **sneaked** some alcohol **into** the party.*

   More examples:

   ❑ (1) The student was ten minutes late for class so he tried to ***sneak into*** class when the teacher's back was turned.

   ❑ (2) The man tried to ***sneak*** the package ***into*** the airplane but was caught by the stewardess.

Sneak out
(separable or inseparable depending on usage):

1. *(inseparable)* To leave a building, event, or restricted area without being seen or heard, as in this example: *Some of the boys sat near the door because they wanted to **sneak out** of class early.*

2. *(separable)* To cause something or someone to exit or depart someplace without the knowledge of those in authority, as in this example: *The refugees **sneaked** their families **out** of the country.*

More examples:

❑ (1) The girl tried to ***sneak out*** of the restaurant without paying her bill.

❑ (2) The man tried to ***sneak*** the drugs ***out*** of the country but was caught during the security check at the airport.

Sort out
(separable):

1. To solve or to try to understand a problem or difficulty, as in this example: *The teacher stopped the argument between the two students and tried to **sort out** what the problem was.*

2. To organize or separate things out into smaller, manageable groups, as in this example: *Before washing the clothes, my mother **sorted** them **out** according to color.*

More examples:

❑ (1) The customer was arguing with the store clerk, so the store manager came over to ***sort out*** the problem.

❑ (2) We had over 20 packages to mail, so we ***sorted*** them ***out*** according to destination and brought them to the post office.

Space out
(separable):

1. To separate things or people so as to be more or less equal distance from each other, as in this example: *When I came home from shopping, I **spaced** everything I bought **out** on the table.*

2. *(slang or informal)* To lose your focus or train of thought, to be confused about or forget something, as in this example: *While driving to work, I **spaced out** and turned down the wrong street.*

More examples:

❑ (1) I brought the mail into the house and ***spaced*** it ***out*** on the table so I could have a look at it.

❑ (2) Oh, I totally ***spaced out*** and forgot to invite my best friend to the party.

Stand around
(inseparable):

1. To stand here or there without purpose, without getting anything done; sometimes used when expressing frustration with workers not getting any work done, as in this example: *We have a lot of work to do and you guys are just **standing around**.*

   More examples:
   ❑ (1) I wasn't sure about what I was supposed to do, so I ***stood around*** for most of the day.
   ❑ (1) We just ***stood around*** waiting for our friends to arrive.

Stand for
(inseparable):

1. To tolerate or put up with, as in this example: *One thing that my teacher won't **stand for** is his students not doing their homework.*
2. To represent or to symbolize, as in this example: *The flag of your country **stands for** the unity of the people of your country.*

   More examples:
   ❑ (1) The people in our neighborhood won't ***stand for*** a lot of noise.
   ❑ (2) The symbol or the eagle on my company ID card ***stands for*** my company.

Stand up
(inseparable or separable, depending on usage):

1. *(inseparable)* To remain true or valid, sound or durable, as in this example: *The car looks good but it will not **stand up** to hard driving.*
2. *(separable)* To position yourself or something in an upright, standing, vertical position, as in this example: *The hunter **stood** his rifle **up** in the corner or his cabin.*

3. To speak out for, to fight for, or to defend something or someone, as in this example: *I **stood up** for my sister when she was accused of stealing because she is not a thief.*

   More examples:
   - (1) The book was old and falling apart. It didn't **stand up** well to repeated use.
   - (2) I **stood** the package **up** in the corner while I removed the wrapping.
   - (3) It is important for a person to **stand up** for his or her rights.

Start off
(inseparable):

1. Expresses: *the beginning* or *in the beginning*; to begin, as in this example: *We **started off** dinner with a nice salad.*

   More examples:
   - (1) My sister was in a bad mood, she **started off** the day by being late for school.
   - (1) The celebration **started off** very nicely, but it soon rained and everyone had to find shelter.

Start out
(inseparable):

1. Expresses "the beginning" or "in the beginning" usually as it relates to an action, event, or activity of some kind; we tend to use start out when we are talking about the beginning of an activity that was planned or when we are telling a store about what happened during an activity in the past, as in this example: *We **started out** by going to the Vatican when we were in Rome, but did not have time to see everything in Vatican City.*

   More examples:
   - (1) When you don't have experience with a new job, you usually **start out** by doing small, easy jobs until you have more knowledge.
   - (1) Most employees **start out** at a low salary and then gradually make more money as they become more experienced.

Start over
(separable):

1. To begin again; to do something over, to do something again after already having done it, as in this example: *After the great earthquake destroyed our business, we had to **start over** again.*

   More examples:
   - ❑ (1) The student asked the teacher if he could ***start*** the exam ***over*** because there was too much noise outside the classroom and he couldn't concentrate.
   - ❑ (1) I couldn't understand what the girl was saying so I asked her to ***start over*** and speak more slowly.

Start up
(separable):

1. To initiate something, usually a business, club, organization, or other formal group, as in this example: *After finishing school he **started up** a new business.*

2. To initiate the operation of a mechanical or electrical motor or computer, as in this example: *She **started up** the car engine and drove to the food market.*

   More examples:
   - ❑ (1) We ***started up*** a new club for English students.
   - ❑ (2) I pushed the button and ***started up*** the computer.

Stay off
(inseparable):

1. Many times used in demands or commands, ***stay off*** means to not step on, climb on or generally be on something else or on a restricted area, as in this example: *Please **stay off** the grass!*

2. To keep a distance from, as in this example: *Let's not talk about the negative things about our vacation; let's **stay off** that subject.*

   More examples:
   - ❑ (1) Please ***stay off*** the new bicycle until we have made all of the adjustments.

❏ (2) When we meet our friends tonight, let's not talk about work; let's ***stay off*** that subject.

Stay out
(inseparable):

1. To ***stay out*** of something means to distance yourself from something, to not get involved with something, often referring to a tricky or difficult problem or something involving other people besides yourself, as in this example: *My sister told me to **stay out** of her personal affairs; she said she could solve her own problems.*

2. To remain away from, usually, home or work, as in this example: *I asked my mother if I could **stay out** until 4am in the morning.*

   More examples:
   ❏ (1) My father warned me that it was always best to ***stay out*** of other people's affairs.
   ❏ (2) What a great party! We ***stayed out*** all night.

Stay up
(inseparable):

1. To remain awake beyond the time when you would normally go to bed, as in this example: *My sister and I **stayed up** to see the special program on TV.*

2. To remain at a certain elevation; to remain at a certain high position, as in this example: *With the strong winds, the kite **stayed up** for two hours.*

   More examples:
   ❏ (1) My family ***stayed up*** for the fourth of July all-night celebration.
   ❏ (2) The house was very old and rotted. We didn't know how long it would ***stay up***.

Step on
(inseparable):

1. To walk or tread on, as in this example: *Be careful not to **step on** any glass with your bare feet.*

2. Can also be used, as in a command, to mean to hurry up, go faster, or to increase speed, as in this example: *Come on, **step on** it! We have to hurry up and get ready if we want to arrive at the theater on time.*

   More examples:
   - ❑ (1) Be careful not to ***step on*** the cat's tail!
   - ❑ (2) We are going to have to ***step on*** it if we are going to arrive at school in time for the exam.

Stick around
(inseparable):

1. To remain somewhere longer than expected, as in this example: *After school was over, we **stuck around** for another hour.*

   More examples:
   - ❑ (1) Hey, ***stick around***; don't go home yet! We are going to have some coffee in about ten minutes.
   - ❑ (1) We ***stuck around*** after work because we wanted to finish our project.

Stick out
(inseparable):

1. To be obvious, to be prominent; something sticks out when it is more obvious than other things, as in this example: *His red pants really **stuck out**.*

2. Can also be used to express enduring something, or being patient with usually a long process, as in this example: *The show was so boring, but we **stuck** it **out** until the end.*

   More examples:
   - ❑ (1) I had wonderful memories of my vacation to Asia, but the memory that ***stuck out*** was of all of the beautiful temples.
   - ❑ (2) Work was boring today. After 3pm there was nothing to do; we had to ***stick*** it ***out*** until 5pm.

Stick to
(separable):

1. To continue doing, believing, or behaving in a certain way; *stick to* has the feeling of "not changing" or steadfastness, as in this example: *Even though his friend's idea sounded better, he decided to* **stick to** *his idea and do it his way.*

2. To remain attached to something, as in this example: *It just finished raining and mud was* **sticking to** *both sides of the car.*

3. To focus, to remain on subject, as in this example: *It is important for a writer to* **stick to** *the subject he is writing about and not distract the reader with other information.*

   More examples:
   - ❑ (1) If you feel you are right, then you must **stick to** your way of doing things.
   - ❑ (2) I **stuck** the announcement **to** the bulletin board with a thumb tack.
   - ❑ (3) The teacher told the students to **stick to** the subject in their essay and not write about things that had nothing to do with the topic.

Stick up
(separable):

1. To post or put up something for everyone to see, as in this example: *She* **stuck** *the notice* **up** *on the bulletin board.*

2. To rob, usually with a weapon, as in this example: *The robbers* **stuck up** *a bank and stole $2 million.*

3. To protrude or to be above a surface, as in this example: *Be careful not to step on the nails* **sticking up** *from the boards on the floor.*

   More examples:
   - ❑ (1) The teacher **stuck** the students' finished homework assignments **up** on the wall for everyone to see.
   - ❑ (2) The robber **stuck up** the tourist and took his wallet.
   - ❑ (3) We just removed the carpet in the living room. Be careful walking in that room because there are still some nails **sticking up** out of the floor.

Stick with
(separable and inseparable depending on usage):

1. *(inseparable)* To stick with something is to continue to do something the way you have always done it, as in this example: *My sister still **sticks with** her old way of making lamb curry, even though it is easier to make it my way.*

2. *(inseparable)* To continue to use something that you have been using, as in this example: *I'm not getting a new cellular phone. I'm going to **stick with** my old cellular phone because it is more reliable.*

3. *(inseparable)* To remain close to other people, as in this example: *It's really crowded here at the theater. **Stick with** me and I'll find our seats.*

4. *(separable)* To put someone in a position where they have to do something or endure something, as in this example: *I apologized to my colleague for **sticking** him **with** all the work. I had to go home early because of an emergency.*

More examples:
- (1) The people of that country have **stuck with** their traditions for hundreds of years.
- (2) I don't like a wireless mouse for my computer. I'm going to **stick with** the old style mouse with the wire attached.
- (3) The three orphans **stuck with** each other during their childhood.
- (4) The boss **stuck** the new employee **with** a big project.

Stop off
(inseparable):

1. As you travel to a destination you stop briefly to visit with or do something, as in this example: *On my way home, I **stopped off** at the grocery store to buy some eggs.*

More examples:
- (1) On my way to the supermarket I **stopped off** at my friend's house for a brief conversation.
- (1) On my way to school, I **stopped off** at the convenience store to buy some coffee.

Stop over
(inseparable):

1. As you travel to a destination, usually by plane, you stop briefly, and then continue on your way, as in this example: *On our way to Europe, we **stopped over** in Chicago for one night.*

   More examples:
   - ❑ (1) On our way to Asia, we ***stopped over*** in Hawaii for a couple of days.
   - ❑ (1) The plane ***stopped over*** in New York to make some repairs to the engine.

Straighten out
(separable):

1. To correct, to make correct, as in this example: *We had a problem with our airline ticket reservations but the clerk **straightened** it **out**.*

2. To make straight; to mechanically change a curved or crooked item so that it is straight, as in this example: *My car antenna was bent, so I **straightened** it **out**.*

3. *(informal)* To straighten someone out is to do or say something to someone that causes them to change their behavior or to understand something better, as in this example: *One of the students was acting foolishly so the teacher went over, said something to him, and **straightened** him **out**.*

   More examples:
   - ❑ (1) There was a misunderstanding about the homework assignment, but the teacher ***straightened*** us ***out*** about it.
   - ❑ (2) Marcus ***straightened out*** his rear bicycle wheel by tightening up some of the spokes.
   - ❑ (3) One of the students was throwing paper at another student until the teacher came over and ***straightened*** him ***out*** about his behavior.

Straighten up
(separable):

1. To clean up or organize something, as in this example: *My mother told me to **straighten up** my room.*

2. To change something that is bent or crooked to being straight, as in this example: *Your drawing is good but some of the lines are crooked. Please **straighten up** your lines.*

More examples:

❑ (1) Before we can have a party, we have to ***straighten up*** our apartment.

❑ (2) Students, please sit straight in your chairs. Do not curve or hunch your backs, please. Please ***straighten up*** in your seats.

Stress out
(separable):

1. *(informal)* To be worried, anxious or nervous about something, as in this example: *I was really **stressed out** about adopting a child from the orphanage.*

   More examples:

   ❑ (1) The students were ***stressed out*** about taking the important exam.

   ❑ (1) Some of the members of our soccer team were really ***stressed out*** about the upcoming game.

Switch off
(separable):

1. To stop the power to something, to turn off, to stop the operation of something, as in this example: *When we left the classroom, we **switched off** the lights.*

   More examples:

   ❑ (1) After cutting the grass, Toshiko ***switched off*** the lawn mower and put it back in the garage.

   ❑ (1) When you are finished using the computer, please ***switch*** it ***off***. Thank you.

Switch on
(separable):

1. To allow power to energize something, to turn something on, to begin the operation of something, as in this example: *Upon entering the classroom, we **switched on** the lights.*

   More examples:

   ❑ (1) Jean went into the computer room and ***switched on*** the computer.

   ❑ (1) Please put the dishes in the dishwasher and then ***switch*** it ***on***.

Chapter 11 review
Phrasal verbs beginning with the letter S

*Instructions: read and /or listen carefully to the sentences below. Fill in the blank spaces with the correct **preposition, particle,** or **adverb**. The answers can be found in this chapter (above).*

1. We screwed the part _____ the car motor and then started ____ the motor.

2. I screwed ___ and got a bad grade on the exam.

3. I went to see my doctor _____ my sore arm.

4. After cutting the grass, Toshiko switched ____ the lawn mower and put it back in the garage.

5. The students were stressed _____ about taking the important exam.

6. Before we can have a party, we have to straighten ___ our apartment.

7. Marcus straightened ____ his rear bicycle wheel by tightening up some of the spokes.

8. My classmates sold me ____ and told the teacher I didn't hand in the homework assignment.

9. The students set ___ a table at the science fair.

10. In 1492 Columbus set ___ to find a shorter route to India.

11. The salesman traveled from city to city for his job, but dreamed about the day when he could settle _____ in one location.

12. The boy tried to explain why he as late but his father told him to shut ____.

13. All guests were required to sign ___ at the check-in desk.

14. I have been running around all day and now I just want to slow _____ and take a rest.

15. The man tried to sneak the package _____ the airplane but was caught by the stewardess.

16. The customer was arguing with the store clerk, so the store manager came over to sort _____ the problem.

17. I brought the mail into the house and spaced it _____ on the table so I could have a look at it.

18. We just stood _____ waiting for our friends to arrive.

19. It is important for a person to stand _____ for his or her rights.

20. My sister was in a bad mood, she started _____ the day by being late for school.

Answers: (1) into . . . up; (2) up; (3) about (4) off (5) out; (6) up; (7) out; (8) out; (9) up (10) out; (11) down; (12) up (13) in; (14) down (15) into; (16) out; (17) out; (18) around (19) up; (20) out

Chapter 12 *Phrasal verbs beginning with the letter T*

In this section you will learn how to use many different phrasal verbs beginning with the letter T correctly in a sentence.

There are two kinds of phrasal verbs, separable and inseparable. Separable phrasal verbs can take an object between the verb and the preposition. For example: *My father **picked** **me** **up** after school and drove me home.* Inseparable phrasal verbs cannot take an object between the verb and the preposition. For example: I asked my friends to **come along** with me to the Christmas party. **Come along** cannot be separated by an object.

The numbers in front of the examples that are in parenthesis (), correspond the to number of the explanation found directly above. So, for example: 1. *explanation . . .* refers to (1) *example . . . .* . If there is only one explanation or meaning given for the phrasal verb, then there will be two examples given for the one explanation. Both examples will be marked with (1).

If you have the Focus on English digital audio book version of this book (available separately from www.FOEBooks.com) listen to each of the phrasal verbs, followed by their meanings and then some examples of how they are used in real English sentences.

There will be a review at the end of this chapter.

Phrasal verbs beginning with the letter T

Read and / or listen carefully to the examples, as they will give you a good idea as to how to use the phrasal verb in real English sentences.

Take apart
(separable):

1. To disassemble, to separate into pieces, as in this example: *The workman **took** the washing machine **apart** so that he could repair it.*

2. To dissect for the purpose of analyzing something; to analyze something, as in this example: *The committee took the idea apart to see if there were any problems with it. (Here, take apart, means "analyze.")*

   More examples:
   - ❑ (1) My alarm clock stopped working so I ***took*** it ***apart*** to see if I could repair it.
   - ❑ (2) Our class project was about the idea of freedom. Our group had to ***take apart*** the idea of freedom and then make a presentation about this topic to the class.

Take in
(separable):

1. To accept or receive someone or something as a guest, employee, or an adopted member of the family, as in this example: *My parents **took in** a little boy who lost his parents.*

2. To diminish in size or make smaller; to decrease the size of something, a diameter or overall width, as in this example: *The seamstress **took in** the girl's dress. (Note: A seamstress is a person who sews clothing, makes changes to clothing, or makes new clothing.)*

3. To include as part of something else, as in this example: *The exam **takes in** all of the irregular past tense English verbs.*

4. To deceive, cheat, swindle, defraud someone, as in this example: *The old people were **taken in** by a con artist. They lost all of their money.*

5. To look at or view thoroughly, to look and to take the time to understand what you are looking at; sometimes used to express a sightseeing excursion, as in this example: *Last year we went to Rome and **took in** the sights.*

   More examples:
   - ❑ (1) Last week, Myoung Hoon ***took in*** a stray cat and gave it a new home.
   - ❑ (2) The tailor ***took in*** the man's pants so that they would fit better. (Meaning: A tailor is a man who sews clothing. A seamstress is a

woman who sews clothing. Sometimes clothing is too big for a person, so a tailor or seamstress will change the size of the clothing by making it smaller in places, by taking it in, so that the clothing will feel more comfortable to the person who wears it.)

❑ (3) The new immigration form *takes in* all of the applicant's background information.

❑ (4) My friend Blake discovered that the tickets that he bought for the big soccer match were no good. A swindler *had taken* him *in*. (Meaning: a swindler is a person who deceives others, often taking money from people but giving nothing of value back.)

❑ (5) As I walked into the new building, I slowly *took in* everything that I saw.

Take off
(separable):

1. To remove something from something or someone, as in this example: *The woman **took off** her jacket and put it on the chair.*

2. To give a discount, to deduct some money from a price, as in this example: *Janice bought a dress at the mall. The store **took** 20% **off** the regular price.*

3. *(slang)* To go off in a hurry, as in this example: *Stefan really **took off** when he realized that he was late for class.*

4. Used to talk about a plane leaving the ground, as in this example: *The plane **took off** for Hawaii at 6pm.*

5. To withdraw or discontinue something, as in this example: *The restaurant **took** the tomato soup **off** the menu.*

6. To become very popular, usually a book, movie or music, as in this example: *The movie really **took off**. On the very first day, the movie earned 75 million dollars.*

More examples:

❑ (1) The man entered the building and *took off* his raincoat.

❑ (2) The saleslady *took* 10% *off* of the cost of the clothing because we shop there often.

- ❑ (3) When the robber saw the police coming, he really ***took off***.

- ❑ (4) When the plane ***took off***, I knew that our vacation began.

- ❑ (5) The school ***took*** Mark's name ***off*** of the activities list because he was sick.

- ❑ (6) The new magazine became popular quickly; it really ***took off***!

Take on
(separable):

1. To accept or begin an activity, responsibility, or action, as in this example: *Our group **took on** the responsibility of completing the business project.*

2. To challenge someone or something, as in this example: *Our soccer team **took on** the opposition from across town.*

3. To hire, usually for employment, as in this example: *The company **took on** three new employees.*

   More examples:
   - ❑ (1) The new employee ***took on*** a big workload.
   - ❑ (2) The Dallas Cowboy football team ***took on*** the Miami Dolphin football team.
   - ❑ (3) My boss ***took on*** two more employees to help with the project.

Take out
(separable):

1. To remove something from something or somewhere, or withdraw something, as in this example: *The doctor took the splinter out of my foot.*

2. To apply for and receive a license, permit, or other formal authorization, as in this example: *In our State, you have to **take out** a license before you can hunt.*

3. To escort, as on a romantic date, as in this example: *I **took** my girlfriend **out** to the movies last night.*

4. To let out or vent your emotional feelings on someone or something, as in this example: *Mary did poorly on the exam. When she got home she **took** her frustration **out on** the dog. The dog had no idea why Mary was yelling at him.*

   More examples:

- ❑ (1) We ***took*** the fast food ***out*** and ate it at the park.

- ❑ (2) In most cities, you have to ***take out*** a special permit in order to build a house.

- ❑ (3) I ***took*** my wife ***out*** for our anniversary.

- ❑ (4) I couldn't believe that the policeman gave me a ticket. When I got home, I was in a bad mood. I ***took*** my anger ***out on*** everyone who talked to me.

Take over
(separable):

1. To assume control of, or management of, something, as in this example: *A new manager **took over** our department.*

   More examples:
   - ❑ (1) A new company ***took over*** the management of the building.
   - ❑ (1) When mom was on vacation, dad ***took over*** the care of the children.

Take to
(inseparable):

1. To like something, or to become attached to something, as in this example: *The family really **took to** their new home, meeting neighbors and making new friends.*

2. To escape to, seek refuge or seek safety, as in this example: *The flood waters were rising quickly. Everyone had to **take to** the hills.*

   More examples:
   - ❑ (1) Rafael really ***took to*** his brand new car.
   - ❑ (2) The military invasion forced the refugees to ***take to*** safer territory over the border.

Take up
(separable):

1. To raise something; to make something higher as with clothing alteration, as in this example: *The seamstress **took up** the hem on Sally's dress because it was too long.*

2. To accept a bet or a challenge; usually used with the preposition ***on***, as in this example: *I **took** him **up** on his bet that I couldn't finish the marathon.*

   (*Meaning: Someone bet me that I could not finish the marathon. I said that I could. I **took** him **up** on his bet, meaning I accepted his bet. If I finish the marathon, then he has to pay me money.*)

3. To begin again, to resume something, as in this example: *This discussion is very important but we have to go to class now. Let's **take** this **up** later when we have time.*

4. To use up or exhaust something; to use up room or space, as in this example: *We can only fit thirty people in this room. More than that will **take up** too much space.*

5. To develop an interest in something, like a hobby, activity, sport, etc., as in this example: *I **took up** skiing last year and now I really like it.*

   More examples:
   - (1) The tailor ***took up*** the hem on Jim's new pants.
   - (2) Hiro bet me $5.00 I couldn't jump over that fence. I ***took him*** up on his bet.
   - (3) Look, it's getting late and we should talk about this more. Let's ***take*** this ***up*** again tomorrow afternoon at the coffee shop.
   - (4) I'm sorry, but there is no more sugar. We baked a cake last night and that ***took up*** all the sugar that we had.
   - (5) My wife ***took up*** knitting. She is now knitting a new blanket for our bed.

Talk down to
(inseparable):

1. To talk to someone with insulting, belittling condescension; to let someone know that you think very little of them; at act of superiority, as in this example: *The owner of the large home often **talked down to** his servants.*

   More examples:
   - (1) The student who had the highest grade on the exam often ***talked down to*** the other students.

❏ (1) The famous actress would sometimes ***talk down to*** her fans.

Talk into
(separable):

1. To convince someone to do something that they probably didn't want to do, as in this example: *My friend **talked** me **into** going with him to the horror movie. I usually don't watch horror movies.*

   More examples:
   ❏ (1) My wife ***talked*** me ***into*** going shopping with her.
   ❏ (1) My sister ***talked*** me ***into*** helping her wash the dishes.

Talk out of
(separable):

1. To convince someone not to do something that sometimes they felt they needed to do, as in this example: *My friend **talked** me **out of** going with him to the horror movie because he wanted to be alone with his girlfriend. I really wanted to see that movie.*

   More examples:
   ❏ (1) My boss ***talked*** me ***out of*** quitting my job.
   ❏ (1) Sun Wa ***talked*** her friend, Christina, ***out of*** spending money on a new car.

Tear down
(separable):

1. To demolish, raze, or level something to the ground, as in this example: *The construction team **tore down** the building so that they could build a new one.*
2. Sometimes used to mean 'take something apart,' usually a motor, as in this example: *The mechanic **tore down** the engine to see what was wrong with it.*

   More examples:
   ❏ (1) Hey, what happened to your house? Oh, they ***tore*** it ***down***. They are going to build a new one starting next week.
   ❏ (2) We ***tore down*** the motorcycle engine and put new parts in it.

Tear off
(separable):

1. To rip or remove with force, something that is flexible, as in this example: *My brother **tore** the top **off** of the cereal box.*

2. *(informal)* To leave hurriedly, as in this example: *The kids **tore off** when they heard the ice cream truck coming.*

   More examples:
   - ❑ (1) The workers **tore** the **roof** off of the house so that they could put a new one on.
   - ❑ (2) The orphan stole an apple from the fruit stand and then **tore off** into the crowd.

Tear up
(separable):

1. To rip something up, as paper, cardboard or other flexible material, as in this example: *Walter Lu **tore up** the bill from the water company because he already paid them.*

2. *(informal)* To have a wild party or celebration that ends up damaging the party area, as in this example: *The students partied all night long. They had a great time, but they really **tore up** the place.*

   More examples:
   - ❑ (1) She was so angry about her grades that she **tore up** her grades report.
   - ❑ (2) The guests had a too much alcohol to drink and the party got very wild. They really **tore up** the party room and the pool area.

Tell apart
(separable):

1. To see the difference between one thing or person and another, to distinguish between, as in this example: *The twins were identical. I couldn't **tell** them **apart**.*

   More examples:
   - ❑ (1) I don't taste any difference between this drink and that drink. I can't **tell** them **apart**.

❏ (1) I can't remember the names of the two cats. They are so similar, I can't *tell* them *apart*.

Think about
(inseparable):

1. To spend time considering something; to focus on something in your thoughts, as in this example: *After the exam, I thought about the questions that I might have gotten wrong.*

   More examples:

   ❏ (1) The salesman wanted to sell me the computer, but I wanted to *think about* it first.

   ❏ (1) Before getting married, you need to *think about* it. (Meaning: Carefully consider what it means to be married.)

Think ahead
(inseparable):

1. When thinking about something, think about what might be needed in the future or what the consequences of an action will be in the future or what will happen in the future, as in this example: *When starting a new business, always* ***think ahead***.

   More examples:

   ❏ (1) When planning a project, *think ahead*. What will the problems be? What will you need to complete the project?

   ❏ (1) If you *think ahead*, you will avoid a lot of problems.

Think over
(separable):

1. To consider carefully, as in this example: *Before I buy this new house, I want to* ***think*** *it* ***over***.

   More examples:

   ❏ (1) Don't quit your job yet. ***Think*** it ***over***, maybe you can find a way to get the things you want at your company.

❑   (1) My teacher gave me a choice: take the exam, or stay at the same level for the next term. I have to ***think*** this ***over***.

Throw away
(separable):

1. To discard something or dispose of something, as in this example: *After opening the present, I **threw away** the gift-wrapping.*

2. To foolishly discard something, as in this example: *He **threw away** his whole life because of his drug habit.*

   More examples:
   ❑   (1) Bridget ***threw away*** the old batteries and installed new ones in her MP3 player.

   ❑   (2) After he got angry with his boss, he knew he ***threw away*** his chance at a promotion.

Throw out
(separable):

1. To discard something or dispose of something that is not needed, as in this example: *After opening the present, I **threw out** the gift-wrapping.*

2 To force someone to leave a place or a position, especially in an abrupt manner, as in this example: *The judge at the tennis match **threw** the player **out** of the game because the player was not following the rules.*

3. Used to talk about the cause of a pain or an injury, usually when doing something physical; when bones in a part of the body are not properly lined up or out of alignment, as in this example: *I **threw** my back **out** yesterday carrying that heavy sofa.*

4. In the sport of baseball, a player puts another player out by touching him with the ball, as in this example: *The First baseman **threw out** the runner.*

   More examples:
   ❑   (1) I opened the package of gum and ***threw out*** the wrapper.

   ❑   (2) The people did not like the new leader and ***threw*** him ***out*** of office during the next election.

   ❑   (3) The woman ***threw out*** her back when she lifted the child.

❑ (4) The pitcher ***threw out*** the runner on second base.

Throw up
(separable or inseparable depending on usage):

1. *(inseparable)* To vomit, as in this example: *After drinking whiskey all night, Kelly got sick and **threw up** in the bathroom.*

2. *(separable)* To build something very quickly and without care, as in this example: *The house was poorly built; they **threw** it **up** in about a week.*

   More examples:

   ❑ (1) Alicia was sick all day. She ***threw up*** twice.

   ❑ (2) The building was hastily constructed. They ***threw*** it ***up*** in three weeks. We don't think that it is safe.

Track down
(separable):

1. To find someone or something after searching, as in this example: *We finally **tracked down** the sales report. We couldn't find it for two weeks.*

   More examples:

   ❑ (1) The reporter ***tracked*** the politician ***down*** and asked him some questions.

   ❑ (1) Our company has spent a lot of time ***tracking down*** an electronics engineer.

Trade in
(separable):

1. Some businesses will accept an older item as partial payment towards a new item purchased from them, as in this example: *When we bought our new car we got a discount because we **traded in** our old car.*

   More examples:

   ❑ (1) The computer store allowed me to ***trade in*** my old laptop as partial payment for a new one.

   ❑ (1) Our school allows us to ***trade in*** our old text books for newer ones. We can save a lot of money on books this way.

Trick into
(separable):

1. Similar in meaning to con into; to use deceit, or to fool someone into doing something they probably would not have done, as in this example: *The salesman **tricked** me **into** buying a used car that needed repairs.*

   More examples:
   ❑ (1) On April fools day I was **tricked into** believing that there was no school the next day.

   ❑ (1) Be careful of con men, because they will **trick** you **into** buying things that are worthless.

Try on
(separable):

1. To wear a piece of clothing to test it, to see if it fits properly and it looks good on you, as in this example: *My friend **tried on** the new shirt, but it didn't fit and the color was ugly.*

   More examples:
   ❑ (1) Rita Chen **tried on** the new dress and she loved it.
   ❑ (1) Mark **tried on** the pants but they were too big.

Try out
(separable):

1. To use or test something before purchasing it or before committing to it, as in this example: *Alex **tried out** the new skis, but he didn't like them.*

2. When you want to join a competition or team, sometimes you have to demonstrate your abilities in a qualifying test; to demonstrate to qualify for an athletic event or team, as in this example: *Before joining the bicycle club, you have to **try out** by riding 25 miles in just one hour. If you can't do this, you can't join the club.*

   More examples:
   ❑ (1) Tom **tried out** the new surfboard before he purchased it from the store.

❑ (2) Sue Chan ***tried out*** for the swimming team and made it. ("Made it" means that she was successful.)

Turn around
(separable):

1. To reverse your direction, to change your orientation completely, or to look in the opposite direction, as in this example: *Oh no, you drove past the theater!* ***Turn around*** *and go back.*

2. To change the condition of something or a situation for the positive, as in this example: *Last year we were losing money in our business, but this year we have* ***turned around*** *and made a profit.*

More examples:

❑ (1) ***Turn around*** and look who is coming towards us.

❑ (2) Our team was losing the game, but in the last five minutes we have completely ***turned around***. Now we are winning.

Turn down
(separable):

1. To decline or refuse to accept something; usually used when someone makes you an offer, as in this example: *Rodney made me an offer of $10,000 for my car, but I* ***turned*** *him* ***down*** *because the offer was too low.*

2. To reduce or diminish the speed, volume, intensity or flow of something, as in this example: ***Turn down*** *the volume on that radio, it's too loud!*

More examples:

❑ (1) My friend offered to drive me to the concert, but I ***turned*** him ***down*** because my girlfriend is going to drive me there.

❑ (2) There is too much water flowing into the swimming pool; please ***turn*** the water ***down***!

Turn in
(separable):

1. To return or hand something back, similar to *hand in*, as in this example: *The students* ***turned in*** *their homework.*

2. To alert the authorities, the police or other public agency, about where a criminal is hiding or is located; also used when you have captured a wanted criminal and you deliver the criminal to the police, as in this example: *I spotted the thief going into an apartment so I called the police and **turned** him **in***.

More examples:

❑ (1) After I finished filling out the form, I ***turned*** it ***in*** to the clerk.

❑ (2) The police are offering a $1,000 reward for the capture of the bandit. If you ***turn*** this bandit ***in*** you get $1,000!

Turn into
(separable):

1. To become, or change into, to change, as in this example: *After the man drank the smoking chemical he **turned into** a monster!*

More examples:

❑ (1) It was raining this morning, but now it's sunny; boy, it's really ***turned into*** a nice day!

❑ (1) Wow, the construction company did a good job of restoring that old building; they ***turned*** it ***into*** something very beautiful.

Turn off
(separable):

1. To stop the operation of something, like a mechanical or electrical device, or stop the flow of something, or to shut off, as in this example: *Before leaving the factory, we **turned off** the machines and then turned off the lights.*

2. To leave, divert off of, or move off of a path, road, or route that you had been traveling, as in this example: *We **turned off** the road at the second stop light and then drove into the driveway.*

3. *(informal)* When something or someone causes you to feel dislike, displeasure, revulsion, or boredom, as in this example: *We were really **turned off** by the movie. It was so boring.*

More examples:

❑ (1) It's 2 o'clock in the morning, would you please ***turn off*** your television!

❑ (2) Travel down Main Street until you get to 5th Avenue, then ***turn off*** at 5th Avenue and travel for 5 miles. The library is on your right .

❑ (3) Alison was really ***turned off*** by the group of people at the pub, so she left early.

Turn on
(separable):

1. To start or initiate the operation of something, like a mechanical or electrical device, or start the flow of something, or to switch on, as in this example: *Upon entering the factory, we **turned on** the lights and then turned on the machines.*

2. To leave, divert off of, or move off of a path, road, or route that you had been traveling on and then onto another road, path, route or street, as in this example: *We **turned on** to Queen Street from Cyprus Boulevard.*

3. *(informal)* To excite or interest, , as in this example: *We were really **turned on** by the movie. It was well done.*

   More examples:
   ❑ (1) It's 8 o'clock in the morning, would you please ***turn on*** the news.

   ❑ (2) Travel down Main Street until you get to 5th Avenue, then ***turn onto*** 5th Avenue and travel for 5 miles. The library is on your right.

   ❑ (3) Alison was really ***turned on*** by all of the interesting people at the party.

Turn out
(inseparable or separable depending on usage):

1. *(separable)* Similar to turn off, put usually refers to lights, as in this example: *Please **turn out** the lights when you leave the classroom.*

2. *(inseparable)* Used to talk about the number of people arriving and being at an event, as in this example: *Many people **turned out** for the birthday celebration.*

3. *(separable)* To produce or manufacture, as in this example: *The automobile company **turns out** thousands of vehicles every year.*

4. *(inseparable)* To discover that someone or something is a certain way, as in this example: *The student **turned out** to be a nice person and a hard worker.*

5. *(inseparable)* To end up, to result in, as in this example: *We didn't think the pizza would be good, but actually the pizza **turned out** to be delicious.*

More examples:

- (1) We have too many lights on in the house. Please **turn out** the lights in the living room.
- (2) Over 400 people **turned out** for the political meeting.
- (3) The computer company **turns out** thousands of computers every month.
- (4) We thought the policeman was going to me nasty, but he **turned out** to be a good guy.
- (5) The cake **turned out** good even though we didn't put enough sugar in it.

Turn over
(separable):

1. To give something to someone, usually with the meaning to surrender something to someone else, as in this example: *When I left the company, I had to **turn over** the keys to the office to the boss.*

2. Used to talk about the rate at which employees leave and join a company; when one person leaves a company and a new person is hired, as in this example: *The fast food company **turned over** its employees very quickly. Sometimes there were two new positions open every week.*

3. To change the position of something so that the bottom becomes the top and the top the bottom, as in this example: *The cook **turned** the sausages **over** so that both sides would cook evenly.*

4. Can be used to express the rate of sales of an item, as in this example: *That item **turns over** very quickly, so it is very important to order more as soon as possible.*

More examples:

❑ (1) The punishment for drinking and driving is the loss of your driver's license. You have to ***turn*** your license ***over*** to the authorities if you are caught drinking and driving.

❑ (2) The company was difficult to work for and they ***turned*** their employees ***over*** very quickly.

❑ (3) When you make pan cakes you have to ***turn*** them ***over*** so that both sides cook.

❑ (4) The unagi sushi sells very quickly; lots of people buy it and it ***turns over*** very quickly. Because of this, we have to make a lot of unagi sushi.

Turn up
(inseparable or separable depending on usage):

1. *(separable)*To increase the volume level or level of energy, as in the volume of a radio or other electronic device, as in this example: *I can't hear what they are saying on the TV, could you **turn** it **up**?*

2. *(inseparable)* To show up, appear, to arrive somewhere, as in this example: *A lot of people **turned up** for the party. I hope we have enough food.*

More examples:

❑ (1) Please ***turn up*** the news, that sounds interesting. (Note: Americans say ***turn up*** the news, or turn up the announcement when they mean ***turn up*** the volume of the radio or TV that is playing the news or announcement.)

❑ (2) Fifteen people ***turned up*** for the ceremony.

Chapter 12 <u>review</u>
Phrasal verbs beginning with the letter T

*Instructions: read and /or listen carefully to the sentences below. Fill in the blank spaces with the correct **preposition, particle,** or **adverb**. The answers can be found in this chapter (above).*

1. My alarm clock stopped working so I took it _____ to see if I could repair it.

2. Fifteen people turned ___ for the ceremony.

3. The company was difficult to work for and they turned their employees _____ very quickly.

4. The cake turned _____ good even though we didn't put enough sugar in it.

5. It's 8 o'clock in the morning, would you please turn _____ the news.

6. The workers tore the roof _____ of the house so that they could put a new one on.

7. She was so angry about her grades that she tore _____ her grades report.

8. I don't taste any difference between this drink and that drink. I can't tell them _____.

9. The salesman wanted to sell me the computer, but I wanted to think _____ it first.

10. The famous actress would sometimes talk _____ to her fans.

11. The tailor took _____ the hem on Jim's new pants.

12. My wife talked me _____ going shopping with her.

13. My boss talked me _____ of quitting my job.

14. If you think _____, you will avoid a lot of problems.

15. Don't quit your job yet. Think it _____, maybe you can find a way to get the things you want at your company.

16. Bridget threw _____ the old batteries and installed new ones in her MP3 player.

17. The woman threw _____ her back when she lifted the child.

18. Alicia was sick all day. She threw ___ twice.

19. The reporter tracked the politician _____ and asked him some questions.

20. The computer store allowed me to trade _____ my old laptop as partial payment for a new one.

Answers: (1) apart (2) out; (3) around (4) out (5) on; (6) off; (7) up; (8) apart; (9) about (10) down; (11) up; (12) into (13) out; (14) ahead (15) over; (16) out; (17) out; (18) up (19) down; (20) in

Chapter 13 *Phrasal verbs beginning with the letter U, W, and Z*

In this section you will learn how to use many different phrasal verbs beginning with the letters U, W, and Z correctly in a sentence.

There are two kinds of phrasal verbs, separable and inseparable. Separable phrasal verbs can take an object between the verb and the preposition. For example: *My father **picked** me **up** after school and drove me home.* Inseparable phrasal verbs cannot take an object between the verb and the preposition. For example: I asked my friends to ***come along*** with me to the Christmas party. ***Come along*** cannot be separated by an object.

The numbers in front of the examples that are in parenthesis (), correspond the to number of the explanation found directly above. So, for example: 1. *explanation . . .* refers to (1) *example . . . .* If there is only one explanation or meaning given for the phrasal verb, then there will be two examples given for the one explanation. Both examples will be marked with (1).

If you have the Focus on English digital audio book version of this book (available separately from www.FOEBooks.com) listen to each of the phrasal verbs, followed by their meanings and then some examples of how they are used in real English sentences.

There will be a review at the end of this chapter.

Phrasal verbs beginning with the letters U, W, and Z

Read and / or listen carefully to the examples, as they will give you a good idea as to how to use the phrasal verb in real English sentences.

Use up
(separable):

1. To exhaust the supply of something, as in this example: *I **used up** all of the milk. Is the store still open? I need to get some milk.*

    More examples:
    - ❑   (1) I'm tired. I think I've ***used up*** all of my energy.
    - ❑   (1) In another 3 miles we will have ***used up*** all of our gas.

Wake up
(separable):

1. To awaken, to arouse from sleep, to stop sleeping, as in this example: *I **woke up** at 4 o'clock this morning. I'm really tired.*

2. Sometimes used to express a sudden awareness of something, as in this example: *That exam really **woke** me **up**. I need to study harder.*

    More examples:
    - ❑   (1) My mother ***woke*** me ***up*** to tell me it was time to get ready for the party.
    - ❑   (2) The people keep voting for the wrong leader. They need to ***wake up*** before it is too late.

Warm up
(separable):

1. To make warm; usually used to refer to food and drink, but sometimes refers to people and objects, as in this example: *When I came into the house I **warmed up** a cup of tea.*

2. Sometimes used to express getting more comfortable with someone or something, as in this example: *I **warmed up** to the new committee and became a member.*

    More examples:
    - ❑   (1) Would you please ***warm up*** some coffee for me, I'm late for work.
    - ❑   (2) My friend ***warmed up*** to the idea of playing soccer for another team. He was ready for a change.

Wash off
(separable):

1. To remove dirt, soil, or other undesirable marks or contaminants from something, as in this example: *The car was dirty so I **washed** it **off** with soap and water.*

   More examples:
   - ❑ (1) My father **washed** the salt water **off** the boat after fishing all day.
   - ❑ (1) I **washed off** my car windshield after the long trip.

Wash up
(separable):

1. To clean up, often with soap and water, as in this example: *I **washed up** the fruit and then put it on the table.*

2. To float onto the shore after being in the water for a period of time, as in this example: *The bottle **washed up** onto the shore. Inside the bottle there was a message.*

   More examples:
   - ❑ (1) After dinner, I **washed up** and then went to bed.
   - ❑ (2) There is too much pollution that **washes up** onto the shore.

Watch out
(inseparable):

1. To be vigilant, alert or aware, as in this example: ***Watch out** for the bus, it comes this way every hour.*

2. Used to express the need to be cautious or careful, as in this example: ***Watch out** for falling rocks!*

   More examples:
   - ❑ (1) **Watch out** for the B train, it should be coming through here any moment.
   - ❑ (2) **Watch out**, don't take another step; there's a snake over there!

Wear down
(separable):

1. To breakdown or exhaust by pressure or resistance; become increasingly tired or worn, as in this example: *All of this homework every day is starting to **wear** me **down***.

2. Sometimes used to talk about the process of persuading someone to do or believe something, as in this example: *At first, I didn't want to buy the vacuum cleaner from the salesman, but eventually he **wore** me **down** and I bought one.*

   More examples:
   - ❑ (1) John and Naoko drove their car across the United States. When the arrived in California they discovered that they had **worn down** their tires quite a bit.

   - ❑ (2) Our daughter wanted to stay out late but we didn't think it was a good idea. She asked us many times during the day if she could stay out late and eventually she **wore** us **down** and we said yes.

Wear off
(inseparable):

1. When the effect of something gradually diminishes or gets smaller, as in this example: *The effects of the alcohol gradually **wore off***.

   More examples:
   - ❑ (1) When the drug **wore off**, I really felt pain.

   - ❑ (1) I drank too much coffee. I was glad when the effects of the caffeine finally **wore off**.

Wear out
(separable):

1. To become or to cause something to become unusable or weak, as in this example: *I **wore out** the brakes in my car by traveling down steep hills and mountains.*

2. To become tired, as in this example: *We played soccer all afternoon. We really **wore** ourselves **out**.*

   More examples:
   - ❑ (1) I have to get a new CD player. I **wore out** the old one by playing it so much.

❑ (2) Grandfather had to take a nap. His grandchildren **_wore_** him **_out_** playing in the yard.

Wind up
(separable or inseparable depending on usage):

1. *(inseparable)* Similar to end up or finish up; to experience the results or consequence of something because of something you did, as in this example: *We took the wrong road to town and **wound up** in a place we weren't familiar with.*

2. *(separable)* Similar to wrap up; to take the necessary action to complete something or to cause to come to the end of something, as in this example: *We **wound up** our meeting by shaking hands.*

3. *(separable)* To turn the key or handle on something that is usually attached to a spring, like in a child's toy car, as in this example: *The boy **wound up** his little toy car and then put it on the ground and watched it race away.*

4. *(separable)* To wrap something like rope, line or tape around something like a cylinder or other object, as in this example: *After we flew the kite, we **wound up** the string and went home.*

5. *(inseparable)* In baseball, when the pitcher prepare to throw a ball at the batter, as in this example: *The pitcher **wound up** and then threw a fast ball at the batter.*

   More examples:
   ❑ (1) I didn't study for the exam and **_wound up_** getting a failing grade.
   ❑ (2) Our team **_wound up_** the game with a winning goal.
   ❑ (3) My friend had an old watch that had to be **_wound up_** in order for it to continue to work.
   ❑ (4) The sailor **_wound_** the line **_up_** around a post on the ship.
   ❑ (5) The pitcher **_wound up_** and threw a curve ball.

Wipe off
(separable):

1. To clean a surface; to remove liquid, dirt, dust or other material from a surface, as in this example: *After we finished dinner, I **wiped off** the table.*

More examples:

- ❏ (1) After traveling through the dusty countryside, I **_wiped_** the dust **_off_** the car.

- ❏ (2) We cleaned up the bedroom yesterday. We vacuumed the floor and **_wiped off_** the shelves.

Wipe up
(separable):

1. Usually used to mean a brief cleaning up; sometimes when you spill liquid you wipe it up; to clean up here and there, as in this example: *After feeding the baby, the mother had to **wipe up** around the baby's table.*

   More examples:

   - ❏ (1) These vinyl seats are easy to take care of. If you spill something on them all you have to do is **_wipe_** it **_up_** with a clean towel.

   - ❏ (1) We **_wiped up_** the kitchen after breakfast and then went to the beach.

Work in(to)
(separable):

1. To introduce or insert something or someone into something else like a conversation, a plan, project, or activity, as in this example: *We have to find a way to **work** John **into** the plan.* (Meaning: *We have to find a way to use or let John participate in our plan*)

2. To make an opening in a schedule for someone, as in this example: *The doctor's secretary **worked** the sick woman **into** the doctor's schedule.*

3. To insert or fit by repeatedly and continuously moving something around into something else; to jiggle something to get it into something else, as in this example: *He **worked** the old key **into** the lock.* (Meaning: *The word 'jiggle' means to move something quickly from side to side.*)

   More examples:

   - ❏ (1) We like your idea and we are going to try to **_work_** it **_into_** our project.

   - ❏ (2) The teacher was very busy, but was kind enough to **_work_** me **_into_** his schedule so we could discuss my exam.

❏ (3) The fisherman carefully ***worked*** his hook ***into*** the bait.

Work out
(separable):

1. Used to talk about being successful at something, as in this example: *We sold our home and bought another home that was more beautiful. We're glad now that we sold the old house and bought the new house. It really **worked out** well.*

2. To solve something or to find a solution for something, as in this example: *The student **worked out** the math problem.*

3. Used to talk about a specific result, as in this example: *The answer to the formula **worked out** to be 25.*

4. To participate in strenuous exercise or physical conditioning, as in this example: *I **worked out** at the gym every night.*

   More examples:
   ❏ (1) Studying every night for that exam ***worked out*** perfectly. I got a 97%.
   ❏ (2) At first, our group could not agree on a name for our new company, but we finally ***worked*** it ***out***.
   ❏ (3) It ***worked out*** that we all fit on the same bus. We didn't have to take separate buses to the museum.
   ❏ (4) If you want to be an Olympic athlete, you have to ***work out*** hard.

Work up
(inseparable):

1. To cause to be anxious, excited or emotional about something or someone; to arouse the emotions or to excite, as in this example: *My sister's best friend was injured in a car accident. My sister is all **worked up** about it.*

2. To build proficiency, skill, responsibility or status through work, as in this example: *Jim **worked** his way **up** to vice president of the company.*

3. To build or develop something over time as a result of effort or work, as in this example: *We played soccer all morning. We're hungry. We really **worked up** an appetite for lunch.*

More examples:

- ❏ (1) What's wrong with Klaus? He's all ***worked up*** because he didn't get a good grade on the final exam.

- ❏ (2) Shohei worked hard in his company. He ***worked*** his way ***up*** to manager in just one year.

- ❏ (3) I spent the whole day at the beach and really ***worked up*** a thirst. I could drink a gallon of water right now!

Wrap up
(separable):

1. To complete something, finish with something or bring something to a conclusion, as in this example: *The teacher **wrapped up** the class promptly at 2pm.*

2. To cover something with gift wrap, paper, packaging paper or other kind of wrapper, as in this example: *I **wrapped up** the gifts that I will give my sister on her birthday.*

3. To summarize, as in this example: *The teacher **wrapped up** the class by going over the main points of the lesson.*

   More examples:

   - ❏ (1) We ***wrapped up*** the business meeting at 10 o'clock.

   - ❏ (2) Janice ***wrapped up*** her sister's gift the day before the party.

   - ❏ (3) The manager ***wrapped up*** the business meeting with a brief discussion of our latest sales information.

Write down
(separable):

1. To write or set something on paper, as in this example: *As I gave her my phone number, she **wrote** it **down** on paper.*

   More examples:

   - ❏ (1) The students ***wrote down*** everything the teacher said..

   - ❏ (1) The police officer ***wrote down*** my address.

Write up

(separable):

1. To document something; to write a report or description of, like for a publication, as in this example: *News of the event was **written up** in the newspaper.*

2. To report in writing, like when you break the law for speeding etc., as in this example: *The policeman **wrote** the woman **up** for going to fast.*

   More examples:

   ❑ (1) The idea for the compressed air motor was **written up** in the auto magazine.

   ❑ (2) Kimberly crossed the street while the light was still red. A policeman caught her and **wrote** her **up** for crossing the street against the red light.

Zip up
(separable):

1. To close up an opening, usually in clothing or cloth goods, using a zipper, as in this example: *I **zipped up** my jacket and left the building.*

   More examples:

   ❑ (1) Mom, would you help me **zip up** my dress?

   ❑ (2) I was trying to **zip up** my coat when some material jammed in the zipper. (Meaning: Jammed means to inhibit or get stuck hard in something. Some material from your jacket, or perhaps your shirt, got jammed or stuck in the zipper while you were trying to **zip** it **up**.)

Chapter 13 <u>review</u>

*Phrasal verbs beginning with the letters **U**, **W**, and **Z***

*Instructions: read and /or listen carefully to the sentences below. Fill in the blank spaces with the correct **preposition, particle,** or **adverb**. The answers can be found in this chapter (above).*

1. We like your idea and we are going to try to work it _____ our project.

2. It worked _____ that we all fit on the same bus. We didn't have to take separate buses to the museum.

3. I spent the whole day at the beach and really worked ___ a thirst. I could drink a gallon of water right now!

4. Mom, would you help me zip ___ my dress?

5. The idea for the compressed air motor was written ___ in the auto magazine.

6. Janice wrapped ___ her sister's gift the day before the party.

7. We wiped ___ the kitchen after breakfast and then went to the beach.

8. After traveling through the dusty countryside, I wiped the dust _____ the car.

9. I didn't study for the exam and wound ___ getting a failing grade.

10. When the drug wore _____, I really felt pain.

11. I washed _____ my car windshield after the long trip.

12. Would you please warm ___ some coffee for me, I'm late for work.

13. My mother woke me ___ to tell me it was time to get ready for the party.

14. I'm tired. I think I've used ___ all of my energy.

15. John and Naoko drove their car across the United States. When the arrived in California they discovered that they had worn _____ their tires quite a bit.

Answers: (1) into (2) out; (3) up (4) up (5) up; (6) up; (7) up; (8) off; (9) up (10) off; (11) off; (12) up (13) up; (14) up; (15) out

Book 3 – *Gerunds and Infinitives*
Gerunds and Infinitives for Real Life English

Book 3 - Quick-Find Menu

Introduction

Focus on English© Mini Series Book
Making the difficult parts of learning English easy

Mastering the use of gerunds and
infinitives after certain English verbs

How to correctly use gerunds (verb + ing) and infinitives (to + base verb) after certain common English verbs. Organized by verb in alphabetical order.

This Focus on English© book contains a comprehensive listing of common English verbs that are followed by the correct usage of gerunds and infinitives after them. The student will find explanations for each of the verb combinations, followed by examples of their correct usage in a sentence.

Each chapter is followed by a practice and review section, which is designed to help the student reinforce the lessons from the previous chapter.

If the student has the Focus on English© audio book that accompanies this book (available separately from www.FOEBooks.com, or the student's school store) he or she will find that each of the examples will be read twice to allow the student to speak the example along with the teacher.

This method helps the student remember the lesson more easily and also helps the student with pronunciation. Focus on English© audio books are a convenient way for the student to study, review and practice the difficult areas of English while they are traveling, on the go, or anywhere.

Chapter 1

Correct usage of some common English verbs that are followed by gerunds

In this first chapter you will learn how to use gerunds correctly after certain common English verbs in typical English sentences.

Read and / or listen to each of the common English verbs below, followed by their meanings as they are used in sentences with gerunds, and then some examples of how they are used in common English sentences followed by a gerund.

Remember that the meanings being given for the verbs are the meanings when the verbs are used with a gerund.

Common English Verbs followed by gerunds

Read and / or listen carefully to the examples, as they will give you a good idea as to how to use the common verb-gerund combinations in real English sentences.

After the examples are given for each verb, you have a chance to practice what have learned. In the "Now you try" sections, fill in the blank space with the correct form of the word given in parenthesis ( ). The answer to the "now you try" section is found in the examples given for the verb.

There is a review section at the end of this chapter. The answers to the review section are found in this chapter in the examples given for each verb.

Acknowledge (+ gerund)

To admit to doing something, or to admit to the existence of something or someone.

Examples of usage with a gerund:

❑ My teacher asked me if I had studied English before. I **_acknowledged studying_** English while attending high school.

❑ The secretary asked me if I had paid the fee. I **_acknowledged having paid_** the fee.

_Now you try: The man acknowledged (smoke) _____ in the building._

Admit (+ gerund)

To acknowledge or grant doing something, or to acknowledge the existence of something or someone.

Examples of usage with a gerund:

❑ I **_admitted using_** marijuana when I was in high school.

❑ I **_admitted_** not **_studying_** for the exam.

_Now you try: Tomoko admitted (work) _____ for the government._

Appreciate (+ gerund)

To recognize the quality, significance or greatness of something or someone.

Examples of usage with a gerund:

❑ I **_appreciated being_** able to study English in Hawaii.

❑ Lana **_appreciated having_** the chance to travel to Europe last year.

Now you try: Lana appreciated (work) _____ for the good company.

Avoid: (+ gerund)
To stay clear of something or someone.

Examples of usage with a gerund:

❑ Students usually ***avoid going*** to expensive restaurants.

❑ Soo Woo ***avoids doing*** exercises in the evening.

Now you try: Adam avoided (walk) _____ to work because of his injury.

Can't help: (+ gerund)
An inability to refrain from doing something.

Examples of usage with a gerund:

❑ My sister ***can't help eating*** delicious chocolates.

❑ Jason ***couldn't help going*** to the pub with his friends every night.

Now you try: Alice can't help (eat) _____ chocolate.

Celebrate: (+ gerund)
To observe an important occasion, usually with festivity.

Examples of usage with a gerund:

❑ My classmates and I ***celebrated graduating*** from university.

❑ Kaori ***celebrated getting*** married.

Now you try: The team celebrated (win) _____ the tournament.

Consider: *(+ gerund)*
To think carefully about or give careful thought to something;

Examples of usage with a gerund:

❑ My sister ***considered attending*** university after graduating from high school.

❑ Mika ***considered studying*** English in Hawaii.

Now you try: *Alex considered (work)* _____ *for the good company.*

Delay: (+ gerund)
To postpone until a later time; defer.

Examples of usage with a gerund:

❑ We ***delayed going*** to the theater because we wanted to look at the sunset.

❑ Susan ***delayed studying*** for the exam because she had other work to do.

Now you try: *The student delayed (register)* _____ *at the new school.*

Deny: (+ gerund)
To refuse to acknowledge.

Examples of usage with a gerund:

❑ Cindy ***denied smoking*** cigarettes when she was younger.

❑ The policeman stopped Toshiko for driving through the red light, but Toshiko ***denied driving*** through the red light.

Now you try: Juan denied (use) _____ marijuana.

Detest: *(+ gerund)*
To dislike intensely.

Examples of usage with a gerund:

❑ The children ***detested eating*** Brussels sprouts.

❑ The commuters ***detested driving*** in the bad weather.

Now you try: Christina detests (talk) _____ to people who are not honest.

Discontinue: *(+ gerund)*
To put a stop to; to terminate.

Examples of usage with a gerund:

❑ The store ***discontinued selling*** the laptop computers.

❑ Mayumi ***discontinued shopping*** at the computer store.

Now you try: Megumi discontinued (study) _____ at the school because of illness.

Discuss: *(+ gerund)*
To speak with others about something or someone; to talk something over.

Examples of usage with a gerund:

❑ My wife and I ***discussed going*** to dinner tonight.

❑ Sam ***discussed getting*** a raise with his boss.

Now you try: Sandra discussed (work) _____ for another company.

Dislike: *(+ gerund)*
To not be pleasing; to regard something or someone with displeasure.

Examples of usage with a gerund:

❑ My brother ***dislikes taking*** out the garbage.

❑ The daughter ***dislikes doing*** the dishes.

Now you try: Fred disliked (have) _____ to go to work every day.

Dispute: *(+ gerund)*
*To disagre(****plus verb + gerund****)e about something; argue about or debate something.*

Examples of usage with a gerund:

❑ Alison's friends called her a gossip, but Alison ***disputes being*** a gossip.

❑ Sun Wa said that her brother sprayed her with the water hose, but her brother ***disputes spraying*** her with a water hose.

Now you try: Frankie disputed (be) _____ lazy.

Endure: *(+ gerund)*
To continue on or continue doing something despite difficulties and hardships.

Examples of usage with a gerund:

❑ Andrew could not ***endure going*** to school again without having nice clothes to wear.

❑ The runners ***endured racing*** in the hot sun to finish the competition.

Now you try: Donny endured (work) _____ for the bad company.

Enjoy: (+ gerund)
To receive pleasure or satisfaction from doing something.

Examples of usage with a gerund:

❑ My girlfriend and I ***enjoy hiking*** in the mountains.

❑ We ***enjoy going*** to the beach.

Now you try: Eddie enjoyed (go) _____ surfing every day.

Escape: (+ gerund)
To get free of something; to break out of the confines of something.

Examples of usage with a gerund:

❑ The little dog narrowly ***escaped getting*** hit by a car.

❑ We ***escaped having*** to go to the boring company meeting.

Now you try: The criminal escaped (get) _____ caught by the police.

Explain: (+ gerund)
To make something clear, plain, and understandable through written or spoken communication.

Examples of usage with a gerund:

❑ How do you ***explain being*** late to class every morning this week? I have been late because my car is being repaired and won't be finished until tomorrow.

❑ How do you ***explain getting*** such a poor grade on the exam? I didn't study.

Now you try: The child explained (have) _____ his hand in the cookie jar.

Feel like: *(+ gerund)*
To have the desire to do something; to be in the mood to do something.

Examples of usage with a gerund:

❑ I don't feel ***like doing*** homework tonight.

❑ No one on the soccer team ***felt like having*** a hard workout yesterday.

Now you try: Gladys felt like (eat) _____ a piece of cake.

Finish: *(+ gerund)*
To complete something.

Examples of usage with a gerund:

❑ Two of the students didn't ***finish taking*** the exam.

❑ Shino ***finished shopping*** at 6pm.

Now you try: The office workers finished (type) _____ the report.

Give up: *(+ gerund)*
To stop doing something.

Examples of usage with a gerund:

❑ We ***gave up trying*** to drive into the city. The traffic was terrible.

❑ At around 1am I ***gave up studying*** and went to bed.

Now you try: Laura gave up (exercise) _____ and gained ten pounds.

Imagine: *(+ gerund)*
To form a mental image or picture of something.

Examples of usage with a gerund:

❑ We ***imagined going*** to Europe next year. We thought it would be possible.

❑ ***Imagine being*** the leader of a country?

Now you try: We imagined (travel) _____ *around the world.*

Justify: *(+ gerund)*
To demonstrate the validity of something.

Examples of usage with a gerund:

❑ Jack and his wife ***justified spending*** all of that money on a new car by saying that the new car got very good fuel economy.

❑ My colleagues ***justified spending*** so much time on the project by explaining that this project was very important to the company.

Now you try: The owner of the company justified (fire) _____ *many workers by saying that the economy was bad.*

Keep: *(+ gerund)*
To continue to do something.

Examples of usage with a gerund:

❑ The students ***kept going*** to the same pub every night.

❑ My brother and I ***kept going*** to the gym for two years.

Now you try: Kyoko keeps (visit) _____ *the same cities every year on vacation.*

**Mention:** _(+ gerund)_
To refer to or communicate something, usually incidentally, by spoken or written word.

Examples of usage with a gerund:

- ❏ Where did Flora and Bill go? They _**mentioned going**_ to the park.

- ❏ How long has the new student been in the United States? He _**mentioned being**_ here for two years.

_**Now you try: The teacher mentioned (have) _____ homework over the weekend.**_

**Mind:** _(+ gerund)_
To object to.

Examples of usage with a gerund:

- ❏ My sister didn't _**mind going**_ to the store for chips.

- ❏ The repairman didn't _**mind returning**_ to the customer's house to explain how to use the new appliance.

_**Now you try: The students didn't mind (review) _____ the work again.**_

**Miss:** _(+ gerund)_
To feel the lack or loss of something; to lose an opportunity to do something.
Examples of usage with a gerund:

- ❏ I _**miss going**_ to the beach every Sunday. Now I have to work on Sundays.

- ❏ The schoolgirls _**missed seeing**_ the famous movie star because the movie star left the building one hour earlier.

Now you try: After leaving New York City, Nicole missed (run)
_____ *in Central Park every morning.*

<u>*Postpone:*</u> *(+ gerund)*
To delay until a future time.

Examples of usage with a gerund:

❑ We ***postponed having*** the picnic until the rain stopped.

❑ The school ***postponed giving*** the exam until after the holiday.

Now you try: The referee postponed (start) _____ *the game because of rain.*

<u>*Practice:*</u> *(+ gerund)*
To do something repeatedly usually to improve.

Examples of usage with a gerund:

❑ The bicycle team ***practiced racing*** on that course every week.

❑ Successful English students ***practice speaking*** English every day.

Now you try: The soccer team practiced (kick) _____ *the ball into the goal.*

<u>*Prevent:*</u> *(+ gerund)*
To keep something from happening.

Examples of usage with a gerund:

❑ To ***prevent being*** late, leave early.

❑ To ***prevent having*** trouble with the government, pay your taxes.

388

Now you try: To prevent (miss) _____ your flight, arrive at the airport early.

Prohibit: *(+ gerund)*
To not allow or forbid (usually by some authority).

Examples of usage with a gerund:

❑ The law ***prohibits throwing*** trash on the highways.

❑ The school rules ***prohibit smoking*** in the building.

Now you try: The building rules prohibit (sell) _____ in the building without permission.

Quit: (+ gerund)
To stop doing something.

Examples of usage with a gerund:

❑ Yuki ***quit eating*** at the restaurant because the prices were too expensive.

❑ Tom ***quit worrying*** about his business and decided to go to a show.

Now you try: Alfred quit (go) _____ to piano practice because it was too expensive.

Recall: (+ gerund)
To remember or recollect.

Examples of usage with a gerund:

❑ The European students ***recalled going*** to Majorca.

❑ The driver told the policeman that he didn't ***recall seeing*** a red light.

Now you try: The student didn't recall (hear) _____ *about the homework assignment.*

<u>Recommend:</u> *(+ gerund)*
To advise or counsel.

Examples of usage with a gerund:

❑ We don't **_recommend seeing_** the movie because it is too violent.
❑ The young couple went to a counselor to talk about their wedding, but the counselor didn't **_recommend getting_** married because the couple was too young.

Now you try: The teacher recommended (study) _____ *for the exam.*

<u>Regret: (+ gerund)</u>
To be sorry or disappointed about something.

Examples of usage with a gerund:

❑ My girlfriend and I **_regretted going_** to the movie because it was too violent.

❑ The businessman **_regretted_** not **_getting_** more sleep the night before.

Now you try: The criminal regretted (commit) _____ *the crime.*

<u>Report: (+ gerund)</u>
To tell about something, to relate something.

Examples of usage with a gerund:

❑ The scientist **_reported finding_** a new kind of insect.

❑ Our friends ***reported going*** to the street festival last night and really having a good time.

Now you try: The watchman reported (see) _____ some strange activity in building number 5.

Resent: (+ gerund)
To be strongly offended by something or someone.

Examples of usage with a gerund:

❑ The new employee ***resented getting*** all of the hard jobs in the company.

❑ Tomomi ***resented being*** told that she could not play on the school's basketball team.

Now you try: Elena resented (be) _____ told that she would not be hired for the job.

Resist: (+ gerund)
To struggle against something; to oppose with resistance.

Examples of usage with a gerund:

❑ The puppy ***resisted being*** walked on a leash.

❑ Claudia ***resisted traveling*** by plane because she was afraid of flying.

Now you try: Hiroko resisted (learn) _____ to drive because she was afraid of having an accident.

Risk: (+ gerund)
To take a chance at something, especially when there are possible negative consequences to failure.

Examples of usage with a gerund:

❑ Military air pilots often ***risk flying*** into dangerous areas to complete their mission.

❑ I didn't study for the exam, but I will ***risk taking*** it because I will not have another chance.

Now you try: Julie risked (spend) _____ her money on jewelry sold on the Internet.

Suggest: *(+ gerund)*
To offer advice in a polite way.

Examples of usage with a gerund:

❑ Cindy's friends didn't have anything to do so Markus ***suggested going*** to the museum.

❑ My mom ***suggested having*** my brother's birthday party at the beach.

Now you try: The weatherman suggested (take) _____ an umbrella with you because of the possibility of rain.

Chapter 1 <u>review</u>

Correct usage of some common English verbs that are followed by gerunds

*Instructions: read and /or listen carefully to the sentences below. Fill in the blank spaces with either the correct **infinitive** (to + base verb) or **gerund** (base verb + ing). The base verb is given in parenthesis. Answers can be found in chapter 1, above.*

1. Jean and I discussed (go)_____ to the movies tonight.

2. The store discontinued (sell)_____ the laptop computers.

3. Andrew could not endure (go)_____ to school again without having nice clothes to wear.

4. We enjoy (go)_____ to the beach.

5. The little dog narrowly escaped (get)_____ hit by a car.

6. How do you explain (get)_____ such a poor grade on the exam?

7. I don't feel like (do)_____ homework tonight.

8. Two of the students didn't finish (take)_____ the exam.

9. We gave up (try)_____ to drive into the city. The traffic was terrible.

10. Jack and his wife justified (spend)_____ all of that money on a new car by saying that the new car got very good fuel economy.

11. My brother dislikes (take)_____ out the garbage.

12. Sun Wah said that her brother sprayed her with the water hose, but her brother disputes (spray)_____ her with a water hose.

13. We enjoy (go)_____ to the beach.

14. We escaped (have)_____ to go to the boring company meeting.

15. Cindy denied (smoke)_____ cigarettes when she was younger.

16. The commuters detested (drive)_____ in the bad weather.

17. The store discontinued (sell)_____ the laptop computers.

18. Kaori celebrated (get)_____ married.

19. Students usually avoid (go)_____ to expensive restaurants.

20. I admitted not (study)_____ for the exam.

Chapter 2

Correct usage of some common English verbs that are followed by infinitives

In this chapter you will learn how we use infinitives correctly after certain common English verbs in typical English sentences.

Read and / or listen to each of the common English verbs below, followed by their meanings **as they are used in sentences with infinitives**, and then some examples of how they are used in real English sentences with infinitives.

After the examples are given for each verb, you have a chance to practice what have learned. In the "Now you try" sections, fill in the blank space with the correct form of the word given in parenthesis ( ). The answer to the "now you try" section is found in the examples given for the verb.

Remember that the meanings being given for the verbs are the meanings when the verbs are used with an infinitive.

Common English Verbs followed by infinitives

Read and / or listen carefully to the examples, as they will give you a good idea as to how to use the common verb-infinitive combinations in real English sentences.

There is a review section at the end of this chapter. The answers to the review section are found in this chapter in the examples given for each verb.

Afford: *(+ infinitive)*
To be in a position to do something financially or because of the availability of other resources.

Examples of usage with an infinitive:

- ❏ The cost of a ticket to the concert was too expensive. We couldn't _**afford to go**_ to the concert.

- ❏ Wednesday's class will be very important. We can't _**afford to miss**_ this class.

Now you try: The family couldn't afford (buy) _____ a new house.

Agree: *(+ infinitive)*
To allow something to happen, to consent to something.

Examples of usage with an infinitive:

- ❏ The governor _**agreed to repair**_ the roads.

- ❏ Megumi _**agreed to study**_ harder for the TOEIC exam.

Now you try: Alicia agreed (spend) _____ more time at home.

Appear: **(+ infinitive)**
To seem to do or be something.

Examples of usage with an infinitive:

- ❏ When I looked out of the window, it _**appeared to be**_ raining, but when I went outside the rain had stopped.

- ❏ Being famous appears to be wonderful, but there are many problems.

Now you try: The weather doesn't appear (be) _____ good, so we'll have our picnic next week.

<u>Ask</u>: *(+ infinitive)*
To put a question to someone.

Examples of usage with an infinitive:

❑ The student ***asked to leave*** class early.

❑ Our party lasted until 2 o'clock in the morning. The neighbors ***asked us to be*** quiet.

Now you try: The team member asked (be) _____ absent from the game because of illness.

<u>**Arrange:**</u> *(+ infinitive)*
To plan or organize for something; to make provisions for something.

Examples of usage with an infinitive:

❑ My wife and I ***arranged to fly*** to London next week.

❑ For my brother's birthday, I ***arranged to have a party at his favorite restaurant.***

Now you try: The manager arranged (have) _____ the meeting at 10am.

<u>**Attempt:**</u> *(+ infinitive)*
To try.

Examples of usage with an infinitive:

❑ The cat ***attempted to jump*** from the floor to the tabletop, but missed and fell to the floor.

❑ When I was in Japan, I ***attempted to pay*** the cashier at the food store with U.S. dollars. She said that she only accepted Japanese yen.

Now you try: The athlete attempted (break) _____ the world record.

Can't afford: *(+ infinitive)*
To not be able to give up or jeopardize something, often having to do with a lack of time or money.

Examples of usage with an infinitive:

❑ We ***couldn't afford to buy*** a new house.

❑ Students often ***can't afford to eat*** at a restaurant every day.

Now you try: Jane just lost her job and cannot afford (buy) _____ the new dress.

Can't wait: *(+ infinitive)*
To be impatient about some upcoming event, action, or occurrence.

Examples of usage with an infinitive:

❑ I ***can't wait to travel*** to Europe this summer.

❑ The children ***couldn't wait to taste*** the cake that their mom just baked. Their mother told them that they would have to be patient and wait until dinner.

Now you try: Alex couldn't wait (drive) _____ his new car.

Care: *(+ infinitive)*
To have the desire to do something.

Examples of usage with an infinitive:

❑ My husband asked me if I wanted to go to the movies tonight. I told him that I didn't **_care to go_** to the movies tonight.

❑ The waitress asked us if we **_cared to have_** more coffee.

Now you try: We ate so many snacks that we didn't care (eat) _____ dinner.

Choose: (+ infinitive)
To make a decision about choice; to prefer over other things.

Examples of usage with an infinitive:

❑ I don't **_choose to stay out_** late because I have to get up early in the morning.

❑ The restaurant gave us the choice of a buffet or a la carte. We **_chose to order_** from the a la carte menu.

Now you try: After the company meeting, Herbert didn't choose (stay) _____ and chat with his colleagues.

Consent: (+ infinitive)
To give permission.

Examples of usage with an infinitive:

❑ Professional athletes must **_consent to be_** tested for illegal drugs.

❑ The students in the English school **_consented to speak_** English only during school hours.

Now you try: The doctor asked the patient to consent (have) _____ the special medical treatment.

(🧑‍🏫Note: in American English, it is very common to use ***consent to*** plus a gerund, as in: *Professional athletes must consent to being tested for illegal drugs.*)

<u>***Decide:***</u> *(+ infinitive)*
To reach a decision.

Examples of usage with an infinitive:

❑ The Liu family ***decided to drive*** to the beach.

❑ The engine in Greg's car has not been working correctly. Yesterday, Greg ***decided to try*** to repair the engine.

Now you try: The police decided (arrest) _____ the man who was caught running away from the robbery.

<u>***Deserve:***</u> *(+ infinitive)*
To be worthy of something.

Examples of usage with an infinitive:

❑ My sister ***deserved to win*** the Best Student award at our school because she was a straight A student.

❑ All human beings ***deserve to be treated*** with respect.

Now you try: All citizens deserve (vote) _____ for their leader.

<u>***Expect:***</u> *(+ infinitive)*
To anticipate a certain outcome; to consider due.

Examples of usage with an infinitive:

- ❑ I ***expected to be*** skiing in the mountains this winter, but now it looks like I will not be able to go.

- ❑ The tennis star ***expected to win*** her match at the tournament, but her competitor won the match.

Now you try: Mary expected (win) _____ the marathon, but she hurt her foot and had to drop out of the race.

Fail: *(+ infinitive)*
To fall short of expectations; to be unable.

Examples of usage with an infinitive:

- ❑ I ***fail to see*** the humor in homelessness.

- ❑ Her boss ***failed to see*** why she couldn't come to work on time.

Now you try: The student failed (complete) _____ the homework assignment.

Grow: *(+ infinitive)*
To increase in amount.

Examples of usage with an infinitive:

- ❑ My daughter has ***grown to like*** playing the violin.

- ❑ Over time, the members of the group ***grew to trust*** one another.

Now you try: The brother and sister grew (respect) _____ each other.

Help: *(+ infinitive)*
To assist.

Examples of usage with an infinitive:

❑ My travels in America **_helped to give_** me a strong foundation in English.

❑ Alice's experience in life **_helped to make_** her a better person.

Now you try: The financial crisis helped (bring down) _____ the government.

<u>Hope:</u> *(+ infinitive)*
To expect and desire.

Examples of usage with an infinitive:

❑ We **_hope to travel_** to China in late May.

❑ The members of the team **_hoped to win_** their next big tournament.

Now you try: My friends hoped (visit) _____ Hawaii during their vacation.

<u>Hurry:</u> *(+ infinitive)*
To hasten or go faster, usually to accomplish something.

Examples of usage with an infinitive:

❑ The tickets to the concert were selling quickly, so we **_hurried to buy_** the tickets.

❑ Alicia and Martin were late for class, so they **_hurried to get_** to class.

Now you try: The shoppers hurried (buy) _____ the products on sale.

Intend: (+ *infinitive*)
To plan on or have in mind to do.

Examples of usage with an infinitive:

❏ We ***intend to travel*** around the world within the next five years.

❏ The professor of science ***intended to prove*** that global warming was a threat to humanity.

Now you try: Hiro intends (purchase) _____ a new car.

Learn: (+ *infinitive*)
To acquire experience, an ability or a skill.

Examples of usage with an infinitive:

❏ Over the years, we ***learned to travel*** more economically.

❏ In Rome, we ***learned to use*** the public transportation to get around the city.

Now you try: The students learned (speak) _____ English well.

Manage: (+ *infinitive*)
To succeed in accomplishing or completing something, sometimes by hard work or in spite of difficulties, sometimes by luck.

Examples of usage with an infinitive:

❏ After searching for three hours, we ***managed to find*** the theater.

❏ I managed to get a job with the corporation with the help of some of my friends.

*Now you try: **Three students managed (get)** _____ **a good grade on the exam.***

Mean: *(+ infinitive)*
To have the intention.

> **Examples of usage with an infinitive:**

- ❑ When I was in class today I **_meant to tell_** the teacher that I would be absent tomorrow.

- ❑ The doctor didn't **_mean to harm_** the patient, but the patient became extremely ill after taking the medication.

*Now you try: **The little boy didn't mean (break)** _____ **the cookie jar when he was reaching for a cookie.***

Need: *(+ infinitive)*
To have necessity or obligation.

> **Examples of usage with an infinitive:**

- ❑ Before going to work, I **_needed to stop_** at the drugstore and get some aspirin.

- ❑ I **_needed to get_** a high grade on the exam in order to get a passing grade for the course.

*Now you try: **You don't need (spend)** _____ **a lot of money for nice clothing.***

Offer: **(+ infinitive)**
To propose or put forward some action, usually as a benefit to someone.

Examples of usage with an infinitive:

❑ The women ***offered to give*** the old man her seat on the train.

❑ My boss ***offered to give*** me a raise if I stayed with the company.

Now you try: The boy offered (help) _____ the old woman across the street.

Pay: *(+ infinitive)*
To be profitable or worthwhile.

Examples of usage with an infinitive:

❑ It doesn't ***pay to break*** the law.

❑ It ***pays to be alert*** when driving a vehicle.

Now you try: It pays (be) _____ careful when crossing the street.

Plan: *(+ infinitive)*
To have the intention, usually to do something.

Examples of usage with an infinitive:

❑ I ***plan to attend*** university next year.

❑ The government plans to cut back services to the poor in two years.

Now you try: We plan (go) _____ to China for our vacation.

Prepare: *(+ infinitive)*
To be ready, usually to do something.

Examples of usage with an infinitive:

❑ The author is ***prepared to defend*** the ideas in his new book.

❏ My cousin is ***preparing to visit*** Hawaii next week.

Now you try: The hikers were not prepared (hike) _____ for such a long time.

<u>*Pretend:*</u> *(+ infinitive)*
To feign or to give a false appearance of.

Examples of usage with an infinitive:

❏ The well-dressed man ***pretended to be*** the president of a large country.

❏ My sister ***pretended to be*** sleepy so that she wouldn't have to go with us to the theater.

Now you try: James pretended (know) _____ how to repair car motors to impress his girlfriend.

<u>***Promise:***</u> *(+ infinitive)*
To commit, agree to, or pledge, usually to do something.

Examples of usage with an infinitive:

❏ I ***promised to help*** my friend with his homework.

❏ The politician ***promised to get rid of*** the crime in his city.

Now you try: Timmy's mother promised (take) _____ him to the movies.

<u>*Refuse:*</u> *(+ infinitive)*
To indicate unwillingness to do, accept, give or allow something.

402

Examples of usage with an infinitive:

❑ Our team was losing the match 1-0, but we ***refused to give up***.

❑ My friend's mother ***refused to give*** her permission to go to Barbados over the summer.

Now you try: Kaori refused (spend) _____ a lot of money for rent.

Request: *(+ infinitive) (+ infinitive)*
To ask for or express a desire for something.

Examples of usage with an infinitive:

❑ Students were ***requested to be*** on time for class.

❑ Cynthia and Yuki ***requested to be*** absent from class next week so that they could go to Europe.

Now you try: We were requested (leave) _____ the building because we were smoking.

Seem: *(+ infinitive)*
To appear or give the impression of being or doing something.

Examples of usage with an infinitive:

❑ World leaders ***seem to agree*** that global warming is an important issue.

❑ We have a choice: we can go to our favorite pub tonight, or we can go to the movies. The pub idea ***seems to be*** a better choice because all of our friends will be there tonight.

Now you try: We take good care of our dogs and they seem (be) _____ happy.

Want: *(+ infinitive)*
To express a strong desire for something.

Examples of usage with an infinitive:

- People around the world ***want to have*** peace.

- Craig's sister ***wants to date*** Craig's best friend.

Now you try: *The children want (play) _____ in the park.*

Wish: *(+ infinitive)*
To prefer something.

Examples of usage with an infinitive:

- When we entered the restaurant, the hostess asked us if we ***wished to sit*** by a window.

- The secretary asked me if I ***wished to see*** a doctor, when I entered the office.

Now you try: *The tour guide asked us if we wished (have) _____ lunch at noon.*

Would like: *(+ infinitive)*
Used to express a polite request; to express a polite preference for something.

Examples of usage with an infinitive:

- We told the travel agent that we ***would like to leave*** for London in the spring.

- There are some people in the world who ***would like to travel*** to the moon in a space ship.

Now you try: **Everyone would like (have) _____ peace in the world.**

Chapter 2 <u>review</u>

Correct usage of some common English verbs that are followed by infinitives

*Instructions: read and / or listen carefully to the sentences below. Fill in the blank spaces with either the correct **infinitive** (to + base verb) or **gerund** (base verb + ing). The base verb is given in parenthesis. Answers can be found in chapter 2, above.*

1. Wednesday's class will be very important. We can't afford (miss)_____ this class.

2. The governor agreed (repair)_____ the roads.

3. The lumberjack plans (cut)_____ down the tree.

4. I needed (get)_____ a high grade on the exam in order to get a passing grade for the course.

5. The women offered (give)_____ the old man her seat on the train.

6. My cousin is preparing (visit)_____ Hawaii next week.

7. My sister pretended (be)_____ sleepy so that she wouldn't have to go with us to the theater.

8. I promised (help)_____ my friend with his homework.

9. My friend's mother refused (give)_____ her permission to go to Barbados over the summer.

10. World leaders seem (agree)_____ that global warming is an important issue.

11. Craig's sister wants (date)_____ Craig's best friend.

12. There are some people in the world who would like (travel)_____ to the moon in a space ship.

13. The government plans (cut)_____ back services to the poor in two years.

14. When I was in class today I meant (tell)_____ the teacher that I would be absent tomorrow.

15. After searching for three hours, we managed (find)_____ the theater.

16. Alicia and Martin were late for class, so they hurried (get)_____ to school.

17. The professor of science intended (prove)_____ that global warming was a threat to humanity.

18. We hope (travel)_____ to China in late May.

19. Over time, the members of the group grew (trust)_____ one another.

20. My sister deserved (win)_____ the Best Student award at our school because she was a straight A student.

(Answers to the review questions are found above in chapter 2.)

Chapter 3

Correct usage of some common English verbs that can be followed by either gerunds or infinitives

In this chapter you will learn how we use certain verbs that are followed by either infinitives or gerunds in typical English sentences.

Read and / or listen to each of the common English verbs below, followed by their meanings as they are used in sentences with either infinitives or gerunds, and then followed by some examples of how they are used in real English sentences with both infinitives and gerunds.

Remember that the meanings being given for the verbs are the meanings when the verbs are used with either an infinitive or a gerund.

Common English Verbs that can be followed by either gerunds or infinitives

Read and / or listen carefully to the examples, as they will give you a good idea as to how to use the common verb-infinitive / verb-gerund combinations in real English sentences.

After the examples are given for each verb, you have a chance to practice what have learned. In the "Now you try" sections, fill in the blank space with the correct form of the word given in parenthesis ( ). The answer to the "now you try" section is found in the examples given for the verb.

There is a review section at the end of this chapter. The answers to the review section are found in this chapter in the examples given for each verb.

<u>Begin:</u> *(followed by either gerends or infinitives)*
To start or commence doing something.

Examples of usage with a gerund or an infinitive:

❏ The ticket agent ***<u>began counting</u>*** the ticket receipts on the table.

❏ In an intermediate level English class, students ***<u>begin to learn</u>*** about more complex English sentence structure.

Now you try: The teacher began (talk) _____ about gerunds and infinitives.

<u>Can't stand:</u> *(followed by either gerends or infinitives)*
To dislike intensely.

Examples of usage with a gerund or an infinitive:

❏ It's time for Wilma to quit her job. She says that she ***<u>can't stand going</u>*** to work in the morning.

❏ Some people ***<u>can't stand to listen</u>*** to politicians who don't tell the truth.

Now you try: Albert couldn't stand (do) _____ exercises.

<u>Continue:</u> *(followed by either gerends or infinitives)*
To go on or persist with something.

Examples of usage with a gerund or an infinitive:

❏ Many people don't have savings, so they have to ***<u>continue working</u>*** without a rest in order to pay bills .

❏ The storm ***<u>continued to devastate</u>*** the city long after nightfall.

Now you try: The students continued (study) _____ *English for three years.*

Forget: *(followed by either gerends or infinitives)*

(Note: _**forget**_ has different meanings depending on whether you use it with a gerund or you use it with an infinitive. Please read the meanings below in order to understand how this word is used with infinitives and gerunds)

Used with an infinitive, _**forget**_ means you didn't remember to do something *at the time the action should have been completed*. Used with a gerund, _**forget**_ means that you *didn't recall doing something that should have been done in the past*.

Examples of usage with a gerund or an infinitive:

❑   I'm not sure if the door was locked or not. I couldn't remember if I locked the door when we left. I _**forgot locking**_ the door.

❑   The door wasn't locked. I _**forgot to lock**_ the door when we left.

Now you try: I forgot (put) _____ *the keys to the car in my pocket. (couldn't recall)*

Try another: I forgot (put) _____ *the keys to the car in my pocket. (didn't remember to do something)*

Hate: *(followed by either gerends or infinitives)*
To detest; extreme dislike of something.

Examples of usage with a gerund or an infinitive:

❑   I _**hate going**_ to the dentist!

❑   Our dog *__hates to go__* for a walk.

Now you try: I hate (put) _____ sugar in my green tea.

__Like:__ *(followed by either gerends or infinitives)*
To prefer, to enjoy.

>   **Examples of usage with a gerund or an infinitive:**

❑   I *__like going__* to the mall!

❑   My colleagues *__like to go__* to a restaurant for lunch.

Now you try: I like (put) _____ milk on my cereal in the morning.

__Love:__ *(followed by either gerends or infinitives)*
Intense preference for something or to do something.

>   **Examples of usage with a gerund or an infinitive:**

❑   I *__love going__* hiking.

❑   My girlfriend and I *__love to walk__* on the beach.

Now you try: Jean loves (play) _____ tennis.

__Prefer:__ *(followed by either gerends or infinitives)*
To choose to.

>   **Examples of usage with a gerund or an infinitive:**

❑   Many Americans *__prefer drinking__* coffee.

❑   My friend *__prefers to drive__* a car that doesn't pollute the air.

Now you try: Alice prefers (do) _____ *her homework in the early morning hours.*

Remember: *(followed by either gerends or infinitives)*

(Note: ***remember*** has different meanings depending on whether you use it with a gerund or you use it with an infinitive. Please read the meanings below in order to understand how this word is used with infinitives and gerunds)

Used with an infinitive, ***remember*** means you remembered to do something *at the time the action should have been completed*. Used with a gerund, ***remember*** means that you *recalled doing something that should have been done in the past*.

Examples of usage with a gerund or an infinitive:

- Don't worry, the apartment is locked up. I ***remember locking*** it when we left. (Means that I now have the memory of locking the door when we left in the past.)

- The door wasn't locked. I didn't ***remember to lock*** the door when we left. (Means that at the time when we left the apartment, I didn't remember to lock the door.)

Now you try: Andrew remembered (put) _____ *the garbage outside. (remembered to do something)*

Try another: Jane remembered (put) _____ *the garbage outside. (had a memory of doing something; recalled doing something)*

Start: *(followed by either gerends or infinitives)*
To begin an activity or a movement.

Examples of usage with a gerund or an infinitive:

❑ My cousin Alice ***started doing*** her homework at 8 o'clock in the evening.

❑ People are ***starting to understand*** that pollution is not good for the environment.

Now you try: Kyoko started (study) _____ English about two years ago.

___Stop:___ *(followed by either gerends or infinitives)*

(Note: ***stop*** has different meanings depending on whether you use it with a gerund or you use it with an infinitive. Please read the meanings below in order to understand how this word is used with infinitives and gerunds)

Used with an infinitive, **stop** means you ***paused or took time out from something you were doing in order to do something else***. Used with a gerund, __*stop*__ means that you ***discontinued doing something***.

Examples of usage with a gerund or an infinitive:

❑ My sister ***stopped smoking*** last week.

❑ On the way to work, I ***stopped to pick*** up a newspaper.

Now you try: Matthias stopped (exercise) _____ about three weeks ago and now he is gaining weight. (quit doing something)

Try another: Nicole stopped (give) _____ some money to the homeless man. (paused to do something)

**Try:** _(followed by either gerends or infinitives)_
To attempt to do something.

Examples of usage with a gerund or an infinitive:

❏ Jim Bowman _**tried going**_ to a doctor for his illness, but the doctor could not help him.

❏ The athlete _**tried to break**_ a new world record.

_**Now you try: Stephan tried (help)** _____ **his friend with the car repair.**_

Chapter 3 <u>review</u>

Correct usage of some common English verbs that can be followed by either gerunds or infinitives

*Instructions: read and / or listen carefully to the sentences below. Fill in the blank spaces with either the correct **infinitive** (to + base verb) or **gerund** (base verb + ing). The base verb is given in parenthesis. Answers can be found in chapter 3, above.*

1. My girlfriend and I love (walk)_____ on the beach.

2. Our dog hates (go)_____ for a walk.

3. My colleagues like (go)_____ to a restaurant for lunch.

4. Many Americans prefer (drink)_____ coffee.

5. The door wasn't locked. I forgot (lock)_____ the door when we left (remembered not doing something).

6. I'm not sure if the door was locked or not. I couldn't remember if I locked the door when we left. I forgot (lock)_____ the door.

7. Many people don't have savings, so they have to continue (work)_____ without a rest in order to pay bills.

8. It's time for Wilma to quit her job. She says that she can't stand (go)_____ to work in the morning.

9. In an intermediate level English class, students begin (learn)_____ about more complex English sentence structure.

10. Don't worry, the apartment is locked up. I remember (lock)_____ it when we left.

Chapter 4

Correct usage of some common English verbs that are followed by objects and then an infinitive: **common verb + object + infinitive**

In this chapter you will learn how we use common English verbs that are typically followed by an object and then by an infinitive.

Read and / or listen to each of the common English verbs below, followed by their meanings as they are used in sentences with an object and then an infinitive, and then followed by some examples of how they are used in real English sentences. Each example will be spoken twice. You can practice and reinforce your knowledge, if you have the Focus On English audio book that accompanies this book (www.FOEBooks.com), by repeating the examples with the teacher.

Remember that the meanings being given for the verbs are the meanings when the verbs are used in the following way: common verb + object + infinitive.

Common English Verbs followed by object + infinitive

Read and / or listen carefully to the examples, as they will give you a good idea as to how to use the common ***verb + object + infinitive*** combinations in real English sentences.

After the examples are given for each verb, you have a chance to practice what have learned. In the "Now you try" sections, fill in the blank space with the correct form of the word given in parenthesis ( ). The answer to the "now you try" section is found in the examples given for the verb.

There is a review section at the end of this chapter. The answers to the review section are found in this chapter in the examples given for each verb.

Advise: *(plus object + infinitive)*
To recommend or give counsel.

> **Examples of usage with an object + an infinitive:**

> ❏ The airline stewardess ***advised the passengers to fasten*** their seatbelts.

> ❏ After two days of rain, the weatherman ***advised people to evacuate*** their homes because of possible flooding.

Now you try: Marco's parents advised him (study) _____ for the exam.

Allow: *(plus object + infinitive)*
To permit or let someone or something do something.

> **Examples of usage with an object + an infinitive:**

> ❏ The school rules ***allowed us to smoke*** outside the building.

> ❏ The sign in the park did not ***allow us to bring*** alcohol into the park.

Now you try: Ann allowed the girl (try) _____ her new bicycle.

Ask: *(plus object + infinitive)*
(Note: ***ask*** can also be followed by an infinitive without using an object)
To inquire or put a question to someone.

> **Examples of usage with an object + an infinitive:**

- The homeless person ***asked us to give*** him some money.

- Renata ***asked her colleague to help*** her with a project.

Now you try: The boss asked us (finish) _____ *the project as soon as possible.*

Cause: *(plus object + infinitive)*
To bring about or produce a consequence, action, or behavior.

Examples of usage with an object + an infinitive:

- Bad weather ***caused us to postpone*** the picnic in the park.

- High fuel prices ***caused us to consider*** taking the bus to work instead of driving.

Now you try: The weather caused us (postpone) _____ *the picnic.*

Choose: *(plus object + infinitive)*
(Note: ***choose*** can also be followed by an infinitive without using an object) To prefer, to make a selection.

Examples of usage with an object + an infinitive:

- We all ***chose Kazu to sing*** the next song at the karaoke party.

- Ingrid ***chose math to be*** her university major.

Now you try: The teacher chose Megume (answer) _____ *the question.*

Convince: *(plus object + infinitive)*
To persuade to do something.

Examples of usage with an object + an infinitive:

- ❏ The bad grade on the exam ***convinced him to study*** harder.

- ❏ I ***convinced my boss to give*** me a raise.

Now you try: *Ted convinced his brother (give up)* _____ *smoking.*

Encourage: *(plus object + infinitive)*
To stimulate.

Examples of usage with an object + an infinitive:

- ❏ The government ***encouraged everyone to go*** out and vote.

- ❏ High demand for our product ***encouraged us to increase*** manufacturing.

Now you try: *We encouraged our team (win)* _____ *the match.*

Expect: *(plus object + infinitive)*
(Note: ***expect*** can also be followed by an infinitive without using an object) To anticipate that something will happen.

Examples of usage with an object + an infinitive:

- ❏ His boss ***expected him to complete*** the project by 5 o'clock.

- ❏ My teacher ***expected me to do*** the homework for tomorrow.

Now you try: *Eri expected her friend (help)* _____ *organize the wedding.*

Forbid: *(plus object + infinitive)*
To command someone not to do something.

Examples of usage with an object + an infinitive:

❑   Airline rules ***forbid us to smoke*** on the plane.

❑   Signs at the Vatican ***forbid visitors to enter*** certain areas.

Now you try: The law forbids people (cross) _____ the street against a red light.

___Force:___ *(plus object + infinitive)*
To coerce or put someone under pressure to do something.

Examples of usage with an object + an infinitive:

❑   High food prices have ***forced the people of this village to grow*** their own food.

❑   Floodwater entering our homes ***forced us to evacuate*** to higher ground.

Now you try: The police forced the robber (surrender) _____.

___Help:___ *(plus object + infinitive)*
(Note: ***help*** can also be followed by an infinitive without using an object) To give aid or assistance to someone.

Examples of usage with an object + an infinitive:

❑   Janice locked her keys in the car. The technician ***helped her to get*** back into her car.

❑   Talking with native speakers every day, really ***helped us to learn*** English quickly.

Now you try: Janis helped us (understand) _____ the difficult math problem.

Hire: (plus object + infinitive)
To enlist the services of someone, usually for pay.

Examples of usage with an object + an infinitive:

❑ The company ***hired him to manage*** their accounting department.

❑ The government ***hired a consultant to help*** complete an environmental project.

Now you try: The company hired him (work) _____ in the sales department.

Invite: (plus object + infinitive)
To request or to welcome.

Examples of usage with an object + an infinitive:

❑ My cousin ***invited me to attend*** a surprise birthday party for her sister.

❑ Because of my high grades in high school, the university ***invited me to enroll*** for the fall term.

Now you try: The bride invited all of her friends (attend) _____ the wedding.

Need: (plus object + infinitive)
(Note: ***need*** can also be followed by an infinitive without using an object) To require something.

Examples of usage with an object + an infinitive:

❑ Andrew ***needed his sister to help*** him with his homework.

❑ The construction company ***needed the crane to lift*** materials to the high floors.

Now you try: Barry needed his wife (pick) _____ him up from work at 5pm.

<u>**Order:**</u> *(plus object + infinitive)*
To make a strong request.

> **Examples of usage with an object + an infinitive:**

> ❑ The president of the company ***ordered his employees to work*** harder.

> ❑ When we arrived at our hotel room, I ***ordered the bellhop to put*** our luggage on the bed.

Now you try: The judge ordered the thief (go) _____ to jail.

<u>**Pay:**</u> *(plus object + infinitive)*

(Note: ***pay*** can also be followed by an infinitive without using an object) To compensate; to be worth; to be valuable.

> **Examples of usage with an object + an infinitive:**

> ❑ Mr. Jones ***paid the man to cut*** his lawn.

> ❑ My father ***paid me to work*** for his company.

Now you try: Annja paid the mechanic (repair) _____ her car.

<u>**Permit:**</u> *(plus object + infinitive)*
To allow.

> **Examples of usage with an object + an infinitive:**

> ❑ The museum guard wouldn't ***permit the students to touch*** the painting.

- During our vacation, our tour group was ***permitted to spend*** extra time in the castle.

Now you try: The teacher permitted the student (take) _____ the exam one week after the other students.

Persuade: *(plus object + infinitive)*
To convince someone to do something.

Examples of usage with an object + an infinitive:

- The shop clerk ***persuaded me to buy*** a second pair of pants.
- My teacher ***persuaded me to study*** extra hard for the upcoming exam.

Now you try: The store clerk persuaded the customer (buy) _____ the expensive computer.

Remind: *(plus object + infinitive)*
To cause someone to remember something.

Examples of usage with an object + an infinitive:

- Signs in the park ***reminded people*** not ***to feed*** the birds.
- The airline reservations clerk ***reminded us to be*** at the airport at least two hours early.

Now you try: My boss reminded me (go) _____ to work early on Monday.

Require: *(plus object + infinitive)*
To impose an obligation or to command.

Examples of usage with an object + an infinitive:

- International travel *__requires us to carry__* a passport.

- Company rules *__require us to clock__* in when we come to work every morning.

Now you try: The government requires you (pay) _____ taxes.

Teach: (plus object + infinitive)
To instruct.

Examples of usage with an object + an infinitive:

- Our car was broken into and a wallet was stolen from the front seat. This experience *__taught us to be__* more careful about leaving personal belongings in the car.

- The boy *__taught his dog to lie down__* on command.

Now you try: The instructor taught us (speak) _____ English more fluently.

Tell: (plus object + infinitive)
To communicate something to someone, usually orally.

Examples of usage with an object + an infinitive:

- The lifeguard at the swimming pool *__told us__* not *__to swim__* in the deep section of the pool.

- The fireman *__told the onlookers to move__* back away from the fire trucks.

Now you try: Her mother told her (clean) _____ her room.

**Urge:** _(plus object + infinitive)_
To press or express importance about the need to do something.

Examples of usage with an object + an infinitive:

- His company _**urged him to study**_ English so that he could have a good career.

- The coach _**urged the team to put**_ more pressure on the pposition.

**Now you try:** _**The manager urged his employees (work)**_ _____ _**hard on the project.**_

**Want:** _(plus object + infinitive)_
(Note: _**want**_ can also be followed by an infinitive without using an object) To have a strong desire for.

Examples of usage with an object + an infinitive:

- Is that policeman following us? Yes, he _**wants us to stop**_ at the side of the road.
- The people of the city _**want the mayor to reduce**_ crime.

**Now you try:** _**Kelly wanted her friend (shop)**_ _____ _**with her at the mall in town.**_

**Warn:** _(plus object + infinitive)_
To caution.

Examples of usage with an object + an infinitive:

- A tsunami was approaching the city. The loud speakers _**warned the people to go**_ to higher ground!

- The signs _**warned us**_ not _**to smoke**_ in the building.

Now you try: The policeman warned us not (drive) _____ over the speed limit.

Would like: *(plus object + infinitive)*

(Note: ***would like*** can also be followed by an infinitive without using an object) Polite form: to desire; to prefer.

Examples of usage with an object + an infinitive:

❑ The boss ***would like us to meet*** with him tomorrow morning.

❑ The bartender ***would like us to pay*** our bill.

Now you try: Paula would like her friends (go) _____ shopping with her.

Chapter 4 <u>review</u>

Correct usage of some common English verbs that are followed by objects and then an infinitive: **common verb + object + infinitive**

Instructions: read and / or listen carefully to the sentences below. Fill in the blank spaces with either the correct infinitive (to + base verb) or gerund (base verb + ing). The base verb is given in parenthesis. Answers can be found in chapter 4, above.

1. Company rules require us (clock)_____ in when we come to work every morning.

2. The boy taught his dog (lie)_____ down on command.

3. Is that policeman following us? Yes, he wants us (stop)_____ at the side of the road.

4. The signs warned us not (smoke)_____ in the building.

5. The bartender would like us (pay)_____ our bill.

6. The airline reservations clerk reminded us (be)_____ at the airport at least two hours early.

7. My teacher persuaded me (study)_____ extra hard for the upcoming exam.

8. During our vacation, our tour group was permitted (spend)_____ extra time in the castle.

9. My father paid me (work)_____ for his company.

10. The president of the company ordered his employees (work)_____ harder.

11. Andrew needed his sister (help)_____ him with his homework.

12. My cousin invited me (attend)_____ a surprise birthday party for her sister.

13. The company hired him (manage)_____ their accounting department.

14. High food prices have forced the people of this village (grow)_____ their own food.

15. Airline rules forbid us (smoke)_____ on the plane.

16. My teacher expected me (do)_____ the homework for tomorrow.

17. Bad weather caused us (postpone)_____ the picnic in the park.

18. I convinced my boss (give)_____ me a raise.

19. High demand for our product encouraged us (increase)_____ manufacturing.

20. The school rules allowed us (smoke)_____ outside the building.

Chapter 5

Correct usage of some common English verbs that are followed by objects and then a gerund: **common verb + object + gerund**

In this chapter you will learn how we use common English verbs that are typically followed by an object and then by a gerund. While this combination is usually used in more informal everyday English speech, it is very common.

Read and / or listen to each of the common English verbs below, followed by their meanings as they are used in sentences with an object and then a gerund, and then some examples of how they are used in real English sentences.

Remember that the meanings being given for the verbs are the meanings when the verbs are used in this way: common verb + object + gerund.

Common English Verbs followed by an object and then followed by a gerund

---

Read and / or listen carefully to the examples, as they will give you a good idea as to how to use the common *verb + object + gerund* combinations in real English sentences. There is a review section at the end of this chapter.

After the examples are given for each verb, you have a chance to practice what have learned. In the "Now you try" sections, fill in the blank space with the correct form of the word given in parenthesis ( ). The answer to the "now you try" section is found in the examples given for the verb.
There is a review section at the end of this chapter. The answers to the review section are found in this chapter in the examples given for each verb.

<u>*Catch:*</u> *(with object+gerund)*
To see or witness someone doing something.

Examples of usage with an object + a gerund:

❏ "I'd better not ***catch you going*** out after 10 o'clock in the evening," said the mother to her daughter.

❏ Our two dogs were lost, but I ***caught them walking*** down by the river and brought them back to our house.

Now you try: Yumi's mother caught her (come) _____ home after midnight.

<u>*See:*</u> *(with object+gerund)*
To witness or observe.

Examples of usage with an object + a gerund:

❏ I ***saw Julia walking*** to school this morning. It looked like she was walking with a limp.

❏ I ***saw my friend Charlie driving*** to work this morning.

Now you try: Stefan saw Hilda (drive) _____ a brand new car.

<u>*Spend:*</u> *(with object+gerund)*
To use up or utilize.

Examples of usage with an object + a gerund:

❏ It was a beautiful evening so my boyfriend and I ***spent time walking*** around the neighborhood.

❑ We spent a lot of money at the mall last night. We ***spent money buying*** clothes and computer stuff.

Now you try: Cynthia's boyfriend spent his money (buy) _____ Cynthia a new car.

___

Witnes: *(with object+gerund)*
To observe.

Examples of usage with an object + a gerund:

❑ The police asked the clerk if he saw the thieves who robbed the store. The clerk said that he had ***witnessed two men running*** from the building about 7:30pm.

❑ We were very lucky to be at the beach so that we could ***witness the sun going*** down.

Now you try: Three people witnessed the men (run) _____ from the bank.

Chapter 5 <u>review</u>

English verbs that are followed by objects and then a gerund

*Instructions: read and / or listen carefully to the sentences below. Fill in the blank spaces with either the correct **infinitive** (to + base verb) or **gerund** (base verb + ing). The base verb is given in parenthesis. Answers can be found in chapter 5, above.*

- "I'd better not catch you (go)_____ out after 10 o'clock in the evening," said the mother to her daughter.

- I saw my friend Charlie (drive)_____ to work this morning.

- We spent a lot of money at the mall last night. We spent money (buy)_____ clothes and computer stuff.

- The police asked the clerk if he saw the thieves who robbed the store. The clerk said that he had witnessed two men (run)_____ from the building about 7:30pm.

- Our two dogs were lost, but I caught them (walk)_____ down by the river and brought them back to our house.

Book 4 – English Irregular Verbs Made Easy

Use English Irregular Verbs Correctly in Every Sentence

Book 4 - Quick-Find Menu

Write (base), **wrote** (simple past), **written** (past participle);   519

Introduction

A Guide to English Irregular English Verbs
English irregular verbs: definitions, explanations, examples of usage and practice reviews.

Using irregular English verbs correctly: when and how to use them in correct English sentences.

You will find in this Focus on English© text a comprehensive listing of irregular English verbs and a complete guide to their correct usage. The student will find explanations and / or meanings for each of the irregular verbs, followed by examples of their correct usage in a sentence in the simple present tense, simple past tense, and an example of how to use the past participle. If the student has the Focus on English© audio book that accompanies this book (available from their school store or from www.FOEBooks.com) he or she will find that each of the examples will be read twice to allow the student to speak the example along with the teacher. This method helps the student to remember the lesson more easily and also helps the student with pronunciation. Focus on English© audio books are also convenient ways for the student to study, review and practice the difficult areas of English while they are on the go.

Chapter 1 *Irregular verbs beginning with the letters A, B, and C*

In this and following sections you will learn how to correctly use irregular English verbs in sentences.

You will have a chance to learn many things about irregular English verbs in this lesson. First, you will see the three important forms for the verb: base form (just the verb itself without conjugation), the simple past form, and the past participle form.

You will then see some common definitions for the verb, many with examples of use.

After you read the definitions, there are examples of use of the verb. One example for the simple present, one example for the simple past, and one example using the past participle (usually in the present perfect tense).

If you have the Focus on English© mp3 audio book that accompanies this lesson (available separately from www.FOEBooks.com), listen to each of the irregular verbs, followed by their meanings along with some examples of how they are used in real English sentences. Each example will be spoken twice. You can practice and reinforce your knowledge by repeating the examples with the teacher on the Focus on English© audio book.

Irregular verbs beginning with the letters A, B, and C
---

*Note: most of the past participle examples are demonstrated in the **present perfect** tense which is made up of the helper verb **have** or **has** plus the irregular verb in the **past participle** form.*

Irregular verbs beginning with A

Arise *(base)*, *arose* *(simple past)*, *arisen* *(past participle)*;
some common meanings: 1. To wake up; 2. To ascend or go up; 3. To sit in an upright position.

Examples:

❑ (Simple Present) Anthony *arises* every morning and has coffee.

❑ (Simple Past) Anthony *arose* yesterday and had a bowl of cereal.

❑ (Past Participle) Anthony has *arisen* and has had a bowl of cereal.

Now you try: (Simple Past) My sister _____ this morning and brushed her teeth.

Awake *(base)*, *awoke* *(simple past)*, *awoken* *(past participle)*;
some common meanings: 1. To rouse from sleep; 2. To become aware of something.

Examples:

❑ (Simple Present) Sandra *awakes* to the sound of her alarm clock every morning at 7 o'clock.

❑ (Simple Past) Sandra *awoke* very early in the morning yesterday.

❑ (Past Participle) Sandra has *awoken* and has had her breakfast.

Note: The verb *awaken*, which is a regular verb, can be used in the exact same way as *awake*. In some English-speaking areas, it is much more common to use the word *awaken*. For example, it would be more common to say: Sandra *awakens* to the sound of her alarm clock every morning.

Now you try: (Past Participle, Present Perfect) Jim ___ _____ and has already taken a shower.

Irregular verbs beginning with B

_Be_ *(base),* **_was/were_** *(simple past),* **_been_** *(past participle);*
some common meanings: 1. To exist; 2. To occupy a specific place; 3 To take place *(and many more meanings).*

> **Examples:**

> ❑ (Simple Present) I **_am_** in the city every day except for Saturday and Sunday.

> ❑ (Simple Past) I **_was_** in Italy last year. We **_were_** in France last September.

> ❑ (Past Participle) I have **_been_** in Tokyo, Japan.

Now you try: (Simple Present) She ___ in the building every day except for Sunday.

Beat *(base),* **_beat_** *(simple past),* **_beaten_** *(past participle);*
some common meanings: 1. To strike repeatedly, to pound, to flap; 2. To prevail over another, as in a competition; 3 To arrive or finish before another *(and other meanings).*

> **Examples:**

> ❑ (Simple Present) I **_beat_** my friend to work every morning. We leave our homes at the same time, but he drives more slowly.

> ❑ (Simple Past) Our team **_beat_** the other team last year. I hope they don't beat us this year.

> ❑ (Past Participle) We have **_beaten_** that team for two years now.

Now you try: (Simple Past) Our team _____ their team last year.

Become *(base),* **_became_** *(simple past),* **_become_** *(past participle);*
some common meanings: 1. To change into, transform into, or grow into over time *(and other meanings)*

Examples:

- (Simple Present) Alice ***becomes*** nervous when she walks through the city at night.

- (Simple Past) Last year Kyoko ***became*** the first female police officer to win the special award for bravery.

- (Past Participle) Over the past three years, our school basketball team has ***become*** a strong team.

Now you try: (past participle, present perfect) Over the past two years, I ___ _____ a better student.

Begin *(base),* ***began*** *(simple past),* ***begun*** *(past participle);*
 some common meanings: 1. To start or commence; to take the first step in doing something *(and other meanings)*

Examples:

- (Simple Present) The class always ***begins*** at 8 o'clock in the morning.

- (Simple Past) Stefan ***began*** his English studies last month.

- (Past Participle) You are late. We have already ***begun*** working on our group project.

Now you try: (simple past) Kaori _____ her English training two years ago.

Bend *(base),* ***bent*** *(simple past),* ***bent*** *(past participle);*
some common meanings: 1. To force something to curve or change shape; 2. To create tension by applying force *(and other meanings)*

Examples:

- (Simple Present) Ironworkers ***bend*** steel rods into different shapes while they build tall buildings.

❑ (Simple Past) Hiro ***bent*** his golf club when he threw it against the tree.

❑ (Past Participle) This is the second time you have ***bent*** this knife. Please be more careful.

Now you try: (Simple Past) Mayumi _____ her golf club when she hit the ground.

Bet *(base),* ***bet*** *(simple past),* ***bet*** *(past participle);*
some common meanings: 1. To wager; 2. Something valuable risked on an uncertain outcome

Examples:

❑ (Simple Present) When people go to Las Vegas, they go to the casinos and ***bet*** money.

❑ (Simple Past) Last week, Tanya ***bet*** her husband that she could arrive home from work before he did.

❑ (Past Participle) Jill and her husband like to go to the horse races at night. The have ***bet*** on horse races for three years.

Now you try: (Simple Past) Hiroko _____ her friend that she could pass the exam.

Bleed (base), ***bled*** (simple past), ***bled*** (past participle); some common meanings: 1. To lose blood; 2. To drain. *(and other meanings)*

Examples:

❑ (Simple Present) When traveling to high altitudes, some people's noses ***bleed***.

❑ (Simple Past) Janice cut herself cutting up vegetables for dinner. She ***bled*** for about two minutes before she put a bandage on the wound.

❑ (Past Participle) The mechanic has **_bled_** the fluid from the brake system and is now ready to replace the brakes.

Now you try: (Simple Past) Cynthia cut herself by accident and _____ for about two minutes before she put a bandage on the wound.

Bite *(base),* **_bit_** *(simple past),* **_bitten_** *(past participle);*
some common meanings: 1. To grip, cut, or tear, sometimes with one's teeth, or with a tool or other object; 2. Sometimes used to refer to sting. *(and other meanings)*

Examples:

❑ (Simple Present) Just before the sun goes down, the mosquitoes really **_bite_**.

❑ (Simple Past) Alex **_bit_** his lip when he jumped over the puddle.

❑ (Past Participle) That dog is very dangerous. It has **_bitten_** many people.

Now you try: (Simple Past) Ted's dog _____ the stranger.

Blow *(base),* **_blew_** *(simple past),* **_blown_** *(past participle);*
some common meanings: 1. To push or expel air from the mouth or from something; 2. Refers to the movement of air as from the wind or in weather. *(and other meanings)*

Examples:

❑ (Simple Present) The wind **_blows_** from the north every September.

❑ (Simple Past) During her birthday party, Yuki **_blew_** out the candles on her cake.

❑ (Past Participle) The wind has **_blown_** hard for two days.

Now you try: (Past participle. present perfect) The wind ___ _____ very little in the past two days.

__Burst__ (base), __burst__ (simple past), __burst__ (past participle);
some common meanings: 1. To explode or fly apart usually because of some internal pressure; 2. To arrive suddenly and unexpectedly. *(and other meanings)*

   Examples:

   ❑ (Simple Present) Every time we blow up these cheap balloons, they __*burst*__!

   ❑ (Simple Past) Wendy __*burst*__ into the room and demanded to speak to the manager.

   ❑ (Past Participle) This is the second time a tire has __*burst*__ on my car!

Now you try: (Simple Past) The manager _____ into the room and fired everyone.

__Break__ (base), __broke__ (simple past), __broken__ (past participle);
some common meanings: 1. To divide into pieces usually by force of bending or applying pressure, as in snap off; 2. To cause to separate or divide into pieces, usually violently or suddenly. 3. To cause to stop functioning. *(and other meanings)*

   Examples:

   ❑ (Simple Present) I __*break*__ my pencil tip every time I take an exam.

   ❑ (Simple Past) Hiroko dropped and __*broke*__ her best dinner plate during dinner last night.

   ❑ (Past Participle) My sister and I have __*broken*__ three computers in the past eight months. We have to be more careful when we use a computer.

Now you try: (Simple Past) Mika _____ her sewing machine yesterday.

Bring *(base),* ***brought*** *(simple past),* ***brought*** *(past participle);*
some common meanings: 1. To take or carry something with you; 2. To cause to occur or happen. *(and other meanings)*

Examples:

- (Simple Present) Yukiko ***brings*** her favorite pen to school with her every day.
- (Simple Past) Claudia ***brought*** her boyfriend to the party with her.
- (Past Participle) This is the third time that Tom has ***brought*** good grades home from school.

Now you try: (Past Participle, Present Perfect) This is the second time that Jennifer has ___ _____ a red dress home from the mall.

Build *(base),* ***built*** *(simple past),* ***built*** *(past participle);*
some common meanings: 1. To create, form or construct something ; 2. To make stronger, increase, or improve upon something by gradually adding to it. *(and other meanings)*

Examples:

- (Simple Present) The Ajax Construction Company ***builds*** houses.
- (Simple Past) He ***built*** his good reputation with hard work.
- (Past Participle) Jim and Nigel have ***built*** three race cars together.

Now you try: (Past Participle, Present Perfect) Don's company ___ _____ three homes.

Burn *(base),* ***burned*** *(simple past),* ***burned*** *(past participle);*
some common meanings: 1. To light, ignite, or destroy with fire; 2. To consume fuel. *(and other meanings)*

Examples:

- ❑ (Simple Present) Wood, paper and plastic ***burn*** when set on fire.

- ❑ (Simple Past) The man ***burned*** all of his money and moved to an island in the Pacific Ocean.

- ❑ (Past Participle) Driving to California, we have ***burned*** about thirty gallons of fuel since this morning.

Now you try: (Simple Past) After cleaning his yard, Alex _____ the trash in his back yard.

Buy *(base),* ***bought*** *(simple past),* ***bought*** *(past participle);*
one common meaning: 1. To purchase, acquire, or get something in exchange for money or something of similar value.

Examples:

- ❑ (Simple Present) Rosie usually ***buys*** flour and vegetables when she goes to the food store.

- ❑ (Simple Past) Simone ***bought*** the new bathing suit last week.

- ❑ (Past Participle) The manager of the soccer team has ***bought*** at least fifty soccer balls this year.

Now you try: (Simple Past) Simon _____ a new car suit last week.

Irregular verbs beginning with C

Catch *(base),* ***caught*** *(simple past),* ***caught*** *(past participle);*
some common meanings: 1. To take hold of, capture, or seize usually after a chase; 2. To become infected by something, usually illness. *(and other meanings)*

Examples:

- ❑ (Simple Present) The early bird always ***catches*** the worm.

- ❑ (Simple Past) The fishermen ***caught*** many fish when they went to sea.

- ❑ (Past Participle) Many of the students in the class have **_caught_** a cold this has week.

Now you try: (Simple Past) We _____ a frog by the lake.

Choose *(base),* **_chose_** *(simple past),* **_chosen_** *(past participle);*
some common meanings: 1. To select from a number of possibilities; 2. To prefer something or someone. *(and other meanings)*

Examples:

- ❑ (Simple Present) She always **_chooses_** the funny programs when she watches TV.

- ❑ (Simple Past) Danielle **_chose_** a very nice restaurant for dinner last night.

- ❑ (Past Participle) The manager has **_chosen_** Frank to organize the company party.

Now you try: (Simple Past) Albert _____ a nice color for his new car.

Come *(base),* **_came_** *(simple past),* **_come_** *(past participle);*
some common meanings: 1. To move or advance towards something or someone; 2. To arrive at or reach a location, understanding or condition. *(and many other meanings)*

Examples:

- ❑ (Simple Present) She **_comes_** to class late every day.

- ❑ (Simple Past) Nicole **_came_** to New York City about three years ago.

- ❑ (Past Participle) The students have **_come_** to understand that they must study hard in this class.

Now you try: (Simple Past) Frank _____ to Honolulu about a year ago.

<u>Cost</u> *(base),* <u>***cost***</u> *(simple past),* <u>***cost***</u> *(past participle);*
some common meanings: 1. To require payment or have as a price; 2. To estimate or determine the value of something (to cost out something). *(and many other meanings)*

Examples:

❑   (Simple Present) The new sports car ***costs*** $150,000.

❑   (Simple Past) When they bought that house last year, it ***cost*** a lot of money.

❑   (Past Participle) His bad behavior has ***cost*** him his freedom. Now he must spend time in jail.

Now you try: (Past Participle, Present Perfect) The apples _____ always _____ one dollar per pound.

<u>Cling</u> *(base),* <u>***clung***</u> *(simple past),* <u>***clung***</u> *(past participle);*
some common meanings: 1. To hold on to, stick to, or adhere to something or someone; 2. To stay close to one another. *(and other meanings)*

Examples:

❑   (Simple Present) The children ***cling*** to their mother's side as they walk through the city.

❑   (Simple Past) Pieces of cheese ***clung*** to the empty pizza plate.

❑   (Past Participle) He has ***clung*** to that old bible for twenty five years.

Now you try: (Simple Past) Allison _____ to the side of the pool while she talked to her friend.

Creep *(base),* ***crept*** *(simple past),* ***crept*** *(past participle);*
some common meanings: 1. To move along very slowly or cautiously; 2. To move along with the body close to the ground. *(and other meanings)*

> **Examples:**

- ❏ (Simple Present) The traffic always ***creeps*** along during rush hour.

- ❏ (Simple Past)   The little boy ***crept*** into the kitchen to take a cookie from the cookie jar.

- ❏ (Past Participle) That snake has ***crept*** slowly towards the bird for five minutes.

Now you try: (Simple Past) The cat _____ towards the little bird.

Cut *(base),* ***cut*** *(simple past),* ***cut*** *(past participle);*
some common meanings: 1. To sever or penetrate with something sharp; 2. To separate from something else; to reduce in size or length, as in cut one's hair. *(and other meanings)*

> **Examples:**

- ❏ (Simple Present)   The family is poor so the mother always ***cuts*** her children's hair.

- ❏ (Simple Past) Janice ***cut*** her finger with the knife.

- ❏ (Past Participle) Barbara has ***cut*** hair at the same beauty salon for ten years.

Now you try: (Simple Past) Janice _____ the birthday cake.

Chapter 1 Review
*Irregular verbs beginning with the letters **A**, **B** and **C***

*Directions: If the verb is used correctly in the sentence check "Correct", if it is not used correctly check "Incorrect". If the sentence is **correct**, then check the correct verb tense box: <u>present</u>, <u>past</u>, or <u>past participle</u>. If the verb is "Incorrect," check the box next to the verb tense that **should** be used in the correct version of the sentence. Answers can be found on the bottom of the page, at the end of the exercise.*

1. *Anthony **<u>arised</u>** yesterday and had a bowl of cereal.* □*Correct* □*Incorrect* □*Present* □*Past* □*Past Participle*

2. The little boy **<u>crept</u>** into the kitchen to take a cookie from the cookie jar. □*Correct* □*Incorrect* □*Present* □*Past* □*Past Participle*

3. Janice **<u>cutted</u>** her finger with the knife. □*Correct* □*Incorrect* □*Present* □*Past* □*Past Participle*

4. The manager of the soccer team has **<u>bought</u>** at least fifty soccer balls this year. □*Correct* □*Incorrect* □*Present* □*Past* □*Past Participle*

5. Danielle **<u>chose</u>** a very nice restaurant for dinner last night. □*Correct* □*Incorrect* □*Present* □*Past* □*Past Participle*

6. The fishermen **<u>catched</u>** many fish when they went to sea. □*Correct* □*Incorrect* □*Present* □*Past* □*Past Participle*

7. The man **<u>burned</u>** all of his money and moved to an island in the Pacific Ocean. □*Correct* □*Incorrect* □*Present* □*Past* □*Past Participle*

8. Claudia **_brought_** her boyfriend to the party with her. ☐*Correct*
   ☐*Incorrect* ☐*Present* ☐*Past* ☐*Past Participle*

9. My sister and I have **_broken_** three computers in the past eight months.
   ☐*Correct* ☐*Incorrect* ☐*Present* ☐*Past* ☐*Past Participle*

10. Every time we **_blow_** up these cheap balloons, they burst! ☐*Correct*
    ☐*Incorrect* ☐*Present* ☐*Past* ☐*Past Participle*

11. That dog is very dangerous. It has **_bitten_** many people. ☐*Correct*
    ☐*Incorrect* ☐*Present* ☐*Past* ☐*Past Participle*

12. She **_bled_** for about two minutes before she put a bandage on the wound.
    ☐*Correct* ☐*Incorrect* ☐*Present* ☐*Past* ☐*Past Participle*

13. Last week, Tanya **_betted_** her husband that she could arrive home from
    work before he did. ☐*Correct*   ☐*Incorrect*   ☐*Present*   ☐*Past*
    ☐*Past Participle*

14. You are late. We have already **_begun_** working on our group project.
    ☐*Correct* ☐*Incorrect* ☐*Present* ☐*Past* ☐*Past Participle*

15. Last year Kyoko **_became_** the first female police officer to win the
    special award for bravery. ☐*Correct*   ☐*Incorrect*   ☐*Present*   ☐*Past*
    ☐*Past Participle*

Answers: 1.Incorrect / Past; 2. Correct / Past; 3. Incorrect / Past; 4. Correct / Past Participle; 5. Correct / Past; 6. Incorrect / Past; 7. Correct / Past; 8. Correct / Past; 9. Correct / Past Participle; 10. Correct / Present; 11. Correct / Past Participle; 12. Correct / Past; 13. Incorrect / Past; 14. Correct / Past Participle; 15. Correct / Past

Chapter 2 *Irregular verbs beginning with the letters D, E and F*

Again, in this chapter, after you read the definitions, there are examples of use of the verb. One example for the simple present, one example for the simple past, and one example using the past participle (usually in the present perfect tense).

If you have the Focus on English© mp3 audio book that accompanies this lesson (available separately from www.FOEBooks.com), listen to each of the irregular verbs, followed by their meanings along with some examples of how they are used in real English sentences. Each example will be spoken twice. You can practice and reinforce your knowledge by repeating the examples with the teacher on the Focus on English© audio book.

Irregular verbs beginning with the letters D, E and F

Note*: most of the past participle examples are demonstrated in the **present perfect** tense which is made up of the helper verb **have** or **has** plus the irregular verb in the **past participle** form.*

Irregular verbs beginning with D

__Dig__ *(base),* ***dug*** *(simple past),* ***dug*** *(past participle);*
some common meanings: 1. To penetrate a surface (usually soil, rock, sand, etc) by turning it over or removing it; 2. To poke or force down into something. *(and other meanings)*

Examples:

- (Simple Present) A dog ***digs*** a hole to bury its bone.

- (Simple Past) The backpack ***dug*** into Allan's back, but he continued walking.

❑ (Past Participle) The treasure hunters have ***dug*** for weeks but have not discovered treasure.

Now you try: (Simple Past) The workers _____ the hole.

Dive *(base),* ***dove*** *(simple past),* ***dived*** *(past participle);*
some common meanings: 1. To plunge, usually headfirst, into water or air; 2. To drop sharply and rapidly, as in prices. *(and other meanings)*

Examples:

❑ (Simple Present) Whenever my sister goes to the swimming pool, she ***dives*** into the deep end.

❑ (Simple Past) The bungee jumper ***dove*** off the bridge.

❑ (Past Participle) The price of fuel has ***dived*** another ten cents per liter since yesterday.

Now you try: (Past Participle, Present Perfect) The price of potatoes ___ _____ another penny a pound.

Do *(base),* ***did*** *(simple past),* ***done*** *(past participle);*
some common meanings: 1. To perform, put into motion, or execute something; 2. To carry out, undertake or commit; 3. To have as your employment, occupation, or profession (as in: "What do you do?"). *(and other meanings)*

Examples:

❑ (Simple Present) We usually ***do*** the dishes before we go to bed.

❑ (Simple Past) I don't want to go to the movies tonight. I ***did*** that last night.

❑ (Past Participle) It is time to stop working because we have ***done*** enough work for today. Let's go home.

Now you try: (Past Participle, Present Perfect) We'__ _____ enough today. Let's go have a drink.

Deal *(base),* **_dealt_** *(simple past),* **_dealt_** *(past participle);*
some common meanings: 1. To distribute something to a number of recipients; 2. To be about or concerned with (as in a book that **_deals_** with English grammar); 3. To do business in a particular area (he **_deals_** in diamonds). *(and other meanings)*

> **Examples:**

> ❏ (Simple Present) My father has a computer store. He **_deals_** in business computers.

> ❏ (Simple Past) That was a good movie last night. It **_dealt_** with the story of two lovers.

> ❏ (Past Participle) I have **_dealt_** the cards, now let's play!

Now you try: (Simple Past) Chapter fourteen _____ with phrasal verbs.

Draw *(base),* **_drew_** *(simple past),* **_drawn_** *(past participle);*
some common meanings: 1. To pull or drag something; 2. To sketch, illustrate or paint; 3. To attract interest in something or someone. *(and other meanings)*

> **Examples:**

> ❏ (Simple Present) The horses **_draw_** (pull) the cart.

> ❏ (Simple Past) My sister **_drew_** that picture.

> ❏ (Past Participle) The movie was very popular. It has **_drawn_** (attracted) thousands of viewers.

Now you try: (Simple Past) My friend _____ the diagram.

Dream *(base)*, ***dreamed*** *(simple past)*, ***dreamed*** *(past participle)*
 some common meanings: 1. To experience thoughts and images while sleeping; 2. To hope for something in the future. *(and other meanings)*

> **Examples:**

- ❑ (Simple Present) Michelle ***dreams*** of the day when she can travel to asia.

- ❑ (Simple Past) Last night I ***dreamed*** I was in Hawaii.

- ❑ (Past Participle)   All of her life, Keiko has ***dreamed*** of becoming a ballerina.

Now you try: (Simple Past) I fell asleep and _____ I was flying.

Drink *(base)*, ***drank*** *(simple past)*, ***drunk*** *(past participle)*;
some common meanings: 1. To take in or swallow liquid; 2. To absorb (as a sponge absorbs water). *(and other meanings)*

> **Examples:**
- ❑ (Simple Present) Jonah ***drinks*** a cup of green tea every day.
- ❑ (Simple Past) I have a headache. I think we ***drank*** too much beer last night.
- ❑ (Past Participle) That juice is delicious. I've ***drunk*** that before while visiting the United States.

Now you try: (Past Participle, Present Participle) We'___ _____ six cans of beer since we've been here.

Drive *(base)*, ***drove*** *(simple past)*, ***driven*** *(past participle)*;

some common meanings: 1. To guide or control a motor vehicle; 2. To force, push, move or propel something. *(and other meanings)*

Examples:

- ❏ (Simple Present) Three of our students **_drive_** to school every day.

- ❏ (Simple Past) The cowboys **_drove_** the herd of horses across the desert.

- ❏ (Past Participle) I have **_driven_** to Los Angeles three times.

Now you try: (Simple Past) I _____ the car to Cape Town.

Irregular verbs beginning with E

Eat *(base)*, **_ate_** *(simple past)*, **_eaten_** *(past participle);*
some common meanings: 1. To consume or take food into the body; 2. To use up, to deplete (as, for example, fuel). *(and other meanings)*

Examples:

- ❏ (Simple Present) Students **_eat_** two meals per day at the school cafeteria.

- ❏ (Simple Past) We **_ate_** lobster for dinner last night.

- ❏ (Past Participle) Our vacation in Italy has **_eaten_** up all of our money.

Now you try: (Simple Past) They _____ vanilla ice cream for dessert.

Irregular verbs beginning with F

Fall (base), **_fell_** (simple past), **_fallen_** (past participle); some common meanings: 1. To drop, tumble, descend towards the ground or lower position; 2. To drop, as in value or worth. *(and other meanings)*

Examples:

- ❑ (Simple Present) When a surfer _**falls**_ off of his surfboard, the wave covers him up.

- ❑ (Simple Past) I laughed so hard I _**fell**_ off of my chair.

- ❑ (Past Participle) The price of food has _**fallen**_ again today.

Now you try: (Simple Past) Peter _____ off his horse but wasn't hurt.

**Feed** *(base),* _**fed**_ *(simple past),* _**fed**_ *(past participle);*
some common meanings: 1. To give food; 2. To supply. *(and other meanings)*

Examples:

- ❑ (Simple Present) Denise _**feeds**_ her cat twice a day.

- ❑ (Simple Past) I _**fed**_ the carpenter wood as he built the house.
  (Meaning: I supplied the carpenter with wood.)

- ❑ (Past Participle) Over the past years, I have _**fed**_ my dogs well. They eat twice a day and I give them treats.

Now you try: (Simple Past) I _____ my dog some hamburger.

**Feel** *(base),* _**felt**_ *(simple past),* _**felt**_ *(past participle);*
some common meanings: 1. To be aware of something through your physical sense of touch; 2. To be emotionally aware of something; 3. To perceive your own physical condition (as in _**feeling**_ tired). *(and other meanings)*

Examples:

- ❑ (Simple Present) I _**feel**_ good after walking on the beach.

- ❑ (Simple Past) The surface of the furniture _**felt**_ very smooth.

- ❑ (Past Participle) I have _**felt**_ sad since my cat died.

Now you try: (Past Participle, Present Perfect) She ____ _____ sad since her boyfriend left her.

Fight *(base),* **fought** *(simple past),* **fought** *(past participle);*
 some common meanings: 1. To struggle against someone or something, physically or with words; 2. To work very hard to achieve something. *(and other meanings)*

> **Examples:**
> ❑ (Simple Present) Workers sometimes **fight** for higher salaries.
> ❑ (Simple Past) Jane **fought** with the storeowner about the high price of the food in his store.
> ❑ (Past Participle) My uncle has **fought** in two wars.

Now you try: (Simple Past) Kimberly _____ with her colleagues about the project.

Fit *(base),* **fit** *(simple past),* **fit** *(past participle);*
some common meanings: 1. To be the right size for something; 2. To be right for something, or be suited or acceptable for something. *(and other meanings)*

> **Examples:**
>
> ❑ (Simple Present) A size seven dress always **fits** her.
>
> ❑ (Simple Past) Paul never went with us because he didn't **fit** in with our group of friends.
>
> ❑ (Past Participle) All ten of us have **fit** into that car at the same time!

Now you try: (Simple Past) The dress _____ Silvia perfectly.

Find *(base),* ***found*** *(simple past),* ***found*** *(past participle);*
some common meanings: 1. To discover, or to discover after searching; 2. To become more aware of something *(I found English to be very helpful). (and other meanings)*

> **Examples:**

- ❏ (Simple Present) I always ***find*** money in the washing machine.

- ❏ (Simple Past) I ***found*** my car keys on the kitchen table.

- ❏ (Past Participle) I have ***found*** that learning English can be very useful.

Now you try: (Simple Past) Sally _____ the wallet in the street.

Flee *(base),* ***fled*** *(simple past),* ***fled*** *(past participle);*
a common meaning: 1. To run away from something. *(and other meanings)*

> **Examples:**

- ❏ (Simple Present) The cat always ***flees*** from the dog when the dog comes in the house.

- ❏ (Simple Past) The bank robber ***fled*** from the police.

- ❏ (Past Participle) The people of the town have ***fled*** from the rising floodwaters.

Now you try: (Past Participle) The people of our city ____ _____ to safety from the tycoon.

Fling *(base),* ***flung*** *(simple past),* ***flung*** *(past participle);*
a common meaning: 1. To toss or throw something, usually without care. *(and other meanings)*

> **Examples:**

- ❏ (Simple Present) Alice usually ***flings*** her coat on the chair when she comes home from work.

- (Simple Past) I ***flung*** my hat at the table but the hat landed on the floor.

- (Past Participle) The witness told us that the robber had ***flung*** a wallet into the trash while fleeing from the police.

Now you try: (Simple Past) Dana _____ the horseshoe at the peg, but she missed.

Fly *(base),* ***flew*** *(simple past),* ***flown*** *(past participle);*
some common meanings: 1. To travel, float or move through the air above the ground; 2. To display a flag *(we flew our country's flag).*   *(and other meanings)*

 Examples:

- (Simple Present) This airline usually ***flies*** every day.

- (Simple Past) I ***flew*** to New York to meet my friend.

- (Past Participle)   I have ***flown*** with the same airline company for twenty years.

Now you try: (Simple Past) My friends _____ to Hong Kong for vacation.

Forbid *(base),* ***forbade*** *(simple past),* ***forbidden*** *(past participle);*
some common meanings: 1. To not be allowed to do something; to prevent someone from doing something *(often used as a command).*

 Examples:

- (Simple Present) School rules ***forbid*** smoking in the building.

- (Simple Past) Her mother ***forbade*** her to go to the party.

- (Past Participle) She was ***forbidden*** to travel across the border.

Now you try: (Simple Past) The doctor _____ *him to leave the hospital.*

__*Forget*__ *(base),* __*forgot*__ *(simple past),* __*forgotten*__ *(past participle);*
a common meaning: 1. To be unable to remember something.

> **Examples:**

> ❑ (Simple Present) Janine sometimes __*forgets*__ to bring a pencil to school.

> ❑ (Simple Past) I __*forgot*__ to pay for the meal at the restaurant!

> ❑ (Past Participle) The party has been so much fun that we have __*forgotten*__ what time it is.

Now you try: (Past Participle, Present Perfect) We'___ _____ to buy a present for our friend's wedding party.

__*Forgive*__ *(base),* __*forgave*__ *(simple past),* __*forgiven*__ *(past participle); a common meaning: 1. To excuse or pardon someone or something.

> **Examples:**

> ❑ (Simple Present) The manager __*forgives*__ employees who are late because of bad weather.

> ❑ (Simple Past) The shop owner __*forgave*__ the poor woman for stealing an apple.

> ❑ (Past Participle) Sally has __*forgiven*__ her boyfriend for arriving late for their date.

Now you try: (Simple Past) The manager _____ *the employee for making a mistake.*

Freeze (base), *froze* (simple past), *frozen* (past participle); a common meaning: 1. To become ice; 2. To be very cold; 3. To be stuck or immobile.

Examples:

❑ (Simple Present) Water *freezes* at 32 degrees Fahrenheit, 0 degrees Celsius.

❑ (Simple Past) The weather was cold and Yuko *froze* without a jacket on.

❑ (Past Participle) I was walking in the mall when someone called my name. As soon as I heard their voice, I *froze*. It was an old friend from many years ago.

Now you try: (Simple Past) The water _____ quickly in the freezer.

Chapter 2 Review
*Irregular verbs beginning with the letters **D**, **E** and **F***

*Directions: If the verb is used correctly in the sentence check "Correct", if it is not used correctly check "Incorrect". If the sentence is **correct**, then check the correct verb tense box: <u>present</u>, <u>past</u>, or <u>past participle</u>. If the verb is "Incorrect," check the box next to the verb tense that **should** be used in the correct version of the sentence. Answers can be found on the bottom of the page, at the end of the exercise.*

1. The worker **<u>dug</u>** a hole in the ground this morning. ☐*Correct* ☐*Incorrect*
   ☐*Present* ☐*Past* ☐*Past Participle*

2. The teacher has **<u>forgaven</u>** the student for being late. ☐*Correct*
   ☐*Incorrect* ☐*Present* ☐*Past* ☐*Past Participle*

3. The weather was cold and the water on the walkway **<u>froze</u>**. ☐*Correct*
   ☐*Incorrect* ☐*Present* ☐*Past* ☐*Past Participle*

4. Her mother **<u>forbade</u>** her to go to the party last night. ☐*Correct*
   ☐*Incorrect* ☐*Present* ☐*Past* ☐*Past Participle*

5. I think we have **<u>forgotten</u>** our keys. ☐*Correct* ☐*Incorrect* ☐*Present*
   ☐*Past* ☐*Past Participle*

6. Anna **<u>fed</u>** her baby some milk this morning. ☐*Correct* ☐*Incorrect*
   ☐*Present* ☐*Past* ☐*Past Participle*

7. I laughed so hard I **<u>fell</u>** off of my chair. ☐*Correct* ☐*Incorrect* ☐*Present*
   ☐*Past* ☐*Past Participle*

8. The taxi driver **<u>drove</u>** me to the concert. ☐*Correct* ☐*Incorrect* ☐*Present*
   ☐*Past* ☐*Past Participle*

9. We **_eated_** fish for dinner last night. □*Correct* □*Incorrect* □*Present* □*Past* □*Past Participle*

10. All of her life, Keiko has **_dreamed_** of becoming a ballerina. □*Correct* □*Incorrect* □*Present* □*Past* □*Past Participle*

11. After running, we **_drinked_** a lot of water. □*Correct* □*Incorrect* □*Present* □*Past* □*Past Participle*

12. The little boy **_drew_** a picture of his sister. □*Correct* □*Incorrect* □*Present* □*Past* □*Past Participle*

13. I have **_dealt_** the cards, now let's play! □*Correct* □*Incorrect* □*Present* □*Past* □*Past Participle*

14. I **_did_** yoga for three hours yesterday. □*Correct* □*Incorrect* □*Present* □*Past* □*Past Participle*

15. The bungee jumper **_dove_** off the bridge. □*Correct* □*Incorrect* □*Present* □*Past* □*Past Participle*

Answers: 1. Correct / Past; 2. Incorrect / Past Participle; 3. Correct / Past; 4. Correct / Past; 5. Correct / Past Participle; 6. Correct / Past; 7. Correct / Past; 8. Correct / Past; 9. Incorrect / Past; 10. Correct / Past Participle; 11. Incorrect / Past; 12. Correct / Past; 13. Correct / Past Participle; 14. Correct / Past; 15. Correct / Past

Chapter 3 *Irregular verbs beginning with the letters G, H and K*

Again, in this chapter, after you read the definitions, there are examples of use of the verb. One example for the simple present, one example for the simple past, and one example using the past participle (usually in the present perfect tense).

If you have the Focus on English© mp3 audio book that accompanies this lesson (available separately from www.FOEBooks.com), listen to each of the irregular verbs, followed by their meanings along with some examples of how they are used in real English sentences. Each example will be spoken twice. You can practice and reinforce your knowledge by repeating the examples with the teacher on the Focus on English© audio book.

Irregular verbs beginning with the letters G, H and K
---

*Note: most of the past participle examples are demonstrated in the **present perfect** tense which is made up of the helper verb **have** or **has** plus the irregular verb in the **past participle** form.*

Irregular verbs beginning with G

Get *(base),* **_got_** *(simple past),* **_gotten_** *or* **_got_** *(past participle);*
some common meanings: 1. To receive something; 2. To purchase or buy something; 3. To arrive at or reach a destination; 4. To possess or own something *(when used with the present perfect tense, as in: We've got $10.);* 5 To become *(to change into an emotional state like angry or mad, as in: He got angry when they told him the price.). (and other meanings)*

Examples:

- ❏ (Simple Present) Rafael always **_gets_** a soft drink when he goes to the store.

- ❏ (Simple Past) My sister **_got_** a cold last week, but she is fine now.

- ❏ (Past Participle) We haven't **_gotten_** to New York yet. The pilot said that we should be there in five more hours.

Now you try: (Simple Past) Everyone in the class _____ a cold two weeks ago.

_Go_ *(base),* **_went_** *(simple past),* **_gone_** *(past participle);*
some common meanings: 1. To move or travel; 2. To function or work properly *(as in: the car won't go because the motor isn't working);* 3. To pass from person to person (as in: the rumor was going around the town.). *(and other meanings)*

Examples:

- ❏ (Simple Present) Tobias **_goes_** to Hawaii every year.

- ❏ (Simple Past) We **_went_** to Asia last year.

- ❏ (Past Participle) They haven't **_gone_** to the movies in a month.

Now you try: (Past Participle, Present Perfect) Calvin ____ _____ to work in two days.

Grind *(base),* **_ground_** *(simple past),* **_ground_** *(past participle);*
 some common meanings: 1. To crush something into small particles, powder or dust; 2. To rub two surfaces together in a harsh way *(The wheels on that wagon grind.). (and other meanings)*

Examples:

- ❏ (Simple Present) Fijians **_grind_** kava root to make a powder.

- ❏ (Simple Past) The flour factory **_ground_** some wheat to make flour.

❑   (Past Participle) We haven't **_ground_** our own coffee for two weeks.

Now you try: (Past Participle, Present Perfect) Patricia _____n't *_____ the coffee yet.*

Grow *(base),* **_grew_** *(simple past),* **_grown_** *(past participle);*
some common meanings: 1. To expand, gain or increase in size; 2. To become *(as in: he grew angry.). (and other meanings)*

   Examples:

❑   (Simple Present) Corn **_grows_** very quickly.

❑   (Simple Past) They **_grew_** flowers in that plant nursery, but now they grow trees.

❑   (Past Participle) During the years or their friendship they have **_grown_** to trust each other.

Now you try: (Simple Past) The children _____ quickly and always needed new clothes.

Give *(base),* **_gave_** *(simple past),* **_given_** *(past participle);*
some common meanings: 1. To transfer something from one person to another; 2. to convey *(the word convey means to transfer, give over to someone, or transmit via speech, as in: I gave him my best regards.). (and other meanings)*

   Examples:

❑   (Simple Present) The grocery clerk always **_gives_** me a free apple when I shop at his store.

❑   (Simple Past) They **_gave_** him a beautiful birthday present.

❑   (Past Participle) My company has **_given_** me a raise in pay this year.

Now you try: (Simple Past) My sister _____ me a nice present for the holiday.

Irregular verbs beginning with H

Hang *(base),* **_hung_** *(simple past),* **_hung_** *(past participle);*
some common meanings: 1. To suspend something from above or a higher position; 2. To stop functioning in the middle of operation *(as in: the computer program always hangs when loading up). (and other meanings)*

Examples:

❏ (Simple Present) He always **_hangs_** his hat on the chair.

❏ (Simple Past) They **_hung_** the rope from the tree.

❏ (Past Participle) The art museum has **_hung_** all of its best paintings on that wall.

Now you try: (Simple Past) The boy _____ the rope from the branch.

Have *(base),* **_had_** *(simple past),* **_had_** *(past participle);*
some common meanings: 1. To be in possession of; 2. To cause to do something *(as in: I had my car cleaned at the carwash). (and other meanings)*

Examples:

❏ (Simple Present) Angelina **_has_** two children.

❏ (Simple Past) The children **_had_** a good time at the beach.

❏ (Past Participle) Albert has **_had_** many good opportunities to learn English.

Now you try: (Past Participle, Present Perfect) The students _____ _____ many good opportunities to practice English.

Hear (base), *__heard__* (simple past), *__heard__* (past participle);
some common meanings: 1. To sense, perceive or be aware of sound (by ear); 2. To learn about something *(as in: I heard that we are having an exam on Tuesday). (and other meanings)*

Examples:

- ❑ (Simple Present) Some animals *__hear__* very well.

- ❑ (Simple Past) When we went to the beach we *__heard__* the sound of children playing.

- ❑ (Past Participle) I've never *__heard__* of that before!

Now you try: (Simple Past) The police _____ the robber inside the house.

Hide (base), *__hid__* (simple past), *__hidden__* (past participle);
some common meanings: 1. To conceal something, to put or keep from being seen; 2. To seek refuge *(as in: The refugees hid in the jungle.). (and other meanings)*

Examples:

- ❑ (Simple Present) When I travel, I always *__hide__* money in my shoe.

- ❑ (Simple Past) Jack *__hid__* his spare car key under his front bumper.

- ❑ (Past Participle) The stars are *__hidden__* by the bright lights of the city.

Now you try: (Simple Past) Kathleen _____ her money under her mattress.

Hit (base), *__hit__* (simple past), *__hit__* (past participle);
some common meanings: 1. To strike something or someone; 2. To reach *(as in: He hit 25 on his last birthday.). (and other meanings)*

Examples:

❑ (Simple Present) When some people ***hit*** old age, they are in very good health.

❑ (Simple Past) Jackie ***hit*** the curb with her tire while driving.

❑ (Past Participle) The amount of poverty in some countries has ***hit*** a new, higher level.

Now you try: (Simple Past) Tom _____ the ball with his bat.

Hold *(base)*, ***held*** *(simple past)*, ***held*** *(past participle)*;
some common meanings: 1. To have something or to keep in one's grasp; 2. To contain something *(as in: The fuel tank holds gasoline). (and other meanings)*

Examples:

❑ (Simple Present) This jar ***holds*** two liters of water.

❑ (Simple Past) Steve ***held*** his fishing pole in one hand and a beer in the other hand.

❑ (Past Participle) Jim has ***held*** many important positions in his company.

Now you try: (Past Participle, Present Perfect) Dennis ___ _____ the same position in his company for nine years.

Hurt *(base)*, ***hurt*** *(simple past)*, ***hurt*** *(past participle)*;
some common meanings: 1. To injure or cause physical pain; 2. To damage *(as in: The soccer player's bad behavior hurt the team.). (and other meanings)*

Examples:

❑ (Simple Present) Her poor job record ***hurts*** her chances of getting a good job in the future.

- ❑ (Simple Past) Steve **_hurt_** his finger with the fishing hook.

- ❑ (Past Participle) Our company was **_hurt_** by poor economic conditions.

Now you try: (Simple Past) Sal _____ his foot when he fell.

Irregular verbs beginning with K

Keep *(base),* **_kept_** *(simple past),* **_kept_** *(past participle);*
some common meanings: 1. To hold onto something; to retain possession of something; 2. To continue to do something *(as in: She kept walking even though her foot hurt.)*; 3.   To take care of *(as in: We have kept dogs for two years.) (and other meanings)*

Examples:

- ❑ (Simple Present) William always **_keeps_** a credit card with him.

- ❑ (Simple Past) My girlfriend **_kept_** asking me for my picture.

- ❑ (Past Participle) Yumiko has **_kept_** a cat for five years.

Now you try: (Past Participle, Present Perfect) Yuki ___ _____ two dogs for more than a year.

Kneel *(base),* **_knelt_** *(simple past),* **_knelt_** *(past participle);*
a common meaning: 1. To go down on or rest on both knees.

Examples:

- ❑ (Simple Present) Many people **_kneel_** and pray at the sacred wall.

- ❑ (Simple Past) After the race, the runner **_knelt_** in the grass to catch his breath.

- ❑ (Past Participle) Many people have **_knelt_** at this alter.

Now you try: (Simple Past) The people _____ in the temple.

Knit *(base),* ***knit / knitted*** *(simple past),* ***knit / knitted*** *(past participle);*
some common meanings: 1. To join closely; 2. To make or weave a fabric with thread or yarn. *(and other meanings)*

> **Examples:**

- ❏ (Simple Present) You ***knit*** with two knitting needles and colorful yarn.

- ❏ (Simple Past) She ***knitted*** a beautiful blanket for her friend.

- ❏ (Past Participle) These sweaters were ***knitted*** by my friend.

Now you try: (Simple Past) Her mother _____ *her a beautiful sweater.*

Know *(base),* ***knew*** *(simple past),* ***known*** *(past participle);*
some common meanings: 1. To be familiar with something, to have an understanding of something or to have something fixed in the mind; 2. To be acquainted with someone or something. *(and other meanings)*

> **Examples:**

- ❏ (Simple Present) All of you ***know*** what the rules are for taking exams: no talking, no books on your desk and cell phones off.

- ❏ (Simple Past) I ***knew*** her when she was just a little girl.

- ❏ (Past Participle) We have ***known*** each other for ten years.

Now you try: (Simple Past) I _____ *that teacher from my other school.*

Chapter 3 Review
Irregular verbs beginning with the letters **G, H** *and* **K**

Directions: If the verb is used correctly in the sentence check "Correct", if it is not used correctly check "Incorrect". If the sentence is **correct***, then check the correct verb tense box:* <u>present</u>, <u>past</u>, *or* <u>past participle</u>. *If the verb is "Incorrect," check the box next to the verb tense that* **should** *be used in the correct version of the sentence. Answers can be found on the bottom of the page, at the end of the exercise.*

1. We haven't **<u>gotten</u>** our change yet from the cashier. □*Correct* □*Incorrect* □*Present* □*Past* □*Past Participle*

2. We **<u>gone</u>** to Europe last year. □*Correct* □*Incorrect* □*Present* □*Past* □*Past Participle*

3. My girlfriend **<u>kept</u>** asking me for my picture. □*Correct* □*Incorrect* □*Present* □*Past* □*Past Participle*

4. She **<u>knitted</u>** a beautiful sweater for her friend. □*Correct* □*Incorrect* □*Present* □*Past* □*Past Participle*

5. I **<u>knew</u>** her when she was just a little girl. □*Correct* □*Incorrect* □*Present* □*Past* □*Past Participle*

6. Jim has **<u>held</u>** many important positions in his company. □*Correct* □*Incorrect* □*Present* □*Past* □*Past Participle*

7. Jack **<u>hitted</u>** the ball with his bat. □*Correct* □*Incorrect* □*Present* □*Past* □*Past Participle*

8. Julia **<u>hid</u>** the present under the table. □*Correct* □*Incorrect* □*Present* □*Past* □*Past Participle*

9. We **_heard_** the fireworks last night. □*Correct* □*Incorrect* □*Present* □*Past* □*Past Participle*

10. She always **_hangs_** her jacket in the closet. □*Correct* □*Incorrect* □*Present* □*Past* □*Past Participle*

11. They **_gived_** him a beautiful birthday present. □*Correct* □*Incorrect* □*Present* □*Past* □*Past Participle*

12. They **_grew_** fruit in their back yard last year. □*Correct* □*Incorrect* □*Present* □*Past* □*Past Participle*

13. The flour factory **_grinds_** wheat into flour. □*Correct* □*Incorrect* □*Present* □*Past* □*Past Participle*

14. Albert has **_had_** many good opportunities to learn English. □*Correct* □*Incorrect* □*Present* □*Past* □*Past Participle*

15. Cynthia **_hurted_** her finger with the hammer. □*Correct* □*Incorrect* □*Present* □*Past* □*Past Participle*

Answers: 1. Correct / Past Participle; 2. Incorrect / Past; 3. Correct / Past; 4. Correct / Past; 5. Correct / Past; 6. Correct / Past Participle; 7. Incorrect / Past; 8. Correct / Past; 9. Correct / Past; 10. Correct / Present; 11. Incorrect / Past; 12. Correct / Past; 13. Correct / Present; 14. Correct / Past Participle; 15. Incorrect / Past

Chapter 4 *Irregular verbs beginning with the letters L, M, P and Q*

Again, in this chapter, after you read the definitions, there are examples of use of the verb. One example for the simple present, one example for the simple past, and one example using the past participle (usually in the present perfect tense).

If you have the Focus on English© mp3 audio book that accompanies this lesson (available separately from www.FOEBooks.com), listen to each of the irregular verbs, followed by their meanings along with some examples of how they are used in real English sentences. Each example will be spoken twice. You can practice and reinforce your knowledge by repeating the examples with the teacher on the Focus on English© audio book.

Irregular verbs beginning with the letters L, M, P and Q

*Note: most of the past participle examples are demonstrated in the **present perfect** tense which is made up of the helper verb **have** or **has** plus the irregular verb in the **past participle** form.*

Irregular verbs beginning with L

*Lay (base), **laid** (simple past), **laid** (past participle);*
some common meanings: 1. To cause to lie down; 2. To put, place or set something onto a surface *(as in: I always lay the book on the table when I come home). (and other meanings)*

Examples:

❑ (Simple Present) In the evening, the mother ***lays*** her baby in its bed to sleep.

❑ (Simple Past) She ***laid*** the pencil down on her book.

❑ (Past Participle) Bricks are ***laid*** on cement to form a wall.

Now you try: (Simple Past) The teacher _____ the book down on his desk.

Lie *(base),* ***lay*** *(simple past),* ***lain*** *(past participle);*
some common meanings: 1. To recline; 2. To occupy a position, place or location *(as in: The United States lies between Canada and Mexico on the North American continent.). (and other meanings)*

Examples:

❑ (Simple Present) The Hawaiian Islands ***lie*** in the Pacific Ocean.

❑ (Simple Past) The dog ***lay*** outside all day.

❑ (Past Participle) The books have ***lain*** on the shelf for two years.

Now you try: (Simple Past) The baby _____ inside its crib.

Note: the word ***lay*** is different from the word ***lie*** in the following ways:
- ***Lay*** means to actively put or place something on something else.
- ***Lie*** means the act of reclining or laying horizontal on a surface
- ***Lay*** uses ***laid*** for its simple past and past participle
- ***Lie*** uses ***lay*** for its simple past and ***lain*** for its past participle.

Note: the word, ***lie***, as in, to not tell the truth, is a regular English verb and uses ***lied*** for its simple past and past participle. There is no difference in pronunciation between ***lie*** (to recline) and ***lie*** (to not tell the truth).

Lead *(base),* ***led*** *(simple past),* ***led*** *(past participle);*
some common meanings: 1. To guide, direct or show the way; 2. To live one's life *(as in: She led a life of devotion to her family.). (and other meanings)*

Examples:

❑ (Simple Present) The tour guide leads visitors through the museum.

❑ (Simple Past) The teacher led his students through the difficult chapter.

❑ (Past Participle) The captain has led his men into many battles.

Now you try: (Simple Past) Alfred _____ us to the pub with the good beer.

Leap *(base),* ***leapt*** *(simple past),* ***leapt*** *(past participle);*
some common meanings: 1. To spring or jump, usually upward; 2. To move quickly *(as in: He leapt into action.). (and other meanings)*

Examples:

❑ (Simple Present) Frogs often ***leap*** from one giant leaf to another.

❑ (Simple Past) The hikers ***leapt*** over the stream.

❑ (Past Participle) We've ***leapt*** over many fallen tree branches during our hike.

Now you try: (Past Participle, Present Perfect) They'___ _____ over several rocks during their mountain walk.

Lend *(base),* ***lent*** *(simple past),* ***lent*** *(past participle);*
some common meanings: 1. To allow someone to use something temporarily; 2. To give off, or assist in creating an affect *(as in: The wood trim lent a warm feeling to the house.). (and other meanings)*

Examples:

❑ (Simple Present) My friend always asks me if he can borrow my book. I always ***lend*** him my book.

❑ (Simple Past) Mark ***lent*** me his flashlight yesterday.

- ❑ (Past Participle) Over the years, the library has **_lent_** many books to people.

Now you try: (Simple Past) Alice _____ me ten dollars to buy the book.

Let *(base),* **_let_** *(simple past),* **_let_** *(past participle);*
some common meanings: 1. To allow or permit something; 2. To release from *(as in: I stepped on my sister's toe and she let out a yell.). (and other meanings)*

Examples:

- ❑ (Simple Present) The teacher **_lets_** us take a break at 10 o'clock.

- ❑ (Simple Past) Marshall **_let_** the dog in one hour ago.

- ❑ (Past Participle) The shopkeeper has always **_let_** us pay by credit card.

Now you try: (Simple Past) The teacher _____ the students in the class even though they were late.

Light *(base),* **_lit_** */* **_lighted_** *(simple past),* **_lit_** */* **_lighted_** *(past participle);*
a common meaning: 1. To cause to give off light, to illuminate something *(and other meanings).*

Examples:

- ❑ (Simple Present) We always **_light_** a candle before the ceremony.

- ❑ (Simple Past) Harvey **_lit_** the campfire.

- ❑ (Past Participle) The monks of the temple have **_lit_** the same lamp for many years.

Now you try: (Past Participle, Present Perfect) We _____ ____ the candles and we are ready for the party.

Lose *(base),* ***lost*** *(simple past),* ***lost*** *(past participle);*
some common meanings: 1. To misplace or mislay something so that you are unable to find it; 2. To no longer have control of something *(as in: I lost my driver's license because I had too many violations.) (and other meanings).*

Examples:

- ❏ (Simple Present) He always ***loses*** his books on the very first day of class.

- ❏ (Simple Past) I ***lost*** my car keys yesterday.

- ❏ (Past Participle) Sam has ***lost*** his contact lenses and now cannot see well enough to drive.

Now you try: (Simple Past) She _____ her purse last night.

Irregular verbs beginning with M

Make *(base),* ***made*** *(simple past),* ***made*** *(past participle);*
some common meanings: 1. To create, build, construct; 2. To cause something to come about *(as in: Her mother made her change her clothes.); 3. To earn (and other meanings).*

Examples:

- ❏ (Simple Present) The company ***makes*** car tires.

- ❏ (Simple Past) Allison ***made*** a wonderful dinner last night.

- ❏ (Past Participle) Jill has ***made*** a lot of money in her business.

Now you try: (Simple Past) Mother _____ a wonderful pasta for the party.

Mean *(base),* ***Meant*** *(simple past),* ***Meant*** *(past participle);*
 some common meanings: 1. To Signify or represent; 2. To have as an intention *(as in: He meant go tell the teacher he would be late, but he*

forgot.); 3. Used to indicate value *(as in: Her necklace meant a lot to her).* *(and other meanings).*

Examples:

❏ (Simple Present) The word food ___means___ something to eat.

❏ (Simple Past) I ___meant___ to stop and buy milk, but I forgot.

❏ (Past Participle) Kyoko's job has always ___meant___ a lot to her.

Now you try: (Simple Past) Jon _____ to go shopping before he went home, but forgot.

___Meet___ *(base),* ___Met___ *(simple past),* ___Met___ *(past participle);*
some common meanings: 1. To come together by chance or by arrangement; 2. To assemble *(as in: The group met to discuss important issues.).*   *(and other meanings).*

Examples:

❏ (Simple Present) The group ___meets___ every Monday at 7pm.

❏ (Simple Past) I ___met___ my friend Al at the pub.

❏ (Past Participle) Class has always ___met___ at 8:30am.

Now you try: (Simple Past) We _____ our friends at the party.

Irregular verbs beginning with P

___Pay___ *(base),* ___paid___ *(simple past),* ___paid___ *(past participle);*
some common meanings: 1. To compensate or reimburse for something with money or something of value; 2. To give or bestow *(as in: She paid the waiter a complement for his good service.).*   *(and other meanings).*

Examples:

- ❑ (Simple Present) First you ***pay*** the cashier, and then you can go inside the theater.

- ❑ (Simple Past) I ***paid*** too much money for that car.

- ❑ (Past Participle) We have already ***paid*** the waiter for our dinner.

Now you try: (Simple Past) The company _____ us one million dollars for the products.

Prove *(base),* ***proved*** *(simple past),* ***proven*** *(past participle);*
a common meaning: 1. To demonstrate that something is true, to authenticate, to verify. *(and other meanings).*

Examples:

- ❑ (Simple Present) Students ***prove*** they are 18 years old by showing their ID cards at the door.

- ❑ (Simple Past) I ***proved*** to my girlfriend that I loved her by giving her a ring.

- ❑ (Past Participle) I have taken a driving test and have ***proven*** that I am a good driver.

Now you try: (Past Participle, Present Perfect) Scientists _____ _____ that the climate is becoming warmer.

Put *(base),* ***put*** *(simple past),* ***put*** *(past participle);*
some common meanings: 1. To place or set something in a location; 2. To wager or bet *(as in: I'll put $25 on the black horse);* 3. To express in words *(as in: Put very simply, you're fired!).* *(and other meanings).*

Examples:

- ❑ (Simple Present) We usually ***put*** a donation in the box.

- ❑ (Simple Past) Tim ***put*** his homework on the teacher's desk yesterday.

❑ (Past Participle)   Jamie has **_put_** all of her books in her locker and has gone to lunch.

Now you try: (Simple Past) The student _____ his finished exam on the teacher's desk.

Irregular verbs beginning with Q

Quit *(base),* **_quit_** *(simple past),* **_quit_** *(past participle);*
a common meaning: 1. To stop doing something, to terminate.   *(and other meanings).*

Examples:

❑ (Simple Present) People usually **_quit_** their jobs for good reasons.

❑ (Simple Past) Jason **_quit_** playing soccer because of an injury.

❑ (Past Participle) Three people have **_quit_** our company this week.

Now you try: (Simple Past) Don _____ working when he was 70 years old.

Chapter 4 Review
*Irregular verbs beginning with the letters **L**, **M**, **P** and **Q***

*Directions: If the verb is used correctly in the sentence check "Correct", if it is not used correctly check "Incorrect". If the sentence is **correct**, then check the correct verb tense box: present, past, or past participle. If the verb is "Incorrect," check the box next to the verb tense that **should** be used in the correct version of the sentence. Answers can be found on the bottom of the page, at the end of the exercise.*

1. Jason **_quit_** playing soccer because of an injury. ☐*Correct* ☐*Incorrect*
   ☐*Present* ☐*Past* ☐*Past Participle*

2. Jamie has **_put_** all of her books in her locker and has gone to lunch.
   ☐*Correct* ☐*Incorrect* ☐*Present* ☐*Past* ☐*Past Participle*

3. She **_lain_** the pencil down on her book. ☐*Correct* ☐*Incorrect* ☐*Present*
   ☐*Past* ☐*Past Participle*

4. The Hawaiian Islands **_lay_** in the Pacific Ocean. ☐*Correct* ☐*Incorrect*
   ☐*Present* ☐*Past* ☐*Past Participle*

5. The teacher **_led_** his students through the difficult chapters. ☐*Correct*
   ☐*Incorrect* ☐*Present* ☐*Past* ☐*Past Participle*

6. We've **_leapt_** over many fallen tree branches during our hike. ☐*Correct*
   ☐*Incorrect* ☐*Present* ☐*Past* ☐*Past Participle*

7. My friend always **_asks_** me if he can borrow my book. ☐*Correct*
   ☐*Incorrect* ☐*Present* ☐*Past* ☐*Past Participle*

8. Marshall **_let_** the dog into the house one hour ago. ☐*Correct* ☐*Incorrect*
   ☐*Present* ☐*Past* ☐*Past Participle*

9. The monks of the temple have **_lit_** the same lamp for many years. ☐*Correct* ☐*Incorrect* ☐*Present* ☐*Past* ☐*Past Participle*

10. I **_lost_** my car keys yesterday. ☐*Correct* ☐*Incorrect* ☐*Present* ☐*Past* ☐*Past Participle*

11. I **_meant_** to stop and buy milk, but I forgot. ☐*Correct* ☐*Incorrect* ☐*Present* ☐*Past* ☐*Past Participle*

12. I **_met_** my friend Al at the pub. ☐*Correct* ☐*Incorrect* ☐*Present* ☐*Past* ☐*Past Participle*

13. We have already **_paid_** the waiter for our dinner. ☐*Correct* ☐*Incorrect* ☐*Present* ☐*Past* ☐*Past Participle*

14. Tim **_put_** his homework on the teacher's desk yesterday. ☐*Correct* ☐*Incorrect* ☐*Present* ☐*Past* ☐*Past Participle*

15. Three people have **_quit_** our company this week. ☐*Correct* ☐*Incorrect* ☐*Present* ☐*Past* ☐*Past Participle*

Answers: 1. Correct / Past; 2. Correct / Past Participle; 3. Incorrect / Past; 4. Incorrect / Present (lie); 5. Correct / Past; 6. Correct / Past Participle; 7. Correct / Present; 8. Correct / Past; 9. Correct / Past Participle; 10. Correct / Past; 11. Correct / Past; 12. Correct / Past; 13. Correct / Past Participle; 14. Correct / Past; 15. Correct / Past Participle.

Chapter 5 *Irregular verbs beginning with the letters R and S*

Again, in this chapter, after you read the definitions, there are examples of use of the verb. One example for the simple present, one example for the simple past, and one example using the past participle (usually in the present perfect tense).

If you have the Focus on English© mp3 audio book that accompanies this lesson (available separately from www.FOEBooks.com), listen to each of the irregular verbs, followed by their meanings along with some examples of how they are used in real English sentences. Each example will be spoken twice. You can practice and reinforce your knowledge by repeating the examples with the teacher on the Focus on English© audio book.

Irregular verbs beginning with the letters R and S

---

*Note: most of the past participle examples are demonstrated in the **present perfect** tense which is made up of the helper verb **have** or **has** plus the irregular verb in the **past participle** form.*

Irregular verbs beginning with R

<u>Read</u> *(base),* **<u>read</u>** *(simple past),* **<u>read</u>** *(past participle);*
some common meanings: 1. To look at and understand the meanings of words and sentences; 2. To decipher the meaning of *(as in: The captain read the sky for signs of bad weather.) (and other meanings).*

> **Examples:**

- ❏ (Simple Present) Always **<u>read</u>** the instructions before taking an exam.

- ❏ (Simple Past) Yesterday, Peggy **<u>read</u>** four chapters from her history book.

❑ (Past Participle) One of the students in our class has **_read_** hundreds of books over the past two years.

Now you try: (Past Participle, Present Perfect) The English professor _____ _____ all of our essays.

Ride *(base),* **_rode_** *(simple past),* **_ridden_** *(past participle);*
some common meanings: 1. To be carried by a vehicle or on the back of a horse or other animal; 2. To travel along *(as in: We rode the rails in many parts of Europe.) (and other meanings).*

Examples:

❑ (Simple Present) Thousands of people in Tokyo **_ride_** the subway every day.

❑ (Simple Past) He **_rode_** the bus to work yesterday.

❑ (Past Participle) My brothers and I have **_ridden_** the train to school since the beginning of the year.

Now you try: (simple past) Jennifer _____ a taxi to work last week.

Rise *(base),* **_rose_** *(simple past),* **_risen_** *(past participle);*
a common meaning: 1. To come up, increase or ascend from a lower position. *(and other meanings).*

Examples:

❑ (Simple Present) In the winter, the sun **_rises_** later in the morning.

❑ (Simple Past) The homeless man **_rose_** to his feet and walked towards the city.

❑ (Past Participle) Albert has **_risen_** to the position of manager in a very short period of time.

Now you try: (Simple Present) The sun usually _____ in the east.

Run *(base),* ***ran*** *(simple past),* ***run*** *(past participle);*
some common meanings: 1. To move swiftly on foot; 2. To flee or retreat from; 3. To make a short trip to somewhere; 4. To operate or cause to function; 5. To be offered as or to offer oneself as a political candidate. *(and other meanings).*

Examples:

❑ (Simple Present) Eileen and Dan **_run_** for two miles every day.

❑ (Simple Past) I **_ran_** to the store and bought a package of chewing gum this morning.

❑ (Past Participle) Roger has **_run_** for president of our club three times in the past.

Irregular verbs beginning with S

Say *(base),* ***said*** *(simple past),* ***said*** *(past participle);*
some common meanings: 1. To express something in words; 2. To indicate or show *(as in: the clock says it's time to eat.). (and other meanings).*

Examples:

❑ (Simple Present) People sometimes **_say_** things that hurt other people.

❑ (Simple Past) I just read the sign and it **_said_** that we couldn't park here.

❑ (Past Participle) The teacher has **_said_**, at least three times, that the test will be given on Friday.

Now you try: (Simple Past) The sign _____ no smoking.

See *(base),* ***saw*** *(simple past),* ***seen*** *(past participle);*

some common meanings: 1. To perceive or sense images through the eye; 2. To understand or comprehend something *(as in: I see what you are talking about now.). (and other meanings).*

Examples:

❑ (Simple Present) The eagle has good eyesight and **_sees_** very tiny animals on the ground.

❑ (Simple Past) We **_saw_** the solar eclipse yesterday afternoon.

❑ (Past Participle) That old man has **_seen_** many things in his life.

Now you try: (Simple Past) The girls _____ the snake crawl into the bushes.

Seek *(base),* **_sought_** *(simple past),* **_sought_** *(past participle);*
 some common meanings: 1. To look for or search for; 2. To want to reach or obtain a certain goal *(as in: Alice seeks a degree in nursing.). (and other meanings).*

Examples:

❑ (Simple Present) During a hot day, horses and cows **_seek_** the shade of a tree.

❑ (Simple Past) Margaret **_sought_** a good book on gardening.

❑ (Past Participle) Many companies have **_sought_** good employees, but good employees are hard to find.

Now you try: (Simple Past) The police _____ a man wearing a dark coat and sunglasses.

Sell *(base),* **_sold_** *(simple past),* **_sold_** *(past participle);*
some common meanings: 1. To exchange or deliver something for something else of value; 2. To persuade someone about something or to do something

(as in: The car salesman sold the customer on buying all of the accessories for the vehicle.). (and other meanings).

Examples:

❑ (Simple Present) A furniture emporium is a big store that **_sells_** furniture.

❑ (Simple Past) Claudio **_sold_** his motor scooter last week.

❑ (Past Participle) We are too late. The store has **_sold_** all of it's English text books.

Now you try: (Past Participle, Present Perfect) We are too late. The grocery store _____ _____ all of it's bananas.

Send *(base),* **_sent_** *(simple past),* **_sent_** *(past participle);*
some common meanings: 1. To mail, ship, dispatch, or transmit something to someone else; 2. To broadcast *(as in: The police sent the message by radio.). (and other meanings).*

Examples:

❑ (Simple Present) My grandmother **_sends_** me a gift for my birthday every year.

❑ (Simple Past) The businessman **_sent_** a check to his supplier.

❑ (Past Participle) The package was **_sent_** yesterday.

Now you try: (Simple Past) I _____ a check to the tax department last week.

Set *(base),* **_set_** *(simple past),* **_set_** *(past participle);*
some common meanings: 1. To put something in a position or location, to place; 2. To adjust something for proper operation *(as in: The operator set*

the machine to cut thin slices.); To establish (as in: The runner set a new world record.) (and other meanings).

Examples:

- (Simple Present) When Mary gets home at night, she always **_sets_** her books on her desk.

- (Simple Past) Mark **_set_** his calculator on his car seat yesterday, but now he is unable to find it.

- (Past Participle) The swimmer has **_set_** two world records.

Now you try: (Simple Past) I _____ a check to the tax department last week.

Sew *(base),* **_sewed_** *(simple past),* **_sewn_** *(past participle);*
a common meaning: 1. To join, attach, or repair by stitching with needle and thread *(and other meanings).*

Examples:

- (Simple Present) Many people **_sew_** as a hobby.

- (Simple Past) The seamstress **_sewed_** the button on the dress.

- (Past Participle) His mother has **_sewn_** many buttons onto his shirts.

Now you try: (Simple Past) Her mother _____ the tear in her shorts.

Shake *(base),* **_shook_** *(simple past),* **_shaken_** *(past participle);*
some common meanings: 1. To cause something to jerk, vibrate or move back and forth in a jerky motion; 2. To disturb or make someone very uneasy *(as in: The family was shaken by the loss of their home to fire.) (and other meanings).*

Examples:

- ❏ (Simple Present) An earthquake ***shakes*** the ground, which sometimes causes buildings to fall.

- ❏ (Simple Past) Robbie ***shook*** the vending machine to get his candy.

- ❏ (Past Participle) The airline passengers were ***shaken*** by the plane's sudden drop in altitude.

Now you try: (Simple Past) Rafael _____ his boots to let the dirt fall out.

Shave *(base),* ***shaved*** *(simple past),* ***shaven*** *(past participle);*
some common meanings: 1. To remove facial or body hair, usually with a razor; 2. To remove a small amount of something *(as in: The carpenter shaved a little bit of wood from the end of the plank.) (and other meanings).*

Examples:

- ❏ (Simple Present) Alex gets up every morning and ***shaves*** his face.

- ❏ (Simple Past) The nurse ***shaved*** the hair from around the wound on her arm.

- ❏ (Past Participle) The homeless man hasn't ***shaven*** for two years.

Now you try: (Simple Past) Bob _____ his face early this morning.

Shine *(base),* ***shone / shined*** *(simple past),* ***shone / shined*** *(past participle);*
some common meanings: 1. To make something bright and glossy; 2. To aim a beam of light *(as in: The policeman shone the flashlight on the building.); 3. To emit light (and other meanings).*

Examples:

- ❏ (Simple Present) The sun ***shines*** brightly.

- ❏ (Simple Past) The campers ***shone*** their light on the tree.

❑ (Past Participle) The housekeeper has **_shined_** the kitchen table and the dining room table.

Now you try: (Past Participle, Present Perfect) The cleaning lady _____ _____ all of the table surfaces.

Shoot *(base),* **_shot_** *(simple past),* **_shot_** *(past participle);*
 some common meanings: 1. To discharge or fire a weapon (gun or other weapon); 2. To hit with a bullet or other projectile, sometimes causing injury or damage; 3.   To film, videotape, or photograph something *(and other meanings).*

Examples:

❑ (Simple Present) Soldiers **_shoot_** at a paper target for practice.

❑ (Simple Past) The hunter **_shot_** the deer.

❑ (Past Participle) The film was **_shot_** in the desert.

Now you try: (Simple Past) The boy _____ the rifle.

Show *(base),* **_showed_** *(simple past),* **_shown_** *(past participle);*
some common meanings: 1. To direct someone's attention to something or to display something; 2.   To guide, direct, or lead someone *(and other meanings).*

Examples:

❑ (Simple Present) The tour guide **_shows_** the tourists the old building.

❑ (Simple Past) The real estate agent **_showed_** the woman the apartment.

❑ (Past Participle) The film was **_shown_** in the theater.

Now you try: (Simple Past) Alicia _____ her friends her new dog.

Shrink *(base),* ***shrank / shrunk*** *(simple past),* ***shrunk*** *(past participle);*
some common meanings: 1. To reduce in size; 2. To reduce in value *(and other meanings).*

Examples:

- ❑ (Simple Present) Cotton t-shirts sometimes ***shrink*** when you wash them.

- ❑ (Simple Past) When I washed the t-shirt it ***shrank***.

- ❑ (Past Participle) The value of the dollar has ***shrunk*** over the past two years.

Now you try: (Simple Past) When I washed my socks, they _____!

Shut *(base),* ***shut*** *(simple past),* ***shut*** *(past participle);*
some common meanings: 1. To close or block entrance to something; 2. To confine or restrict something or someone to an enclosed space *(as in: The prisoners of war were shut in a small room.) (and other meanings).*

Examples:

- ❑ (Simple Present) We always ***shut*** the door when we come in the house.

- ❑ (Simple Past) After she got out of the taxi, she ***shut*** the door.

- ❑ (Past Participle) We have always ***shut*** the windows when we've left the building.

Now you try: (Simple Past) After she left the house, she _____ the door.

Sing *(base),* ***sang*** *(simple past),* ***sung*** *(past participle);*
a common meaning: 1. To make sounds or word in musical tones; to perform songs *(and other meanings).*

Examples:

- ❏ (Simple Present) I always **_sing_** in the shower. It makes me feel good.

- ❏ (Simple Past) It was a beautiful day. The birds **_sang_** and the sun shone.

- ❏ (Past Participle) Wendy has a beautiful voice. She has **_sung_** with some famous groups.

Now you try: (Past Participle, Present Perfect) We _____ _____ a lot of songs during karaoke parties.

Sink *(base)*, **_sank_** *(simple past)*, **_sunk_** *(past participle)*;
some common meanings: 1. To fall, drop or descend to a lower level; 2. To make an impression *(as in: It finally sank in that I would not be able to complete the course this year.) (and other meanings).*

Examples:

- ❏ (Simple Present) Huge waves at sea **_sink_** big ships.

- ❏ (Simple Past) I dropped a penny into the glass of water and it **_sank_** to the bottom.

- ❏ (Past Participle) The sun has **_sunk_** in the west.

Now you try: (Simple Past) I dropped my glasses into the pool and they _____ to the bottom.

Sit *(base)*, **_sat_** *(simple past)*, **_sat_** *(past participle)*;
some common meanings: 1. To change from one position (standing, lying, kneeling, etc.), to placing your hindquarters onto a surface and resting in that position; 2. Can be used to mean located or situated somewhere *(as in: The company building sits on the corner or Elm Street and Vine Road.) (and other meanings).*

Examples:

- ❑ (Simple Present) The teacher usually **_sits_** in the front of the room.

- ❑ (Simple Past) My girlfriend and I **_sat_** in the last row of the movie theater.

- ❑ (Past Participle) Many important people have **_sat_** in the seats at the U.N building.

Now you try: (Simple Past) Our friends _____ together at the dinner table.

Sleep *(base),* **_slept_** *(simple past),* **_slept_** *(past participle);*
a common meaning: 1. To be in a state of unconscious rest *(and other meanings).*

Examples:

- ❑ (Simple Present) My brother usually **_sleeps_** late on Sundays.

- ❑ (Simple Past) Alice **_slept_** until 10am this morning and was late for work.

- ❑ (Past Participle) Many important leaders have **_slept_** in that hotel.

Now you try: (Past Participle, Present Perfect) We ___ _____ in at least ten hotels during our vacation.

Slide *(base),* **_slid_** *(simple past),* **_slid_** *(past participle);*
some common meanings: 1. To glide, skim or slip over a, usually, smooth surface; 2. To move downward *(as in: The price of fuel has slid to a lower price.) (and other meanings).*

Examples:

- ❑ (Simple Present) Polar bears often **_slide_** on the ice and snow.

- ❑ (Simple Past) The car **_slid_** off the road and hit a tree.

❑ (Past Participle) Prices for computers have **_slid_** to new, lower prices over the past two years.

Now you try: (Simple Past) The children _____ down the water slide.

Speak *(base),* **_spoke_** *(simple past),* **_spoken_** *(past participle);*
some common meanings: 1. To communicate thoughts, ideas, and opinions orally, with words; 2. To communicate without using words *(as in: Her eyes spoke of great sadness.) (and other meanings).*

Examples:

❑ (Simple Present) My boyfriend lives in France, but I **_speak_** to him everyday by telephone.

❑ (Simple Past) The politician **_spoke_** to the crowd last night.

❑ (Past Participle) The movie star has **_spoken_** to the press four times today.

Now you try: (Simple Past) The teacher _____ to the student after class.

Speed *(base),* **_sped_** *(simple past),* **_sped_** *(past participle);*
a common meaning: 1. To cause to move quickly, to hasten *(and other meanings).*

Examples:

❑ (Simple Present) Alicia **_speeds_** to work in her car every morning because she is late.

❑ (Simple Past) The police car **_sped_** through the town.

❑ (Past Participle) Many cyclists have **_sped_** through the down during the race.

Now you try: (Simple Past) The motorcycle _____ along the road.

500

Spend *(base),* ***spent*** *(simple past),* ***spent*** *(past participle);*
a common meaning: 1. To use up, pay out, expend (energy, time, money, resources) *(and other meanings).*

> **Examples:**

- ❑ (Simple Present) Jacques ***spends*** a lot of money on school.

- ❑ (Simple Past) We ***spent*** $40 on dinner last night.

- ❑ (Past Participle) We have already ***spent*** too much money on shopping today. I only have $10 left!

Now you try: (Simple Past) Marta _____ $500 for food yesterday.

Spill *(base),* ***spilled*** *(simple past),* ***spilled*** *(past participle);*
a common meaning: 1. To cause something (often liquid) to run out of a container, often without control *(and other meanings).*

> **Examples:**

- ❑ (Simple Present) Jamie always ***spills*** her beer when she drinks too much.

- ❑ (Simple Past) The nurse knocked over the bottle and ***spilled*** the medicine.

- ❑ (Past Participle) Too much blood has been ***spilled*** in war.

Now you try: (Simple Past) John accidentally _____ his medicine on the table.

Spin *(base),* ***spun*** *(simple past),* ***spun*** *(past participle);*
some common meanings: 1. To cause to rotate quickly, twirl or whirl; 2. To draw out and twist fiber to make thread or yarn *(and other meanings).*

> **Examples:**

❑ (Simple Present) The cloth factory **_spins_** cotton to make thread. The thread is used to make clothing.

❑ (Simple Past) The speeding car **_spun_** out of control.

❑ (Past Participle) For many years, the women of the village have **_spun_** thread to make clothing.

Now you try: (Simple Past) The wheels of the car _____ quickly as the car sped down the road.

Spit *(base),* **_spit / spat_** *(simple past),* **_spat_** *(past participle);*
some common meanings: 1. To eject saliva from the mouth, or to eject something as if it came from the mouth, such as a projectile; 2. To release or emit something forcefully and suddenly *(as in: She was angry and spit out her feelings to the others.) (and other meanings).*

Examples:
❑ (Simple Present) The volcano **_spits_** out hot lava every day.
❑ (Simple Past) The criminal **_spat_** on the ground and then ran away.
❑ (Past Participle) The cat has **_spit_** at the dog two times, and now the dog will not attack.

Now you try: (Simple Past) The food tasted terrible and some people _____ it out onto their plate.

Split *(base),* **_split_** *(simple past),* **_split_** *(past participle);*
some common meanings: 1. To separate, to divide in half; 2. To divide evenly, as with profits *(as in: At the end of the year the two business owners split the profits.) (and other meanings).*

Examples:

❑ (Simple Present) When we go to the fruit stand the clerk **_splits_** an apple and gives one half to me and the other half to my brother.

- ❑ (Simple Past) The camper **_split_** the log and threw one half into the fire.

- ❑ (Past Participle) We have owned our business together for five years. We have always **_split_** the earnings equally.

Now you try: (Past Participle, Present Perfect) Husbands and wives _____ always _____ their financial responsibilities in half.

Spread *(base),* **_Spread_** *(simple past),* **_Spread_** *(past participle);*
some common meanings: 1. To make wider or move to or more objects or people further apart; 2. To cover with a layer of something *(as in: She spread butter on the bread.) (and other meanings).*

Examples:

- ❑ (Simple Present) Adrian always **_spreads_** his muffins with honey in the morning.

- ❑ (Simple Past) Yesterday, the boy **_spread_** the pieces of the puzzle on the table.

- ❑ (Past Participle) The children have **_spread_** their toys on the floor.

Now you try: (Simple Past) Her mother _____ butter on the toast.

Spring *(base),* **_Sprang_** *(simple past),* **_Sprung_** *(past participle);*
some common meanings: 1. To leap, jump or bound; 2. To move or occur suddenly *(as in: The police sprung into action.) (and other meanings).*

Examples:

- ❑ (Simple Present) The competitor **_springs_** forward when the starting gun is fired.

- ❑ (Simple Past) The faucet **_sprung_** a leak. *(Meaning: The faucet began leaking suddenly.)*

❏ (Past Participle) Some campers have gotten lost in the mountains, but rescuers have __*sprung*__ into action to rescue them.

Now you try: (Simple Past) When he heard the loud noise, he _____ from his seat and ran to the window.

__*Stand*__ *(base),* __*stood*__ *(simple past),* __*stood*__ *(past participle);*
some common meanings: 1. To rise to and maintain an upright vertical position; 2. To rise to an upright position on the feet *(and other meanings).*

Examples:

❏ (Simple Present) The broom always __*stands*__ in the corner with the other cleaning tools.

❏ (Simple Past) We __*stood*__ in line at the theater for two hours.

❏ (Past Participle) We've __*stood*__ here for fifteen minutes waiting for a bus.

Now you try: (Past Participle, Present Perfect) I'____ _____ here for an hour waiting for my friends.

__*Steal*__ *(base),* __*stole*__ *(simple past),* __*stolen*__ *(past participle);*
some common meanings: 1. To take something without permission; 2. To draw attention to something or someone unexpectedly because of some action *(as in: The magic show was wonderful, but the clown stole the show with his act.) (and other meanings).*

Examples:

❏ (Simple Present) My girlfriend always __*steals*__ popcorn out of my popcorn bag when we are at the movies. *(Note: The word* __*steal*__ *usually means* take without permission, *but is often used among friends* *to mean that one person has borrowed something without asking, but it was okay to do this.)*

- ❏ (Simple Past) Last night, someone **_stole_** the soccer ball from our front yard.

- ❏ (Past Participle) The dolphins have always **_stolen_** the show at the aquarium.

Now you try: (Simple Past) The thief _____ the woman's purse.

Stick *(base),* **_stuck_** *(simple past),* **_stuck_** *(past participle);*
some common meanings: 1. To puncture, penetrate, prod or pierce, sometimes with a sharp object; 2. To place the blame or responsibility for some action or deed on someone *(as in: My friends stuck me with the bill at the restaurant.);* 3. To put, thrust or push something somewhere *(as in: He stuck the mail in the mailbox and rushed away.);* 4. To glue or cause to adhere something to a surface *(and other meanings).*

Examples:

- ❏ (Simple Present) The mail clerk **_sticks_** the mail in the post office boxes every day.

- ❏ (Simple Past) I **_stuck_** the stamp on the envelop and placed the letter in the mailbox.

- ❏ (Past Participle) The secretary has **_stuck_** mailing labels on one hundred envelopes.

Now you try: (Simple Past) I _____ the notice on the bulletin board.

Stink *(base),* **_stank / stunk_** *(simple past),* **_stunk_** *(past participle);*
some common meanings: 1. To give off a bad or unpleasant odor; 2. To be highly offensive, untrustworthy, or of really poor quality *(as in: His business practices stink.) (and other meanings).*

Examples:

❑ (Simple Present) That cheese always ***stinks***.

❑ (Simple Past) That movie ***stunk*** last night.

❑ (Past Participle) This is not the first time he has come to work smelling like that. He has ***stunk*** like that for weeks.

Now you try: (Simple Past) The rotting food _____.

Sting *(base),* ***stung*** *(simple past),* ***stung*** *(past participle);*
a common meaning: 1. To cause to feel a sharp pain, like when pricked or stuck with a needle, or the stinger part of certain insects like bees *(and other meanings).*

Examples:

❑ (Simple Present) The wasp ***stings*** when it feels threatened.

❑ (Simple Past) During the inoculation, the needle ***stung*** my arm.

❑ (Past Participle, Present Perfect) The bees in this area have ***stung*** many people.

Now you try: (Past Participle) The wasps living in our back wall ____ _____ me several times.

Strike *(base),* ***struck*** *(simple past),* ***struck*** *(past participle);*
some common meanings: 1. To hit or cause to contact something violently; 2. To collide with or crash into something *(as in: He struck his head on the lamp overhead.)*; 3. To stop work for an employer in protest of work conditions or low wages *(and other meanings).*

Examples:

❑ (Simple Present) The golfer swings his club and ***strikes*** the ball perfectly.

- ❏ (Simple Past) Cynthia ***struck*** her knee on the leg of the dining room table.

- ❏ (Past Participle) This is the second time I have ***struck*** my head on that beam.

Now you try: (Simple Past) He was too tall for the doorway and he _____ his head when he entered the building.

Swear *(base),* ***swore*** *(simple past),* ***sworn*** *(past participle);*
some common meanings: 1. To make a promise, vow or oath, usually declaring loyalty, honesty or truth; 2. To curse or use bad or profane language *(and other meanings).*

Examples:

- ❏ (Simple Present) The new members ***swear*** an oath of loyalty to their club.

- ❏ (Simple Past) Last time I came to this place I ***swore*** I would never return, but I came back anyway.

- ❏ (Past Participle) The witness has ***sworn*** that he is telling the truth.

Now you try: (Simple Past) When the man hit his hand with the hammer, he _____.

Sweep *(base),* ***swept*** *(simple past),* ***swept*** *(past participle);*
some common meanings: 1. To clear away or clean an area as with a broom or brush; 2. To search usually with the help of more than one person or with technical aids; 3. To clear away everything as with a storm or flood *(as in: The flood swept away the houses.) (and other meanings).*

Examples:

- ❑ (Simple Present)　My mother always *__sweeps__* the kitchen in the morning.

- ❑ (Simple Past)　The storm *__swept__* the coastline causing much damage.

- ❑ (Past Participle)　The police have *__swept__* the building for bombs and now it is safe to reenter.

Now you try: (Simple Past) The maid _____ the kitchen.

__Swim__ (base), __swam__ (simple past), __swum__ (past participle);
a common meaning:　1.　To move through the water using the power of limbs, fins, tails, etc., *(and other meanings).*

Examples:

- ❑ (Simple Present)　Eric *__swims__* in the pool every day.

- ❑ (Simple Past)　My girlfriend and I *__swam__* in the ocean last night.

- ❑ (Past Participle)　The competitors have *__swum__* fourteen laps in the pool since three o'clock.

Now you try: (Simple Past) Andy _____ in the pool last week.

__Swing__ (base), __swung__ (simple past), __swung__ (past participle);
some common meanings:　1.　To hit at something with a sweeping motion; 2. To move back and forth while suspended from something (as in: The children swung from a rope in the tree.) *(and other meanings).*

Examples:

- ❑ (Simple Present)　The golfer *__swings__* his golf club to hit the ball.

- ❑ (Simple Past)　We *__swung__* back and forth in the swing that hung from the tree. (　Meaning:　a *swing* is a seat connected to ropes that are tied to a tree branch.)

❏ (Past Participle) The baseball player has ***swung*** at the ball three times and has missed each time!

Now you try: (Simple Past) The man _____ the axe to cut the tree down.

Chapter 5 Review
Irregular verbs beginning with the letters **R** *and* **S**

Directions: If the verb is used correctly in the sentence check "Correct", if it is not used correctly check "Incorrect". If the sentence is **correct***, then check the correct verb tense box:* <u>present</u>*,* <u>past</u>*, or* <u>past participle</u>*. If the verb is "Incorrect," check the box next to the verb tense that* **should** *be used in the correct version of the sentence. Answers can be found on the bottom of the page, at the end of the exercise.*

1. The girl <u>**swore**</u> at her classmate after school. ☐*Correct*   ☐*Incorrect*
   ☐*Present*   ☐*Past*   ☐*Past Participle*

2. The waves from the ocean <u>**swept**</u> the coastline. ☐*Correct*   ☐*Incorrect*
   ☐*Present*   ☐*Past*   ☐*Past Participle*

3. My friends and I <u>**swimmed**</u> in the ocean after school.   ☐*Correct*
   ☐*Incorrect* ☐*Present*   ☐*Past*   ☐*Past Participle*

4. Cynthia <u>**struck**</u> her knee on the leg of the dining room table. ☐*Correct*
   ☐*Incorrect* ☐*Present*   ☐*Past*   ☐*Past Participle*

5. The bee <u>**stung**</u> the little girl earlier today. ☐*Correct*   ☐*Incorrect*
   ☐*Present*   ☐*Past*   ☐*Past Participle*

6. The man <u>**sticked**</u> the stick in the ground about an hour ago. ☐*Correct*
   ☐*Incorrect* ☐*Present*   ☐*Past*   ☐*Past Participle*

7. Last night, someone <u>**stole**</u> the radio from Adam's car.   ☐*Correct*
   ☐*Incorrect* ☐*Present*   ☐*Past*   ☐*Past Participle*

8. We <u>**stood**</u> in line at the concert hall for three hours to buy tickets.
   ☐*Correct*   ☐*Incorrect*   ☐*Present*   ☐*Past*   ☐*Past Participle*

9. Albert ***spreaded*** butter and honey on his toast this morning. □*Correct* □*Incorrect* □*Present* □*Past* □*Past Participle*

10. The teenager ***spun*** the wheels of his car, which made a loud noise. □*Correct* □*Incorrect* □*Present* □*Past* □*Past Participle*

11. We ***spent*** $50 on food today. □*Correct* □*Incorrect* □*Present* □*Past* □*Past Participle*

12. The police car ***sped*** through the town last night. □*Correct* □*Incorrect* □*Present* □*Past* □*Past Participle*

13. Allison usually ***speaks*** to her friend every day by telephone. □*Correct* □*Incorrect* □*Present* □*Past* □*Past Participle*

14. The plate ***slided*** off the table and fell to the floor. □*Correct* □*Incorrect* □*Present* □*Past* □*Past Participle*

15. It was a beautiful day. The birds ***sang*** and the sun shone. □*Correct* □*Incorrect* □*Present* □*Past* □*Past Participle*

Answers: 1. Correct / Past; 2. Correct / Past; 3. Incorrect / Past; 4. Correct / Past; 5. Correct / Past; 6. Incorrect / Past; 7. Correct / Past; 8. Correct / Past; 9. Incorrect / Past; 10. Correct / Past; 11. Correct / Past; 12. Correct / Past; 13. Correct / Present; 14. Incorrect / Past; 15. Correct / Past

Chapter 6 Irregular verbs beginning with the letters T, U and W

Again, in this chapter, after you read the definitions, there are examples of use of the verb. One example for the simple present, one example for the simple past, and one example using the past participle (usually in the present perfect tense).

If you have the Focus on English© mp3 audio book that accompanies this lesson (available separately from www.FOEBooks.com), listen to each of the irregular verbs, followed by their meanings along with some examples of how they are used in real English sentences. Each example will be spoken twice. You can practice and reinforce your knowledge by repeating the examples with the teacher on the Focus on English© audio book.

Irregular verbs beginning with the letters T, U and W

*Note: most of the past participle examples are demonstrated in the **present perfect** tense which is made up of the helper verb **have** or **has** plus the irregular verb in the **past participle** form.*

Irregular verbs beginning with T

<u>**Take**</u> *(base),* <u>***took***</u> *(simple past),* <u>***taken***</u> *(past participle);*
some common meanings: 1. To get into your possession, to seize, to get hold of; 2. To draw in or absorb (as in: She stood on the beach and took in the beautiful sunset.); 3. To sit for an exam (as in: We took an exam yesterday.) *(and other meanings).*

   Examples:

- ❏ (Simple Present)   Someone **_takes_** your ticket at the door before you enter the theater.

- ❏ (Simple Past) She **_took_** an apple from the apple tree.

- ❏ (Past Participle) We have **_taken_** three exams over the past two weeks.

Now you try: (Past Participle, Present Perfect) Janet _____ _____ *three pieces of candy from the candy dish.*

Teach *(base),* **_taught_** *(simple past),* **_taught_** *(past participle);*
some common meanings: 1. To share knowledge or skill with someone; 2. To give instruction or training, especially as a profession *(and other meanings).*

Examples:

- ❏ (Simple Present)   The red ESL textbook **_teaches_** you basic English grammar.

- ❏ (Simple Past)   Adam **_taught_** English to intermediate level English students.

- ❏ (Past Participle) Kelly has **_taught_** English for ten years.

Now you try: (Simple Past) Andrew _____ *students how to speak English.*

Tear *(base),* **_tore_** *(simple past),* **_torn_** *(past participle);*
some common meanings: 1. To pull something apart or into pieces by force; to rend 2. To separate or divide by force *(and other meanings).*

Examples:

- ❏ (Simple Present) When you walk into the theater, the ticket taker **_tears_** your ticket in half and gives you the bottom half.

❑ (Simple Past) Alexis **_tore_** her boyfriend's love letter in half when she discovered he was dating another girl.

❑ (Past Participle) Sun Wah has **_torn_** her stocking while walking through the bushes.

Now you try: (Simple Past) Rene _____ a page our of the magazine.

Tell *(base),* **_told_** *(simple past),* **_told_** *(past participle);*
some common meanings: 1. To express something with words; to convey by language; to give an account of something 2. To discover something by watching or observation *(as in: She could tell he was lying because he could not look at her.) (and other meanings).*

Examples:

❑ (Simple Present) Every day our teacher **_tells_** us that studying is important.

❑ (Simple Past) The old man **_told_** us the story about the ghost that lives in the woods.

❑ (Past Participle) Jenny has **_told_** the police about the robbery.

Now you try: (Simple Past) Our boss _____ us to complete the project by Wednesday.

Think *(base),* **_thought_** *(simple past),* **_thought_** *(past participle);*
some common meanings: 1. When you form thoughts in your mind; to ponder 2. To visualize or imagine *(as in: Think how beautiful it will be in Hawaii.);* 3. To form an opinion *(as in: Everyone thought the movie was terrible.) (and other meanings).*

Examples:

❑ (Simple Present) Karen **_thinks_** that money grows on trees!

❑ (Simple Past) Allison didn't come prepared for the exam. She ***thought*** the exam was next week.

❑ (Past Participle) Our committee has ***thought*** of many solutions to the problem, but the governor has approved none of them.

Now you try: (Simple Past) Aiko _____ she could learn English easily.

Throw *(base),* ***threw*** *(simple past),* ***thrown*** *(past participle);*
some common meanings: 1. To hurl, fling, or toss an object through the air; 2. To put something on or take something off hastily or in a hurry *(as in: I threw on a coat and went outside.)*; 3. To move a lever or switch from one side to the other *(as in: He threw the switch and the lights came on.)* *(and other meanings).*

Examples:

❑ (Simple Present) He ***throws*** a baseball really well!

❑ (Simple Past) After the picnic we ***threw*** our garbage in the trash.

❑ (Past Participle) We have ***thrown*** all of our beer cans into the trash since the end of the party.

Now you try: (Simple Past) James _____ his old notebook into the trash.

Irregular verbs beginning with U

Understand *(base),* ***understood*** *(simple past),* ***understood*** *(past participle);*
some common meanings: 1. When you comprehend the meaning of something 2. To have sympathy or tolerance for something said or done *(as in: I understand it has been a difficult time for you.)* *(and other meanings).*

Examples:

- ❑ (Simple Present) All of our employees ***understand*** that tomorrow we only have to work a half day.

- ❑ (Simple Past) The student ***understood*** the lesson but still had a question for the teacher.

- ❑ (Past Participle) Gloria hasn't ***understood*** the teacher since the course began.

Now you try: (Past Participle, Present Perfect) None of the new students _____ _____ the homework assignments since last week.

Upset *(base),* ***upset*** *(simple past),* ***upset*** *(past participle);*
some common meanings: 1. To overturn or capsize; 2. To cause someone distress, or to disturb someone or something *(as in: I upset the people in the audience.) (and other meanings)*.

Examples:

- ❑ (Simple Present) The cat always ***upsets*** the flower vase when she jumps up on the table.

- ❑ (Simple Past) Kim ***upset*** his girlfriend when he told her he was leaving.

- ❑ (Past Participle) The speaker at the conference has ***upset*** everyone with his comments.

Now you try: (Simple Past) Raul _____ his parents with his bad grades from school.

Irregular verbs beginning with W

Wake *(base),* ***woke*** *(simple past),* ***woken*** *(past participle);*

some common meanings: 1. To rouse from sleep, to stop sleeping; 2. To become alert *(as in: The yelling woke him up and he realized that the manager was serious.) (and other meanings).*

Examples:

- ❑ (Simple Present) Jill's dog likes to sleep. She **_wakes_** her dog up to go for a walk every morning.

- ❑ (Simple Past) On Saturday morning, he **_woke_** to the news that a typhoon was approaching his city.

- ❑ (Past Participle) The campers have **_woken_** up too late to see the sun rise.

Now you try: (Simple Past) His mother _____ him at 7:00am to go to school.

Wear *(base)*, **_wore_** *(simple past)*, **_worn_** *(past participle)*; some common meanings: 1. To have on, as with clothing; 2. To damage, diminish in usefulness, or erode something over time *(as in: The tires of his car wore down over the long trip.) (and other meanings).*

Examples:

- ❑ (Simple Present) All of this walking around the city wears me out.

- ❑ (Simple Past) She wore a beautiful gown for the wedding.

- ❑ (Past Participle) I have worn this shirt too many times. I need a new shirt.

Now you try: (Simple Past) He _____ a plaid pair of pants to the meeting.

Weave *(base)*, **_wove_** *(simple past)*, **_woven_** *(past participle)*;

some common meanings: 1. To interlace threads or yarn into cloth or a cloth product; 2. To make up something or contrive something *(as in: He wove an interesting story about his trip overseas.) (and other meanings).*

Examples:

❏ (Simple Present)   The woman **_weaves_** a beautiful blanket from wool threads.

❏ (Simple Past)   The island native **_wove_** a beautiful basket from palm leaves.

❏ (Past Participle)   Eric has **_woven_** a belt from strips of leather.

Now you try: (Simple Past) The women _____ baskets for fruit and vegetables.

Weep *(base),* **_wept_** *(simple past),* **_wept_** *(past participle);*
some common meanings: 1. To cry or she tears as an expression of emotion; 2. To leak slowly *(as in: Some water wept from pipe joint.) (and other meanings).*

Examples:

❏ (Simple Present)   The bride's maid always **_weeps_** during the wedding.

❏ (Simple Past)   Ginger **_wept_** when she lost her cat.

❏ (Past Participle)   Jennifer has **_wept_** with joy since learning that she was admitted to the university.

Now you try: (Past Participle, Present Perfect) The mother ____ _____ many times because of her misfortune.

Win *(base),* **_won_** *(simple past),* **_won_** *(past participle);*

some common meanings: 1. To achieve success or victory through effort; 2. To achieve success through luck *(as in: I won the lottery!)* *(and other meanings).*

Examples:

❑ (Simple Present) Our team **_wins_** a lot because we work hard.

❑ (Simple Past) My uncle Jimmy **_won_** the lottery last week.

❑ (Past Participle) That team has **_won_** four tournaments so far.

Now you try: (Simple Past) Shawn _____ a new car last week.

Wind *(base),* **_wound_** *(simple past),* **_wound_** *(past participle);*
some common meanings: 1. To turn, for example a handle, in a serious of circular motions; 2. To wrap something around another object *(as in: He wound the string around the stick.);* 3. To proceed on a curving or twisting road, path or course *(and other meanings).*

Examples:

❑ (Simple Present) My father **_winds_** his old wristwatch every morning.

❑ (Simple Past) Elizabeth **_wound_** her yarn around the spool.

❑ (Past Participle) The child has **_wound_** up his toy and now he wants to play with it on the floor.

Now you try: (Simple Past) The little girl _____ her kite string onto a spool as the kite came to earth.

Withdraw *(base),* **_withdrew_** *(simple past),* **_withdrawn_** *(past participle);*
some common meanings: 1. To take back, to remove; 2. To go back or retreat on a battlefield *(and other meanings).*

Examples:

- ❏ (Simple Present) Before going shopping, I always ***withdraw*** money from the bank.

- ❏ (Simple Past) The commander ***withdrew*** his men from the battle.

- ❏ (Past Participle) Mr. and Mrs. Jones have ***withdrawn*** their money from the bank.

Now you try: (Simple Past) The soldiers _____ as the enemy advanced.

Wring *(base),* ***wrung*** *(simple past),* ***wrung*** *(past participle);*
some common meanings: 1. When you twist, squeeze or compress something (for example, cloth) usually to remove the liquid from it; 2. To squeeze or grasp your hands as in distress *(and other meanings).*

Examples:

- ❏ (Simple Present) Whenever she finishes an exam, she ***wrings*** her hands worrying about her grade.

- ❏ (Simple Past) The woman ***wrung*** the water out of the towel.

- ❏ (Past Participle) We have ***wrung*** our hands enough worrying about the future.

Now you try: (Simple Past) After falling in the pool, Bobby went home and _____ his clothing and hung it up to dry.

Write *(base),* ***wrote*** *(simple past),* ***written*** *(past participle);*
some common meanings: 1. To form letters or symbols for the purpose of communication; 2. To record on a computer storage device *(as in: When I saved my file the computer wrote it to the hard drive.) (and other meanings).*

Examples:

- ❑ (Simple Present) Dana keeps a diary. She **_writes_** something in her diary every day.

- ❑ (Simple Past) The angry citizens **_wrote_** a letter to the government.

- ❑ (Past Participle) He has **_written_** two books since last year.

Now you try: (Simple Past) I _____ an email to my friend overseas.

Chapter 6 Review
Irregular verbs beginning with the letters **T, U** *and* **W**

Directions: If the verb is used correctly in the sentence check "Correct", if it is not used correctly check "Incorrect". If the sentence is **correct***, then check the correct verb tense box:* <u>present</u>*,* <u>past</u>*, or* <u>past participle</u>*. If the verb is "Incorrect," check the box next to the verb tense that should be used in the correct version of the sentence. Answers can be found on the bottom of the page, at the end of the exercise.*

1. The angry customer **<u>writed</u>** a letter to the president of the company.
    ☐*Correct* ☐*Incorrect* ☐*Present* ☐*Past* ☐*Past Participle*

2. The woman **<u>wrung</u>** the water out of the wash cloth. ☐*Correct* ☐*Incorrect* ☐*Present* ☐*Past* ☐*Past Participle*

3. My sister **<u>won</u>** the lottery last week. ☐*Correct* ☐*Incorrect* ☐*Present* ☐*Past* ☐*Past Participle*

4. Elizabeth **<u>winds</u>** her yarn around the spool last night. ☐*Correct* ☐*Incorrect* ☐*Present* ☐*Past* ☐*Past Participle*

5. Ginger **<u>wept</u>** when she lost her pet bird. ☐*Correct* ☐*Incorrect* ☐*Present* ☐*Past* ☐*Past Participle*

6. The woman **<u>wove</u>** a hat from palm leaves. ☐*Correct* ☐*Incorrect* ☐*Present* ☐*Past* ☐*Past Participle*

7. He **<u>wore</u>** formal clothing for the party. ☐*Correct* ☐*Incorrect* ☐*Present* ☐*Past* ☐*Past Participle*

8. On Saturday morning, he **<u>woke</u>** to the news that a typhoon was approaching his city. ☐*Correct* ☐*Incorrect* ☐*Present* ☐*Past* ☐*Past Participle*

9. The speaker at the conference has **_upset_** everyone with his comments.
   ☐ *Correct* ☐ *Incorrect* ☐ *Present* ☐ *Past* ☐ *Past Participle*

10. The student **_understanded_** the lesson but still had a question for the
    teacher. ☐ *Correct* ☐ *Incorrect* ☐ *Present* ☐ *Past* ☐ *Past Participle*

11. After the picnic we **_throwed_** our garbage in the trash. ☐ *Correct*
    ☐ *Incorrect* ☐ *Present* ☐ *Past* ☐ *Past Participle*

12. Jeff has already **_told_** his friends about his new girlfriend. ☐ *Correct*
    ☐ *Incorrect* ☐ *Present* ☐ *Past* ☐ *Past Participle*

13. The secretary **_teared_** the paper from the pad. ☐ *Correct* ☐ *Incorrect*
    ☐ *Present* ☐ *Past* ☐ *Past Participle*

14. Adam has **_teached_** English to intermediate level English students for three
    years. ☐ *Correct* ☐ *Incorrect* ☐ *Present* ☐ *Past* ☐ *Past Participle*

15. The boy **_took_** an apple from the apple tree. ☐ *Correct* ☐ *Incorrect*
    ☐ *Present* ☐ *Past* ☐ *Past Participle*

Answers: 1. Incorrect / Past; 2. Correct / Past; 3. Correct / Past; 4. Incorrect / Past (wound); 5. Correct / Past; 6. Correct / Past; 7. Correct / Past; 8 Correct / Past; 9. Correct / Past Participle; 10. Incorrect / Past; 11. Incorrect / Past; 12. Correct / Past Participle; 13. Incorrect / Past; 14. Incorrect / Past Participle; 15. Correct / Past

Book 5 - English Articles a, an, and the

How to use English articles correctly in every sentence

Book 5 – Table of Contents

Focus On English© Reference Series
Making the difficult parts of learning English easy

*Using English Articles Correctly: a guide to the correct use of **a**, **an** and **the** with explanations and examples.*

*You will find in this Focus On English Reference Edition a guide to the correct usage of English articles. There is an explanation for each of the rules for using **a**, **an**, and **the**, and then there are examples of their correct usage in a sentence.*

If you have the Focus On English digital audio book for this book (sold separately at www.FOEBooks.com), then you will be able to listen and practice pronunciation along with the teacher. This method helps the student remember the lesson more easily and also helps the student with pronunciation.

A note to students

A free audio book version of this English Articles book can be found here:

Chapter 1 *English articles <u>a</u> and <u>an</u>*

In this section you will learn all of the rules for using the English articles, a and an. Read the rules for usage and the explanations. After each explanation there are examples to help reinforce the correct use of the article in common English sentences.

*Quick rules for **a** and **an** in this chapter:*
- ✓ *Use **a** and **an** with singular, noncount nouns (E.g: I ate **an** egg. She bought **a** dress.)*
- ✓ *Don't use **a** and **an** with plural nouns (E.g: Don't say: I ate **an** eggs)*
- ✓ *Use **a** and **an** to mean 'each one' or 'per' (E.g: I make $20 **an** hour.)*
- ✓ *Use **a** before 'few' or 'little' (E.g: I bought **a** few eggs)*

English articles <u>a</u> and <u>an</u>

Rules, explanations and examples for correct usage of <u>a</u> and <u>an</u>

1. Use <u>***a***</u> and <u>***an***</u> with singular, noncountable nouns (sometimes called noncount nouns).

1a. Use <u>***a***</u> if the noun that follows begins with a consonant *sound*. Use <u>***an***</u> if the noun that follows begins with a vowel *sound*.

Examples:

❑   The student has <u>***a***</u> pencil.

❑   The child has <u>***an***</u> ice cream cone.

❑   The doctor will be finished in <u>***an***</u> hour.

(Note: ***hour*** is pronounced like ***our***)

Now you try (fill in the blank): The boy has _____ egg sandwich.

2. **Don't** use <u>***a***</u> and <u>***an***</u> with plural nouns.
   Examples of what **not** to do:

❑   I ate <u>***an***</u> apples for lunch. (Correct form: I ate apples for lunch.)

❑ I bought *a* computers yesterday. (Correct form: I bought computers yesterday)

> ***Now you try*** *(fill in the blank): We ate _____ bananas for breakfast.*

3. Use *a* or *an* to mean for *each* or *per*.
(Remember: use *a* before consonant *sounds* and *an* before vowel *sounds*).

Examples:

❑ How much money do you make at your job? I make $50 *an* hour.
(Remember: even though hour begins with "h," which is a consonant, hour is *pronounced* with an "o" sound, so we use *an* and do not use *a*.)

❑ How many people arrive at the airport every day? Over 3,000 people *a* day arrive at the airport.

> ***Now you try*** *(fill in the blank): How many students take this exam every week? More than 40 students _____ week take this exam.*

4. Use *a* before the words *few* or *little* to mean *some but not many or much*.
Examples:

❑ How much longer do we have to wait before this train arrives? We have *a* few minutes more to wait.

(Note: use the word *only* or *just* + *a* + *few* or *little* to emphasize the meaning *not much* or *not many* in the sentence.)
Examples:

❑ I'm really late. How much longer do we have to wait before this train arrives? The train should be here in only *a* few minutes. The train should be here in just *a* few minutes.

❑ Be patient just *a* little longer, the train should be here soon.

(Note: when you want to express *almost none* using the words *few* or *little*, then do **not** use an article. **Examples:**

- He is very hungry. He has had little to eat since yesterday. (Meaning: he has eaten almost nothing since yesterday.)

- He is very lonely; he has few friends. (Meaning: he has almost no friends.)

    Now you try *(fill in the blank): Jim has 50 cents. Jim has ___ little money.*

Chapter 1 Review

Directions: Fill in the blanks with a, an, the, or Ø if you think the sentence is correct the way it is. Correct answers can be found by looking back in chapter 1, above.

1. The mechanic will be finished with the repair in _____ hour.

2. The student has _____ pencil in his hand.

3. Abby is eating _____ ice cream cake.

4. That guy has a fast car. It goes 150 miles _____ hour.

5. Excuse me. How long do we have to wait for the bus? You've just got _____ few more minutes.

6. Is the train always this late? The guy at the ticket counter said the train should be arriving in just _____ few minutes; but that was ten minutes ago!

7. Oh, be patient and stop complaining! The train should be here in just _____ little while.

8. The homeless man was very hungry. He has had _____ little to eat.

9. Jenny is staying home again tonight. Almost no one likes her. She has _____ friends, but they don't call her very often.

10. Jeremy bought _____ new car yesterday.

Answers: 1. an; 2. a; 3. an; 4. an; 5. a; 6. a; 7. a; 8. Ø; 9. Ø; 10. a

Chapter 2 *Correct use of the English article **the***

*In this section you will learn the rules for using the English article **the**. Listen to the rules for usage and an explanation. After each explanation there are examples to help reinforce the correct use of the article in common English sentences.*

*Quick rules for **the** in this chapter:*
- ✓ *Use **the** in front of university when 'of ' is part of the university's name (E.g: I went to **the** University of Alabama.)*
- ✓ *Use **the** in front of countries with the words united, union, kingdom, or republic in their name, or countries with the word 'of ' in their name (E.g: He is from **the** Republic of China).*
- ✓ *Use **the** in front of names of oceans, deserts, rivers and seas (E.g: **The** Pacific Ocean is big).*

Correct use of the English article the

Rules, explanations and examples for using the English article *the*

1. Use *__the__* when talking about colleges and universities that have the word *of* in their name. If a college or university does not have the word *of* in its name, then do not use an article before the name.

Examples:

❏ I have applied to *__the__* University of Hawaii

❏ Hawaii Loa College is a good school.

❏ My sister goes to *__the__* University of Florida

❏ Florida State University has a good football team.

> ***Now you try*** *(fill in the blank): _____ University of Iowa has many good students.*

2. Use *__the__* when talking about countries that have the words *united, union, kingdom,* or *republic* in their name. If a country, city or state has the word *of* in

its name, then use **_the_** before the name. Do not use **_the_** before the names of countries, states, or cities that do not have *of* in their name or the words *united*, *union*, *kingdom*, or *republic* in their name.

Examples:

❑ I am studying English in **_the_** United States of America

❑ I will be traveling to **_the_** Kingdom of Tonga next month.

❑ My friend lives in Germany.

❑ Zurich has a good soccer team.

> ***Now you try*** *(fill in the blank):* _____ *Republic of China is very large.*

3. Use **_the_** with the names of oceans, seas, rivers, and deserts.

Examples:

❑ **_The_** Pacific Ocean is the largest body of water in the world.

❑ **_The_** Red Sea passes through Egypt.

❑ **_The_** Mississippi River flows from the northern border of the United States to the southern border.

❑ **_The_** Mohave desert is one of the driest places on earth.

> ***Now you try*** *(fill in the blank):* _____ *Sahara desert is a vast desert of northern Africa.*

3a. Do not use an article for the names of ***single*** lakes, mountains, or islands. Use **_the_** when talking about ***plural*** lakes, mountains or islands.

Examples:

❑ Lake Tahoe is very big.

❑ **_The_** Great Lakes border on the north-central part of the United States and south-central region of Canada.

❑ Mount Shasta is a great place to visit.

❑ On Maui you will find Haleakala Mountain.

❑ ***The*** Himalayas are in Tibet.

❑ ***The*** Hawaiian Islands are beautiful.

> ***Now you try*** *(fill in the blank):* _____ *Lake Huron is in the Great Lakes region.*

4. Use ***the*** when talking about the names of theaters, hotels, motels, buildings, and bridges.

Examples:

❑ A good movie was playing at ***the*** Freeport theater.

❑ We stayed at ***the*** Marriott hotel in Utah.

❑ ***The*** Empire State Building in New York City used to be the tallest building in the world.

❑ Driving across ***the*** Golden Gate Bridge is exciting.

> ***Now you try*** *(fill in the blank): My cousin stayed at* _____ *Sagebrush Inn in Miami.*

4a. Don't use an article in front of the names of hospitals.

Examples:

❑ The accident victims were taken to Saint Mary's Hospital.

❑ I went to Queens Hospital for a checkup.

5. Use ***the*** when talking about the names of museums, zoos, institutes, and companies if the word *company* or *corporation* appears in the company name.

Examples:

❑ ***The*** Museum of Modern Art is a fascinating place.

❑ There are many interesting exhibits in ***the*** Bronx Zoo.

❑ ***The*** Massachusetts Institute of Technology is a good place to study engineering.

❑ ***The*** Microsoft Corporation makes the Windows operating system.

❑ Microsoft makes Word for Windows.

> ***Now you try*** *(fill in the blank): At _____ Institute of Higher Health you can learn about better ways to take care of your health.*

6. Use ***the*** when talking about family names that are followed by a noun or when talking about all the family members by using the last name in the plural form.

Examples:

❑ ***The*** Morita family had a picnic last weekend.

❑ ***The*** Smith clan is very close. (The word *clan* is used to mean *family* in casual English)

❑ ***The*** Schmids have gone to Las Vegas together for a vacation.

> ***Now you try*** *(fill in the blank): _____ Jones family will be coming for dinner.*

7. Use ***the*** when talking about fire, police and emergency services, and military institutions, such as the navy, the army, the air force, the marines, the military.

Examples:

❑ ***The*** fire department arrived 5 minutes after we called them.

❑ ***The*** police could not catch the criminal.

❑ My brother just joined ***the*** navy.

❑ ***The*** military has taken over the government in the small country.

> ***Now you try*** *(fill in the blank): _____ military police could not catch the drunken sailor.*

8. Use ***the*** with nouns that you can identify specifically.

Examples:

- *The* books on the table are English books. Which books? *The* books on the table.

- I bought *the* computers yesterday. Which computers? *The* computers on my desk.

- I bought *the* apples this morning. Which apples? *The* apples in the refrigerator.

8a. You **cannot** use *the* in front of a noun that you cannot specifically identify.

For **example:**

If Hiro says, "I buy *the* apples every week," then we think that Hiro must be pointing to some apples as he is speaking because *the* tells us that Hiro knows exactly which apples he's talking about. If it is true that Hiro is buying *the* apples every week then he must be buying the very same exact apples week after week. (Not likely.)

If you want to tell someone that you buy apples every week, just say: I buy apples every week. The person will know that when you go shopping you usually buy some apples.

Generally, when you want to talk about a plural noun in general, then don't use *the*. Just say, I buy apples every week. (Meaning: generally, I buy apples at least once a week.)

Other examples:

- I wash *the* windows every month. Which windows? *The* windows in my house.

- I wash windows for a cleaning company. Which windows? I don't know exactly which windows until my boss gives me instructions.

  Now you try (fill in the blank): The cleaning lady washes _____ windows when she comes. (Specific windows)

  Try another (fill in the blank): I bought _____ groceries every time I went to that food store.

9. Don't use ***the*** after the *there + be verb* (*there is* or *there are*).

   For example, **<u>do not</u>** say:

❑   There is ***the*** ball in the water. This is **not** correct.

Other examples (**correct** forms):

❑   There is a ball in the water.

❑   There is a pen on the desk.

❑   There are stars in the sky.

   Now you try (fill in the blank): There is _____ duck on the lake.

10. Use ***the*** when you have already talked about a noun in a previous sentence. Examples:

❑   I bought a new computer last Wednesday. ***The*** computer works great!

❑   I bought some apples yesterday. ***The*** apples were delicious.
   Now you try (fill in the blank): My sister bought _____ (general) new mp3 player last night. Unfortunately, _____ mp3 player has a problem!

11.   Use ***the*** when it is very obvious what you are talking about.

   Examples:

❑   My cup fell on ***the*** floor and broke.

❑   Rain fell from ***the*** sky.

❑   Please don't smoke inside ***the*** building!
   Now you try (fill in the blank): My watch fell to _____ floor but, nothing was damaged.

12. Use ***the*** when the noun is identified by a prepositional phrase or an adjective clause. (A prepositional phrase looks like this: ***The*** woman ***in the back of the room*** is my boss. The prepositional phrase begins with a preposition, in this case, ***in***. An adjective clause looks like this: ***The*** policeman ***who gave me a ticket last year***, gave me another ticket today).

   Examples:

❑   ***The*** man ***in the red car*** is driving too fast.

- ❑ **_The_** dress **_on the shelf_** is on sale.

- ❑ **_The_** blouse **_that my mother gave me_** is stained.

- ❑ **_The_** man **_who gave me the money_** has disappeared.

> **_Now you try_** *(fill in the blank):* _____ *ring that my friend gave me doesn't fit.*

12a. Make sure that the adjective clause identifies the noun and makes it specific. Here is an example where the adjective clause does not make the noun specific:

- ❑ We went shopping yesterday to try to find **_a_** computer **_that would help us with our English studies_**. (☝ In this case, we haven't found a specific computer yet, we are still looking, so we use **_a_**, meaning one of many possibilities, to identify the computer.)

13. Use **_the_** when you want to express how good or bad something is (superlatives), but do not use **_the_** when comparing one thing to another.

Examples:

- ❑ That is **_the_** most beautiful flower I've ever seen. (Not: the more beautiful flower . . . .)

- ❑ This is **_the_** worst class I've taken.

> **_Now you try_** *(fill in the blank): That is _____ most incredible dive I've ever seen.*

13a. Do not use **_the_** when comparing things.

Examples:

- ❑ That book is as good as this one.

- ❑ That Lamborghini is just as fast as this Ferrari.

- ❑ This brand of coffee is better than that brand.

13b. Exception: When you are comparing two sets of things in a single sentence (a double comparative) use ***the***.

Example:

❑ ***The*** harder the exam, ***the*** more I like it. (This is a double comparative).

14. Use ***the*** with ***morning***, ***afternoon*** and ***evening*** but **not** with ***night***.

Examples:

❑ I have to wake up early in ***the*** morning to go to work.

❑ We have lunch in ***the*** afternoon.

❑ The stars come out in ***the*** evening.

> ***Now you try*** *(fill in the blank): We usually meet in* _____ *late morning.*

15. Use ***the*** when using ordinal numbers (1st, 2nd, 3rd, 4th, etc.) and words, and words that rank, for example, next and last.

Examples:

❑ This is ***the*** first time I got an A on an exam.

❑ ***The*** second step is too complicated. I have to read the instructions again.

❑ Mom came last year so I think we have to visit her this year. (Specific period of time, no ***the***)

❑ My brother got second prize in the competition. (Prize, no ***the***)

❑ First, place the flour in the bowl. Next, add milk. Finally, mix in sugar. (No ***the*** before ordinal words followed by ideas)

15a. But, do not use ***the*** when using ordinal numbers or words when you talk about ideas.

Example: First, read the summary. Second, write down your comments.

15b. Do not use ***the*** when using ordinal numbers or words when you talk about specific periods of time

Example:

❑ We are going to grandmother's house next spring. My brother came to visit last Christmas.

15c. Do not use *the* when using ordinal numbers or words that refer to prizes

Example:

❑ Congratulations, you won first prize!).

Now you try (fill in the blank): _____ *first step is easy.*

16. Use *the* when you are generalizing about classes of animals (*The* elephant is the largest animal in the animal kingdom.), about musical instruments (*The* violin has a long history.), or about inventions (*The* computer is changing the way we do work.). But, use *the*, *a*, or *an* (interchangeably) when talking in general about the effect or significance of something.

Examples:

❑ *The* snake can be a very dangerous animal. (Meaning the whole class of animals called snake)

❑ *A* snake can be a very dangerous animal (Meaning any individual snake)

❑ *The* guitar was first created by Gaetano Vinaccia in 1779 in Naples, Italy. (Meaning the whole class of instruments called guitar)

❑ *A* guitar can make a very beautiful sound. (Meaning any individual guitar)

❑ *The* computer has changed the way we communicate. (Meaning the whole class of inventions called computer)

❑ *A* computer can be used to send email. (Meaning any particular computer)

Now you try (fill in the blank): _____ *violin makes a very beautiful sound.* *(any)*

17. Use *the* when the noun in the sentence is well known as being the only one of its kind.

Example: We use a telescope to observe ***the sun, the moon, the stars*** and every interesting thing in ***the sky.***

More **examples:**

❏ ***The*** water in the ocean is very salty.

❏ ***The*** air is very clean and sweet smelling.

> *Now you try (fill in the blank):* _____ water is dirty.

18. Use ***the*** when you want to express ideas about a nationality (group of people from a given country) .

Examples:

❏ ***The*** Italians are very good at making wine.

❏ ***The*** Americans like fast food.

❏ ***The*** Japanese produce many fine video products.

❏ ***The*** Germans like good beer.

> *Now you try (fill in the blank):* _____ *Italians love their cheeses and sauces.*

19. Use ***the*** when you want to express ideas about a group or class of people that have some characteristic.

Examples:

❏ ***The*** poor do not have enough money to buy nice clothes.

❏ There is a special program for ***the*** deaf to help them to learn sign language.

❏ The nurse hurried to the accident to help ***the*** injured.

> *Now you try (fill in the blank):* _____ refugees do not have a place to live.

20. Use ***the*** only when the word language appears after a language (example: ***the*** French language), and only when the word religion appears after a religion (example: ***the*** Hindu religion).

Examples:

- The Pope is the head of **_the_** Catholic religion.
- **_The_** Chinese language has many dialects.

> *Now you try (fill in the blank):* _____ *Chinese language is a tonal language.*

21. Use **_the_** before directions like north, south, east and west, if they follow prepositions such as in, to, from, at, on, etc.

Examples:

- The sun is in **_the_** west.
- All of the good restaurants are on **_the_** east side of the city.
- The train should be approaching from **_the_** north.

> *Now you try (fill in the blank): The storm will approach from* _____ *south.*

21. Use **_the_** when you want to talk about large periods of time in the past.

Examples:

- **_The_** Han Dynasty of China lasted over 400 years.
- Dinosaurs ruled the earth during **_the_** Triassic period.

> *Now you try (fill in the blank):* _____ *Pleistocene period lasted over 1.7 million years.*

22. Use **_the_** when you want to talk about special names, titles of nobility, and epithets.

Examples:

- **_The_** Queen of England.
- Catherine **_the_** great.
- Phillip **_the_** talking robot was a popular character in the movie.

> *Now you try (fill in the blank): Henry* _____ *eighth.*

23. Use ***the*** when you want to refer to some place on your body that was struck or touched by something outside of yourself.

Examples:

❑ The bullet struck the man in ***the*** chest.

❑ She tapped the girl on ***the*** shoulder.

❑ He hit the boy on ***the*** head.

> ***Now you try*** *(fill in the blank): The doctor gave the boy a flu shot in* _____ *arm.*

24. Use ***the*** right before the word *same*.

Examples:

❑ She was wearing ***the*** same color dress that I was wearing.

❑ I order ***the*** same kind of food every time I go to that restaurant. A hamburger and French fries.

Now you try *(fill in the blank): The twins were wearing* _____ *same color dresses.*

25. Use ***the*** when talking about ***the*** flu, ***the*** measles, ***the*** Chicken Pox or ***the*** mumps, but ***don't*** use ***the*** to refer to any other disease.

Examples:

❑ She couldn't go to school because she had ***the*** flu.

❑ The ambulance took the girl to the hospital because she had appendicitis.

> ***Now you try*** *(fill in the blank): His aunt went to the doctor because she had* _____ *flu.*

Chapter 2 Review

Directions: Fill in the blanks with a, an, the, or Ø if you think the sentence is correct the way it is. Correct answers can be found back in chapter 2, above.

1. _____ Nassau Community College has a good football team.

2. Allan goes to _____ University of Hawaii.

3. Terry orders ___ same smoothie every time she goes to the smoothie shop.

4. The ambulance took _____ little girl to the hospital because of her serious illness.

5. _____ two women were wearing ____ same style dress at the party.

6. The sun sets in _____ west.

7. The bus will be approaching from _____ east.

8. ___ water in ____ ocean is full of life.

9. Ivan _____ Terrible was a czar in Russian history.

10. _____ Chinese produce many different kinds of products.

11. _____ computers have changed the way we communicate in the world today.

12. The young soldiers have to wake up early in _____ morning.

13. _____ poor often do not have enough money to buy food for their children.

14. Okay students, here are the instructions for the exam: ____ first, write your name on the top of _____ first page.

15. _____ Pope is ____ head of ____ Catholic religion.

16. _____ guitars can make a very beautiful sound.

17. Mastering _____ piano requires a lot of practice.

18. My friend got _____ second prize in the cooking competition.

19. Betsy washes _____ floors in her house every month.

20. The baby's cup fell on _____ floor and broke.

21. _____ Hawaiian Islands are located in _____ Pacific Ocean.

22. We generally have tea in _____ afternoon.

23. Alice bought _____ fruit in the refrigerator this morning.

24. Alice often goes shopping for _____ fruit.

25. There's _____ ball, in the water.

26. _____ rain fell from _____ sky.

27. My aunt visited us _____ last year, so I think we have to visit her this year.

28. _____ Browns have gone to California together for a ski vacation.

29. That is _____ fastest car I've ever ridden in!

30. The doctor tapped _____ boy on _____ knee.

Answers: 1. Ø; 2. the; 3. the; 4. the; 5. the, the; 6. the; 7. the; 8. the, the; 9. the; 10. the; 11. Ø; 12. the; 13. the; 14. Ø, the; 15. the, the, the; 16. Ø; 17. the; 18. Ø; 19. the; 20. the; 21. the, the; 22. the; 23. the; 24. Ø; 25. the; 26. the, the; 27. Ø; 28. the; 29. the; 30. the, the

Chapter 3 *When NOT to use articles*

In this section you will learn the rules for when you do NOT use articles. Listen to the rules for NOT using articles and an explanation why. After each explanation there are examples to help reinforce your understanding.

If you have the Focus On English digital audio book version of this book (for smart phones and other digital audio devices; sold separately at www.FOEBooks.com) you can listen and practice speaking the examples, reinforcing your knowledge by repeating the examples with the teacher on the audio book.

When NOT to use articles

Rules, explanations and examples for NOT using English articles in sentences

1. **Don't** use articles in front of the name of a road, street, lane, boulevard, avenue, etc.
   Examples:

   ❑ Please turn left on **Smith Street** and my house is on the right.

   ❑ We traveled down **Ala Moana Boulevard** until we saw the mall.

   Now you try (fill in the blank): We drove to _____ Main Street and then turned left onto _____ Elm Street.

2. **Don't** use articles in front of abstract nouns like *love, crime, happiness*, etc.
   Examples:

   ❑ Happiness is easy when you live a simple life. (Not "the happiness')

   ❑ The newlywed couple was filled with joy.

   ❑ Everyone wants peace in the world. (Everyone and peace are both abstract nouns in this sentence.)

   Now you try (fill in the blank): People like to have _____ fun in life.

3. **Don't** use articles in front of plural nouns in sentences that are making general statements.

Examples:

❏ Dogs usually like to chase cats.

❏ Vegetables are good for your health.

❏ Hot dogs are made with beef, chicken, or pork.

>   ***Now you try*** *(fill in the blank):* _____ *fish is good to eat and good for your health.*

4. **Don't** use articles in front of the names of malls, parks or stadiums unless the name usually has another identifying noun as part of the name.

Examples:

❏ I love shopping at Ala Moana Shopping Center. (Shopping Center is part of the name of the mall so no article is needed)

❏ I love shopping at ***the*** Ala Moana shopping center. (In this case, shopping center is not part of the name, but identifies Ala Moana as being a shopping center and so we use ***the*** in front of the name.)

❏ We watched the football game at ***the*** stadium.

❏ We watched the football game at Aloha Stadium.

❏ The children played in Central Park.

>   ***Now you try*** *(fill in the blank): We often shop at _____ Town Square shopping center.*

5. **Don't** use articles in front of the names of religions or languages unless they have been identified by another word in the sentence.

Examples:

❏ I speak French.

❏ I speak ***the*** French language.

❏ Hinduism is practiced by many people in India and Indonesia.

❏ The Hindu religion is practiced by many people in India and Indonesia.

Now you try (fill in the blank): Allison speaks _____ Chinese.

6. **Don't** use articles in front of directions like north, south, east, or west when the direction follows an action verb like walk, run, go, head, sail, drive, etc.

Examples:

❑   Go west for about four miles and you will see the store on your right side.

❑   The ship sailed west for two weeks before reaching Japan.

❑   We drove north until we arrived in Canada.

Now you try (fill in the blank): The soldiers hiked _____ west for about ten miles and then rested.

7. **Don't** use articles in front of the names of diseases except for *the flu, the measles, the chicken pox,* and *the mumps*.

Examples:

❑   The man was suffering from Tuberculosis.

❑   The woman had diabetes.

Now you try: A dangerous bone condition is _____ Osteoporosis.

8. **Don't** use articles in front of numbers or letters used for lists.

Examples:

❑   Number 1 on the list is the most important.

❑   Sorry, but I don't understand letter A. (Meaning: I don't understand the question or information following letter A.)

❑   Excuse me, could you please read number 7 again?

Now you try (fill in the blank): We are _____ number 8 on the waiting list.

9. There are many frequently used expressions in English that begin with the action verb *go*. Because they are frequently used, English speakers have cut them short and **don't** use articles in front of the nouns in these kinds of

expressions. **Don't** use articles in front of the nouns in expressions like *go to church*, *go to school*, *go to class*, *go to bed*, *go to jail*, etc.

Examples:

❑   WRONG: I go to the bed every night at 10 o'clock.

❑   CORRECT: I go to bed every night at 10 o'clock.

❑   CORRECT: We go to school to learn English.

❑   CORRECT: The two ladies go to church every Sunday.

Now you try (fill in the blank): We usually go to _____ dinner around 8 o'clock .

Chapter 3 Review

Directions: Fill in the blanks with a, an, the, or Ø if you think the sentence is correct the way it is. Correct answers can be found back in chapter 3, above.

1. My whole family goes to _____ bed at 11pm every night.

2. The two women were suffering from _____ osteoporosis.

3. Go _____ south to Baker Street and then turn left.

4. I am going to _____ New York tomorrow morning.

5. Do you speak _____ Spanish?

6. _____ Buddhist religion is practiced by many people.

7. _____ vegetables are good for you.

8. Fred drove down _____ Howard Avenue looking for a bakery.

9. _____ happiness comes from a simple life.

10. _____ Buddhist monks are praying for _____ peace.

11. We watched the baseball game at _____ Shea Stadium.
12. _____ cats usually don't like dogs.

13. The young couple was filled with _____ joy.

Answers: 1. Ø; 2. Ø, 3. Ø; 4. Ø; 5. Ø; 6. the; 7. Ø; 8. Ø; 9. Ø; 10. the (or Ø); 11. Ø; 12. Ø; 13. Ø

Quick-Find INDEX

Book 6 – English Expressions (advanced)

Some English Expressions for Everyday Real Life

Book 6 - Quick-Find Menu

CHAPTER 2 581

Some common English expressions and idioms when talking about entertainment   581

CHAPTER 3 595

CHAPTER 4 ....**607**

Some common English expressions and idioms when talking about the workplace   **607**

CHAPTER 5 620

Some common English expressions and idioms when talking about romance   620

Preface

English expressions are everywhere in the English language. The correct use of English expressions in English communication can sometimes be difficult and comes with practice. This text was written as a quick reference guide, a primer, and a practice text to help students quickly learn new expressions, and find and correct problem areas. The book was written for high intermediate and advanced learners.

Using English Expressions for Real Life
Stepping Stones to Fluency for Advanced ESL Learners

Understanding the language of sarcasm, clichés, slang, jargon, colloquialisms and informal speech patterns in English.

Using English Expressions for Real Life

Using English Expressions for Real Life was designed for the advanced ESL learner. This book is not an exhaustive list of English idioms and expressions. It is, instead, an approach to understanding how native English speakers articulate their daily concerns, needs, wants and feelings. Most fluent day-to-day American English is spoken via expressions whose meanings are best understood in the context of a specific situation and of American culture in general. This book attempts to give the advanced ESL learner a window onto this world of English expression.

Using English Expressions for Real Life is a wonderful way to explore and practice some of the more common forms of fluent English expression. The book explores common English idioms, sarcasm, clichés, slang, and informal expressions used every day by native speakers in a variety of different situations. The student will find lots of explanations and examples of correct usage in common sentences.

If the student has the Focus on English© audio book version of this book (for smart phones and other digital audio devices; available separately, at no extra charge, at www.FOEBooks.com), the student will be able to listen to the examples along with the teacher. Reading and listening helps the student remember a lesson more easily and also helps the student with pronunciation.

Note to Students: Audio Book

There is an audio book for *Using English Expressions for Real Life* available on our website to all of our students, free of charge. Go here to access this audio book.

How to Use This Book

Each chapter in *Using English Expressions for Real Life* represents a different common communication area in English:

- travel
- entertainment
- business
- the workplace
- romance
- education

Within each of these chapters, the student will learn and understand common English expressions. So that the student can more rapidly understand the expression, there is a quick reference system that allows the student to find meanings fast. How do English speakers use expressions when talking about time and space, feelings, emotion, success and failure? Through a series of clear explanations, simple examples, and review, the student will master the expressions in this book and, more importantly gain valuable understanding about how English speakers build expressions from common English vocabulary.

How does the <u>quick reference</u> system work in this book?

In the table of contents, areas of interest are referenced to a page number. Page numbers, in this book, are in large type at the top of each page, which allow the student to quickly thumb through the book and find the appropriate page.

Individual expressions are numbered. To find the meaning of the expression, simply go to the end of the chapter and find the number. There you will find the meaning.

There is also a quick-find index section at the back of the book, which allows students to quickly find individual expressions of interest.

Introduction

Louise Gibessi is our famous advice and gossip columnist from New York City who writes for our newspaper and our Internet blog called Dear Louise Gibessi (http://www.DearLouiseGibessi.com).

People write to her from all over the world to ask her about personal problems and sometimes problems that they are having when they are using English in real life situations.

Louise Gibessi is famous because she is very *up front** and *tells it like it is.*** She gives advice about **romance**, **business**, **the workplace**, **traveling**, **education**, and **entertainment**.

(**To be up front** means to be completely honest with someone, without hiding any facts.)

(** *To tell it like it is* (slang) means to be completely honest when telling someone something; to describe something to someone by simply telling the facts. Straight talk. Often used to express the reality of something. Often very frank, bordering on impolite.)

In this and following sections you will learn how native English speakers use various idioms and expressions correctly in real life situations.

Chapter 1

Correct usage of some common English expressions and idioms in travel situations

In this first chapter Louise Gibessi's column deals with traveling.

Directions: Read and / or listen to Louise's column and try to understand the general meaning. Don't **stress out*** about **every little thing.**** After you have read (or listened to) the story, you will have a chance to read (or hear) the meanings of the idioms used in the story with some brief examples. After you've learned what everything means, there will be a practice and review session at the end of the chapter. By this time you will be **up to snuff***** on the meanings of all of the idioms and other expressions in the story.

(**stress out**= don't worry)*

*(** **every little thing**= about every detail)*

*(*** **up to snuff**= you will know about or be up to date on)*

Some common English expressions and idioms when talking about travel

---

Below we have reprinted one of Louise Gibessi's recent columns about travel.

<u>TRAVEL</u>

(Here is a letter from a man who is concerned that his mother-in-law wants to be a part of the romantic vacation that he has planned for himself and his wife.)

Dear Louise Gibbesi,

I'm looking forward to my vacation, which is **right around the corner**[1]. I have been thinking about traveling to an island far away in the South Pacific because I really need to **get away from it all**[2].

The **rub**[3] is that my wife wants her mother to go along with us on this vacation and, frankly, I don't want to **open a can of worms**[4] by telling her that her mother is **a pain in the butt**[5] and that I really wouldn't enjoy my vacation with her **in tow**[6]. I **can't just come out and tell**[7] my wife that I don't want her mother around because that would **go over like a lead balloon**[8].

Louise, I'm **chomping at the bit**[9] to **fast track**[10] my South Pacific vacation plans. My job is really stressful and this kind of vacation would be a great way to **chill out**[11]. Having my mother-in-law along would be stressful. How do I **put it to**[12] my wife that **three's a crowd**[13] on this vacation? Signed: **Hogtied**[14] in Minnesota

Louise Gibessi responds:

Dear **Hogtied**[14],

You're **getting all worked up over nothing**[15]. **Contain yourself**[16] and simply **engage your brain**[17]. **Take a pill**[18] and then follow these steps. First, **lay it all on the table**[19] so that your wife can really understand where you are **coming from**[20]. Suggest to her that this vacation should be just for the two of you—a kind of **romantic interlude**[21] or **second honeymoon**[22]. Second, **make a pact**[23] with your **significant other**[24] **to the effect**[25] that mother would be welcome on the next vacation, or the next extended family outing.

Now, stop *making a **mountain out of a molehill**[26]* and start making your vacation plans!

And, ***by the bye**[27]*, ***try your hand at**[28]* learning how to hula when your down there. It's a great way to relax!

1. **_Right around the corner_**: *(idiom)*

   When something is **_right around the corner_** that means that it will happen very soon.

   Examples:
   - My sister's wedding is **_right around the corner_** and I still haven't bought a dress for the occasion.
   - Summer vacation is **_right around the corner_** and the students have already made their summer plans.

2. **_To get away from it all_**: *(idiom)*

   To escape from your normal, everyday life. To go somewhere where life is very different from what you experience in your daily life. To distance yourself from your normal daily life in such a way as to be pleasant and different from what you are normally used to.

   Examples:
   - My job is terrible, my wife is not happy because she wants a new house, and the kids are complaining because they want new video games. Right now, I just want **_to get away from it all_** on some deserted South Pacific island!
   - Some people like **_to get away from it all_** by taking a vacation on a cruise ship.

3. **_The rub_**: *(noun, informal)*

The problem, the obstacle, or the difficulty.

> **Examples:**
> ☐ John and Betty wanted to invite everyone they knew to their party. **_The rub_** was that they had a small apartment and they could only invite a small number of people.
> ☐ Kana loved to going speeding around the city in her sports car. **_The rub_** was that she couldn't afford to pay for all the speeding tickets.

4. **_Open a can of worms_**: *(idiom)*

To introduce more problems, possibly worse problems than those already occurring.

> **Examples:**
> ☐ I really **_opened a can of worms_** when I reminded my girlfriend of the time she flirted with my friend. She then started to remind me of all of the times when I flirted with her friends! What a mess.
> ☐ You are just **_opening a can of worms_** when you start to argue with a policeman about giving you a traffic ticket.

5. **_Pain in the butt_**: *(idiom)*

A person or thing that is very annoying. This is for casual use, usually around people you already are acquainted with.

> **Examples:**
> ☐ The new math class is such a **_pain in the butt_**! We have to do homework every night.
> ☐ I hate it when Becky's friends come over. They're such a **_pain in the butt_**.

6. **In tow**: *(idiom)*

   A person who comes ***in tow*** is a friend or family member of the person who is actually invited. A person who comes ***in tow*** with someone else is usually welcome mainly because of their affiliation with the person who brought them.

   Examples:
   - Sally came to my party last night with her sister ***in tow***.
   - I attended the health seminar with my brother ***in tow***. He came along because he wanted to learn more about nutrition and health.

7. **Can't just come out and tell**: *(idiom)*

   When a person comes out and tells someone something, he or she is being very direct about passing information to someone else. Often, the information is obvious to other people but not to the recipient. Often, the information is embarrassing to the recipient and / or to the people around the recipient. Sometimes coming out and telling someone something can be impolite, embarrassing, or stressful, but usually it is necessary so that the person knows how others are feeling about him or her.

   Examples:
   - Stop laughing! You should just ***come out and tell*** Harry that he has a hole in the back of his pants.
   - Rather than *beat around the bush*, the boss just ***came out and told*** his secretary that she was fired. (*beat around the bush*= being indirect or evasive about telling someone something.)

8. **Go over like a lead balloon**: *(idiom)*

   Information that is not welcome by another person.

   Examples:

- Telling my wife that we would have to skip our vacation this year ***went over like a lead balloon***.
- I told the police officer that the reason why I was speeding was because I had to go to the bathroom. That ***went over like a lead balloon***.

9. ***Chomping at the bit***: *(idiom)*

Really anxious or excited to get started doing something.

Examples:
- I was ***chomping at the bit*** to learn English because then I could communicate with lots of people around the world.
- Our soccer team was ***chomping at the bit*** to win the championship.

10. ***Fast track***: *(idiom)*

To accelerate, to speed up, or make go faster.

Examples:
- My human resources manager decided that I could ***fast track*** my career by taking some courses in English.
- The architect told the builder that he could ***fast track*** the approval of the building plans by changing the design slightly. *(Building plans must first be approved by the government before a building can be built. Sometimes this takes a long time.)*

11. ***Chill out***: *(idiom)*

Usually used as an imperative, ***chill out*** means to relax or be calm. Sometimes this is shortened to just the word *chill*.

Examples:
- We should be home in about ten minutes. ***Chill out***, you can get a drink of water then.

- After school, a group of us go to a pizza place, order pizza and just ***chill out***.

12. ***Put it to (someone)***: *(idiom)*

Means to explain something, usually something that may be difficult to discuss.

Examples:
- Let me ***put it to you*** this way: if you don't study for the exam, you won't pass.
- I couldn't figure out how to ***put it to*** my son that we wouldn't be able to go fishing this weekend.

13. ***Three's a crowd***: *(idiom)*

When a third person is unwelcome. Usually used when a couple wants to be alone or do something by themselves without a third person coming along or being present. The third person could be a friend or relative of one or both members of the couple.

Examples:
- My brother should know by now that when I am with my girlfriend, ***three's a crowd***.
- Jackie had to tell her brother that he couldn't come with her and her boyfriend to the beach. She told him that ***three was a crowd***.

14. ***Hogtied***: *(idiom)*

To disrupt or restrict movement. When you are *hogtied*, you feel restricted about what options you have to resolve an issue.

Examples:
- I was trying to plan our vacation, but everyone wanted to do something different. I really felt ***hogtied***.

□ My brother was having a difficult time finding a birthday gift for his wife because she didn't really need anything. His choices were limited and he felt a little ***hogtied*** because he wanted to get her something nice.

15. **_Getting all worked up over nothing_**: *(idiom)*

When you *get all worked up over nothing*, you get emotional about something that is not very important, or that appears to be more important than it really is.

Examples:
□ This is just a movie. You're ***getting all worked up over nothing***. We're not going to be attacked by aliens from outer space!
□ I thought the test was going to be really hard, but it was easy. I ***got all worked up over nothing***.

16. **_Contain yourself_**: *(idiom)*

Means to control your behavior and relax. Often used playfully, contain yourself is used when someone is over emotional about something.

Examples:
□ ***Contain yourself***! I was only kidding when I said that your favorite movie star was coming to dinner with us.
□ My girlfriend's plane will land in approximately ten minutes. I can hardly ***contain myself***.

17. **_Engage your brain_**: *(idiom)*

When you *engage your brain*, you think rationally. ***Engage your brain*** is another idiom that is often used playfully; sometimes we say this to a person who is being lazy and they appear unwilling to think about something more carefully. (Note: this expression is used among people who are friendly. Saying this to someone you do not know could be insulting.)

Examples:

- Don't worry, you can pass the test. Just ***engage your brain*** and you will see how easy it is.
- Life doesn't have to be difficult. Just ***engage your brain***.

18. ***Take a pill****: (slang)*

Take a pill is another way to say *relax*, or *stay calm*. This term is usually used playfully among people who are acquainted. It can be used sarcastically in some situations.

Examples:

- My wife kept bothering me about going to the doctor for a checkup. I told her to ***take a pill***; I'm too busy for a checkup right now. *(Slightly sarcastic in this context and may not be appreciated by the wife!)*
- I was really excited about seeing my favorite rock band and I couldn't contain my excitement. Finally, my friend told me to ***take a pill*** because we'd be at the concert auditorium in less than ten minutes.

19. ***Lay it all on the table****: (idiom)*

When you ***lay it all on the table***, you are giving someone all of the facts and details about a situation. Many times, you use this expression when there is a misunderstanding that needs to be cleared up, or when something needs to be made more clear.

Examples:

- I ***laid it all on the table*** for him: I couldn't sign the contract unless all of my needs were listed in the contract.
- She just didn't understand the danger of smoking cigarettes so her doctor ***laid it all on the table*** for her.

20. **_Coming from_**: *(idiom)*

The origin / source of your thinking, having to do with your point of view.

Examples:

- I'm not sure where my boss was **_coming from_** when he said I was doing a good job. Was he being sarcastic, or was he sincere?
- When my wife says she loves me, it **_comes from_** her heart.

21. **_Romantic interlude_**:

A pause or segment of someone's life when they are romantic with someone else; a time taken for romance.

Examples:

- My sister and her husband used to watch the sunset together. It was a beautiful **_romantic interlude_** for them.
- Jim's wife had a little **_romantic interlude_** with another man. When Jim found out, he filed for divorce.

22. **_Second honeymoon_**:

After many years of marriage, some couples decide to take a honeymoon for the second time in their lives. The first honeymoon usually occurs right after marriage. A **_second honeymoon_** can occur many years later.

Examples:

- My mother and father took a **_second honeymoon_** after 50 years of marriage.
- My wife and I decided to take a **_second honeymoon_** after 25 years of marriage.

23. **_To make a pact_**: *(idiom)*

To **_make a pact_** with someone is to make an agreement. A pact is usually more binding, stronger than just an agreement.

Examples:

❑ My friend and I **_made a pact_** to always help each other in emergencies.

❑ The two leaders **_made a_** nuclear non-proliferation **_pact_** *(an agreement not to continue to produce nuclear weapons)*.

24. **_Significant other_**: *(idiom)*

Usually your wife or husband. Your significant other can be a girlfriend or a boyfriend.

Examples:

❑ I wanted to go have a few beers with my friends so I called my **_significant other_** to find out if she had any plans for us.

❑ It is possible for your **_significant other_** to be of the same sex in gay relationships.

25. **_To the effect_**: *(idiom)*

Approximately, or something similar to (this idea).

Examples:

❑ I wasn't there when the mayor gave his speech, but he said something **_to the effect_** that taxes would be going up next year.

❑ I couldn't hear exactly what the teacher was saying, but she said something **_to the effect_** that the project would be due soon.

26. **_To make a mountain out of a molehill_**: *(idiom)*

To make a big deal out of something insignificant.

Examples:

- I think they are ***making a mountain out of a molehill*** when they say you have to eat vegetables every single day. I'm sure you can miss a day here and there and not get sick!
- Stefan was ***making a mountain out of a molehill*** when he described the difficulty of the advanced English course at the college.

27. **By the bye**: *(idiom)*

Incidentally.

Examples:

- Yes, I liked the movie too. ***By the bye***, will you be going to the party tomorrow night.
- I normally like eating at good quality restaurants. ***By the bye***, when are you going on your vacation?

28. **To try one's hand at something**: *(idiom)*

To try doing something new.

Examples:

- I'd like to ***try my hand at*** surfing. I heard it was fun and very healthy!
- Alex ***tried his hand at*** carpentry and found that he liked it. Now he is going to school to become a carpenter.

Chapter 1 Practice and Review

Directions: In each of the sentences below, fill in the blank spaces with the word or words that are missing from the expression. Think about the sentence carefully. Which expression best fits? Do not use the same expression twice. There is no answer key. Complete all of the sentences that you know, and then go back and work on the ones that are more difficult.

1. Jill and Harold took a _____ **_honeymoon_** after 25 years of marriage.

2. Our plane will land in Hawaii in approximately ten minutes. I _____ _____ **_contain_** myself.

3. Please _____ **_your brain_** before you take the exam!

4. I had to lay __ ____ **_on the table_** for him so he would understand my position.

5. True giving _____ _____ **_the heart_**.

6. Two is company, but three __ _ **_crowd_**.

7. When we were in high school, my friends and I _____ ___ **_pact_** to stay friends forever.

8. Trying to make plans was impossible because everyone wanted to do something different. I really felt _____**_tied_**.

9. My friend said, "**_Take a_** _____, the test won't be that hard!

10.   **_By the_** _____, will you be competing in the marathon this weekend?

11.   Jean is making **_a_** _____ **_out of a_** _____ when she says that no one will pass the exam.

12.   The vacation in Kauai was a beautiful _____ **_interlude_** for the young couple.

13.   The workers were **_getting_** _____ **_worked_** _____ **_over nothing_** because the company really did not want to fire them.

14.   Adam **_tried his_** _____ ___ painting and found that he didn't like the smell of the paint.

15.   The policeman said something **_to_** _____ **_effect_** that if we didn't leave right now, we would go to jail.

Chapter 2

Correct usage of some common English expressions and idioms used to talk about entertainment.

Directions: Read and / or listen to Louise's column and try to understand the general meaning. Don't ***stress out**** about ***every little thing.***** After you have read (or listened to) the story, you will have a chance to read (or hear) the meanings of the idioms used in the story with some brief examples. After you've learned what everything means, there will be a practice and review session at the end of the chapter. By this time you will be ***up to snuff****** on the meanings of all of the idioms and other expressions in the story.

(**stress out**= don't worry)*

*(** **every little thing**= about every detail)*

*(*** **up to snuff**= you will know about or be up to date on)*

Some common English expressions and idioms when talking about entertainment

---

Below we have reprinted one of Louise Gibessi's recent columns about entertainment.

ENTERTAINMENT

(Here is a letter from a girl who is not happy about her boyfriend's idea of a date)

Dear Louise,

I'm so **sick and tired**[1] of turning on the TV and seeing the **same old thing**[2] on **the tube**[3] night after night. Our TV gets 156 TV Channels of reception—*a little something for everyone*[4], I guess—but **it is all so commercialized**[5].

Anyway, my boyfriend came over the other night and we decided to watch TV and make some popcorn. *I swear*[6], Louise, we must have **flipped through**[7] every channel on my TV at least twice trying to find something that both of us could enjoy.

My boyfriend wanted to watch mixed martial arts fighting and I wanted to watch a mystery show. So we decided to **flip through**[7] the channels until we could find something we both wanted to watch.

Well, after **plowing through**[8] two big bowls of popcorn, **quaffing down**[9] two big bottles of pop, and **flipping through**[7] at least 300 channels, we finally settled on a **reality show**[10] where everyone on the show was lost or something.

It was **so lame**[11]. I think next time we should go to the movies together, or maybe a concert or a play. But **making TV into a date**[12] is really a bad idea.

We are seriously thinking about going to the theater more to see musicals and plays. The problem is that my boyfriend and I can't agree on how we should dress when we go to the theater. My boyfriend says we can dress however we want. I say that there are certain **dress codes**[13] that you have to pay attention to. What is the appropriate attire for live theater performances?

Signed, ready for *a night on the town*[14].

Louise Gibessi responds:

Dear Ready,

I'm glad you two finally *came to your senses*[15]! You are so right! There is so much more to do *out there*[16] than just watch TV!

If you are lucky enough to live in a city that has live theater performances, this is an excellent way to enjoy time together. Take a little time during the week to *check out*[17] the different performance reviews on the Internet or in your local newspaper. Then use the Internet or your local newspaper to find out where and when *it's all happening*[18]. Do *a little homework*[19] during the week and you will be able to plan the perfect weekend for you and your guy.

Here's a little guide on how to dress for *a night out on the town*[14].

If you are in a big city with *big-time*[20] live theatrical performances, then *semi-formal attire*[21] will most likely be the *best call*[22]. If in doubt, why don't you give the theater a call and ask. If you are going to a smaller theater for a live performance, dress in comfortable *smart casuals*[23]. If you are going to a rock concert, then dress like everyone else is going to dress. If you are going to a musical, or a band or orchestral concert then you may want to dress somewhere between *smart casual*[23] and *semi-formal*[21]. Again, if there is a question, *take a stab at*[24] calling the theater and ask someone how people are dressing. If you can't *get through*[25], then check the advertisement on the Internet to see if it may tell you about the *dress code*[13].

The most important thing is to have fun!

1. ***Sick and tired****: (idiom)*

To dislike or be annoyed with something or someone; when you are *sick and tired* of something or someone, you can no longer put up with or tolerate them.

Examples:
- We had five days of rain. Everyone was ***sick and tired*** of the rain.
- Anna was ***sick and tired*** of eating the same food every day, so she decided to try something different.

2. ***Same old thing****: (idiom)*

Something that you do on a regular basis that is so familiar to you that you are bored with it.

Examples:
- I go to work five days per week. I arrive at 8am, make coffee, listen to my phone messages and then go to work. ***Same old thing*** every day.
- Every Friday night Gina's boyfriend takes her to dinner and then they see a movie. ***Same old thing*** every Friday night. Gina wishes she could do something different on Friday nights.

3. ***The tube****: (slang)*

Television, TV.

Examples:
- What's on ***the tube*** tonight? (Meaning: what shows are on television tonight?)
- Don't believe everything you see and hear on ***the tube***.

4. ***A little something for everyone****: (idiom)*

Everyone attending a show or presentation, or involved in an activity will be entertained by or interested in at least some part of the show, presentation or activity.

Examples:

- ❏ Let's go to the circus! The circus usually has ***a little something for everyone***.
- ❏ Our group project ***has a little something for everyone***; everyone will find some part of the project interesting to him or her.

5. ***It's all so commercialized****:*

Produced mainly just to make money, usually with little concern for quality.

Examples:

- ❏ Many of the tourist destinations today are ***so commercialized***. All they care about is taking the tourist's money, and not so much about the quality of the tourist's experience.
- ❏ The Internet is becoming ***so commercialized*** with all of the pop-up advertising and advertising on almost every website.

6. ***I swear . . .****:*

This is an expression that is used to mean: I promise you that this is the truth. This expression usually precedes a statement that you want someone to really believe; used to emphasize something to someone.

Examples:

- ❏ "***I swear***!" said Alice, "I'm not going out on another date with my boyfriend until he gets a new pair of shoes."
- ❏ ***I swear***, if we don't win this soccer match, we are really bad.

7. ***Flipping through****:*

To rapidly change the channels on a TV, usually with a remote control. People often flip through channels to try to find something interesting to watch, or to **kill time*** when the program they are watching was interrupted by a TV commercial. (***Kill time** means to occupy yourself with something while you are waiting for time to pass.)

Examples:

❑ We must have ***flipped through*** 25 channels before we found something interesting to watch on TV.

❑ Every night my father would come home from work, sit in his favorite chair in front of the TV, and just ***flip through*** the TV channels. He never seemed to be interested in watching just one particular thing.

8. **Plowing through***: (slang)*

When you *plow through* something, you do something intently, that is, with single-minded focus. When a person plows through food, they are generally eating large amounts of food rapidly.

Examples:

❑ I ***plowed through*** my homework in 45 minutes so that I would have time to see the concert.

❑ My colleagues and I ***plowed through*** the assignment in two days. Our boss was very proud of us.

9. **Quaffing down***:*

When you *quaff* something *down*, you drink a lot of it quickly, or heartily.

Examples:

❑ We ***quaffed down*** a pitcher of beer and then went to the show. Boy, we were **blitzed**!* (***Blitzed** (slang) means drunk or inebriated.)

❑ The runners were so thirsty after the competition that they ***quaffed down*** over two gallons of lemonade.

10. ***Reality show****:*

This is a television show that does not have a script. There are usually no actors in a reality show, and the idea is to show television audiences a real life situation with the actual people who are in those situations.

Examples:

❑ My friends and I like watching ***reality shows*** because they are more interesting.

❑ There are many ***reality*** TV ***shows*** on American television, and they are often the most popular shows in America.

11. ***So lame****: (slang)*

Something that is *lame* is something that is boring or even stupid (pointless or worthless).

Examples:

❑ Jim's idea to go bird watching on Saturday was ***so lame***. I'd rather go snowboarding!

❑ That television show is ***so lame***! They should replace it with something that is more interesting.

12. ***Making TV into a date****:*

When you make something into something else, you are representing one thing as another. In this case, *making TV into a date* means that you have decided to watch TV on a Friday night with your boyfriend or girlfriend and then you decide to call that a date.

Examples:

❑ Let's go to the park this afternoon and have a picnic. We could ***make this picnic into a*** wonderful ***date***.

□ Mark is famous for ***making TV into a date*** with his female friends.

13. ***Dress codes***:

A set of rules that indicate the approved way to dress in certain situations.

Examples:

□ There is a company meeting tomorrow night at 5pm! The ***dress code*** is casual.

□ The ***dress code*** is often semi-formal for graduation ceremonies.

14. ***A night on the town***: *(idiom)*

Going out for *a night on the town* means you intend to have a lot of fun going to different places throughout the evening; perhaps a combination of visiting several pubs, going to a show, going to a dance or a party, or other celebration.

Examples:

□ I just got a big promotion in my company so I would like to celebrate by going out for ***a night on the town***!

□ Nicole's boyfriend took her out for ***a night on the town*** last night. She's exhausted today!

15. ***Came to your senses***: *(idiom)*

To begin to think clearly, or act in a sensible way.

Examples:

□ When Edward looked at his bank account, he ***came to his senses*** and decided that he could not afford a new car.

□ After his wife caught him with another woman for the third time, she ***came to her senses*** and filed for a divorce.

16. **_Out there_**:

Meaning: in the real world, the larger world beyond personal perception, reality.

Examples:

❏ My counselor told me that I've got to get **_out there_** and find a good job.

❏ After my divorce, my friend told me that I had to get **_out there_** and make some new friends.

17. **_Check out_**: *(slang)*

Meaning: To investigate, look at or examine.

Examples:

❏ Let's go down to the mall and **_check out_** the new cell phones.

❏ Hey, **_check out_** Leonard. He's wearing his new jacket.

18. **_It's all happening_**: *(informal)*

Where *it's all happening* means where [the exciting or interesting] activities are taking place.

Examples:

❏ There is a really cool party happening tonight. **_It's all happening_** at Jean's house.

❏ Where is the concert happening? **_It's all happening_** at the Sports Dome.

19. **_Do a little homework_**: *(informal)*

When you *do a little homework* you do some research about something, or you investigate something to find out more about it.

Examples:

❏ After **_doing a little homework_**, the detective figured out who committed the murder.

- Before she bought the new computer, Cynthia ***did some homework*** to find out which computer was best for her.

20. *Big-time*: *(informal)*

Big-time is an adjective describing something as being at the most prestigious level, or of major significance.

Examples:
- Shows playing on Broadway in New York City are considered ***big-time*** entertainment.
- If you are a really good baseball player, the ***big-time*** professional baseball teams might be interested in hiring you.

21. *Semi-formal attire*:

Semi-formal attire (clothing or dress) is often used to describe one of the dress code categories. When a person is wearing *semi-formal attire,* he is usually wearing a tie and jacket (for men), and she is usually wearing an evening dress (for women).

Examples:
- We are invited to the dance next Friday night. We have to wear ***semi-formal attire***.
- We have been invited to attend the annual celebration with our partner banks at the Old Opera House in Frankfurt. ***Semi-formal*** attire is required.

22. *Best call*: *(informal)*

Your *best call* is you best decision or very best guess. Sometimes we just say *good call*.

Examples:
- I don't know who will win the soccer game tonight. My ***best call*** would be that we will win by just one point.

❑ I think that going to the movies might be our ***best call*** tonight because there isn't any other entertainment that looks very interesting.

23. ***Smart casual attire****:*

Smart casual attire (clothing or dress) is often used to describe one of the dress code categories. When a person is wearing *smart casual attire,* he is usually wearing fashionable pants and shirt outfit (for men), and she is usually wearing a fashionable, but comfortable dress (for women). Smart casual attire differs from casual attire in that casual attire is considered appropriate for everyday activity. Casual in this context means relaxed and not serious. Smart casual means somewhat relaxed but still recognizing that the occasion has some importance.

Examples:

❑ Stefan and Helga were invited to an afternoon party at their yacht club. ***Attire*** for this kind of affair is ***smart casual***.

❑ Keiko is going to a baby shower this evening. She will be wearing ***smart casual attire***.

24. ***Take a stab at****: (idiom)*

When you *take a stab at* something, you try to do it.

Examples:

❑ I would like to ***take a stab at*** learning how to play tennis.

❑ Angelina was a pretty good rock climber, so she ***took a stab at*** climbing the difficult rock face.

25. ***Get through****:*

In the context of this sentence, ***get through*** means to make a successful telephone connection with someone else.

Examples:

- ❑ I called the doctor's office but I couldn't **_get through_** because the line was busy.
- ❑ After the earthquake, the telephone system was down and you couldn't **_get through_** to anyone.

Chapter 2 Practice and Review

Directions: In each of the sentences below, fill in the blank spaces with the word or words that are missing from the expression. Think about the sentence carefully. Which expression best fits? Do not use the same expression twice. There is no answer key. Complete all of the sentences that you know, and then go back and work on the ones that are more difficult.

1. Cathy has really gotten good at soccer. She is ready for the _____-*time* soccer leagues.

2. Jan's mother told her that she should **_get_** _____ **_there_** and make some friends.

3. When the bank clerk told Bill he had no money in his account, Bill _____ **_to his_** _____ and decided that he had better get a job.

4. After **_doing a little_** _____, the girl figured out that her boyfriend was cheating on her.

5. You and I are invited to a dance party next Monday night. We have to wear **_semi_**-_____ attire.

6. I don't know who will win the football game tomorrow, but **_my_** _____ **_call_** would be that we will win by a small margin.

7. Hey, let's go to the shopping center and _____ **_out_** the sales.

8. Her boyfriend took her out for a **_night_** ___ ____ **_town_** yesterday evening.

9. The office workers **plowed** _____ the project in two hours. Our boss gave them a raise for their good work.

10. Maureen would like **to** _____ **a stab at** surfing.

11. Hey, what's happening tonight? It's **all** _____ **at** the pub on the corner of Elm Street and Davis Avenue.

12. My brother must have _____ **through** 100 TV channels before he found a program he liked.

13. I must have drunk ten glasses of beer. Boy, was I _____**ed**!

14. I must have flipped through two hundred channels. There is so much nonsense on **the** _____ today!

15. We have been in our hotel rooms for five days. I think that everyone is _____ **and tired** of being in their hotel rooms.

Chapter 3

Correct usage of some common English expressions and idioms when talking about business situations.

Directions: Read and / or listen to Louise's column and try to understand the general meaning. Don't **stress out*** about **every little thing.**** After you have read (or listened to) the story, you will have a chance to read (or hear) the meanings of the idioms used in the story with some brief examples. After you've learned what everything means, there will be a practice and review session at the end of the chapter. By this time you will be **up to snuff*** on the meanings of all of the idioms and other expressions in the story.

(**stress out**= don't worry)*

*(** **every little thing**= about every detail)*

*(*** **up to snuff**= you will know about or be up to date on)*

Some common English expressions and idioms when talking about business
---

Below we have reprinted one of Louise Gibessi's recent columns about business.

BUSINESS

*(Here is a letter from a business investor who is having a very difficult time with English expressions. He is not using expressions correctly and **really** needs Louise's help)*

Dear Louise,

I would like to **buy some steak in**[1] a company that I feel has a good future. The problem is, I don't think that the **principals**[2] like me very much. I realize that buying into any company is a **calcified risk**[3] but I don't think that this is a **big shot**[4]. I would like to sit down with these guys and *fix up a contract*[5] or at least **push something in the works**[6]. When I talked to the **head honcho**[7], he said that he'd probably want **to throw cold water on**[8] the idea of having more partners right now. I told him that I usually take a hot shower so he need not worry about me.

Louise, **what's your take on**[9] how I can get these guys interested in my offer?
Signed, **Ty Coon**[10]

Louise Gibessi responds:

Dear **Ty Coon**[10],

Are you sure you are ready **to take the plunge**[11] into something so risky? And, I think that I have discovered why it may appear that the **principals**[2] in this company may not **be falling all over**[12] the idea of having you **on board**[13].

First of all, let's fix a few mistakes: it's **buy a stake in**[1], not buy some steak in. Next, it's a **calculated risk**[3], not a calcified risk. Third, it's a **long shot**[4], not a big shot. A big shot is a person! Next, it's **draw up a contract**[5], not fix up a contract! **Fixing a contract**[14] usually means to change a contract illegally! And it's **get something in the works**[6], not push something in the works!

Okay, now that we are ***back on track***[15], I would suggest that you contact the ***big cheese***[16] by phone and schedule a ***face to face appointment***[17]. Tell him what you are ***bringing to the table***[18]. If you have something they want, they will allow you to ***buy in***[19].

And, by the way, to ***throw cold water on***[8] something means to diminish interest in something and has nothing to do with hygiene or showers!

Good luck, Ty. I hope you ***make a killing***[20]!

(Read Ty Coon's corrected letter below. This is what Ty Coon's letter should have sounded like.)

(I would like to ***buy a stake in***[1] a company that I feel has a good future. The problem is, I don't think that the ***principals***[2] like me very much. I realize that buying into any company is a ***calculated risk***[3] but I don't think that this is a ***long shot***[4]. I would like to sit down with these guys and ***draw up a contract***[5] or at least ***get something in the works***[6]. When I talked to the ***head honcho***[7], he said that he'd probably want ***to throw cold water on***[8] the idea of having more partners right now. I told him that I usually take a hot shower so he need not worry about me.

Louise, ***what's your take on***[9] how I can get these guys interested in my offer?
Signed, ***Ty Coon***[10])

Explanations of expressions in this chapter

1. **_To buy a stake in_** *something: (idiom)*
   Means to invest money in part ownership of something.

Examples:

❏ The new computer company is doing very well. I think I would like to ***buy a stake in*** that company.

❏ My friends decided to share the cost of a vacation home in Fiji. After I saw the home, I decided to ***buy a stake in*** it.

2. ***Principal(s)****: (noun)*

The person or people who are in charge of or responsible for something. Often in business, the principals are the people who started the company, or were the first to initiate a partnership investment.

Examples:

❏ The ***principals*** in the company decided to close one of the sales departments because the company was not doing well.

❏ My friend and I wanted to invest a large sum of money in a certain computer company. We called the company on the phone and we were told to contact the ***principals*** for more information.

3. ***Calculated risk****: (idiom)*

You take a calculated risk when you have carefully assessed or analyzed the possibilities for success for something and then do it. Something that might fail, but, because of good analysis, has a good chance of being successful.

Examples:

❏ When athletes use illegal drugs before a competition, they are taking a ***calculated risk*** that they will not be caught.

❏ Jeff decided to dive into the ocean from the cliff. It was a ***calculated risk***. If he failed he could be seriously injured, but, after careful analysis, Jeff felt he would be successful.

4. ***Long shot****: (idiom)*

When the chances for success are not very good.

Examples:

❑ At the horse racing track, Ivan decided to bet on the big black horse. This horse did not do well in the last five races so it was ***a long shot*** to win.

❑ Two of the students from my class decided to stay up very late to study for the exam, which was being given the next day. They knew that if they stayed up late they would be tired the next day, but they also knew that they might have a better chance of success on the exam if they studied more. It was ***a long shot***, but they decided to stay up late and study.

5. ***Draw up a contract****: (idiom)*

To write a contract or an agreement usually to accomplish some goal in business.

Examples:

❑ Hiroko owns a big piece of property in the city and wants to build a building on the property. She called a building contractor and asked him to estimate how much this building would cost. After receiving the estimate, she told the building contractor to draw up a contract so that she can look at it and then sign it

❑ The owner of the football team and the star player drew up a contract and both of them signed it. With the signing of this contract the star player now had a career with this team.

6. ***To get something in the works****: (idiom)*

To take action to develop plans for and implement an idea. To take the steps to change an idea into a reality.

Examples:

❑ For years the city has had an idea to build a new sports arena. This year they are finally ***getting something in the works*** and we may have a new sports arena by next May.

- We've been talking about going to Bali for two years. After our meeting last night, I really feel like we have ***got something in the works now***. It sounds like we will be in Bali by next January.

7. *Head honcho*: *(slang)*

The person in charge. Honcho is slang for leader or person in charge. It is often used playfully. In some regions of the U.S., referring to the person in charge as the head honcho may not be appropriate. If in doubt, just say: *may I see (or talk to) the person in charge?*

Examples:
- I would like to return this item that I purchased yesterday from your store. May I see the ***head honcho***?
- When Kazu first came to this company he was just a stock boy. Now he is the ***head honcho***.

8. *To throw cold water on*: *(idiom)*

To diminish enthusiasm for something. To discourage something.

Examples:
- The boss ***threw cold water on*** the idea of hiring new employees.
- We heard about the violence that was occurring in the country that we were planning to visit. That ***threw cold water on*** our plans to visit that country.

9. *[Someone's]* ***take on*** *[something]*: *(idiom)*

When you ask someone what their take is on something you are asking them for their opinion. So, *what's your take on that* means *what's your opinion about that.*

Examples:
- Allison's ***take on*** the illegal drugs problem is that if someone is caught using illegal drugs, they should be punished in some way.

❑ My teacher asked me what my ***take*** was ***on*** the final exam that was given last Friday. I told him I thought the exam was fair.

10. *Tycoon*: *(noun)*

Ty Coon is a play on words. Ty is a somewhat common American first name, and Coon is a possible last name. The English word *tycoon* means someone who is very successful in business and is worth a lot of money, controls many industries, and is generally very aggressive in business.

Examples:

❑ A very wealthy ***tycoon*** owns the fiber optic cables that deliver our Internet signal.

❑ If you want to be a ***tycoon***, you've got to think ***out of the box*** (means: you have to think differently than most people).

11. *To take the plunge*: *(idiom)*

To take decisive action and do something that may appear a little risky or involved or complicated, but that could be rewarding.

Examples:

❑ We had been dating each other for six years. We decided ***to take the plunge*** and get married.

❑ Learning how to dance was something I always wanted to do. I finally ***took the plunge*** and went to a dance instructor last week.

12. *To fall all over*: *(idiom)*

To be very enthusiastic about accepting or doing something. The feeling of this idiom is that the affected person or people are so excited and enthusiastic about something that they are almost 'drunk' with enthusiasm.

Examples:

- Professional soccer teams in Europe were ***falling all over themselves*** to meet with the new soccer star who was looking for a team to play with.
- Automobile manufacturers were not exactly ***falling all over the idea*** of building more inefficient cars. Gas prices were expected to climb even higher.

13. **On board**: *(idiom)*

Being part of a team, company, staff, or other entity. To *welcome someone* **on board** means to formally accept someone as being part of your group.

Examples:

- Our company will welcome three new employees ***on board*** today during the monthly staff meeting.
- Our department finally got the employee we needed. We have been trying to get this employee ***on board*** for months.

14. **Fix a contract**: *(verb, tr.)*

The word fix can mean to change or alter something so that the outcome or results favors you even though the changes that were made were illegal or unethical. ***Fix*** in this context can mean to change illegally, or at least unethically, so as to favor the person who did the fixing. To fix up a contract means to change a contract in such a way as to favor the person who fixed it up.

Examples:

- The election results were ***fixed*** and, even though he was not popular, the president was elected to office again.
- The accounting balance sheets were ***fixed*** giving the appearance that the company was very successful, when actually the company was losing money.

15. **_Back on track_**: *(idiom)*

To be *on track* to doing something means that you are on schedule, headed towards, or en route to getting something done. When you are *back on track*, you come back to doing what you were doing after being temporarily distracted. Being *back on track* means that you are back to doing what you were doing and you have done all of the work necessary to be on schedule for successful completion.

Examples:

❑ After a two-week vacation in Italy, we are **_back on track_** to completing the work we started before we left for Italy.

❑ Serena was **_back on track_** to getting her project done, after being absent with the flu for one week.

16. **_Big cheese_**: *(idiom)*

The person who is in charge. Similar to head honcho. Often used playfully. Could be construed as disrespectful in formal settings, so be careful where you use this.

Examples:

❑ Who is the **_big cheese_** over at that corporation?

❑ Wally is the **_big cheese_** now, all bow to Wally! (Used playfully and a bit sarcastically in this office setting)

17. **_Face to face_** appointment: *(idiom)*

A face to face meeting is a meeting where people meet in person, as opposed to meeting over the phone or Internet.

Examples:

❑ The two leaders met **_face to face_** to talk about problems in their countries.

❑ I met **_face to face_** with my son's teacher to talk more about my son's progress in school.

18. **_Bring to the table_**: *(idiom)*

Often used in business, bringing something to the table means to come to a meeting or negotiation prepared to offer something of value to the others taking part in the meeting or negotiation. Since meetings or negotiations are often discussed around tables, when you come with your offer or idea it is said that you are bringing that offer or idea to the table.

Examples:
- ❑ Everyone at the meeting was waiting to hear what the others had **_brought to the table_**.
- ❑ The mayor of the city **_brought_** some good ideas **_to the table_**.

19. **_Buy in_**: *(idiom)*

To make an investment in something that is established. To invest time or money in something that was in progress.

Examples:
- ❑ The corporation spent $10 million to **_buy into_** the new computer technology.
- ❑ My friends all bought shares of stock in a local company and asked me if I wanted to **_buy in_** too.

20. **_To make a killing_**: *(idiom)*

To make a lot of money because of an investment. Sometimes people make a lot of money when the stock market goes up. People say: they made a killing on the stock market.

Examples:
- ❑ My parents invested in some real estate about twenty years ago. They really **_made a killing_**.
- ❑ Jan spent $2 on a lottery ticket and won. She **_made a killing_** on the lottery.

Chapter 3 *Practice and Review*

Directions: In each of the sentences below, fill in the blank spaces with the word or words that are missing from the expression. Think about the sentence carefully. Which expression best fits? Do not use the same expression twice. There is no answer key. Complete all of the sentences that you know, and then go back and work on the ones that are more difficult.

1. Who is in charge here? Oliver is the **_big_** _____ in this department.

2. The two business owners **_met_** _____ **_to_** _____ to talk about a partnership.

3. Alice bought the house for $100,000 two years ago. She sold the house for $300,000 last month. She really _____ **_a killing_**.

4. Our project was **_back_** ____ **_track_** after being delayed for the long holiday.

5. All four of us **_bought_** _____ the new business venture.

6. After dating for ten years, the couple decided to _____ **_the plunge_** and get married.

7. Our school welcomed three new teachers _____ **_board_** this past week.

8. Ross and his wife didn't have enough money in their savings, which **_threw_** ____ **_water on_** the idea of buying a new car.

9. The two witnesses that saw the crime had a different **_take_** ___ what happened.

10. We spent $100 on lottery tickets, but winning was a ___long___ _____.

11. We have been planning this vacation for two years. It's time to ___get___ _____ ___in___ _____ ___works___.

12. Cal and Jennifer were the ___prin_____ in the new business venture.

13. Ai was falling all _____ herself to meet the handsome new student.

14. Surfing big waves involves a _____ ___risk___.

15. Heidi and Clem were satisfied with the plans for the house and _____ ___up a___ _____ with the builder.

Chapter 4

Correct usage of some common English expressions and idioms when talking about the workplace

Directions: Read and / or listen to Louise's column and try to understand the general meaning. Don't **stress out*** about **every little thing.**** After you have read (or listened to) the story, you will have a chance to read (or hear) the meanings of the idioms used in the story with some brief examples. After you've learned what everything means, there will be a practice and review session at the end of the chapter. By this time you will be **up to snuff***** on the meanings of all of the idioms and other expressions in the story.

(**stress out**= don't worry)*

*(** **every little thing**= about every detail)*

*(*** **up to snuff**= you will know about or be up to date on)*

Some common English expressions and idioms when talking about the workplace

---

Below we have reprinted one of Louise Gibessi's recent columns about the workplace.

T<small>HE</small> W<small>ORKPLACE</small>

(Here's a letter from a woman who's got a real problem in the office where she works)

Dear Louise,

I work as an admin assistant in the office of a large corporation in Minneapolis, Minnesota. The job **rocks**[1] but one of my coworkers **gets on my nerves**[2]. She is always **badmouthing**[3] other colleagues **behind their backs**[4] and, frankly Louise, she has a hygiene problem that makes her **stand out like a sore thumb**[5]. She practically **bathes in cheap perfume**[6] to cover a **B.O.**[7] problem and she **totally reeks**[8]! **As luck would have it**[9], I have to sit next to this woman most of the day! By the end of the day, I **end up with**[10] a headache from the odor.

Louise, if you can't help me I think I will **loose my mind**[11]. She's got the boss **wrapped around her little finger**[12], so I have to **watch my step**[13] around her. First of all, how can I let her know that it is not okay to **blab**[14] **behind other people's back**[4]? I mean, she really needs to **get this message**[15]. And secondly, how do I **break it to her**[16] that she's really **fouling the air**[17] in our office with her terrible hygiene habits? Signed, **holding my nose**[18] in Minneapolis.

Dear **Holding your nose**[18],

It sounds like this coworker is really **lousing up your day**[19]! The workplace needs to be a comfortable, safe environment for everyone in the office, otherwise work will not get done on time. If your coworker's hygiene problem is as bad as you say, it's **beyond me**[20] that the boss hasn't detected it. I'm sure he or she has! So here's your first **in**[21]:

Arrange a meeting with your boss and don't be afraid **to lay it out**[22]. Explain to him or her that this employee is making it difficult for you to get your work done. It may help to mention that you get headaches from the odor. Remember, your boss has **bigger fish to fry**[23], so keep your conversation brief and to the point. ***Believe me***[24], he or she already knows about the problem. What you will do by talking to him or her is bring the issue ***out into the open***[25].

As for[26] the gossiping problem that this woman has, you would do well not to encourage it! You encourage it when you allow her to gossip to you about other coworkers in the office. Next time she tries gossiping, let her know that you think she would also gossip about you behind your back if she were talking to another colleague. Also, put a ***bug in the ears***[27] of your other colleagues to follow your behavior. The woman will ***get the message***[15].

Good luck! In the next week or so, I hope that your are not having to ***hold your nose***[17] anymore!

1. **Rocks**: *(slang)*

   When something rocks, it is really good, enjoyable, exciting, or interesting.

   Examples:
   - ❑ My new English class really ***rocks***! The teacher is really good and the class is really interesting.
   - ❑ Skiing really ***rocks***! Fresh air, lots of sunshine, fun slopes, and parties at night make this one of my favorite things to do.

2. **Gets on my nerves**: *(idiom)*

   When someone or something gets on your nerves, you are annoyed or bothered.

   Examples:
   - ❑ That new girl in the class talks too much. She really ***gets on my nerves***.
   - ❑ All that construction noise outside is really ***getting on my nerves***.

3. **_Badmouthing_**: *(slang)*

To say bad things about someone or something; despoiling someone's reputation through negative gossip; attempting to discredit something or someone.

Examples:

❑ One of my colleagues is always **_badmouthing_** my favorite soccer team. He's just jealous because my team beat his team in the championships.

❑ Be careful when you **_badmouth_** someone because it may *come back to bite you* (it may harm or make you look bad later on)

4. **_Behind their backs_**: *(idiom) Without them knowing. Doing something or saying something behind someone's back usually has a negative meaning. It means that you are doing or saying something that someone else would not approve of or would not allow.*

Examples:

❑ **_Behind his back_**, people were saying that he was a terrible soccer player and should be removed from the team.

❑ What a gossip says **_behind your back_**, they will rarely *tell you to your face*. (Idiom. Tell you to your face= tell you directly.)

5. **_Stand out like a sore thumb_**: *(idiom)*

When something or someone stands out like a sore thumb, he, she or it is very obvious to everyone. This expression sometimes has a negative feeling.

Examples:

❑ Julie's red dress **_stuck out like a sore thumb_** among all of the black formal dresses at the party.

❑ Jims small car **_stuck out like a sore thumb_** among all of the big pickup trucks.

6. ***Bathes in cheap perfume****:*

(see the definition of hyperbole) Called a hyperbole, this is an expression that exaggerates something in order to emphasize the point the speaker is trying to make. In this case, the girl put a lot of perfume on herself. Whether it is cheap perfume or not may not be known for sure. That she takes a bath in it is most probably not true.

Examples:
- ❑ That guy is so rich he ***bathes in*** money!
- ❑ That woman ***bathes in*** good fortune. She has lots of money, fame, and good friends.

7. ***B.O.****: (abbreviation)*

This abbreviation stands for *body odor*. Abbreviations are occasional used in casual or informal English conversation for effect or brevity.

Examples:
- ❑ Boy, I wish he would take a bath! He's got ***B.O.***
- ❑ To avoid having ***B.O.***, shower daily.

8. ***Totally reeks****: (slang)*

If you *reek* of something you give off or emit it in a very strong way. To *reek* by itself often means to smell very badly. The use of the word *totally* in a slang expression usually means completely.

Examples:
- ❑ After Alfred fell in the dirty pond, he ***totally reeked*** and had to go home and shower.
- ❑ We sat around the campfire all night. By morning we ***totally reeked*** of campfire smoke.

9. ***As luck would have it****: (idiom)*

Dictated by pure luck: sometimes good luck, sometimes bad luck.

Examples:

❑ I didn't study for the exam. ***As luck would have it***, they postponed the exam for another week giving me a chance to study.

❑ The day started out sunny and beautiful so we decided to have a picnic. We packed lots of good food, blankets and games and went to the park. ***As luck would have it***, though, it started raining as soon as we arrived at the park.

10. ***End up with****: (idiom)*

Finish up with a certain result or object.

Examples:

❑ Alexander worked on his car for two months and ***ended up with*** one of the most beautiful cars in his neighborhood.

❑ After investing all of that money in the stock market we ***ended up with*** nothing. We lost all of our money.

11. ***Lose my mind****: (idiom)*

A figure of speech meaning to become very agitated, upset or distraught about something.

Examples:

❑ If I had a job where I had to do the same thing every day, I'd ***lose my mind***.

❑ I thought she was going to ***lose her mind*** when she found out that her boyfriend was dating another girl.

12. ***Wrapped around her little finger****: (idiom)*

To have control over someone, usually because of emotional reasons .

Examples:

❑ Alice had her boyfriend ***wrapped around her little finger***. He would do anything for her.

❑ Jim was a tall, good-looking guy who worked for a big company in New York. His coworkers really didn't like the fact that he often got special favors from his female boss. Some people said that he had her ***wrapped around his little finger***.

13. ***Watch my step****: (idiom)*

To exercise caution; to be careful.
   Examples:
- ❑ A coworker of mine told me that the police were out giving tickets for speeding. He said I'd better ***watch my step*** when I drive home after work.
- ❑ ***Watch your step***, this is a bad neighborhood. Maybe you'd better take another road home.

14. ***Blab****: (informal / casual)*

When you blab you reveal information about other people or things that your probably shouldn't. A person who blabs just talks without giving thought to the content of his or her conversation, often revealing information that is either unnecessary to the listener or considered secret by someone else.
   Examples:
- ❑ I never told her any of my secrets because she likes to ***blab***.
- ❑ Jenny is the neighborhood gossip. She'll ***blab*** about anything.

15. ***Get this message****: (slang)*

When you *get the message* you completely understand the meaning of what someone is trying to communicate to you.
   Examples:
- ❑ The police told those kids last week that they couldn't skateboard in the park. They're doing it again. I don't think they ***got the message***.
- ❑ We saw a very powerful show on TV last night about the dangers of smoking. I don't think my sister ***got the message*** because she is outside smoking right now.

16. ***Break it to her****: (idiom)*

When you break something to someone, you tell them something directly, usually information that is not good news.

Examples:

- A young boy was seriously injured in a car accident and taken to the hospital. The police had to go to the boy's home with this bad news and ***break it to*** his parents.
- My friend didn't get accepted to the university and I'm not sure how to ***break it to*** him.

17. ***Fouling the air****: (slang)*

Polluting the air, in this case with the strong smell of perfume. This has a hint of sarcasm in it.

Examples:

- I hate it when a smoker ***fouls the air*** with his cigarette smoke.
- The smell of French fries and grease ***fouled the air*** around the fast food restaurant.

18. ***Holding my nose****: (idiom)*

Pinching off the openings of your nose with two fingers to prevent a strong smell from entering.

Examples:

- As we walked past the bakery, I ***held my nose*** so I wouldn't have to smell all of that delicious pastry.
- I ***held my nose*** when we went into the horse stable because I don't like the smell of horse stables.

19. ***Lousing up your day****: (idiom)*

Ruining your day. When something is lousing up your day, it is ruining the quality of your day's experience.

Examples:

- ❑ The rain really ***loused up my day*** today. Traffic was heavy and there was flooding downtown making it difficult to go anywhere.
- ❑ I found out that I own $10,000 in taxes. That really ***loused up my day***. *(in this case, put me in a bad mood so that the rest of the day wasn't very pleasant)*

20. ***Beyond me***: *(idiom)*

When something is *beyond you*, that means that you do not understand it.

Examples:
- ❑ Why people use illegal drugs is ***beyond me***.
- ❑ Why Alicia went back with her boyfriend after he cheated on her is ***beyond me***.

21. **In**: *(noun, slang or used in the expression to have an in)*

An opportunity or an opening; *(noun)* a connection to someone or something that has access to what you may want.

Examples:
- ❑ You've got to have an ***in*** to be asked to join that club.
- ❑ I know that you are trying to get accepted into that university. I think you'll have an ***in*** when you show them your excellent grades.

22. ***To lay it out***: *(idiom)*

To be direct and clear when giving someone information.

Examples:
- ❑ The prime minister ***laid it out*** for the people: if they didn't find an alternative energy source soon, their country would be in trouble.
- ❑ The coach of the team ***laid it out*** for the players: they can win the championships if they win the next two games.

23. **_Bigger fish to fry_**: *(idiom)*

More important things to do.
Examples:
❑ I don't have time to listen every little complaint; I've got **_bigger fish to fry_**.
❑ The president of the company has **_bigger fish_** to fry and relies on his managers to direct the day-to-day operation of the company.

24. **_Believe me_**: *(idiom)*

An expression that means *this is true, don't doubt it.*
Examples:
❑ **_Believe me_**, if we didn't have to depend on oil, we would be a lot happier.
❑ **_Believe me_**, a person's quality of life depends on how healthy they are.

25. **_Out into the open_**: *(idiom)*

Something that is there for everyone to observe; not hidden.
Examples:
❑ The issue of companies not hiring people from certain racial backgrounds needs to be brought **_out into the open_** so that this does not happen in the future.
❑ The dangers of using a cellular phone are just now being **_brought out into the open_**.

26. **_As for_**: *(idiom)*

Pertaining to or in regards to.
Examples:
❑ The state should provide more opportunities for less fortunate people to better themselves. **_As for_** wealthy people, well, they can take care of themselves.

❑ Everyone is going to Florida when they retire. ___**As for**___ me, I'm going to the South Pacific.

27. ___**Bug in the ears**___: *(idiom)*

When you put a bug in someone's ear you give them a hint or an idea about something.

Examples:

❑ I put a ___**bug in**___ my boss' ___**ear**___ that I am due for a raise in pay.
❑ My wife put a ___**bug in**___ my ___**ear**___ about the garage needing to be cleaned.

Chapter 4 *Practice and Review*

Directions: In each of the sentences below, fill in the blank spaces with the word or words that are missing from the expression. Think about the sentence carefully. Which expression best fits? Do not use the same expression twice. There is no answer key. Complete all of the sentences that you know, and then go back and work on the ones that are more difficult.

1. I don't have time right now to talk about the weather. I **_have_** _____ **_fish to fry_**.

2. Why people smoke is _____ **_me_**.

3. **_Believe_** _____, a person's quality of life depends on how healthy they are.

4. The lady next door **_likes to_** _____, so don't tell her anything.

5. The smoke from the building fire **_fouled the_** _____ around the city.

6.   We didn't know how to **_break_** ___ ___ **_her_** that she didn't pass the exam.

7. The weather really **_loused_** _____ **_our day_**. It was supposed to be sunny, but, instead, it was stormy.

8. Jim _____ **_a bug_** __ his friend's ear about his poor eating habits.

9. After working on the painting for six months, the artist **_ended_** _____ **_with_** a beautiful work or art.

10. Whew! That dead fish _____ **_reeks_**. It has been there for a week.

11. That new pub really _____s: good music, good food, and cheap drinks.

12. _____ your step, it is dark in that cellar and you may trip on something.

13. There was a warning in the newspaper about the dangers of some prescription drugs. Despite this warning, many people never **get the** _____ that prescription drugs can be very dangerous.

14. It really _____ **on my nerves** when some one leaves their cell phone on in class.

15. Boy, that pink house really _____ **out like a** _____ **thumb**!

Chapter 5

Correct usage of some common English expressions and idioms when talking about romance

Directions: Read and / or listen to Louise's column and try to understand the general meaning. Don't **stress out*** about **every little thing.**** After you have read (or listened to) the story, you will have a chance to read (or hear) the meanings of the idioms used in the story with some brief examples. After you've learned what everything means, there will be a practice and review session at the end of the chapter. By this time you will be **up to snuff***** on the meanings of all of the idioms and other expressions in the story.

(**stress out**= don't worry)*

*(** **every little thing**= about every detail)*

*(*** **up to snuff**= you will know about or be up to date on)*

Some common English expressions and idioms when talking about romance

---

Below we have reprinted one of Louise Gibessi's recent columns about romance.

ROMANCE

*(Here is a letter from a guy in Seattle, Washington, U.S.A., who **has a crush on**[14] a girl in the office where he works)*

Dear Louise,

I asked the pretty black-haired girl who works in the accounting department if she would like to **go out to dinner**[1] with me on Friday night. To my surprise, she said yes! But when I asked her if she wouldn't mind **going Dutch**[2], she really **told me off**[3] and then walked away. I **can't figure out,**[4] what happened! Signed, **Heartbroken**[5] in Seattle

Louise Gibessi responds:

Dear **Heartbroken**[5],

First of all, **get a grip**[6]. When you asked her if she wouldn't mind **going Dutch**[2], you asked her to pay half of the expense of your date at the restaurant. **Look**[7], I'm going to be very **up front with you**[8] here: what a **numbskull**[9] you are! Did you really like this girl? Well, you **can forget it**[10] now because **cheapskate**[11] is not one of the words in a **classy**[12] woman's **vocab**[13]. My advice to you is this: in the future, when you **have a crush on someone**[14] and would like to date this person, please never bring up the subject of who will pay for the date. In many societies around the world the man pays for the dates—especially the first date! Using the expression, **going Dutch**[2], to most women on the first date is like **waving a red flag in front of a bull**[15]. Good luck, and I hope you **find Miss Right**[16] soon.

1. To **go out** to dinner: *(idiom)*

   In a romantic situation, to take someone to dinner on a date. To ask someone to go out with you is to ask someone to accompany you on a date.

   Examples:
   ❑ I asked the girl with the red hair to **go out** with me.

   ❑ My girlfriend and I ***go out*** every Friday night. We usually go to dinner and then see a movie.

2. To ***go Dutch***: *(idiom)*

To split the cost of something, usually in casual situations when two or more people are going to dinner or experiencing other activities together where there are charges involved.

     Examples:
   ❑ My girlfriend and I are trying to save money for our marriage, so when we go out we usually ***go Dutch***.
   ❑ She is a good friend of mine, but there is no romantic interest between us. Sometimes we have lunch together. When we do, we ***go Dutch***.

3. To ***tell someone off***: *(idiom)*

To tell someone off is to get angry with someone and tell them exactly how you feel. This is usually done with a lot of emotion. To tell someone off usually implies a rejection.

     Examples:
   ❑ When I found out that my boyfriend was seeing another woman, I really ***told him off***, and then left him forever.
   ❑ The policeman really ***told*** the driver ***off*** for speeding through the school zone, and then gave him a ticket (cars must go very slowly through a school zone).

4. ***Can't figure out***: *(idiom)*

Unable to understand what is happening or what is going on.

     Examples:

- I ***can't figure out*** why my colleague was fired at work. He was a good worker, always came in on time, and was always respectful to the boss. I just can't figure it out.
- We ***could*** never ***figure out*** why the cat liked to sleep on the top of the refrigerator.

5. *Heartbroken*: (adjective)

Suffering from overwhelming grief or sorrow, many times because of the loss of a loved one or something very important to you.

Examples:
- I was ***heartbroken*** when our dog died.
- Our family was ***heartbroken*** when we heard that our house did not survive the storm.

6. *Get a grip*: (slang)

Is derived from *get a grip on yourself*, which means to calm down and think rationally or become rational. This is often used in a playful, lighthearted way to mean *think realistically!* But using this term with strangers can be considered to be rude and impolite, so be careful when you use this.

Examples:
- My friend was really upset about not getting her work done on time at work. I told her to ***get a grip***, she still has two more days to complete the project.
- My neighbors were upset and panicking after hearing that a hurricane might be coming through our town. I told them to ***get a grip*** and just do what is necessary to prepare themselves.

7. *Look!*: (imperative)

Is derived from *look at me,* which means to pay careful attention to what I am going to say next. This is often used in a serious conversation where there may be a misunderstanding, or where important points need to be understood by the listener. Usually used between people who already know each other or have not met for the first time; but if a stranger is causing you some problem it is possible to begin your comments to him or her with *look!*

Examples:

❑ The kids were running in and out of the house while the adults were trying to have a conversation. Finally, the father said, ***look****, you kids stay outside and play!*

❑ I thought that it was very important that my customer purchased one of our safety devices. I said to him, ***look****, if your building catches fire and you don't have one of these safety devices, many people could be hurt.*

8. To be ***up front with*** someone: (idiom)

To be completely honest with someone without hiding any facts.

Examples:

❑ The doctor was very ***up front with*** us when he was describing our daughter's injuries from the auto accident.

❑ Some people say it is difficult to find a politician who will be ***up front with*** you.

9. ***Numbskull***: (informal, noun)

Often used playfully to mean that a person is not very smart.

Examples:

❑ What a ***numbskull***! He didn't wait for the light to change to green before he crossed the street.

❑ You would have to be a ***numbskull*** not to understand this lesson.

10. You **_can forget it_**: *(slang)*

Sometimes used playfully to mean that your opportunity to do something has come and has now gone, possibly forever. Don't worry about it anymore because that opportunity will not come again.

Examples:
- ❏ You have failed the last three exams. If you think you're going to graduate to the next level, [you can] **_forget it_**.
- ❏ The boy asked the amusement park attendant if he could go on the big roller coaster for free. The attendant answered: *No money?* _You **_can forget it_**.

11. **_Cheapskate_**: *(slang, noun)*

A cheapskate is a person who never wants to pay for anything. This is a person who will buy the cheapest of everything and will rely on his friends or family to pay for things. Sometimes used playfully.

Examples:
- ❏ He's such a **_cheapskate_**. Every time we go to the pub, we end up buying him a drink. He never buys.
- ❏ If you're a **_cheapskate_**, you won't have a girlfriend for long.

12. **_Classy_**: *(informal, adjective)*

Used to mean a person with good taste in clothing and other things in life, as well as conducts themselves in a sophisticated way. A person who is highly stylish and elegant.

Examples:
- ❏ She wears stylish clothing and drives a nice car. She is a **_classy_** lady.
- ❏ The man's good manners, stylish clothing, and expensive car distinguish him as a **_classy_** gentleman.

13. _**Vocab**: (abbreviation for vocabulary, informal)_

Sometimes, in informal or slang speech, speakers will abbreviate certain words. They do this to create a certain effect or to get their point across more quickly. Below are some other words that are sometimes used this way:

Examples:

❑ Body = **_bod._** You can really see what a good **_bod_** she has in that bathing suit.

❑ Body odor = **_B.O._** Showering daily is a good way to prevent **_B.O._**

14. _**To have a crush on someone**: (idiom)_

Means to be romantically interested in someone who usually doesn't know that you feel this way. Crushes are usually temporary for one reason or another, but occasionally they develop into relationships.

Examples:

❑ I **_had a crush on_** my boss, but she was married.

❑ A lot of girls **_have crushes on_** their favorite movie stars.

15. _**To wave a red flag in front of a bull**: (cliché)_

Means to deliberately provoke a dangerous situation. To say or do something that would obviously make someone else mad or very annoyed.

Examples:

❑ Telling that policeman that he should be fired from the police department for giving you a ticket was like **_waving a red flag in front of a bull_**.

❑ My business partner was already upset because our company was not doing well. But when I told him that a close associate was starting another company to compete with ours, it was like **_waving a red flag in front of a bull_**.

16. *To find **Miss Right**: (idiom)*

Comes from the idiom *to find Mr. Right*. To find Miss Right means to find the right woman for someone. To find the person, usually of the opposite sex, who you could best be together with.

Examples:

❑ In order ***to find Miss Right***, you have to look in the right places.

❑ If you want to ***meet Mr. Right***, go where Mr. Right hangs out.

Chapter 5   *Practice and Review*

Directions: In each of the sentences below, fill in the blank spaces with the word or words that are missing from the expression. Think about the sentence carefully. Which expression best fits? Do not use the same expression twice. There is no answer key. Complete all of the sentences that you know, and then go back and work on the ones that are more difficult.

1. The teenager was afraid to be **_up_** _____ **_with_** his problems. Whenever an adult tried to help, he told them that everything was okay.

2. Sylvia has **_a_** _____ **_on_** her classmate, but he doesn't seem interested.

3. Telling the policeman that you only drink a little when you drive, is like waving **_a_** _____ **_flag in_** _____ **_of a bull_**.

4. He always asks his girlfriends to pay half of the restaurant bill. He is such a _____ **_skate_**.

5. People **_can't figure_** _____ why they have to pay so much in taxes.

6. Sam has been trying **_to_** _____ **_Miss Right_** for years, but he hasn't had much luck.

7. He forgot to roll up the windows in his car again, and now it's starting to rain. What a _____ **_skull_**!

8. Alicia's friend was really upset about losing her job. I told her to **_get a_** _____, she will get another one.

9. You don't have the skills of a professional soccer player. You **_can_** _____ **_it_** if you think you will be hired by a professional soccer team.

10. My girlfriend and I are trying to save money for our marriage, so when we go out we usually go Dutch.

11. The mother was growing impatient with her kids: "_____! You kids go outside and play!"

12. The little girl was _____ when her kitten died.

13. The boy asked the girl with the red hair to **_go_** _____ **_to dinner with_** him.

Chapter 6

Correct usage of some common English expressions and idioms when talking about education

Directions: Read and / or listen to Louise's column and try to understand the general meaning. Don't **stress out*** about **every little thing.**** After you have read (or listened to) the story, you will have a chance to read (or hear) the meanings of the idioms used in the story with some brief examples. After you've learned what everything means, there will be a practice and review session at the end of the chapter. By this time you will be **up to snuff***** on the meanings of all of the idioms and other expressions in the story.

(**stress out**= don't worry)*

*(** **every little thing**= about every detail)*

*(*** **up to snuff**= you will know about or be up to date on)*

Some common English expressions and idioms when talking about education

---

Below we have reprinted one of Louise Gibessi's recent columns about education.

EDUCATION

(Here is a letter from an ESL student who is studying English in the United States. Apparently, this student is not too happy with his school.)

Dear Louise Gibbesi,

I am an English student presently studying English in the United States. I'm pretty **gung-ho**[1] about learning English because I want to use English in my profession when I **get back to**[2] my home country. The school that I am going to is okay, but some of the classes **leave a lot to be desired**[3]. In some classes some of the other students in the class are not as enthusiastic about learning English as I am. I have **brought this up**[4] to the teacher, but the teacher doesn't seem to be able to do anything about it. I guess this lack of enthusiasm is a personal decision **on the part of**[5] these students.

One of the other **gripes**[6] I have about my present educational experience is my home stay accommodations. My home stay parents are very nice and they can speak my native language. But, that's the problem! I came to America to learn English but my home stay parents think that this is an opportunity to improve their conversation in my language! Louise, I can't seem to get them to **break this habit**[7] of talking to me in my language. One of the big reasons why I chose home stay accommodations was because I wanted to practice English with my home stay parents. What should I do? Also, regarding my first problem, what can I do to make bigger strides in improving my English in my present situation at my school?

Signed, **down in the dumps**[8] in the USA.

Louise Gibessi responds:

Dear **down in the dumps**[9],

Look on the bright side of things[10]! Being able to study English in America is a **godsend**[11]. After all, this is an English speaking country! And **herein lies**[12] your answer! Make time when you are not going to school to participate in activities around the community. You can find these activities by looking on the Internet or in the local newspaper. **Go out**

and[13] volunteer for something – they're always looking for volunteers. Go to museums, art galleries, and specialty shows where you have a chance to talk to the people who are responsible for the exhibits. Go to street festivals, concerts and local events and *mingle with*[14] the people. Make a trusted friend in America; someone with whom you share the same interests. Remember, you learn to speak English well by speaking English. So don't be bashful, *go for it*[15]!

Here's the skinny[16] on your home stay dilemma. Your home stay parents are not obligated to teach you English. They have signed a contract with your school saying that they would provide a student with clean, safe accommodations within a family environment. There is nothing in that contract that says they have to speak English. Why don't you *sit down with them*[17] and explain your point of view. Then negotiate an arrangement with them where part of the time they can practice your language with them, but most of the time you would prefer to speak English.

That's it *in a nutshell*[18]. Hey, *keep your chin up*[19]! Life is a *bowl of cherries*[20] for you right now!

1. **Gung-ho**: *(idiom)*

    When you are gung-ho you are very eager, motivated and enthusiastic to do something.

    Examples:
    ❑ Our team was really **gung-ho** to win the championships.
    ❑ Molly studied every day for the upcoming exam. She was **gung-ho** to do well on the exam.

2. **Get back to:** *(idiom)*

    To return to somewhere, something or someone.

Examples:

❑ The clerk said she had to answer the phone but that she would ***get back to*** us in a minute.

❑ We won't be ***getting back to*** our home country for three weeks.

3. ***Leave a lot to be desired****: (idiom)*

Inadequate. When you say that something leaves a lot to be desired, you are saying that it is not as good as it could be, inadequate.

Examples:

❑ The food in that restaurant ***left a lot to be desired***.

❑ The manager was thinking about firing Ted because his work ***left a lot to be desired***.

4. ***Brought this up****: (idiom)*

When you bring something up, you introduce it into a discussion.

Examples:

❑ Yesterday I talked to my boss about my job. I ***brought up*** the fact that I had not received a raise in nearly two years.

❑ When I spoke to my friend Jocelyn on Tuesday, she reminded me that I owed her money. That was the second time this week that she has ***brought*** this ***up***.

5. ***On the part o****f: (idiom)*

On the part of means *regarding* or *by.*

Examples:

❑ A lot of hard work ***on the part of*** our employees ensured the profitable year.

❑ Complaining ***on the part of*** some students caused the teacher to change the test date.

6. ***Gripes***: *(noun)*

Complaints.

> **Examples:**
> ❑ One of my ***gripes*** about this town is that there aren't enough entertainment spots.
> ❑ The mayor asked the audience if anyone had a special ***gripe***.
> *(special gripe= a complaint that is particularly important to someone)*

7. ***Break*** *this* ***habit***: *(idiom)*

To end or stop a usually bad habit.

> **Examples:**
> ❑ Kelly has to ***break*** her ***habit*** of smoking.
> ❑ I wish my friend would ***break*** his ***habit*** of interrupting people while they are talking.

8. ***Down in the dumps***: *(idiom)*

When you are *down in the dumps* you are unhappy, sad, kind of melancholy.

> **Examples:**
> ❑ Jean was really ***down in the dumps*** when she found out her flight was cancelled.
> ❑ Jun's sister was really ***down in the dumps*** because she couldn't go to the concert.

10. ***Look on the bright side of things***: *(idiom)*

When you *look on the bright side of things* you attempt to be positive about something; you see the positive side of something.

> **Examples:**

- I know you hate to go to work, but ***look on the bright side of things***: if you didn't have a job, you wouldn't have money to live.
- I like Katy because she is never negative. She always ***looks on the bright side of things***.

11. *Godsend*: (noun)

A *godsend* is something that you need or want that appears in your life unexpectedly or at a good time.

Examples:

- Winning this money was a ***godsend***, now I can pay my bills.
- Hiring that new employee was a ***godsend***, now we have enough people to complete the project.

12. *Herein lies*:

Herein lies means within this place, idea, situation, scenario, or concept something exists: perhaps an answer; perhaps something you have been looking for, or just something of interest.

Examples:

- When learning English, studying is very important. ***Herein lies*** the key to success: studying.
- She said she likes to smoke because it helps her stay slim. ***Herein lies*** the wisdom behind her smoking habit.

13. *Go out and* (do something):

To *go out and* do something is a way of saying that you are taking action to do something.

Examples:

- I got tired of not having a good job so I ***went out and*** took some courses in school.

- My parents said that it was good to know how to speak more than just one language so I ***went out and*** learned another language.

14. ***Mingle with***:

To mix together with or be among individuals in a group.

Examples:
- The older students ***mingled with*** the younger ones at the graduation ceremony.
- Customers and company representatives ***mingled with*** each other at the trade show in Chicago.

15. ***Go for it***: *(idiom)*

When you *go for it*, you use all of your energy and talent towards achieving a certain goal, sometimes without regard for the consequences of failure.

Examples:
- I really wanted to do well in the competition, so when I practiced, I really ***went for it***.
- Sally wanted the job with the fashion designer company but was a little afraid that they might not accept her. Finally, she decided to ***go for it***.

16. ***Here's the skinny***: *(idiom)*

Here's the skinny means here are the details about something.

Examples:
- ***Here's the skinny*** about our itinerary: we're leaving at 6am tomorrow morning and will be at the airport by 8am. Our flight leaves at 10:05 am.

❑ ***Here's the skinny*** about the exam next week: there will be two parts, grammar and composition. Each grammar question will be worth two points.

17. **Sit down with** *them:*

When you *sit down with* someone to have a meeting, you have usually pre-arranged or pre-planned the meeting, and the meeting is usually important to both parties. To *sit down with* someone is to take the time necessary, usually to discuss something important.

Examples:
❑ We ***sat down with*** the union leaders and discussed benefits for the workers.
❑ The human resources director ***sat down with*** the new employee and explained all of the company rules.

18. **In a nutshell***: (idiom)*

To describe something in a few words, concisely.

Examples:
❑ What the cruise director explained to us, ***in a nutshell***, was that we had to be back on the ship by 8pm because the ship was sailing at 8:30pm.
❑ ***In a nutshell***, if you are an athlete and you take performance-enhancing drugs, you are not allowed to compete in the competitions.

19. **Keep your chin up:** *(idiom)*

When you *keep your chin up*, you stay positive in spite of negative circumstances.

Examples:

❏ ***Keep your chin up***, it's a beautiful day today and there are lots of fun things we can do.

❏ Even though it looks like rain, ***keep your chin up*** because there is always sunshine behind every cloud.

20. **Bowl of cherries**: *(idiom)*

When life is a *bowl of cherries*, it is really good.

Examples:

❏ Keep your chin up, life is a ***bowl of cherries*** if you choose to see it that way.

❏ Life during a war is not exactly a ***bowl of cherries***.

Chapter 6 *Practice and Review*

Directions: In each of the sentences below, fill in the blank spaces with the word or words that are missing from the expression. Think about the sentence carefully. Which expression best fits? Do not use the same expression twice. There is no answer key. Complete all of the sentences that you know, and then go back and work on the ones that are more difficult.

1. Our team really **went** _____ **it** and won the match.

2. Getting this new job was a **god**_____, now I can pay my bills.

3. Ursula was really **gung**-___ to do well in the competition.

4. In a **nut**_____, if you smoke, you could end up with cancer.

5. _____ **the habit** of eating too much at dinner might help you lose some weight.

6. The teachers **mingled** _____ the students during the school party.

7. If you lose sometimes, **keep your** _____ **up**, work hard, and you will have better days.

8. Life can be a _____ **of cherries** if you keep a good balance.

9. Work hard and be positive; **herein** _____ **the key to** success.

10. The quality of his work was not so good; it left **a** ____ **to be desired**.

11. One **g**_____ that everyone had on the tour was that the tour guide spoke too quickly.

CPSIA information can be obtained
at www.ICGtesting.com
Printed in the USA
LVHW111748110122
708310LV00006B/414